Radical Islam in Central Asia

The Soviet Bloc and After

Gail Lapidus, Series Editor

German Rule in Russia 1941–1945: A Study of Occupation Policies
by Alexander Dallin

Making and Breaking Democratic Transitions: The Comparative Politics of Russia's Regions
by Vladimir Gel'man, Sergei Ryzhenkov, and Michael Brie, with Vladimir Avdonin, Boris Ovchinnikov, and Igor Semenov

Radical Islam in Central Asia: Between Pen and Rifle
by Vitaly V. Naumkin

Russian Strategic Modernization: Past and Future
by Nikolai Sokov

Dissolution: Sovereignty and the Breakup of the Soviet Union
by Edward W. Walker

Radical Islam in Central Asia

Between Pen and Rifle

Vitaly V. Naumkin

ROWMAN & LITTLEFIELD PUBLISHERS, INC.
Lanham • Boulder • New York • Toronto • Oxford

ROWMAN & LITTLEFIELD PUBLISHERS, INC.

Published in the United States of America
by Rowman & Littlefield Publishers, Inc.
A wholly owned subsidary of The Rowman & Littlefield Publishing Group, Inc.
4501 Forbes Boulevard, Suite 200, Lanham, MD 20706
www.rowmanlittlefield.com

P.O. Box 317, Oxford OX2 9RU, UK

All photos taken by nineteenth-century photographers (pp. 13, 14, 15, 16, 17, 18, 19) were found by the author in three Russian academic archives—those of the Institute of the History of Material Culture, the St. Petersburg Branch of the Institute of Oriental Studies, and the Russian Geographical Society—then published by Garnet Publishing in the series *Caught in Time*, series editor Vitaly Naumkin (*Samarqand*, 1992; *Bukhara*, 1993; *Khiva*, 1993) © Vitaly Naumkin.

British Library Cataloguing-in-Publication Information Available

Library of Congress Cataloging-in-Publication Data

Naumkin, Vitalii Viacheslavovich
  Radical Islam in Central Asia : between pen and rifle / Vitaly V. Naumkin.
    p. cm. — (The Soviet bloc and after)
  Includes bibliographical references and index.
  ISBN 0-7425-2929-0 (cloth : alk. paper) — ISBN 0-7425-2930-4 (pbk. : alk. paper)
  1. Islamic fundamentalism—Asia, Central—History—20th century. 2. Islam and politics—Asia, Central—History—20th century. 3. Hizb al-Tahrir. I. Title. II. Series.
  BP63.A34N38   2005
  320.5'57'0958—dc22
                                                    2004023936

Printed in the United States of America

∞ ™ The paper used in this publication meets the minimum requirements of American National Standard for Information Sciences—Permanence of Paper for Printed Library Materials, ANSI/NISO Z39.48-1992.

Contents

List of Illustrations   vii

Preface   ix

Introduction   xi

Chronology   xv

1 The Roots and Causes of Islamic Radicalism: The History
   of Islam in Central Asia   1

2 The Rise and Fall of the Islamic Movement of Uzbekistan   37

3 The Hizb at-Tahrir al-Islami: A Peaceful Expansion?   127

4 Islamists in Government: The Case of the Islamic Revival
   Party of Tajikistan   201

Conclusion   261

Glossary   271

Index   277

About the Author   285

List of Illustrations

1 Samarqand, the famous Gur-e Amir Mausoleum
   (photo 2002)   11
2 The mausoleum on the grave of Khoja Bahauddin
   Naqshband (photo 2002)   12
3 *Zikr* (photo 1896)   13
4 Khiva, the mosque at the Pahlavan-Ahmad *mazar*
   (photo 1873)   14
5 Amir Abd al-Ahad, ruler of the Bukhara Amirate, 1885–1910
   (photo 1893)   15
6 The Shirbudun Palace (photo 1890s)   16
7 Sayyid Muhammad Rahim II Bahadur Khan (photo 1896)   17
8 Khiva girls (photo 1896)   18
9 Execution in Bukhara (photo 1890s)   19
10 Hajji *domulla* Muhammadjan Hindustani   44
11 Imam Ismail *qari*, Kokand (January 2004)   49
12 Imam Ishaq *qari* with the author in Kokand (January 2004)   55
13 Two suspected members of the Hizb at-Tahrir al-Islami are
   arrested in Tajikistan (April 2000)   165
14 A rally of the Islamic opposition at Shahidon Square in
   Dushanbe (May 1992)   217
15 Sangak Safarov with a group of fighters from the People's
   Guard (1992)   219
16 Document for protection (October 1992)   221
17 Government troops suffer losses during the fighting over
   Tavildara (June 1996)   231

18 Hoji Akbar Turajonzoda returns to Dushanbe after five years
   of exile in Iran (February 1998)   238
19 The start of the military operation to neutralize the
   Sanginov–Muakkalov band in Tajikistan (June 2001)   244
20 Said Abdullo Nuri   245

Preface

This book was conceived in the fall of 2002, when I began preparing to teach a course on Islam in the Soviet successor states in the Department of Political Science at the University of California, Berkeley. I was asked that same semester to write a research paper on a related topic as part of an occasional papers series for the Berkeley Program in Soviet Studies.

By that time, I had already spent many years studying Islam in the Middle East and Central Asia, having begun my academic career by writing a Ph.D. dissertation on medieval Sufism, particularly focused on the works of Abu Hamid al-Ghazali. My dissertation work also led me to translate chapters from al-Ghazali's main theological encyclopedia, *The Revival of the Religious Sciences*, into Russian. I decided that my expertise as a specialist both in the Middle East and in Central Asia might be helpful in contributing to scholarship of one of the most intriguing topics in contemporary international politics. As a young Russian Arabist many years ago, I knew many of the key actors in Central Asian Islam in the late Soviet period, from great muftis to underground teachers. Later, I followed the emergence of the first radical Islamic groups in this region. Many informal meetings with radical Islamic scholars in Uzbekistan—especially in the Ferghana Valley—in the late 1980s and early 1990s helped me in my sincere but sometimes desperate attempts to grasp the hidden and complicated texture of Central Asia's clandestine Islamic movements as they began to gain momentum in the years following the collapse of the Soviet Union.

The personal relationships I had developed over the years, as well as my scholarly background, helped me comprehend the acute political battles in

Tajikistan that eventually led to the devastating civil war that lasted from 1992 to 1997. At the end of 1992, together with several colleagues, I started preparations for launching an American–Russian initiative on Tajikistan undertaken within the framework of the Dartmouth Conference. The project, which began in March 1993, fostered a sustained dialogue between representatives of the conflicting sides in the Tajik conflict. My American counterpart, Harold Saunders of the Kettering Foundation, has been the soul of this long-lasting undertaking. The debates that took place during the many rounds of the inter-Tajik dialogue, along with frequent visits to the region, allowed me to acquire new knowledge on my topic. It is my particular pleasure to thank Harold for sharing his vast expertise with me in the course of our sessions.

My participation in a great number of Islam-related international conferences and seminars in many countries in the West, the Middle East, and Central Asia helped me avoid a one-sided perspective and helped shape my intellectual approach to the topic. It also allowed me to work out the ideas in this book in a broader context and on a comparative basis.

I owe a great debt of gratitude to the many colleagues who provided helpful advice. Of particular benefit were the seminars organized by the Berkeley Program in Soviet and Post-Soviet Studies (BPS) and funded by the Carnegie Corporation of New York that took place during my stay at Berkeley. I also wish to acknowledge the role of Professor Edward Walker, executive director of BPS, who gave me helpful feedback on my Berkeley research paper, which became the bulk of one of the chapters of this book. My deep gratitude goes as well to Professor Gail Lapidus of Stanford University for her active support of my work and her very insightful comments on the manuscript.

I express my sincere thanks to the Rockefeller Foundation, which gave me a unique opportunity to spend several weeks as a resident completing my manuscript in the spring of 2004 at the Villa Serbelloni in Bellagio, Italy. The inspiring atmosphere, the beautiful surroundings of the villa, and the company of many outstanding intellectuals eased the fatigues of this uneasy literary effort.

The publisher and I would like to thank the following for their kind permission to reproduce illustrations: Ni'matulla Ibrahimov and Zahidulla Munavvarov (plates 1, 2, and 10), Photo ITAR-TASS Agency (plates 13, 17, 18, and 19), and Gennady Ratushenko (plates 14, 15, and 20). Photos shown in plates 3, 7, and 8 were taken by I. Volzhinsky; plate 4 by G. Krivtsov; plates 6 and 9 by Hordet; and plate 5 by V. Yasvoin. Photos in plates 11, 12, and 16 were taken by me.

My thanks go last but not least to the many friends from Central Asia and the Middle East who made this difficult endeavor possible.

Introduction

All men of state in the Arab Caliphate in the Middle Ages were classified either as *arbab al-aqlam* (bearers of the pen) or *arbab al-suyuf* (bearers of the sword). Wielding a pen and wielding a sword were male professions, and which one a man wielded determined his place in life and the social hierarchy of the Muslim theocratic state. The union and opposition of these two elements—the intellectual and the martial—have permeated the entire history of the Islamic world, and our times bear witness to the continuing existence of this conflicting dyad in which the relations between its component parts are sometimes shaped very dramatically. This can be clearly demonstrated with the example of political Islam in present-day Central Asia. Naturally enough, the role of the sword has long since been played by the rifle (or, more correctly, the gun).

In the early 1990s, the ideology of political Islam and Islamist organizations started to become an important factor in Central Asian political life. Until the terrorist attacks of September 11, 2001, however, Islamism in Central Asia had received scant attention abroad. That has since changed, and it is now difficult even to discuss Central Asia in the West without reference to Islamist mobilization in the region. Nevertheless, few studies have examined the phenomenon comparatively, to place it in the context of Islamist movements elsewhere.[1]

This volume presents case studies of three key Islamic political organizations in Central Asia: the Islamic Movement of Uzbekistan (IMU), the Hizb at-Tahrir al-Islami, or the Party of Islamic Liberation (HTI), and the Islamic Revival Party of Tajikistan (IRPT).

The IMU was listed by the U.S. State Department as a terrorist organization in 2000. It is a militant and extremist Islamic organization that has operated mostly within the borders of one state (Uzbekistan). Nevertheless, it is closely linked to international Islamic networks. It has also used armed struggle and terrorism in an effort to topple the regime of Uzbekistan president Islam Karimov. Although many of its members were killed or dispersed during the U.S.-led military campaign in Afghanistan, the IMU still has a social base in the Ferghana Valley, a densely populated region that straddles southeast Uzbekistan, southwest Kyrgyzstan, and northern Tajikistan.

The two other radical Islamic movements in Central Asia—the Hizb at-Tahrir al-Islami and the Islamic Revival Party of Tajikistan—are different from the IMU. The HTI has, to date, advocated nonviolent political struggle. Its principal mode of operation has been education and the dissemination of literature. Its goal is the creation of an Islamic state (as a "caliphate") encompassing the entire region of Central Asia and—in the future—the whole Islamic world. Unlike the IMU, the HTI is a true transnational organization that consists of semi-independent branches, only some of which are in Central Asia. In Central Asia, it has been most active in Uzbekistan, Kyrgyzstan, and Tajikistan, although there is evidence of growing HTI activity in southern Kazakhstan.

Despite the fact that the HTI agenda does not appeal directly to the grievances and concerns of the people of Central Asia, it has been increasingly successful in recruiting sympathizers. In part, this is because the people of Central Asia have a strong desire for opening the borders between their states. The "Islamic internationalism" of the HTI is thus more appealing than the particularistic and egoistic nationalism of Central Asia's national governments.

While the IMU has been losing influence in the wake of September 11 and the launching of the global war on terror, the HTI has been gaining in popularity. Central Asia's acute socioeconomic and political problems, as well as the inability of its ruling elites to find a formula for successful modernization and democratization, are increasing social frustration and disaffection. In turn, this provides fuel for Islamists of all types, especially those who do not espouse violence, such as the HTI. (The party seems to have resolved for itself, at least for the time being, the dilemma of pen or rifle in favor of the pen.) The cruel persecution of Islamist activists by Central Asian governments has also created new martyrs, increasing the HTI's popularity and broadening its social support.

The Islamic Revival Party of Tajikistan was established in 1991 as a national organization, making it the first Islamic political party ever registered in Central Asia. It was also the first Islamic party to form an alliance with democratic parties and to participate in presidential elections. Remarkably, in 1992—just one year after the collapse of the USSR—the IRPT briefly became part of a coalition government, although that government proved short-lived. A subsequent outburst of violence radicalized the party, and later it became involved in the Tajik civil war, which broke out in 1992. In 1997, under strong pressure from the international community, the parties to that conflict, including the IRPT, agreed to a peace treaty. The treaty provided for the inclusion of opposition representatives in the government, as well as the incorporation of the opposition's guerrilla units into the armed forces and police. This was a unique example of constructive cooperation between secularists and Islamists in Central Asia.

This volume represents a comparative study of these three Islamic organizations, including the history, the ideology, and the organizational structure; the methods of political, military, and other types of activities; the power bases; the local and transnational links; the influence of external and internal factors; and the dynamics of transformation. This study will help us understand why Islamic political groups, including militant ones, have been able to garner support in moderate Islamic societies such as those of Central Asia. My apprehension regarding the method of research that has to be employed for a successful analysis of this topic is based on the necessity not to confine it to a narrow regional scope but to put it into the context of broader Islamic intellectual-religious strands of thought and to examine how they were transmitted and absorbed in the specific conditions of Central Asia. My previous works on the history of Arab nationalism and Arab national/liberation movements helped me to understand how their political, organizational, and military skills had been effectively used by modern radical Islamic movements, who have also benefited from the human and organizational resources of both nationalist and Marxist organizations.[2] I paid special attention to the role of individual actors, which I consider, if not central, at least equal to that of institutions.

In this study I rely upon many different written sources, including theoretical works by the founders and teachers of radical Islam in the Middle East and Central Asia, materials of local press, a great number of both official and unpublished documents (many of which have not yet been used by the scholars of Central Islam) of various legal and clandestine Islamic groups, and publications from governmental agencies. In addition to these documents, I use the data collected in the course of my long fieldwork in the region and, in particular, interviews with local political actors—Islamic scholars and clerics, political leaders, government officials, academics, and top and rank-and-file radical Islamists.

NOTES

1. Exceptions include a book by the French scholar Olivier Roy, *The New Central Asia: The Creation of Nations* (London: I. B. Tauris, 2000), and one by the Pakistani journalist Ahmed Rashid, *Jihad: The Rise of Militant Islam in Central Asia* (New Haven, CT: Yale University Press, 2002).

2. See Vitaly Naumkin, *Red Wolves of Yemen* (Cambridge: Oleander, 2004).

Chronology

7th century	Arab conquest and the beginning of spread of Islam in Central Asia
700–767	life of Imam al-Nu'man b. Thabit b. Zuta Abu Hanifa
780–855	life of Ahmad b. Muhammad b. Hanbal
875–999	Samanid state with Bukhara as its capital—Islam adopted as this state's official religion
944	death of Abu Mansur al-Maturidi al-Samarqandi, a prominent Islamic scholar
12th century	establishment of the Naqshbandiyya Sufi brotherhood by Yusuf al-Hamadani (d. 1166)
12th century	establishment of the Yasaviyya Sufi brotherhood by Ahmad Yasavi (d. 1166)
1145–1221	life of Najmuddin Qubra, the founder of Qubraviyya brotherhood
1318–1389	life of Bahauddin Naqshband after whom the Naqshbandiyya brotherhood was named
13th century	the Mongol conquest of Central Asia
14th century	reemergence of the role of Islam as the official religion of Central Asia
1336–1405	life of Timur
1394–1449	life of Timur's grandson Ulugh Beg
16th century	emergence of the Bukhara Khanate
17th century	beginning of penetration of the Russian Empire into Central Asia

1827–1897	life of Ahmad Donish, a famous Central Asian enlightener
1860–1870s	incorporation of Central Asia into the Russian Empire
1865	establishment of Russian Governship-General in Turkestan
1868	treaty of Russian protectorate on Bukhara
1873	treaty of Russian protectorate on Khiva
1851–1914	life of Ismail-bek Gasprinski, founder of Jadidism
1878–1931	life of Munavvar *qari* Abdurrashidkhanov, a famous enlightener
1892–1989	life of Muhammadjan Rustamov-Hindustani
late 19th to early 20th century	Jadidist movement
1916	rebellion for independence in Khiva
1913	creation of Ush Zhuz political party
May 1–11, 1917	First All-Russian Muslim Congress
June 1917	Second All-Russian Muslim Congress
October 25, 1917	Bolshevik revolution in Russia
November 1917	Muslim National Assembly
November 1917	declaration of independence of Turkestan
1919–1932	activities of Shami *domulla*
September 1920	declaration of "people's" republics in Bukhara and Khiva
December 1922	creation of the Union of Soviet Socialist Republics (USSR)
1920s	delimitation of borders between the Soviet republics of Central Asia
1928	birth of the Muslim Brotherhood in Egypt
1929	creation of the Tajik Soviet Socialist Republic
1920–1930s	basmachi movement in Central Asia
1930s	repression against local Islam and the religious class in Central Asia
1943	reestablishment of the Spiritual Board of Muslims of Central Asia and Kazakhstan (SADUM), muftiyate and qaziyates in all Central Asian republics
1945	renewal of hajj of Soviet Muslims to Mecca and Medina
1917–1940	pro-Salafi ideas occasionally brought to Central Asia
1950–1970	local proto-Salafis appeared in Central Asia
late 1980s	Salafis operated more openly

1953	the birth of the Hizb at-Tahrir al-Islami (HTI) under Taqi al-Din Nabhani
1977–2003	'Abd al-Qadim Zallum served as the leader of the HTI
1908–1982	life of Ziyauddin Khan Ishan Babakhanov
September 1989	establishment of the Rastokhez society in Tajikistan
February 1990	anti-Armenian demonstrations in Dushanbe
June 9, 1990	constituent conference of all-USSR Islamic Revival Party (IRP) in Astrakhan
August 10, 1990	creation of the Democratic Party of Tajikistan
September 1990	creation of La'li Badakhshon in Tajikistan
October 6, 1990	establishment of the Tajik branch of the IRP
early 1990s	appearance of first HTI cells in Central Asia
early 1990s	activities of the first radical Islamists in Uzbekistan
June 9, 1990	creation of the Islamic Revival Party (IRP) of the USSR
January 1991	creation of a separate IRP for Uzbekistan
early 1990s	formation of Islam Lashkarlari
early 1990s	establishment of Adolat
November 1991	Rahmon Nabiev elected President of Tajikistan
December 4, 1991	official registration of the Islamic Revival Party of Tajikistan (IRPT)
December 8, 1991	collapse of the USSR
March–May 1992	rallies of supporters of the Islamist opposition at the Shahidon square and supporters of the government at the Ozodi square in Dushanbe
May 1992	formation of the government of national reconciliation in Tajikistan, beginning of military confrontation
September 7, 1992	forced resignation of Nabiev, active phase of civil war in Tajikistan
November 16, 1992	election of Emomali Rahmonov as chairman of the presidium of the Tajik Supreme Council, exodus of refugees from Tajikistan
February 1993	all-Muslim Kurultai of Uzbekistan ousted Muhammad Sadiq from the post of Mufti
1993	establishment of the Movement of Islamic Revival of Tajikistan, then the United Tajik Opposition (UTO), beginning of the "second civil war"
1993	ban on the Erk party in Uzbekistan
April 1994	beginning of official negotiations between the Tajik government and the UTO

December 23, 1996   creation of Commission of National Reconciliation
                    in Tajikistan
1996   creation of Islamic Movement of Uzbekistan (IMU)
June 27, 1996   General Agreement on Peace and National Accord
                    signed in Moscow by Rahmonov and Nuri
February 16, 1999   terrorist bombings of government buildings in
                    Tashkent
March 1999   Karimov's appeal to Uzbek militants to lay down
                    their arms in return for pardon
August 1999   IMU incursions into Kyrgyzstan and hostage
                    taking
August–   IMU units fight government troops in the south
   September, 2000 of Kyrgyzstan and the Surkhan Darya region of
                    Uzbekistan
2002   the IMU included in the U.S. Department of State
                    "List of Foreign Terrorist Organizations"
March–April, 2004   series of terrorist attacks in Uzbekistan
July 2004   attacks by suicide bombers on the embassies of the
                    United States and Israel and the office of General
                    Prosecutor in Tashkent

1

The Roots and Causes of Islamic Radicalism: The History of Islam in Central Asia

SOME BASIC CONCEPTS AND TERMS

Although the issue of conceptual tools as applied to Islamic currents and movements is not the subject for this study, a digression is required here to explain certain aspects of nomenclature. For Western researchers of contemporary Islam, it has become conventional to use the term *fundamentalism*,[1] which usually denotes the totality of tendencies in Islam that stand for getting back to the origins of the religion and purging it of subsequent extraneous features. This term, coined with reference to Christianity, encompasses in Islam a broad spectrum of widely diverging currents that are also called *revivalist* as well as *Salafi* (from the Arabic *salaf*, "ancestors")—the latter a much more fitting and authentic term to denote this phenomenon. The main idea of the Salafis, that is to say, Islamic fundamentalists, is that throughout the ages Islam has been distorted, and inadmissible innovations have been incorporated into it. Therefore, in order to purify the religion, one has to revert to its initial "pure" state in the era of the Prophet Muhammad and the four righteous caliphs (*al-Khulafa' al-Rashidun*)—Abu Bakr, 'Umar, 'Uthman, and 'Ali. This era is a source of constant inspiration for all Salafis. But by no means do all of the latter represent political Islam. Right up to recent times, the bulk of the Saudi Salafis, or Wahhabis, followers of Muhammad 'Abd al-Wahhab (1703/04–1797/98), an Arabian preacher whose conceptions have become the official ideology of Saudi Arabia, had not been politicized. Only in the 1960s did they start working intensively outside the kingdom, and the establishment of the World Muslim League gave them a powerful tool for

1

deep penetration into the Islamic world. Other transnational Islamic organizations, including charities, contributed to this process as well (ideologists of the Egyptian and later the Syrian Muslim Brotherhood were severely persecuted in their countries and fled to Saudi Arabia, where they
began to teach at Saudi universities and made a strong contribution to the
politicization of Wahhabism).[2] They would have gotten along well with
the ruling Saudi dynasty had the latter implemented the Wahhabis' ideas
of the "genuine" Islamic order. They, including many famous contemporary Saudi clerics, such as Shaykh 'Abd al-'Aziz b. Baz (d. 1999) or Shaykh
Ibn 'Uthaymin (d. 2001), still have devoted great attention to questions of
ritual (such as the obligatory practice of women wearing the full veil) and
Shari'a law. Some experts even qualify this everyday "quiet" Salafism as
apolitical. But in the same Saudi environment, particularly after the Soviet
invasion of Afghanistan, there arose a militant, jihadist Salafism, whose
most odious exponent is Usama bin Ladin. It is these Salafis who set their
objective as overthrowing the ruling Saudi regime and replacing it with a
purely Islamic one. Nevertheless, in the opinion of Olivier Roy, it is the
West, and not the Arabian regimes, that is the priority object of the Us-
amists' attack. Even so, both the nonjihadist and jihadist varieties of
Salafism are united by the doctrinal conception of *takfir*—an accusation of
godlessness (*kufr*) or anathemization (sometimes translated by Western
scholars as "excommunication") that constitutes a justification for any
tough punitive action toward Muslims who deviate even in an insignificant degree from the practice prescribed by Shari'a.

The term *jihadist* is commonly used by members of radical Islamic
groups themselves. Dr. Muhammad al-Massari, the head of a London-
based Saudi opposition group (Committee for the Defence of Legitimate
Rights) that favors the creation of an Islamic state in Saudi Arabia says:
"The word Wahhabi has become a misnomer. The U.S., for example, uses
it to denote Jihadists."[3] It should be noted that it is not exclusively radical
Salafis who are jihadists, that is, advocates of proclaiming "armed jihad"
(a holy war for Islam). For example, some Palestinian nationalist groups
carrying on armed struggle against Israel under the slogans of jihad, also
with the use of terrorist methods, are not of the Salafi type.

The term *jihadism* may be quite accurate to describe militant Islamic
groups that understand jihad as a war against the infidels, which in their
view menace Islam and Muslims, and against Muslim rulers who (again,
in their view) violate the precepts of Islam. Jihadists stand for a violent
overthrow of governments and resort to methods of violence, terrorism
included. Not all the Salafis, as already noted, are jihadists, but they often
become jihadist.

The term *integrism* underscores the indivisibility of the lay and the spiritual in the ideas of the Salafis, the term *Islamism* implies their adherence

to the idea of introducing Islamic Shari'a as a foundation of life in modern society, and the term *Islamic activism* applies to the radicalism of action in translating Salafi goals into reality.

The term *political Islam*, quite commonly used, underscores the fundamentalist indivisibility of religion and politics, as embodied in the conception of an Islamic state. Finally, the fundamentalists and the Salafis are sometimes likewise all called *Wahhabis*, extending to them a designation applied only to the Saudi Salafis and their cobelievers in other countries.

The founder of Wahhabism, Muhammad 'Abd al-Wahhab, did not create a new Sunni *madhhab* (a legal dogmatic school), being an adherent of Hanbalism, one of the most stringent varieties of Sunnism (named after Ahmad b. Hanbal). The Saudi Wahhabis were called puritans in view of both the austerity of their way of life and—first and foremost—their literal understanding of sacred texts, which did not in fact allow an interpretative explication (with the exception of that sanctioned by Hanbalism).

The application of the term *Wahhabism* to other Salafi tendencies not linked to the ideas of 'Abd al-Wahhab is not quite accurate, although these groups clearly have certain traits in common. It is no coincidence that the term *neo-Wahhabism* has appeared, which is rather frequently used by students of Islam to distinguish contemporary militant, politicized Saudi Wahhabis and various foreign groups coming under Wahhabi influence, as well as some other fundamentalists similar to them, from the traditional Arabian Wahhabis.

Within this research, I employ the term *Salafism* as a common denomination of all the schools of fundamentalist tendencies in Islam (as opposed to the term *fundamentalism*, Salafism is applicable to Islam alone). In so doing, I think it possible to identify, along with the division of Salafism into jihadist and nonjihadist, two other broad trends in it: conservative, or protective, and modernist.

The conservative, or protective, trend incorporates those Salafi schools that are trying as much as possible to "fence" Islam "in" from contemporary life, particularly from the influences of non-Islamic societies, while absolutizing the conception of *bid'a* (innovation) as being totally inadmissible for Islam. *Bid'a* is extended by the conservatives to a vast number of norms, procedures, and actions, including those that were "Islamized" many years ago and have become an organic part of Muslim life. The Salafis' extremely rigorous monotheism (*tawhid*, which was especially pronounced among the Arabian Wahhabis and also—even more markedly—among the "neo-Wahhabi" Taliban) leads, for example, to a renunciation of such customary attributes of modern life as the photographic portrayal of people, or children's toys depicting living creatures (humans or animals). The concept of *tawhid* is so important for the Wahhabis that it cannot be considered the main constructing idea of this trend

of thought. The Saudi Wahhabis often prefer calling themselves "the people of *tawhid*" rather than "Salafis" (and almost never "Wahhabis").[4] In
the puritan understanding of *tawhid*, the depiction of living creatures is
equated with *shirk*, literally translated as "complicity," and signifies that a
man is blasphemously placing himself on the same footing as Allah, apparently encroaching on his sole right to create them. Among radical
Salafi conservatives, *shirk* entails *takfir*. When *takfir* relates to a Muslim, according to radical Salafi ideas, he must be subjected to severe punishment,
right up to his physical elimination. So far, violence is necessary to return
to the Islamic world of the idealized era. In conservative Salafism there
are tougher, uncompromising, and softer moderate tendencies. In the latter trend, attitudes of extreme rigor become diluted. Thus a Wahhabi
scholar (*'alim*) I talked to in Saudi Arabia told me that it was admissible to
hang the photographs of one's parents or other ancestors about one's
lodgings, and this fosters greater piety among believers. Despite the apparent antiquatedness of their ideas, conservatives succeed in recruiting
many young followers. In a letter to a Western newspaper, one former
Saudi radical Wahhabi recollects: "For 11 years, from the age of 16, I was
a Wahhabi extremist. With like-minded companions I set fire to video
stores selling Western movies, and even burned down a charitable society
for widows and orphans in our village because we were convinced it
would lead to the liberation of women."[5] The severity of such a position
notwithstanding, one can see in it a certain fixation on ethics and culture
rather than politics.

It is noteworthy to tackle once more the issue of terms applied by scholars to different currents existing in the modern Saudi Salafism. The politicized Wahhabism (or neo-Wahhabism) is also called *Sahwism*, the term derived from *al-Sahwa al-Islamiyya* (the Islamic Awakening) that became
widespread in the 1970s, as opposed, on the one hand, to traditional, official Wahhabi religious establishment and, on the other hand, to a much
more militant, jihadist brand of Salafism that is frequently referred to as
"neo-Salafism." This jihadist brand was embodied in the activity of
Juhaiman al-'Utaibi and his followers, who in February 1979 occupied the
sacred sanctuary in Mecca. However, there are Salafis who strongly oppose the mere idea of jihad as a violent action based on the concept of *takfir*. Within this trend, a special sort of criticism against jihadism should be
mentioned. As a Saudi writer, Dr. Khalid al-Dukhayl argues, first, the idea
of jihad in Wahhabism was confined to the territory of the centralized
state that its founders had built in the Arabian Peninsula and, second,
given their affiliation with Hanbalism the Wahhabis cannot accept jihad
without the approval of *waliyy al-amr* (head of the religious establishment)
and his official declaration.[6]

It would be appropriate to describe modernist Salafism as a type of "reformism," and this word well expresses the main significance of this doctrine. Islamic reformism, however, has a much broader scope and bears an obvious modernizing, educating, enlightening connotation. The Salafis of this variety also call for a return to primordial Islam, but they level their criticism against musty prejudices and customs incorporated into Islam from the traditional pre-Islamic beliefs and rituals of Islamized nations. Rejecting the norms incompatible with the true values of Islam, these reformers have called on Muslims to utilize the modern scientific and technological achievements of the West in the interests of the Islamic *umma*, to borrow what can be useful for the development of Muslim society, and to modernize the system of school education.

Both the Salafi conservatives and the modernist reformers have confronted the traditionalists (including the Sufis). In the process, the boundaries between the former and the latter have often become blurred, since among the traditionalists there are also "protective" conservatives and modernists. On some issues of dogma and ritual, the Salafis and the traditionalists of various hues find themselves in mutual agreement, while on others their antagonism reaches an extreme point; but a no lesser hostility separates different trends within both Salafism and traditionalism. For instance, the Arabian Wahhabis are irreconcilable opponents of the cult of saints in Islam and the performance of pilgrimages to their tombs, deeming that those making such pilgrimages sinfully commit a deplorable *shirk*. This is directed against the Sufis—adherents of Sufism, a mystical trend in Islam whose essence consisted of the idea of man's communion with Allah. At the same time, when the late nineteenth to early twentieth century saw the emergence of Jadidism (from the Arabic *jadid*, "new")—a revivalist reform movement that had as one objective the creation of a modern-type educational system for Muslims (they called it *usul-i jadid*, or "new foundations," from which their name is derived)[7]— this was unacceptable for both the "protective" Salafis (of the Wahhabi type) and for the conservative traditionalists, the Qadimists (from the Arabic *qadim*, "old"). The Jadidists' argument with the traditionalists was about the content of faith. They opposed the traditionalist principle of *taqlid* (literally "imitation"), which prescribes the blind following of the spiritual authorities, something that was also criticized by the "protective" Salafis.

In a modern Saudi manual, *Teaching to Pray*, translated into Russian and distributed far and wide among Muslims in Russia and other Commonwealth of Independent States (CIS) countries, Dr. 'Abdallah b. Ahmad al-Zayd says: "He who of his own will performs an act of worship (prayer, fast, supplication, vow, sacrifice or plea for salvation) addressed to anyone besides Allah, to a monument or benefactor, falls into polytheism, and this is one of the greatest sins which brings all good acts to naught. He who does this may be killed, while his property may be taken away."[8] It can easily be seen that such a call for murder may be directed against Sufis.

Sometimes it is impossible to draw a clear-cut division between fundamentalists and traditionalists, conservatives and reformers, because of the complexity and multifaceted nature of the theological and juridical arguments in Islam and because of the profusion of schools and tendencies (and also their historical evolution). However, it is not always necessary to do so. It is more fruitful to adopt a case-by-case approach, which requires that a particular current in Islam be examined in a specific place and at a specific time. A proper understanding of our specific place and specific time requires a general excursion into the history of Islam in Central Asia.

THE SPREAD OF ISLAM IN CENTRAL ASIA

In the seventh century, Arab Muslim troops conquered Central Asia, which they called Ma Wara' al-Nahr ("What Is Beyond the River," with "river" referring to Amu Darya, or the Oxus). In Ma Wara' al-Nahr, or Transoxania, which was incorporated into the Arab Caliphate, Islam began to spread. It became the official religion of the Samanid state (875–999), with the city of Bukhara as its capital, which became independent of Baghdad, the capital of the great Abbasid Caliphate. This gave an impetus to further development of Muslim science and education in the region, the spread of Arabic, and also the Islamization of the settled and nomadic populations. In Ma Wara' al-Nahr, a great number of mosques and *madrasas* (Islamic seminaries) were built at that time, and a stratum of educated Muslim clergy and intellectuals was formed. The *faqih*, or "lawyer," and *'alim*, or "scholar" (from *fiqh* and *'ilm*), were the most important personages in that group of intellectuals. *Fiqh* means jurisprudence and regulates religious observances (*'ibadat*), as well as public life, private life, and even business (*mu'amalat*). It includes family law, the law of inheritance, and criminal law. *Tafsir* (interpretation of the Qur'an) and the Hadiths (a record of actions or sayings of the Prophet Muhammad and his companions) were also parts of *fiqh*.

In early Islamic theology, *fiqh* was opposed to *'ilm* (knowledge), and accordingly, *'alim* (plur. *'ulama*) differed from *faqih* (plur. *fuqaha*), but they were close to each other and could be combined in one person. In modern Islam, *fiqh* is more separate from *'ilm*, and *faqih* has the narrower meaning of "canon lawyer or casuist," while *'alim* means "Islamic scholar" in a broad sense.[9]

Islam in Ma Wara' al-Nahr was spread mostly in the form of Sunnism, although a certain part of the local population became adherents of Shi'a and Isma'iliyya. In the epoch when the main *madhhabs*—schools of *fiqh*—in Sunnism were formed, some of them vied for influence in Ma Wara' al-Nahr, but gradually Hanafism displaced the other schools.

Hanafism is one of the four *madhhabs* (Hanafi, Shafi'i, Maliki, Hanbali) in Sunni Islam and is named after Imam al-Nu'man b. Thabit b. Zuta Abu Hanifa (700–767). This school, known by its adherence to the rationalistic methods of judgment, laid down rules in *fiqh*.

Abu Hanifa also exerted a strong influence on the dogmatics of Islam. This school emerged in Iraq and was the dominant doctrine during the reign of the Abbasid Caliphs. Hanafism began to expand to the east of the empire and enjoyed particular success not only in Ma Wara'al-Nahr but also in Khurasan (a province of Iran).

The Hanafites are usually distinguished from other scholars by their application of subjective opinion (*ra'y*). Their tradition flourished in Central Asia, where Abu Mansur al-Maturidi al-Samarqandi (d. 944), one of the most prominent followers of Abu Hanifa, created his school of scholastic theology (*kalam*), which together with that of al-Ash'ari forms the essence of Sunni theology. The Maturidiyya became the form in which Hanafism turned into the dominant *madhhab* in Transoxania in the tenth century. From that time on, only the Hanafi *fuqaha* and *'ulama* were appointed to all the religious posts in the state: *imam-khatib* (imam at a Friday mosque, who was authorized to deliver a sermon, or *khutba*); *muhtasib* (originally market inspector); *mudarris* (teacher at a *madrasa*); and others. The wide use of *ijma'* (a collective, consensual opinion of lawyers that was relied upon) in Hanafism facilitated the Islamization of pre-Islamic norms and traditions, and in the end it helped to escape tensions between the new and old systems of beliefs, thus accelerating the smooth adoption of Islam.

The success of Hanafism arose to a great extent because it was tolerant of pre-Islamic popular customs and rites, many of which were incorporated into Islam. Some norms of *'urf* and *'adat* (tribal and customary law) were recognized as legal, not contradicting *fiqh*. For example, among many Islamized popular customs and rites in Central Asia was the *sayyil*, or *sayyil-bayram*, a festival of spring revelry falling in late April to early May (mostly among the Turcophone peoples of Central Asia). The celebration of the *sayyil* starts with a reading from the Qur'an (a common Islamizing tool) and visits to the graves of ancestors and saints, before ending in mass feasts. The rural clergy adapted this festival to Islamic rituals, but theologians and the *'ulama* see clear traces of pre-Islamic customs in it. Other examples are the tying of colored pieces of cloth to trees and *tugs* (a wooden pole put over the tomb of an ancestor or a saint), the kissing of headstones, and the rubbing of graveside dust over one's face. The religious class was closely connected to traditions not only through the preserving and performance of those Islamized rites and customs but also because it was interwoven with the traditional social structure of the Central Asian society. Divisions into different types of tribal, clan, patronymic, kinship, professional, and other groups lived almost unchanged through centuries. (The scope of this volume does not include the exact classification of these groups from the point of view of anthropological science, although a brief excursion into this system in Tajikistan will be made in chapter 4.) The dwellers of towns and large villages lived in *mahallas*—neighborhoods that functioned sometimes as semi–self-governed units, each with a mosque and a *maktab*, or religious primary school.

The Hanafi clergy and scholars played an important role in the administrative and political life of medieval Central Asia. The head of the Hanafites in Bukhara (*ra'is*) even acquired hereditary power in Bukhara in the eleventh century, which his family wielded until the Mongol conquest in the thirteenth century. As throughout the whole history of the Islamic world, the indissoluble bond between Islam on the one hand and politics and power on the other here has repeatedly been confirmed.

In the tenth to the thirteenth centuries, theologians and lawyers of Ma Wara' al-Nahr, such as al-Nasafi and al-Pazdawi, won great renown. Works by Central Asian lawyers and theologians became the canonical literature of Hanafism, used for teaching at local *madrasas*.

Central Asian Hanafi scholars called themselves *Ahl al-Sunna wal-Jama'a* (People of the Sunna and Concord). This designation goes back to a Hadith where Muhammad says that the Muslim communities will fragment into seventy-three sects (*firqa*), of which only one will remain—*Ahl al-Sunna wal-Jama'a* (the Sufis likewise claimed to be called the same). These Hanafi scholars emphasized their righteousness in such a manner. However, in Islam there was basically no orthodoxy in the sense in which it exists in Christianity: there is no canonization of doctrines, texts (with the exception of the Qur'an), interpretations, or people. Therefore the use of the term "orthodoxy" as applied to certain Sunni conceptions by many Western researchers has to be considered inaccurate. This term is best avoided altogether. The term "clergy," which is sometimes conventionally used to denote the Muslim religious class and actually cannot be shunned here, is a more difficult matter, it being understood that there is, strictly speaking, no clergy in Islam. Islam does not accept the concept of mediation between God and believers. A person who leads a prayer or presents a sermon is a believer who is recognized as having acquired a better knowledge of religion than his cobelievers and hence can be trusted to perform these duties.

The righteousness of any trend was tested by its adherence to the Qur'an; however, each trend interpreted the sacred text in its own way, and at any specific moment in any specific place the trend that supported the state and that the people followed was considered orthodox.

As the Russian scholar Tawfiq Ibrahim accurately remarks, "What Islam cared for was the advancement not of *orthodoxy* ('right faith') but of *orthopraxy* ('right action'). Therefore, Muslim civilization sought to conceptualize, institutionalize, and canonize *fiqh* as practical theology, not *kalam* as dogmatic, theoretical theology. One cannot, however, interpret Muslim law as 'totalitarian'—a juridical qualification, for although it looks all-embracing, in fact, it categorizes the greater part of actions as 'permissible,' that is 'neutral.'"[10]

The controversy, not only between Sunnism and Shi'ism, but also among the various *madhhabs* of Sunnism, at times reached great acuteness. The dispute between the traditionalists and the rationalists took on very harsh forms, sometimes even within the same *madhhab*. Whereas the former made an absolute out of emulating authority (whether books or preceptors), the latter largely relied on methods of reasoning, analogies, and mental conclusions (everything that became the pivot of *kalam*). Traditionalists sharply criticized both the Ash'arites and the Maturidites. In various regions of the Abbasid Caliphate, the Hanafites seriously conflicted with the Hanbalites, followers of Ahmad b. Muhammad b. Hanbal (780–855), who fully depended on the traditional sources of Islam and literal understanding of texts, admitting *ra'y* only as a last resort, when traditional sources could not give an answer to the questions that arose.

Sufism gained wide acceptance in Ma Wara' al-Nahr. Sufi brotherhoods of Central Asia—Naqshbandiyya, Yasaviyya, Qadiriyya, Qubraviyya—exerted the strongest impact on the cultural and sociopolitical life of the region, in which a new stratum of the religious class was formed, the influential leaders and preceptors of Sufi brotherhoods: pirs, ishans,[11] and shaykhs.[12]

In the opinion of Ashirbek Muminov, a researcher from Uzbekistan, the sources of future collisions within the religious class can be traced to the early stages in the penetration of Islam into Central Asia. Thus if the residents of large urban centers, after having adopted Islam, became *mawali*—a distinctive estate group standing below the Arabs, being their "clients"—then the inhabitants of outlying rural and mountain regions of Ma Wara' al-Nahr made use of the Qahtanid (South Arabian) tradition, which was in common currency among the conquerors, to assert their own Yemeni origins. Pre-Islamic holy places started being transformed into Islamic ones, and the characters of the Qahtanid Tubba' tradition (As'ad al-Kamil and others) became the objects of worship.[13]

Thus the local cult of saints absorbed the strata of both local and Arab mythology, while the incorporation of local elements into Islam was probably one of the reasons the new religion swiftly took root in the local soil.

A similar judgment can be made about the Muslim "clergy" that was in process of being formed after the conquest. It absorbed members of the former, pre-Islamic elite and priesthood. Parallels with the present inevitably suggest themselves: the Soviet party and state *nomenklatura* in our times effectively inscribed itself into the new order, becoming its foundation. The activity of the Karakhanids (840–1212), who turned the tombs of their progenitors into holy places of Islam, was an example of effective transformation in the period of Islamization in Central Asia.[14] The holy places served as a platform for Sufism, whose roots in the entire Muslim world went back to non-Islamic influence. Let us turn once again to the conclusion of Muminov, who remarked that, first, "the founders of brotherhoods were direct ancestors of well-known persons buried near the holy places," second, "the inception of Sufi brotherhoods was the result of long intellectual activity of the so-called rural clergy," and, third, "all the activity of the shaykhs proceeded in *hanqahs* [hostelries] near the holy places."[15] Thus if one is to agree with these explanations, the dichotomy "urban–rural clergy" had already been formed in the Middle Ages, in the era of Islamization.

The Mongol conquest of the thirteenth century was a catastrophe for Central Asian civilization. Bukhara, by that time one of the greatest cultural centers of the Muslim world, was almost destroyed. Now its mosques and *madrasas* were lying in ruins. It was only later, in the fourteenth century, that the role of Islam as the official religion of Central Asia began to reemerge. By that time, the Mongol conquerors had also become Muslims: Islam became the state religion of the Golden Horde under Khan Uzbek (1313–1341). But in that era, it was no longer the *'ulama*, as it was before the conquest, but Sufi shaykhs and ishans who played a paramount role in the religious class. Sufi symbols and rituals—"tombs of saints", or *mazars*; *zikr* ("remembrance," a custom to glorify Allah with certain brief, prescribed phrases), and dervishes—became the quintessence of popular Islam, joining together the diverse ethnic groups of the population. Sufi dervishes (*qalandars*) had no homes and lived in *hanqahs*. Members of the Naqshbandiyya brotherhood were often addressed as hajjis (pilgrims).

The region again became one of the centers of Islam under Timur (1336–1405) and the Timurids (especially under Timur's grandson, Ulugh Beg, 1394–1449), when masterpieces of Muslim architecture—mosques, mausoleums, and *madrasas*, such as the Shah-i Zinda ensemble, the Bibi Khanum mosque, the Gur-e Amir Mausoleum, and the Ulugh Beg *madrasa*—were built. The Bukhara Khanate emerged in the sixteenth century after a chief of a confederation of Uzbek tribes, Shaybani Khan, established his sovereignty over a part of Ma Wara' al-Nahr. Central Asia became an arena of intensive rivalry between the diverse ethnic and tribal groups, local dynasties, and foreign power centers. The Bukhara Khanate was ruled consequently by the Uzbek tribal dynasties of Shaybanids, Janids, and finally Mangyts (1753–1920). Unlike the first two dynasties, the Mangyts (the founder of this dynasty was Muhammad Rahim) were not recognized as descendants of Genghis Khan and therefore could not bear the title of khans and were called amirs, thus the Bukhara state under their rule was an amirate (and only traditionally addressed in some sources as a khanate).

Toward the time of the region's conquest by the Russian Empire, in Central Asia there existed several khanates, the main ones being Bukhara, Kokand, and Khiva, where Islam of a Hanafi Sunni variety remained the official religion. Traditionalism was a prevailing trend in the religious education and scholarly discourse. The students of Islam were receiving religious knowledge mostly by memorizing the sacred texts. The religious class held strong positions in these states—for example, the chief judge (qazi kalon) of Bukhara, who headed the hierarchy of qadis (or qazis), was one of the most influential people in the state. Sufi shaykhs and ishans retained a strong influence on public life and affairs of state.

Samarqand. The famous Gur-e Amir Mausoleum (photo 2002). Built under Amir Timur after the tragic death of his grandson Muhammad Sultan in 1403.

The mausoleum on the grave of Khoja Bahauddin Naqshband
(1318–1389), after whom the Naqshbandiyya Sufi brotherhood
was named, in the village of Kasro Arifon, Bukhara (photo
2002). Built in 1554 by Abd al-Aziz I, the Khan of Bukhara.

Zikr (photo 1896).

ISLAM IN CENTRAL ASIA AS PART OF
THE RUSSIAN EMPIRE AND THE USSR

Russia had begun to penetrate into Central Asia from the times of Peter the Great (1689–1725), but the conquest of the region took place in the second half of the nineteenth century, when a substantial part of it was annexed to the empire in the form of the Turkestan Governorship-General (which included the former Kokand Khanate), Bukhara and Khiva becoming Russia's protectorates. Despite the policy of containing the influence of Islam, it remained a significant power even in Turkestan. In 1908 in Turkestan there were 2,571 jum'a mosques (big mosques for Friday prayers), 8,812 neighborhood (mahalla) mosques, 1,211 mazars with 1,142 shaykhs, 6,102 maktabs (religious primary schools) for male students and 801 for female students, 336 madrasas, and 14,375 other schools, with 103,377 students in all these schools.[16] By the time of the Bolshevik revolution in Russia in 1917, the religious class in Central Asia comprised numerous groups of ministers at mosques (imams and mullas), supervisors of religious endowments (mutawallis), muftis, men of law (muhtasibs—originally, market inspectors—and qadis, or qazis), theologians and scholars ('ulama), keepers of mazars, mudarrises, traditional religious authorities (Sufi shaykhs, ishans, pirs), and so on. The overwhelming majority of the "clergy" belonged to privileged classes of Central Asian society.

Khiva. The mosque at the Pahlavan-Ahmad mazar (photo 1873). The tomb cupola is surrounded by goats' skulls with horns.

In the prerevolutionary era, the population of Central Asia was traditionally divided into *ok-suyak* "blue blood"(literally, "white bone") and *koracha* "mob." In a very general sense, *ok-suyak* comprised sayyids and khojas, the structure of this estate being different in various regions of Central Asia. Sayyids claimed descent from the Prophet Muhammad, just as sayyids or sharifs in most countries of the Muslim East did, tracing their origin to 'Ali b. Abi Talib, who married the Prophet's daughter Fatima and had children by her. Khojas claimed descent from the "righteous caliphs" (the first four caliphs ruling the Arab Caliphate after the Prophet's death, including 'Ali) or even from Arabs in general. Members of the third group were called *tura* and viewed as descendants of the great Mongol conqueror Genghis Khan. The *tura* estate appeared in Central Asia after the Mongol conquest and became part and parcel of the aristocratic estate groups of the population. In some parts of the region, the honorific title *mir* was used also to address those who were recognized as descendants of the first three righteous caliphs (the descendants of the forth one, as mentioned, being sayyids). The homonymic term was used to designate provincial governors, who were in other places called *begs* (*beks*).

In the late nineteenth and early twentieth centuries, the dynamics of religious life in Central Asia were largely shaped by the above-mentioned con-

Amir Abd al-Ahad, the ruler of the Bukhara Amirate in 1885–1910, succeeded by Sayyid Mir-Alim, the last amir of Bukhara, who ruled in 1910–1920 (photo 1893).

flict between the Jadidist modernizers and the Qadimist (from Arabic *qadim*—old) conservatives. The conservatives were dominating the sphere of religious education. Since the epoch of the Timurids until the twentieth century, as Uzbek scholars remark, the traditionalist system of religious education existed without changes. "On the whole, 'the scholastic isolation' in the system of medieval education may be viewed as one of the parameters of entrenched traditionalization of both theology and society. But even the available set of theological sciences in many *madrasas* (especially small ones) gradually began to be more and more confined to applied subjects whose knowledge could be useful in the mosques and in the judicial and legislative spheres, for example, in the profession of local *qadi* (these were, for instance, the rules of reading the Qur'an, initial knowledge of the Hadiths, and the fundamentals of *fiqh*)."[17] The term *scholastic* is not quite an appropriate word to describe the system of education in the religious schools and seminaries of Central Asia. Scholasticism, due to its connection with *kalam*, implies a certain degree of rationalistic speculation. However, this

The Shirbudun Palace. The amir's harem (photo 1890s).

system did not include any sort of theoretical discourse and was based almost exclusively on learning texts by heart, strictly following opinions of
religious authorities on the basis of a *taqlid* (imitation, exact following). So I
prefer to describe this system of education rather as rigidly dogmatic and
pedantic.[18] As I mentioned earlier, there were a lot of *madrasas* in the territory of the khanates of Bukhara and Khiva before the Russian colonization,
but most of them were small and comprised from two to six *hujras*.[19] The
conservation of dogmatic traditionalism in the Central Asian societies was
to a great extent facilitated also by the local social structure based on the importance of various patronage networks and solidarity groups (clans, extended families, tribes, regional communities, neighborhoods, etc.).

Before the colonization, there existed a system of state inspection of the
functioning of *madrasas* in all Central Asian khanates through the institution of *sadrs, shaykh al-islams,* and so forth. This system spread to inspection of the *madrasas'* financial activity in the form of the reports of
mutawallis—inspectors of expenses, payment for the work of *mudarrises,*
fellowships for students, charitable dinners, and so forth. After the Russian conquest of the Kokand Khanate in 1876, the inspection system was
liquidated, and the colonial administration confined its control to *waqfs*
(property or money donated for charitable or religious purposes) so as to
prevent any violations in the sphere of taxation. The tsarist administration also watched over the appointment of *mudarrises* and the checking
of their political loyalty.[20]

Sayyid Muhammad Rahim II Bahadur Khan, the ruler of the Khiva Khanate in 1865–1910, with his ministers (photo 1896).

A number of religious figures, particularly in the Bukharan Amirate, shared some proto-Salafi views. They were the third party in the struggle between the already mentioned Jadidists and the Qadimists, such as the Vaisov Group (the Vaisites) in the late nineteenth and early twentieth centuries in Tatarstan. The Vaisites (whose founder had spent a good deal of time in Turkestan) once called on the people to behead seventy thousand government-appointed mullas, and similar appeals were later issued by Bukharan fundamentalists, who called on believers to extirpate all modernists. The Vaisites, as a Tatar researcher writes, "proposed a mythical version of the Muslim *umma* (community, or people) of the first centuries of the *Hijra*." In addition, they "insisted that they had the right to call for armed struggle."[21] Taking into account the historical interrelationships between Turkestani and Volga Tatar Islam, the Vaisite ideology can be considered as one of the sources of modern Central Asian Salafism.

Khiva girls (photo 1896).

It was important for the fate of political Islam in Central Asia that in the early twentieth century a few Islamic political parties were established there: their experience became part of the region's ideological and political heritage. Among them was *Ush Zhuz* (Three Hordes), which was founded in the Syr Darya region in 1913 by the mullas of Bukhara and local merchants. In 1916, the residents of Khiva excited a rebellion for independence, which was followed by the inhabitants of Turkestan protesting against a decision by the tsarist government to mobilize some of the population as part of the army. The rebellion proclaimed Islamic slogans. In the Jizak area (in today's Uzbekistan), one of the local ishans, Ishan Nazir khoja, proclaimed jihad against Russia.

Islam's involvement in politics notably increased with the downfall of tsarism as a result of the February 1917 revolution, which ushered in some progress toward democratization of Russia's internal political life. On May 1–11, 1917, the First All-Russian Muslim Congress set up a Muslim Central Agency, a Muslim Central Council (Milli Shuro), and an Executive Committee (Ikomus). The Second Congress, in June 1917, also decided to set up a Muslim Military Council (Harbi Shuro) and an All-Russia Muslim Directorate (Milli Idare) and to hold a Muslim National Assembly in November 1917. The Second Congress exhibited a strong tendency toward pan-Islamism, while the Military Council started recruiting soldiers into a Muslim army.

Further growth of this activity was prevented by the Bolshevik revolution in October 1917, which struck a blow at the position of Islam in Central

Execution in Bukhara (photo 1890s).

Asia, the whole of which subsequently became part of the Soviet Union. In the beginning, the Turkestan Autonomous Soviet Republic, a constituent unit of the Russian Federation, was established. The People's Soviet Republics of Bukhara and Khorezm, the latter of which had concluded treaties with the Russian Federation, remained outside of its jurisdiction until 1924. In the mid-1920s, during the process of "national-territorial delimitation," the region was divided into a number of union republics on an ethnic basis, and new boundaries were demarcated.

The Bolshevik administration tried to boost the formation of Soviet republics by promoting titular ethnic groups, some of which had not even existed before the Bolshevik revolution of 1917 under the names they were given or within the boundaries they were assigned. For example, several ethnic groups were ordered to form a united Uzbek nation, and the Iranian-speaking groups of the eastern part of Central Asia were included in the Tajik nation. Borders between the republics were also demarcated without any consideration for historic realities. It should be recognized that such situations arose not only because of some designs of the party and state leadership but also due to the absence of any natural borders between many ethnic groups that could be used as bases for demarcation. The demarcation process was also influenced by the lobbying activities of local Communist leaders who demanded administrative power over particular territory. Probably, it was impossible to find an ideal way to implement the idea of nation-state building as it was planned, given that these republics, whatever the borders, in any case would have widely dispersed ethnic populations. This being so, the borders drawn between these territorial-state entities did not correspond to the borderlines of ethnic settlements.

In the initial postrevolutionary period, the Bolshevik government felt a need for support by the Muslim population, and hence the government took serious steps to meet Muslim wishes, proclaiming freedom and inviolability of their rights, customs, and traditions. A significant section of educated Muslims, especially Jadids and some mullas, and peasants and nomads responded to the slogans of the new regime and backed the revolution. Many Islamic reformers naïvely believed that socialism would bring national liberation to their peoples. While the Bolsheviks regarded the empire's Orthodox clergy as one of their main enemies, as it had been one of the pillars of the former regime, in the Muslim religious class they saw an ally, albeit temporary. The tactic of attracting Muslims brought its reward, but an offensive against Islam, soon unleashed by the authorities, and the ensuing upsurge of nationalism caused a swelling in the ranks of an armed resistance movement, which took the name of basmachi ("robbers"), of a jihadist nature hostile to the Sovietization of Central Asia. The ishans, shaykhs, and 'ulama were the first to declare war on the atheistic power. The basmachi movement was not finally crushed until the mid-1930s.

Facing defeat, basmachi leaders called on citizens who supported them to escape from repression by performing the Hijra (migration), as the Prophet Muhammad had done in his time, to dar al-Islam, "lands of Islam," or by going on a hajj. Thus in certain Muslim countries (Afghanistan, Saudi Arabia), a substantial Central Asian diaspora was formed whose representatives in the future, at the end of the twentieth century, would play an important role in diffusing political Islam throughout the newly independent states of Central Asia.

Relying upon Jadidist intellectuals, who supported the Bolshevik revolution, the Communist authorities decided to reform the traditional system of general and religious education. A moderate Jadidist, Munavvar qari Abdurrashidkhanov (b. 1878; he was executed in 1931), was authorized to be in charge of the implementation of important changes. "All educational institutions, which tried to oppose reforms, were deprived of waqf properties, or simply closed. The consequences of reforms were soon reflected on the traditional system of education. First of all, the teaching of religious sciences began to be conducted in national languages (Uzbek and Tajik) with the use of a new system of Arabic script (usul-i jadid), instead of the traditional Persian or Chagatai written language. The new generation of theologians and their supporters increasingly began using this script."[22]

In the 1930s, the state meted out the harshest repressive measures against local Islam and particularly the religious class. Many mosques were destroyed, many madrasas were closed, and many members of the religious class were subjected to reprisals. Many of those Jadids who supported the regime, served it, or even entered the Communist Party perished during purges. Official Islam was placed under tight state control, an active atheism was pursued, and Sufi brotherhoods were persecuted. However, popular Islam endured and went into hiding, into private life. Even many party and government functionaries, officially atheists, especially in the period after World War II when there was no mass repression, secretly observed Islamic rites, including those such as the performance of *ziyarat* to the tombs of saints.

There is still a broadly held opinion that in Soviet times Islam in Central Asia existed only in its official form (the Spiritual Board of Muslims, or SADUM; the Bukharan *madrasa*, reopened only in 1945; the Islamic Institute in Tashkent; and a few government-controlled mosques) and in the form of popular Islam. However, as will be shown in the next chapter, Islam also existed as an informal system of spiritual education, parallel to the official one. This alternative system of religious education, in the absence of a relevant official one, was embodied in the form of private underground teaching courses that emerged in the Ferghana Valley under the name *hujra* (Arabic for "room"). Since then, *hujra* has carried two different meanings: (1) a room in a *madrasa* where a student of Islam lives and studies and (2) an informal private school bearing the name of the teacher, as explained in the next chapter.

Islam also existed as theological—dogmatic and legal—thought. Moreover, within this parallel discourse, a polemic was carried on between champions of different views, sometimes reaching a point of bitter confrontation, while among the exponents of this unofficial Islam there were—at least through the 1960–1970s—adherents of political Islam. The hidden history of Central Asian Islam in the Soviet period has yet to be studied, but it is beyond doubt that the discovery of new facts and materials and their profound analysis may reveal a lot of new surprises.

In analyzing the roots of Islamic radicalism in this region, one has to bear in mind a multiplicity of approaches and explanations for this phenomenon in general. I'll try to formulate in a generalized form the main contending explanations as I see them, though in some cases they remain implicit and cannot be reduced to or even exemplified by particular statements of certain individuals.

THE ROOTS OF ISLAMIC RADICALISM: CONTENDING APPROACHES AND EXPLANATIONS

Economic approaches stress the importance of socioeconomic conditions as the cause of Islamic militancy. The general assumption is that poverty, underdevelopment, unemployment, and other grievances give birth to extremism. These economic explanations can be further subdivided into "static" and "dynamic" models.

The static approach, which emphasizes conditions at a particular moment, is unconvincing for a number of reasons. First, it cannot explain why radicalism is on the rise and able to mobilize supporters in some countries but not others where economic conditions are equally dire. Second, it cannot explain why extremism, including Islamic radicalism, appears in societies that are relatively developed socioeconomically. Moreover, statistical analyses confirm that a low standard of living has no direct or significant effect on the rise of Islamic extremism. Saudi Arabia, for example, is one of the wealthiest countries in the Middle East, but the Saudis are nevertheless among the strongest supporters of Islamic radicalism. On the other end of the spectrum, Mauritania is one of the poorest Muslim countries on earth, but it does not appear to be prone to religious extremism. Also, many leaders of the most extremist Islamist groups have originated from distinguished and wealthy families and have received good modern educations, as was the case with founders of Communist and leftist extremist movements of the past (capitalist Engels, aristocrat count Kropotkin, landlord Castro, Sorbonne graduate Pol Pot, and so forth). Usama bin Ladin's family's enterprise is widely known as one of the wealthiest corporations in Saudi Arabia, and his right arm in al-Qa'ida, Ayman al-Zawahiri, himself a physician, belongs to the family of rectors of one of the most famous Egyptian universities.

In an effort to address these shortcomings, some scholars have offered a more convincing approach based on economic factors. The emphasis here is on relative economic deprivation. A significant decline in living standards, it is argued, often engenders extremism. While this economic explanation seems more appealing, it does not seem to explain the rise of Islamic militancy over the past several decades. For example, Uzbekistan has become a hotbed for the most ferocious Islamic movements in Central Asia, despite the fact that its decline in living standards has been less than that of some other Central Asian countries in the post-Soviet period.[23]

The idea of social justice is relevant to this explanation. "There is a profound sense of injustice and humiliation in the Islamic world," believes Jason Burke, a well-known specialist in al-Qa'ida. "Injustice has a particular religious significance in Islam, and that's an absolutely huge part of the militants' appeal."[24] These words can be applied to the present situation in Central Asia, where a feeling of injustice is constantly feeding all radical Islamist movements.

An alternative hypothesis stresses not economic but *political* deprivation. Frustration and discontent arise from the lack of participation, oppressive regimes, widespread corruption, and the pressure of patronage networks. Graham Fuller is right when he observes, "For many reasons political Islam still remains the only realistic major alternative to most of today's authoritarian regimes."[25] However, this approach also cannot explain all cases: there are many very authoritarian regimes that do not ignite Islamic militancy, as in Turkmenistan. All these speculations belong to the family of grievance-based explanations. Their authors in one way or another are preoccupied with the prevailing importance of economic, social, political, and other structural precipitating factors for Islamic radicalism.

The *ideological* explanation, which has become particularly popular in the West since September 11, argues that Islam as a religion, or at least some schools of thought within Islam that are usually called fundamentalist or Salafi, contains ideas that profess intolerance and hatred of non-Muslims as well as of Muslims who supposedly violate the norms of "authentic" Islam. There is also concern about the efforts by some Islamic schools of thought to spread their influence to states where Muslims are not a majority. For example, a radical cleric in Tatarstan (Russia), Nurulla Muflikhunov, has asserted, "*Kafirs* (infidels) who are friendly with Muslims do not acquire *iman* (Islamic faith), whereas Muslims who are friendly with *kafirs* lose their faith, appear before Allah as *kafirs* themselves and are punished accordingly." He has also stated, "Those who do not adopt Islam are the enemies of Allah and of Muslims. . . ."[26]

Some scholars, however, do not view Salafism, regardless of divisions within it, as responsible for militancy. John Esposito, for example, has argued, "Islamic modernists and movements like the Muslim Brotherhood of Egypt and Pakistan's *Jamiat-i-Islami* worked to combine religious reform and political mobilization."[27] Still others point out that political mobilization does not necessarily turn Islamic activists into perpetrators or advocates of violence. In the words of François Burgat, "The Quran can 'explain' Usama bin Ladin no more than the Bible can 'explain' the IRA."[28] This view is supported by the existence of nonviolent Salafi organizations such as Jamaat-i-Tabligh (in Pakistan) or the existence of a clear-cut moderate trend (parallel to the radical one) within the North Caucasian Salafist movement that was headed by the late Ahmed *qadi* Akhtaev (d. March 1998).

In accordance with such a view, the expanded version of jihad that Islamic extremists have embraced has little to do with the roots of Islam to which the Salafis appeal. Many Western scholars have argued that the ideas of terrorist jihadists such as Usama bin Ladin are in fact deviations from "true Islam." For example, John Esposito argues that terrorists ignore classical Islamic criteria for a just jihad.[29] Most Islamic clerics also blame the "global terrorist jihadists" in Palestine, Kashmir, Chechnya, and elsewhere for violating basic Islamic principles. They point out that "big jihad" (which means violent struggle against the enemies of Islam, in contrast to the "small jihad," which means the personal effort of an individual Muslim to enforce belief within himself) is justified only when the existence of Muslims is threatened, when their rights are violated, or when their land is taken from them.

While it may be fruitless to try to convince people who are determined to take the lives of their enemies and die in the process that their commitment is not justified by Islamic teachings, it is true that there is nothing in Islam that justifies suicide attacks in the name of God. As Bernard Lewis has noted, suicide attacks are prohibited by a number of passages from the traditions of the Prophet, such as "Whoever kills himself in any way will be tormented in that way in Hell" and "Whoever kills himself in any way in this world will be tormented with it on the day of the resurrection."[30] Nor are suicide attacks exclusive to Islam. Many non-Muslims have engaged in the practice, including European partisans during World War II, Japanese kamikaze pilots, nationalists in today's India and Sri Lanka, and so on. The key elements here are the motivations underlying suicide attacks and the driving force that justifies them in the minds of those who carry them out.

One cannot but see that radical Islamic organizations sometimes fill the vacuum formed in the political spectrum. Thus "many Arabs see in revitalized Islam an alternative to defeated Arab nationalism and stifled leftist ideologies. This probably explains the ease with which many Lebanese Shi'i communists and Arab nationalists shifted to Hizbullah in the 1980s."[31] Not only Arab nationalists (Nasserists, Ba'thists, and the MAN members) after the decline of this movement but also former Marxists and other leftists after the collapse of communism in Eastern Europe shifted to radical Islamism in the Middle East. All of them underwent the process of re-Islamization.[32]

Behavioral and *psychological* explanations interpret these motivations. Behavioral explanations view Islamic extremism as a specific type of behavior based on exclusion and intolerance of outsiders. However, as Ernest Gellner has observed in reference to similar claims about ethnic violence, such motivations "are common to all human groups, and cannot serve to define either tribe or nation."[33] Nor are these motivations unique to confessional groups. Boundaries drawn by the Salafis between "us" (true Muslims) and "them" (bad Muslims or infidels) are clearly of a psychological nature; but this observation is unable to help us understand when, why, or how those boundaries are drawn.

Psychological explanations hold that people behave emotionally rather than rationally. Emotions, for example, are said to have overwhelmed the rational concerns of the Afghans when they welcomed the obscurantist Taliban after they seized power in Afghanistan. The Afghan people supposedly saw the Taliban as pious Muslims and sincere defenders of public order and social justice, in contrast to the corrupt mujahedeen, who came to power in Kabul after the collapse of the pro-Soviet government. A second psychological approach, which is very close to the behavioral one, might be useful for understanding the underlying causes of the emergence of "classical" Salafism in the central Saudi Arabian region of Nejd in the eighteenth century; the psychological features of Arabia's Bedouins, combined with their societal peculiarities, may help explain why Salafism, a strict and puritanical form of Islamic belief, first appeared and then spread. Nevertheless, behavioral approaches usually overestimate the autonomy of motives, emotions, and impulses, and they underestimate the structural causes of puritanical and violent streams in Islam. They also fail to interpret militancy and extremism in the obvious absence of autonomous impulses in many cases, which is why an adequate understanding of violence is required.

Functionalist explanations view Islam as a tool for pursuing political goals. A parallel can be drawn here between interpretations of religious and ethnic violence. As Randall Galvert has argued: "Under the right conditions, ethnic violence can be perpetrated through the efforts of political leaders striving cynically to gain or hold office. And under the right conditions, ethnic conflict can be suppressed or eliminated by the action of politicians seeking to maintain democracy, peace, and economic development."[34] A special line of argument in this category stresses the linkage between religion and ethnicity. Islamic radicalism, it is asserted, is merely an expression of ethnic strife. In the view of Gellner and others, nationalism emerged as a reaction to industrialization and the uprooting of people from their local communities because kinship and religion were no longer capable of organizing people.[35] A similar uprooting took place in Central Asia during the Soviet period. The Communists tried to supplant nationalism with their doctrine imposed from above because they regarded it as extremely dangerous. Islam and Islamic networks survived because the Communists did not believe that Islam was as dangerous as nationalism. After communism collapsed, the peoples of Central Asia suffered an identity crisis, and Islam became one of the most important components of new identity that eventually emerged for Muslims in the region. The rise of Islamic militancy, it is argued, was directly rooted in the self-assertiveness of nations searching for a collective identity.

A group of researchers have been exploring the issue in the framework of social movement theory. Quintan Wiktorowicz defines the main purpose of these studies as "to propose social movement theory as a unifying framework and agenda that can provide effective modes of inquiry to further the boundaries of research on Islamic activism. Whereas the majority of studies on Islamic activism tend to assume that a particular set of grievances, translated into religious idioms and symbols, engenders mobilization, various generations of social movement theory and concomitant debates have demonstrated that other factors are inextricably linked to mobilization processes, including resource availability, framing resonance, and shifts in opportunity structures."[36]

The intimate relationship between radical Islam and ethnonationalism has various forms. In Palestine and in Iraq, groups who are fighting almost entirely for national causes resort to Islamism not because of their devotion to the Islamist ideas but for the sake of enhancing mobilization. This, however, cannot exclude the existence of groups with national agenda but with genuine Salafist strife. Groups working for ethnonational causes and transnational groups can interact, as in the case of Central Asia. Some scholars deny for international jihadists serious commitment to various national causes. As O. Roy suggests, "targets of international jihadist terrorism are almost exclusively Western, and though jihadist groups may profess support for various causes, such as Iraqi and Palestinian liberation, they largely avoid becoming deeply involved in such strategies due to a lack of enthusiasm for nationalist goals."[37]

Many general conclusions that have been made about ethnic movements can be applied to religious ones. For example, Ted Robert Gurr's catalog of violent protest lasting over five years and involving ethnically defined minorities could be applied to sectarian violence.[38] Gurr distinguishes among (1) political banditry, sporadic terrorism, and unsuccessful coups by or on behalf of the groups; (2) campaigns of terrorism and successful coups by or on behalf of terrorist groups; (3) small-scale guerrilla activity or other forms of small-scale violence; (4) guerilla activity involving more than one thousand armed fighters carrying out frequent armed attacks over a substantial area and groups involved in revolutionary or international warfare that is not specifically or mainly concerned with group issues; and (5) protracted civil war fought by military units with base areas. Applying these categories to Islamist mobilization in Central Asia, we can say that the violent conflict in Tajikistan fits into categories four and five at its various stages from 1992 to 1997 (see chapter 4).[39] The activities of the first radical Islamists in Uzbekistan in the beginning of the 1990s, by contrast, fits into category one, while the subsequent incursions of Islamists into Uzbekistan generally fit category two.[40] Similarly, parallels can be drawn between the composition of Islamist movements and nationalist ones. For example, Islamists can be divided in the same kind of categories that Alexander Motyl has identified for nationalists: "martyrs," "fanatics," "true believers," and "believers of convenience."[41]

Security explanations emphasize the feeling of vulnerability and insecurity that generates social resentment in Islamic societies faced with technological and cultural penetration by secular and transnational Western civilization, Westernization, and modernization. The demonstration effect due to the growth of the mass media intensifies the feelings of insecurity and inferiority. The "clash of civilizations" thesis (a formulation coined by Samuel Huntington) is a variety of this approach.[42] Rejection of Western culture, or at least some of its components, is common to many Islamic societies, and the desire to protect the authenticity of the Islamic culture, order, and way of life may be conducive to extremist thinking and behavior. But some scholars, notably Olivier Roy, have noted that many members of extremist Islamic groups and terrorist networks are well integrated into Western societies, received their education at Western universities, and were re-Islamized in the West. This observation undermines security-oriented explanations. However, it also fails to interpret those cases where extremists were not in direct contact with the West.

Agency-based approaches emphasize the role of individual political actors in the emergence of Islamic militancy. Political actors can be divided into ideologists, teachers (guides), organizers, field commanders, financiers, and "diplomats" (recruiters of external support). These roles, however, are often combined in one person, who may primarily be an organizer at one moment but a commander at another. In general, political actors of all types have played an important role in mobilizing religious militancy throughout the Islamic world. Abul-Ala Maududi was an ideologist whose role has been widely recognized by other Salafi scholars and politicians, and his books, translated into Arabic from Urdu, received a broad response in the Arab world. Although in 1941 he created a mainstream organization, Jamiat-i Islami, in what is now Pakistan, he remained primarily an ideologist whose ideas are even now inspiring Salafis rather than an organizer. Hasan al-Banna, who founded the Muslim Brotherhood in Egypt in 1928, seems to have played an organizational role, which is as important as his theorizing. Sayyid Qutb, a writer who inspired Islamist radicals in Egypt, as well all over the world, and was eventually executed by the secular nationalist government of Gamal Abdel Nasser in 1966, was in fact not a fighter, the claims of the Egyptian government notwithstanding (he also remained within the mainstream of the Muslim Brotherhood). Rustamov-Hindustani in Central Asia (see chapter 2) was a moderate thinker and a teacher who did not call for violence or the creation of an Islamic state. His teachings nevertheless served as the basis for a later generation of ideologists of militant Islam. Post-Soviet Central Asia has had a number of different types of Islamist activists, such as Tahir Yuldashev or Juma Hojiev (Namangani), who founded the IMU. The former head of Tajikistan's qaziate, Hoji Akbar Turajonzoda, was and still is a skillful politician and diplomat.

Some observers have downplayed the role of human agents in Central Asia, arguing that a lack of theoretical knowledge, political experience, and organizational expertise have made agency less important. Many emphasize *institutional* factors instead. For them, human agents do not act independently of their social environment. Institutions matter most, they argue, because they support collectively shared systems of meanings that shape agents' activities.

I do not want to exaggerate the role of human agents in the militant Islamic movements elsewhere, and in Central Asia in particular, so as to avoid any overpersonalization of the existing phenomenon. But still the role of personalities who are able to mobilize support and resources from inside and outside, to lead the fight, and to make decisions is great (several theories were even constructed on the idea of the importance of support and resource mobilization).

In connection with the role of human agents and institutions, a question arises of why a fairly significant part of Muslim societies is inclined to support "the Islamic project." Whether the reason for this phenomenon is rooted in the effectiveness of the Islamic appeal itself, in the deeply implanted tradition animated by it, in the specificity of the political culture, in the particular mentality of the people, or in the efficiency of recruitment is difficult to affirm with confidence. Maybe Islamism merely occupies the place of all other protest ideologies, both those that have lost their appeal (Marxism in Central Asia) but left the mass of their erstwhile supporters "without anchor" and those that have not yet reached the Central Asian region (antiglobalism, environmentalism, etc.). One can hardly agree with the qualification of any radical Islamism as an antisystemic current. On the contrary, Islamism's emergence performs a certain social regulatory function, helping the system to renovate itself.

Sometimes historical memory is included in the inventory of explanations of Islamic extremism. S. Haddad and H. Khashan argue that "the destruction of the Islamic Caliphate some 80 years ago, the inception of European colonialism in Muslim and Arab lands, and Western endorsement of the creation of a Jewish state in Palestine seem to better explain political Islam's grudge against the West than the simplistic socioeconomic argument."[43] They support the suggestion of Bruce B. Lawrence that the long-term consequences of colonialism on Arab and Muslim peoples "have yet to be exhausted."[44] Thus a version of a postponed anticolonial rebellion under the Islamic banner was put forward. Close to this version is the already mentioned version of "civilizational repulse," which Nissim Rejwan denotes as a general Muslim response to the West that confirmed its efforts "to dominate and subvert Muslim societies through economic and cultural power."[45]

A question might arise here regarding to what degree different explanations of motivations behind Islamic extremism are linked to different views about its goals. A digression into this category might contribute to the clarification of existing controversies in theorizing about causes of radicalism, but I prefer to tackle this issue in the process of the empirical case studies. It is also evident that political interests of local, regional, and global state actors influence theoretical discourse (for example, a reference to international terrorist networks became a de rigueur ritual for almost all leaders who examine the issue of Islamic radicalism).

None of the approaches in this incomplete list provides a full and adequate explanation of Islamic radicalism in general or in Central Asia in particular. A combination of approaches, or compromises among different explanations, might be more productive (although, at the same time, any inventory-oriented approach aimed at setting up the list of roots and causes is of limited value).[46] So, in my view, it is more constructive to leave theory aside until we regard the empirical case of the Central Asian Islamic groups and consider what light their history throws on theoretical discourse.

THE IMPORTANCE OF THE CULTURE
OF VIOLENCE AND DETERMINISM

First, however, I would like to address the question of *violence as culture*, an approach that has received little attention in the literature on Islamist militancy but that I think has particular explanatory power. Not surprisingly, many members of radical Islamic movements in the Soviet successor states have been former wrestlers, boxers, special forces officers, and so on. The Adolat movement, which emerged in the Uzbek part of the Ferghana Valley at the beginning of the 1990s, for example, consisted primarily of young specialists in martial arts. The most notorious field commander of the Uzbek Islamists, Juma Hojiev (Namangani), served with Soviet forces in Afghanistan, as did many of the Islamist field commanders in Tajikistan. Still others were specialists in contact sports. In a Russian republic, Dagestan, a prominent political Islamic activist, Nadirshah Khachilaev (assassinated in 2003), was a famous wrestling champion.

All these people were what Charles Tilly has called "specialists in violence."[47] These specialists may operate inside and with the government, or they may operate outside and against it. On many occasions, their principal role is not to employ violence but to threaten it. In the case of post-Soviet Islamist movements, demonstrative ritual acts play a particularly important role in solidifying the reputation of experts in violence. They also make clear the inevitability of punishment in case of noncompliance. For example, Juma Namangani captured and decapitated fighters who decided to return to their villages upon the declaration of an amnesty by the government, which reinforced his image as a fearless, determined, and cruel commander and also confirmed that those who betrayed "the cause of jihad" would be ruthlessly punished.

Though not the only political actors in Islamic movements, the specialists in violence are of great importance in reproducing the general culture of violence. Violent rituals, which have become a feature of Central Asian political life, are playing a significant role in this process. In this regard, a comparison can be drawn between Central Asia and the Caucasus. In the Caucasus, violent public rituals play an even more significant role in creating "strong" images of public figures, and they thereby help mobilize people politically. Televised public executions and floggings organized by Chechen separatists during the break between the two wars with Moscow (1996–1999) and the decapitation of a policeman by Islamic radicals in the Ferghana Valley are lucid examples of such actions. Another purpose of these acts is to signal the commitment of Islamic radicals to a certain code of honor and the tradition of the blood feud. Cutting the ears off deceased enemies during the Tajik civil war was another vivid and frightening example.

Specialists in violence have been recruited not only by Islamists but by secular forces as well. During the first phase of the civil war in Tajikistan in 1992, for example, many former racketeers and criminals took the side of the secular opposition to the Islamic Revival Party. In doing so, they sided with certain solidarity groups and regional elites. Sangak Safarov, the leader of the Popular Front (which was responsible for the victory of the Kulyabi–Leninabadi–Hissari alliance over the Gharm–Karategin–Pamir bloc of Islamists and "democrats") had spent twenty-three years in jail on criminal charges. After the victory over the Islamists, some former racketeers were rewarded by appointment to ministerial posts; this included Yaqub Salimov, who became Tajikistan's interior minister (he was later deposed from his post, accused of plotting against the state, arrested in Moscow in 2003 at the request of the government of Tajikistan, and handed over to the Tajik authorities).

A factor that helps maintain a culture of violence in Central Asia and, indeed, throughout the post-Soviet space is the high level of militarization of society, which is a legacy of the Soviet period. A great number of former army, police, security specialists, and others were trained in the use of weapons and fighting by the Soviet regime. Many of these people have since entered politics, business, or the civil service. Still others became unemployed, which has meant that they are subject to recruitment by political actors.

A special subdivision of the violence practiced by Central Asian Islamic radicals is what could be called opportunistic violence. This category usually includes hostage taking, looting, and enslavement. The point is to use violence so as to take revenge, make profits, or scare people. In some cases, opportunistic violence turns into a full-scale lucrative business. For certain nationalist and radical Islamic movements, opportunistic violence is so common that observers describe them as business operations. Such is the case with part of the Chechen separatist movement, as well as with the IMU, widely known for hostage-taking and drug-trafficking operations. Involvement in hostage taking or drug trafficking, however, does not necessarily mean that the participating parties are merely criminal gangs. It may be that this is a "business on the side," one that is particularly attractive because of the huge inequalities in post-Soviet societies.

Religious determinism as expressed in religious doctrines is also an important factor shaping individual and group behavior, including violent behavior. In medieval Islam, a broad debate unfolded between Jabriyya and Qadiriyya in regard to the question of free will. Are the Muslims free in their actions or is everything predestined by Allah? If the latter, do the Muslims bear responsibility for what they do? Jabriyya asserted that individuals could not be responsible for their deeds because Allah guides people in this world and predetermines all that happens. Qadiriyya, in contrast, held that Allah gives believers a choice of actions within a certain range. By choosing within that range, individuals realize their free will. They will be either rewarded or punished on the Day of Judgment for the choices they make. This debate continues among Islamic scholars and theologians today, and it is quite relevant to the interpretation of the behavior of certain Muslim groups and to the ways in which Islam is used to mobilize people politically.

A comparison can be drawn here between Islam and Buddhism to illustrate this mechanism by which religious determinism is used for political purposes. Unlike Islam, Buddhism offers no constraints on individual behavior, and thus it appears that it lacks the means for justifying group behavior. It might be assumed, then, that there is no room in Buddhist teachings for even the possibility of free will. But such an assumption would be wrong, because the concept of karma makes the believers' attitudes toward life entirely deterministic. Nadezhda Bektimirova, a Russian specialist on Buddhism, explains that some of the members of the Buddhist *sangha* (community of monks) "declared that the Pol Pot genocidal regime is the result of karma of the Khmer people, that is to say, a retribution for ancestors' past sinful deeds, particularly for the wars of conquest against its neighbors in the period of Angkor Empire."[48] The concept of "personal karma" helped Cambodians explain their long suffering from the horrible Pol Pot experiments.

Determinism, as well as the notions of responsibility and divine reward, are therefore part of any religion, and they can be employed in one way or another for the purposes of political mobilization. Mobilization for collective violence and the response to it are both directly linked to these motivations, and they help explain the emergence and evolution of radical Islamism in the dominant state in Central Asia—Uzbekistan.

NOTES

1. The term "Islamic fundamentalism" did not exist in Arabic, and was introduced into the language only in light of the need to translate a concept that appeared in English. For this purpose, the word *usuliyyah* (from *usul,* "fundamentals") began to be used in Arabic.

2. The expansion became especially wide after the shocking rise of oil prices in 1973, when the Saudis could afford to spend billions of dollars outside the kingdom. The successful mobilization of jihad, supported by the United States, against the Soviet invasion of Afghanistan, as a recent survey of Islam by the *Economist* asserts, made the Islamic internationalists believe that they could destroy a superpower, and "Muslim identification with the entire *umma*" became much stronger. "In the Name of God," *Economist,* September 13, 2003, 12.

3. Mahan Abedin, "A Saudi Oppositionist's View," *Terrorism Monitor* 1, no. 7 (December 4, 2003): 1.

4. The founder of the Kingdom of Saudi Arabia, 'Abd al-'Aziz Al Sa'ud, said on May 11, 1929: "They call us the 'Wahhabis' and they call our creed a 'Wahhabi' one, as if it were a special one, . . . and this is an extremely erroneous allegation that has arisen from the false propaganda launched by those who had ill feelings as well as ill intentions towards the movement. We are not proclaiming a new creed or a new dogma. Muhammad bin Abdul Wahhab did not come with anything new. Our creed is the creed of those good people who preceded us and which came in the Book of God (the Qur'an) as well as that of his Messenger (the prophet Muhammad, prayer and peace be upon him)." Fouad Al-Farsy, *Modernity and Tradition: The Saudi Equation* (St. Peter Port, England: Knight Communications, 1999), 27.

5. Mansour al-Noqaidan, "Telling the Truth, Facing the Whip," *International Herald Tribune,* November 29–30, 2003, 8. Noqaidan is a remarkable public figure in Saudi Arabia. A journalist in his thirties, he is a former "neo-Salafi," as he refers to himself as of the jihadist brand of Salafis, who later turned into a bitter critic of the Wahhabi dogma, including the concept of *takfir,* which he considers responsible for the act of violence.

6. Khalid al-Dukhayl, "Al-Wahhabiyya: Ru'ya Mukhtalifa" (Wahhabism: A different vision), *Al-Ittihad,* March 7, 2004.

7. For instance, the Crimean Tatar Jadid enlightener Ismail Bei Gasprali, or Gasprinsky (1851–1914), called for relinquishing the outdated, stale manner of teaching in *maktabs* (Islamic schools) by mullas, deeming it necessary to study Russian so as to "educate our children and let them rise in the world" *Terjuman* (Bakhchisarai, Russia), January 31, 1913.

8. 'Abdullah b. Ahmad al-Zayd, *Obucheniye Molitve* (Teaching to pray), translated in 1996 into Russian (Ministry of Waqfs, al-Da'wa and Guidance in cooperation with the welfare organization of Ibrahim b. 'Abd al-'Aziz al-Barahimi, Kingdom of Saudi Arabia, n.d.).

9. "*Fiqh*," by I. Goldziher, and "*'Ilm*," by D. B. Macdonald, in *Shorter Encyclopaedia of Islam*, ed. H. A. R. Gibb and J. H. Kramers (Leiden, Netherlands: Brill, 1974).

10. Tawfiq Ibrahim, "Osnovnie tsennosti i instituty klassicheskogo islama" (Main values and institutions of classical Islam), in *Rossiya i musul'manskii mir* 10, no. 136 (2003): 139–40.

11. Ishan is an honorific title applied throughout Central Asia to spiritual leaders. In most cases, the title is inherited, but on occasion it can be acquired as a result of piety and religious knowledge. Ishans are usually members of the families of shaykhs or leaders of certain Sufi brotherhoods or branches, although some of them do not have direct ties to the brotherhoods or branches.

12. Islam in Central Asia had been rather closely connected with Volga Islam, and so it is interesting to compare the structure of the religious class in these two regions. On the evidence of Russian researchers, *fuqaha'* and *'ulama*, not to mention imams and *mu'azzins*, appeared in Volga Bulgaria after the adoption of Islam as early as the tenth century. After the Mongol conquest in the thirteenth century, the role of Sufism, as in Central Asia, began to grow (see M. K. Garipov, Politika Rossiiskogo gosudarstva v etnokonfessional'noi sfere v kontse XVIII–nachale XX vv.: opyt Dukhovnogo upravleniya musul'man [The policy of the Russian state in the ethnoconfessional sphere in the late eighteenth–early twentieth centuries] PhD dissertation, Kazan State University, 2003), in particular that of Naqshbandiyya, Qubraviyya, and Yasaviyya. The shaykhs of the Sufi orders began to occupy the foremost place in the religious elite, and *qadis* and muftis appeared. Along with them, this elite included sayyids—descendants of the Prophet Muhammad.

13. See Ashirbek Muminov, "Svyatye mesta v Islame" (Holy places in Islam), *Mayak Vostoka*, nos. 1–2 (1996): 15–16.

14. Muminov, "Svyatye mesta," 17. In one of the genealogies, the Karakhanids were declared ancestors of Imam Muhammad in al-Hanafiyya. *Safi al-Din Urung Quylaqi*, "*Nasab-name*," ed. A. Muminov and Z. Zhandarbekov (Turkistan, 1992).

15. Muminov, "Svyatye mesta," 18.

16. Ludmila Polonskaya and Alexei Malashenko, *Islam in Central Asia* (Reading, England: Ithaca Press, 1994), 42.

17. Bakhtiyar Babajanov, Ashirbek Muminov, and Martha Brill Olcott, "Muhammadjon Hindustani i religioznaya sreda yego epokhi" (Muhammadjan Hindustani and the religious environment of his epoch). *Vostok-Oriens*, no. 5 (September–October 2004), 46.

18. The quality of religious education at the official institutions such as Mir-i Arab *madrasa* in Bukhara has been always attested as low, although it has improved in the 1990s. One of the religious authorities of Namangan, 'Umar Khan *domulla*, said to a group of Uzbek scholars that after the graduation from *hujra*, he spent about a year as a worker at the Mir-i Arab *madrasa* in Bukhara planning to enroll in it, but was surprised when he found out that he knew more than its graduates. Ishaq *qari* of Kokand told me that the level of a student who had studied in his *hujra* one and one-half years was equal to the level of a Mir-i Arab graduate (interview in Kokand on January 10, 2004).

19. Babajanov, Muminov, and Olcott, "Hindustani," 46.

20. Babajanov, Muminov, and Olcott, "Hindustani," 46–47.

21. Aidar Khabutdinov, *Millet Orenburgskogo Dukhovnogo Sobraniya v kontse 18–19 vekakh* (The millet of the Orenburg Spiritual Assembly at the end of the 18th–19th centuries) (Kazan, Russia: Iman Publishing House, 2000), 89.

22. Babajanov, Muminov, and Olcott, "Hindustani," 48.

23. According to Alec Rasizade, the collapse of social services, poor public health care, poor public education, massive unemployment, and crippling poverty all "offer militant Islamic groups ripe ground for recruitment" (Alec Rasizade, "The New 'Great Game' in Central Asia after Afghanistan," *Alternatives: Turkish Journal of International Relations* 1, no. 2, Summer 2002, 54). This author believes this direct linkage between poverty and Islamic radicalism is proved by the absence of Islamic radicalism in such oppressive places as Turkmenistan, where the government provides free gas, free electricity, free water, free heating and other utilities, almost free apartments, and free public transportation. But one would hardly support the suggestion that the population of Turkmenistan enjoys high living standards. An average Turkmen family finds it none the easier to make ends meet than, for example, an Uzbek family, which has no such benefits.

24. Jason Burke, "Al Qaeda Today and the Real Roots of Terrorism," *Terrorism Monitor*, February 12, 2004, 2.

25. Graham E. Fuller, *The Future of Political Islam* (New York: Palgrave Macmillan, 2003), 15.

26. N. Muflikhunov, *Kniga propovedei i nastavlenii* (Kazan, Russia: Iman Publishing House, 1998), 143–44; Dmitrii Makarov and Rafik Mukhametshin, "Official and Unofficial Islam," in *Islam in Post-Soviet Russia: Public and Private Faces*, ed. Hilary Pilkington and Galina Yemelianova (London: Routledge Curzon, 2003), 123.

27. John L. Esposito, *Unholy War: Terror in the Name of Islam* (Oxford: Oxford University Press, 2002), 49.

28. François Burgat, *Face to Face with Political Islam* (London: I. B. Taurus, 2003), xv.

29. Esposito, *Unholy War*, 157.

30. Bernard Lewis, *Crisis of Islam: Holy War and Unholy Terror* (New York: Modern Library, 2003), 153–54. It is not quite clear whether Lewis is addressing suicide bombers here and telling them that they have misunderstood Islam or is addressing Westerners who consider Islam responsible for suicide attacks.

31. Simon Haddad and Hilal Khashan, "Islam and Terrorism, Lebanese Muslim Views on September 11," *Journal of Conflict Resolution* 46, no. 6 (December 2002): 814.

32. F. Burgat examined the paths of three remarkable characters to Islamism. Famous Egyptian intellectual 'Adil Husayn was imprisoned for about eleven years as a Communist militant, then switched from Marxism to Nasserism and finally to Islamism to become secretary of the Egyptian Labor Party. Another Egyptian thinker and writer, Tariq al-Bishri, underwent a similar transformation, departing from Arab nationalism for Islamism when he understood that "nothing protects the Arabism of an Egyptian better than Islam." One of the most prominent leaders of modern political Islam in the Middle East, Rashid Ghannushi from Tunisia, in his own words on the night of June 15, 1966, "took a final decision to pass from the world of Arab nationalism and Nasserism to Islam" (Burgat, *Face to Face*, 24–42). The list of such ideological converts is not exhausted by these personalities. I know a lot of people of the same ilk in Egypt, Yemen, Palestine, and some other states.

33. Ernest Gellner, *Nations and Nationalism* (Oxford: Blackwell, 1983), 99.

34. Randall Galvert, "Identity, Expression and Rational-Choice Theory," in *Political Science: The State of the Discipline*, ed. Ira Katznelson and Helen V. Milner (Washington, DC: Norton, 2002), 592.

35. See Gellner, *Nations and Nationalism*.

36. Quintan Wiktorowicz, "Introduction," in *Islamic Activism: A Social Movement Theory Approach*, ed. Quintan Wiktorowicz (Bloomington: Indiana University Press, 2004), 4.

37. Expert: US Failure to Comprehend Islamic Radical Motivations Undermines Democratization Hopes for Middle East, Central Asia, *EurasiaNet: Eurasia Insight*, May 13, 2004, at www.eurasianet.org/departments/recaps/articles/eav051304.shtml, 2.

38. Ted Robert Gurr, *Minorities at Risk: A Global View of Ethnopolitical Conflicts* (Washington, DC: United States Institute of Peace Press, 1993), and *Peoples Versus States: Minorities at Risk in the New Century* (Washington, DC: United States Institute of Peace Press, 2000). Charles Tilly has criticized Gurr for failing to distinguish between violence inflicted by governmental agents and their allies on the one hand and violence perpetrated by dissident groups on the other. See Charles Tilly, *The Politics of Collective Violence* (Cambridge: Cambridge University Press, 2003), 64.

39. The Tajik conflict, in my view, was not directly related to Islam. Indeed, most analysts of the Tajik conflict take a functionalist approach toward the role of Islam in the conflict, arguing that Islam was only an instrument of political mobilization. Others deny that Islam had any role whatsoever. Olivier Roy, for example, has argued that the basis for political mobilization in Tajikistan has always been regional, not ideological or religious (as stated in several public presentations). However, it is more appropriate to argue that it was a conflict between regional elites competing over redistribution of wealth and power than to argue that it was a conflict between regions per se, given the traditional political passivity of the majority of the population and the lack of direct interest on its part in the competition. Moreover, the Islamic factor cannot be ignored. Islam was used instrumentally for political mobilization and as a genuine system of values and concepts around which some groups of the population rallied. In addition, Roy argues that Islamic identity is constructed purely for the sake of political goals of a primarily nationalist nature, which I also disagree with.

40. The same Islamic groups were involved in similar violent clashes with government forces in Kyrgyzstan and Tajikistan at the end of 1990s. These events are described in the next chapter of this book.

41. Alexander Motyl, *Sovietology, Rationality, Nationality* (New York: Columbia University Press, 1990), 37–39.

42. The clash of civilizations thesis can also be viewed as a *culturalist* argument. However, a deep feeling of insecurity is the overwhelming factor that is adduced to explain the supposed clash of civilizations, and therefore I prefer to categorize it as security oriented.

43. Haddad and Khashan, "Islam and Terrorism," 814.

44. Bruce B. Lawrence, *Defenders of God: The Fundamentalist Revolt against the Modern Age* (San Francisco: Harper & Row, 1989), 201.

45. Nissim Rejwan, *The Many Faces of Islam* (Gainesville: University Press of Florida, 2000), 137.

46. Quintan Wiktorowicz, for example, observed that some scholars turned to social movement theory to escape the narrowness of such an approach (see Quintan Wiktorowicz, "Joining the Cause: Al-Muhajirun and Radical Islam," a paper presented to the conference "The Roots of Islamic Radicalism," Yale University, May 8–9, 2004, at www.yale.edu/polisci/info/conferences/Islamic%20Radicalism/). In a case study of this radical Islamic group, based in Britain, Wiktorowicz accepted a grievance-based explanation, but only as a cognitive opening, which is necessarily followed by religious seeking and frame alignment, which "all affect the prospect of successful socialization." Socialization, in its turn, "is needed to indoctrinate individuals into the movement ideology" (23). This author focused on the process of persuasion, thus adding an important perspective to the general debate on Islamic radicalism. The scope of Al-Muhajirun is a bit narrow but still helpful. It is worth mentioning that the future recruits in Britain suffered from identity crisis; they were "trapped between two competing socialization environments: a) secular British society and institutions that proposed equity but in reality offered discrimination; and b) the traditional home with its passive religious values and narrow focus on the Muslim community and rituals" (14). It would have been extremely interesting to know whether all recruits for the al-Qa'ida cause in the West also experienced discrimination as those *muhajirs* who were interviewed by Wiktorowicz. As in the case of leftist revolutionaries and Arab nationalists earlier, at least some of them might have been well established in the Western society.

47. Tilly, *Collective Violence*, 35.

48. Nadezhda Bektimirova, *The Cambodian Sangha's Involvement in Politics: Challenges and Consequences*, paper presented at the Center for Southeast Asia Studies, University of California, Berkeley, May 7, 2003, 9–10.

2

The Rise and Fall of the Islamic Movement of Uzbekistan

The rise of militant Islamism in Central Asia is usually linked to the Islamic Movement of Uzbekistan (IMU), which came into existence in the second half of the 1990s, created by groups of the Ferghana Salafis, who had started their activities long before this time.

The history of Islamism in modern Uzbekistan can be broken up into several periods. The first spanned the years from the Bolshevik revolution in 1917 and Sovietization of the region until the aftermath of World War II. In that first period, puritans, mostly immigrants from the Middle East, brought pro-Salafi ideas to Central Asia. The second period spanned the years from 1950 to 1970, when the first local proto-Salafis appeared in the region. However, they were relatively isolated at the time, and they proved unable to propagate their ideas or have any influence on public life. The third period covered 1970 to the late 1980s, when a relatively less repressive Soviet rule enabled the Salafis to recruit more disciples and teach them privately at underground *madrasas*. Also during this period, the Salafis began to address "trusted" audiences and distribute tapes of sermons and lessons to them. They did not, however, call for jihad or direct struggle against the Soviet regime. Instead, they concentrated on promoting Islamic knowledge, piety, devotion, and morals, and as a result, the broader political influence of these teachers was limited. The fourth period took place at the end of the 1980s, at which point the Salafis started to operate more openly. With strong support from abroad, they began to occupy significant positions in mosques and *madrasas*. They also began to propagate a stricter, more puritanical, and more conservative form of Islam. The fifth period covered the early 1990s, after the collapse of the

USSR, when the Salafis began to organize in the Ferghana Valley, calling for the adoption of Shari'a and the creation of an Islamic state. They continued, however, to advocate dialogue with the authorities, and in general they eschewed violence during this period. The sixth period started in 1992, after a government crackdown on Islamic activists in Ferghana. Many were forced to flee to Tajikistan and Afghanistan, where they formed an alliance with the Tajik Islamic opposition in its struggle against the Tajik government. The seventh period ran from the middle of the 1990s until 1997, when the United Tajik Opposition (the UTO) entered into negotiations with the government and then signed an agreement ending the Tajik civil war (see chapter 4). It was at that point that the IMU was established. Shortly thereafter, during the eight period (1997–2001), the IMU undertook a series of armed attacks and began seizing hostages. The final period started after September 11, 2001. IMU guerrillas fought on the side of the Taliban against the U.S.-led coalition, and as a result, some militants were killed while others fled to Pakistan. In the period since the fall of the Taliban, their activities have been substantially reduced.

As explained in chapter 1, most Central Asians adhered to the Hanafi school of Sunni Islam, which agreed well with local traditions and customs, thus forming a local traditionalist environment. It existed in the form of "popular Islam" throughout the years of Soviet rule, despite persecutions and massive atheist propaganda. Jadidists' attempts to reform the existing system of religious education and science were suppressed by the Communist authorities. A number of local religious authorities developed a tendency, which can be characterized as proto-Salafi, to take a tougher stance on "popular" Islam, Sufi customs, 'urf, and 'adat. It remains unclear to what extent this trend could be a consequence of the impact of Wahhabism. Wahhabi influences may have arrived during this period via contacts with Saudi Arabia, but it is also possible that Salafi tendencies were a natural development of the thought of the Central Asian Islamic heritage.

Saudi influence cannot be entirely excluded, despite the fact that contacts were limited and the clergy was under the strict control of the state and its agencies, especially the KGB. In fact, Saudi influence existed at least to some degree, both through limited contacts and through literature. Saudi Arabia acted as a magnet, not only because it was a country in which the holy places of Islam were to be found and that had powerful financial resources, but also because a significant part of its inhabitants (estimated to number no less than three hundred thousand) had originally come from Central Asia, mostly from Uzbekistan, as descendants of pilgrims who had settled there in prerevolutionary times and as *basmachis* (armed jihadist rebels against Soviet rule) who took refuge there after their defeat in Soviet times.

Some Uzbek researchers argue that the first signs of Salafism in the post-war period were linked to the name of Ziyauddin Khan Ishan Babakhanov.[1]

THE LIFE AND SERMONS OF THE BABAKHAN FAMILY

The ancestors of the Babakhan muftis settled in the *mahalla* Hazrat-i Imam in Tashkent, close to the shrine of the famous theologian of Ma Wara' al-Nahr, Imam al-Qaffal al-Shashi, who professed the Shafi'i *madhhab* of Sunnism and received the title of Hastimam in the tenth century. Traditionally settling in that *mahalla* were many *fuqaha* and *'ulama*. According to Shamsuddin b. Ziyauddin Khan, his grandfather, Shaykh Ishan Babakhan b. Abdulmajid Khan, had been a follower of Naqshbandiyya—the most popular Sufi order in Central Asia.[2] However, some local students of Central Asian Sufism presume that the forebears of the Babakhans were actually Yasaviyya shaykhs.[3] Shamsuddin's evidence suggests that the later generations of the Babakhans positioned themselves as hereditary Naqshbandiyya ishans. However, the Babakhans of the Soviet period showed no sympathies for Sufism whatsoever. The opinion of Martha Brill Olcott (who, incidentally, erroneously calls Ziyauddin the first mufti) that Babakhan assisted in training Naqshbandiyya Sufis[4] can scarcely be buttressed by facts, and it is also contested by present-day Central Asian students of Islam. Shaykh Babakhan's grandfather, Ayyub Khan b. Yunus Khan, had been a well-known *faqih* and a long-time teacher in the Mui Mubarak *madrasa*, bearing an honorary title of *shaykh al-islam*. His father, Abdulla b. Burkhan Ishan, taught in the same *madrasa*. Shaykh Babakhan studied in Bukhara, in the Mir Arab *madrasa* and, in the judgment of people who knew him, was a true knower of Islamic dogmatics (*'aqa'id*), law (*fiqh*), interpretation of the Qur'an (*tafsir*), the Hadiths, and so forth.

In 1943, Stalin, desiring to use Islam, as he did Orthodoxy, for mobilizing the population to fight the fascist aggressor, decided to reestablish the muftiate that had existed at the time of the Russian Empire—the Spiritual Board of Muslims of Central Asia and Kazakhstan (SADUM). Ishan Babakhan became mufti of five Central Asian republics, and his son, Shaykh Ziyauddin Khan, became SADUM executive secretary. The five SADUM representative offices in all these republics were headed by qazis. Ziyauddin Khan came to head the qaziate of Uzbekistan. Shaykh Babakhan served as a mufti until his death in 1957, when that post was filled by his son Ziyauddin Khan, who had previously served as *imam-khatib* of the Mui Mubarak mosque.[5]

Ziyauddin Khan was born in 1908, and was brought up for a religious career. By the age of twelve, he had learned the Qur'an by heart, then, as was customary, he set about studying the *tafsir* and the Hadith. In 1920 he became enrolled in the Tashkent Kukaltash *madrasa* and also took private lessons. In the words of Ziyauddin himself, it was the theologian Shaykh Muhammad b. Sa'id 'Abd al-Wahid al-'Asali al-Shami al-Tarabulsi, who at that time came to Tashkent from the Middle East, who then played the decisive role in influencing Ziyauddin's future as an Islamic scholar. According to the local tradition, Shami came to be called Shami *domulla* (*domulla* from Sham, which means "Syria" in a broad sense of that term, that is, including Lebanon; the latter part of his name, al-Tarabulsi, "a man of Tripoli," indicates that the divine was a native of Tripoli, i.e., in fact a Lebanese). In his lessons, Shami attached particular attention to the heritage of the leading medieval collector of the Hadiths—Imam al-Bukhari.

Al-Shami al-Tarabulsi is a very enigmatic, and as yet little known, figure in Central Asian Islamic thought of the twentieth century. It is not clear who invited him to Tashkent in the early 1920s or why. Judging by scattered facts, he was invited by the Turkestani Bolsheviks themselves, who were even then launching a campaign of struggle against traditional Islam. Perhaps the local revolutionaries took to al-Tarabulsi as a partisan of Islamic puritanism, that is, Salafism, who might become their ally in an offensive against the popular Sufi Islam, which the Bolsheviks likened to stagnation and obscurantism. Sufism was dangerous for the Bolsheviks due to its mass following, the popularity of its preceptors, its mobilizing potential, and its uncontrolled character. Could his arrival have been the result of an accidental convergence of circumstances or a willful decision of someone of power who was charmed by the spell of the Salafi theologian and became his secret admirer? Could it be that al-Tarabulsi sympathized with the revolutionary movement and therefore found himself in Tashkent and received a friendly welcome there? There are arguments in favor of each of these theories, though the evidence is insufficient to draw a conclusion.[6] Thus there are grounds to consider that, even if al-Tarabulsi was not a "pure" Salafi, at any rate he did not, among other things, oppose the worship of the holy places, and he accepted many rites and customs of popular Islam. There are also arguments in favor of an assumption about his left-wing sympathies (after all, did he not understand *where* he was going?). A. K. Muminov has informed me that he has discovered unpublished Shami *domulla*'s paper *Abu Dharr al-Qafari wa-l-ishtirakiyyah* (Abu Dharr al-Qafari and Socialism) indicating his socialist sympathies. For the Bolsheviks in those times, the veneration of Sufi ishans, the worship of holy places, and loyalty to the traditional rural clergy were the main threats. The spread of religious knowledge per se had not yet been anathematized, and the left sought their allies among a section of the clergy sympathetic to them.[7]

Shamsuddin Babakhanov was the first Uzbek scholar who disclosed and publicized the role of Shami *domulla*. It is regrettable that contemporary Uzbek scholars do not give Babakhanov's contribution to general knowledge about Islam in Central Asia during the Soviet period enough credit. Shami *domulla* supposedly was active in 1919–1932 and died in exile in 1940.[8] An article presented for publication mentions that Shami *domulla* not only supported the campaign of destroying *mazars*, in which Communist authorities saw "hotbeds of religious superstitions," but even personally participated together with his disciple in the destruction of at least one *mazar*. It reminds us of a similar campaign carried out by the Saudi Wahhabis. We shall never know what was the real motivation of Shami *domulla* and people like him: whether they considered this act appropriate because of its accordance with their Salafi beliefs, because they favored the Bolsheviks' fervent attacking of "nests of ignorance," or because of mere opportunism.

It is not by chance that Shamsuddin sees merit in "the man of Tripoli" first and foremost for his restoration of the legacy of Imam al-Bukhari—the author of the most authoritative and reliable *Al-Sahih* collection of the Hadiths (Shami *domulla* even wrote a poem about al-Bukhari)—which is an indication of the desire, typical of all the Salafites, to go back to the fundamental origins of religion, purified of later borrowings.[9] It was possibly al-Tarabulsi's tutorship that in part won the future mufti over to an Islam not overburdened by Islamized popular customs. The exponents of this tendency were not puritan Hanbalites, and they stuck to their adherence to the Hanafi *madhhab*.[10] Nonetheless, Ziyauddin, having become a mufti, later voiced disapproval in his fatwas of certain precepts of popular Islam, an act that afforded ground to some Central Asian researchers to consider him all but "the first fundamentalist" of Uzbekistan (I shall revert to Ziyauddin's fatwas).[11]

Although the future mufti studied under many other adepts of Islam, his grandson believes that it is to al-Tarabulsi that he owes his transformation into a genuine Islamic scholar.

It is believed in circles close to the Babakhan family that one of the *mudarrises* of the same orientation as Shami *domulla*, a Russian convert named al-Qiziljari, exerted a great influence on Ziyauddin Khan. Also, mentioned with the clerics who taught Ziyauddin Khan were Hasan-Khazrat in the *'ilm al-tafsir* and Shah-Qiyas *qari* in the *qira'a*.[12]

The year 1945 saw the renewal of the hajj of Soviet Muslims to Mecca and Medina with the first group of pilgrims led by Ishan Babakhan, whose son came to the holy places with him. This initiated renewed contacts with Muslims abroad (though under vigilant control of the state), and in 1947 Ziyauddin Khan set off for a yearly probation to the Arab countries: first to Cairo, to Al-Azhar University, then to Mecca and Medina. His stay in Saudi

Arabia, after which he retained a lifelong gratitude to his teachers from that country, gives one more occasion for contemporary Uzbek researchers to search for traces of "Wahhabi" influence in his subsequent activity.[13]

Some of the present-day Central Asian imams and religious scholars, especially those traditionalists who are antagonistic to Salafism, blame Ziyauddin Khan Babakhanov for the alleged introduction of "Wahhabism." According to Imam Ishaq *qari*, who I spoke to in Kokand in 2004 (I'll come back to him later), right up to Babakhanov's taking office in the muftiate, "no one in Central Asia had heard of Hanbalism, which runs counter to the Hanafi foundations of local Islam."[14] Then, as trips to the holy places of Islam by Central Asian pilgrims started, through them the Saudis "began to use any loophole to advance their Hanbali ideas into the region." With the assistance of the mufti, Ishaq *qari* asserts, hundreds of thousands of books of "alien persuasion" were annually brought to Tashkent from Saudi Arabia in that period. These books were used in the teaching of students, while some officials assisted in the distribution of this literature, conniving at the penetration of Wahhabism. Ishan Babakhan himself, Ishaq *qari* recalls, was handing out Saudi literature right and left.

Now let us turn to certain theses of Mufti Ziyauddin's fatwas. In the fatwa on the *mahr* and the *kalym*, he reproaches those Muslims who make it a custom to organize sumptuous weddings, while the size of the *mahr* reaches astounding proportions: "in the guise of the *mahr*, in essence we witness a regeneration of the pagan pre-Islamic custom of purchase and sale of brides—the *kalym*."[15] The mufti recommended the Central Asian Muslims to henceforth avoid such pernicious customs.

In the fatwa on the funeral ritual, the mufti quotes one of the books on Shari'a, which says, "As for the funeral repasts arranged by the household of the deceased for the people presenting their condolences on the third and seventh days of his death, they are the vestiges of pagans and heretics."[16] Later, the mufti assailed the noisy demonstrative mourning (especially by women), "which can even arouse the anger of Allah," tracing it to the rites of ancient Turks and to the pre-Islamic past. The mufti also urged his flock to cut down on extravagant treats during the commemoration ceremony, saying in addition that it is not members of the deceased person's family but neighbors and distant relatives who should cook food for the guests.[17]

Similar admonitions are to be found in the fatwa on the vanity of banquets on occasion of the *khatna* (circumcision) rite. According to the mufti, such banquets "in no way conform to the dictates of Islamic Shari'a." There is no telling whether or not a certain puritanism of these fatwas was a result of the mufti's latent "fundamentalist" sympathies, a social mandate, or both. Significant in this sense is the fatwa on the attendance of tombs and cemeteries, as it is known that both the classic Wahhabis and the contemporary Central Asian and North Caucasian "neo-Wahhabis" make precisely the ritual of pilgrimage to the tombs of local saints their principal target, which in their opinion is not only "an innovation" (*bid'a*), but also a sinful infringement of monotheism. The mufti writes that the Prophet Muhammad "had forbidden to implore the deceased to assist the living in their worldly affairs."[18] He concludes that "turning the tombs of the saints, or *mazars*, into places of pilgrimage and sacrifice manifestly runs counter to the dictates of Shari'a."[19] The mufti writes that "people are sometimes transforming places declared holy into zones of recreation and manifestations,"[20] which surely "does not befit the Muslims" at all. Nor does applying to "sham doctors, fortune-tellers, wise women, conjurers and quacks" on the part of the Muslims conform to monotheism. In a fatwa on these, the mufti calls on the Muslims to relinquish their services. "It is astonishing," wrote the mufti, "that many of these impostors are women."[21] It is possible that women are mentioned here because they often carry informal authority and constitute a menace for the official clergy, owing to their influence on the believers.

If such puritanism could be pleasing to the Salafis' hearts, one cannot fail to see that it was also useful for the authorities, to which the mufti retained complete loyalty (the worship of the saints' tombs distracted the population from the official ideology, while the ministers of popular Islam by their popularity challenged the party and government *nomenklatura*). I assume that when Ziyauddin Khan attacked traditional beliefs as "superstitions" and called for the adherence to the Qur'an and Hadiths, he was guided not by the intention to spread Wahhabism but by the necessity to comply with the directives of the Communist government authorities whom he had to be loyal to. Most post-Soviet revivalists later blamed muftis and imams of the Soviet epoch for their collaborationism and servility to the party–state bureaucracy, but it should be noted that their position was based on the presumption of survival of *umma* and its religious institutions. Contemporary scholars even recall in this regard the concept of *idtirar* (*iztirar*) "compelled obligation."[22] Be this as it may, if criticism of "popular" Islam by Mufti Ziyauddin was not directly associated with the penetration of Salafi Islam into the Soviet republics of Central Asia, it nonetheless fertilized the local soil to grow the seeds of Salafism in the post-Soviet future.

THE EARLY PROTO-SALAFI IDEOLOGISTS: MAULAWI HINDUSTANI AND OTHERS

Beginning at the end of the 1970s, some of the Uzbek *'ulama* showed signs of dissatisfaction with the Hanafi doctrine and moving toward Hanbalism.

Hajji domulla *Muhammadjan Hindustani.*

These *'ulama* had been educated by several prominent teachers of Islam who had until recently remained unknown abroad due to the almost underground character of their activities under Soviet rule. A significant role among those teachers was played by Maulawi Hindustani.

The biography of Muhammadjan Rustamov-Hindustani (1892–1989) sheds light on the unique fate of an important unofficial Islamic enlightener of Central Asia in the twentieth century; this story intricately combines elements of the historical past of this region, the influences of the foreign schools of Islam, and the new Central Asian reality.[23]

Muhammadjan was born in 1892 in the *kishlak* of Chorbogh (or Chahar Bagh, meaning "four gardens") on the outskirts of Kokand[24] to a village mulla named Rustam, who wanted his son to become a *qari*, a reader of the Qur'an. Muhammadjan started learning the Qur'an by heart under the guidance of a local mulla and completed it in 1904–1906 in Kokand. He continued his religious education, perfected his Arabic with the help of Zikriyo *qari,* and also trained at the Mingoyim *madrasa* in Kokand, then in Bukhara. Bukhara in those times, an amirate that was not formally part of the Russian Empire, as the home to Mir-i Arab *madrasa,* was a center of attraction for all Central Asian youth who strove to become religious scholars.

In Bukhara, young Muhammadjan could see a struggle between renovators—*ravshangaran* (local jadidists and their sympathizers) and conservatives (qadimists). The renovators then succeeded in opening a New School in Bukhara where modern secular subjects were taught alongside religious ones. Under pressure from the Qaziate headed by the qazi kalon, Mulla Burhanuddin, Amir Abdul Ahad was compelled to rescind his consent for this school to function. Not only did the conservatives want to prevent the spread of contemporary knowledge among the youth, but also some of them opposed even such attributes of modernity as the telephone, the railroad, and the bicycle. Relations between Amir Abdul Ahad and the Bukharan religious class resembled those between the Saudi king 'Abd al-'Aziz b. Sa'ud and the *ikhwan* in the period of the formation of the Saudi state in Arabia in the 1920s–1930s. Amir Alim Khan, who replaced Abdul Ahad after the latter's death, was initially inclined to support the renovators, but he, too, was compelled to cave in to the conservative mullas, a turn manifested in particular in his decision to ban the publication of the first Bukharan secular newspaper, *Bukhara-e Sharif* (The Noble Bukhara), which appeared in 1912.

The struggle between renovators and conservatives was a precursor of the battles that began to break out in Central Asia nearly a century later, after the Central Asian republics were granted independence. This struggle undoubtedly laid an imprint on the formation of Muhammadjan's views. During World War I, he set off for Afghanistan, where he continued his religious education, this time under the eminent *'alim* from Mazar-i Sharif, Muhammad Ghaus Saidzade. Here Muhammadjan perfected his knowledge of Arabic and Persian and studied Arab grammar, versification, logic, scholastic theology (*kalam*), dogmatics, and interpretation of the Qur'an (*tafsir*), including the commentary of the famous seventeenth- to eighteenth-century poet Mirza 'Abd al-Qadir Bedil (1644–1721), whose works have become classic for all Central Asian students of Islam.

Soon the gifted student went to Tashkent to assist his teacher Muhammad Ghaus, who bore the title of qazi-*domulla* here, in giving classes in the Kukaltash *madrasa*. After the new king of Afghanistan came to power, the qazi-*domulla* was invited to come back to his homeland, was appointed the qazi kalon of Jalalabad, and brought Muhammadjan with him. After three years as a judge, the teacher fell sick and bequeathed to Muhammadjan to bury him and then go to India to continue his studies.

For eight years Muhammadjan studied in the Uthmaniya *madrasa* in the city of Ajmir in Rajasthan. By chance, he met his father there as the latter was setting off for the hajj, and Muhammadjan saw him off for a long journey. His father died in Mecca, and after burying him, Muhammadjan again went to India and finished his studies in the *madrasa*, after which he returned to his homeland via Afghanistan in 1927.

By that time all of Central Asia had for several years been part of the Soviet Union and under Communist rule. The *basmachi* movement was still waging a struggle against the Soviet power but was already doomed to defeat. Many of Muhammadjan's compatriots had emigrated, having been dispersed in the countries of the Muslim East. Their descendants, citizens of Saudi Arabia, Pakistan, Afghanistan, and Turkey, were bound to play a major role in the Islamic renaissance in Central Asia and in the efforts to form Central Asian Islamic activism in the late twentieth century. In 1929 Muhammadjan became *imam-khatib* in a mosque in the Red Labor *mahalla* of Kokand and started a family.

This relatively quiet period in the life of Hindustani ("the Indian," as he was now called) came to an end in the early 1930s. The country was in the grip of repression of religion and the clergy. Muhammadjan was arrested, but fortunately, he was soon released. As all those who are released, he urgently needed employment. Muhammadjan took a post for an organization that gathered silk cocoons. But as happened to all the former clergymen, he was often summoned for questioning. Sometimes early in the morning Hindustani would go to graze cows, holding a work of Bedil close to hand. According to Domulla Burhanuddin,[25] the Maulawi was summoned to the prosecutor, who, chiding him, said, "We shall destroy all of you, turban-wearers, enemies of the state." Hindustani replied, "Those who wear a turban are not enemies of the state. Better look for enemies of the state among those who hold office." In the Soviet Union of the 1930s, a lot of "enemies" were indeed found among officeholders.

Two years later, Hindustani thought it better to move from Kokand to Albig, Angren district, not far from Tashkent (it was an irony of fate that it was in Angren that clashes between Uzbekistan government forces and the Islamic fighters took place in the 1990s), where he engaged in agricultural labor. But his reputation as an authoritative Muslim scholar who was called a Maulawi constantly put his life in danger.

Hindustani's adopted son Ubaydulla recalls: "Until 1936 we stayed in Angren. At that time my own sister Azizkhan was born. Now we lived for one month in one village, for two months in another. Living in a single place was dangerous. Very hard times had set in and living conditions became extremely bad. We had only one Kyrgyz *yurt* and a donkey that was all the property we had. We loaded this *yurt* upon the donkey and roamed from one place to the other. We set up the *yurt* and lived in it. We had one cauldron, but inside the *yurt* we could not lay a fire under it. In this cauldron not only did we cook meals, but also bake bread."[26]

In 1936 Hindustani was forced to move to another *kishlak*—Aq-Chul—but there he was arrested and sentenced to three years in a labor camp. The Maulawi served his time first in the Urals, in Sverdlovsk (Yekaterinburg), where he was engaged in logging, then in the Far East, in the town of Tygda (near the Amur River), where he worked at a plant that produced railroad ties.

Despite living in the harsh conditions of labor camps, the Maulawi survived and in 1941 again returned to Kokand, where he worked at the local oil and fat plant until 1943. In that year he was enlisted into the army and sent to Semipalatinsk (Kazakhstan) and then to the Soviet–German front. Muhammadjan was wounded in the arm during combat and had to lie in the hospital for a few months. After convalescence, he was sent to a labor front (nonuniformed conscripts used for nonfrontline logistical and support work) in Kemerovo. His ordeal was far from over, however. For two years Muhammadjan grazed sheep. "I consoled myself," he writes in his autobiography, "by remembering that the Prophet himself in his time tended rams. When a man tends sheep, he becomes soft and kind. It was an enormous blessing for me that I became a shepherd. This enabled me to recollect the forgotten *suras* of the Qur'an, repeat them and completely retrace them. In the morning I drove the sheep into the forest and repeated particular *suras* of the Qur'an out loud. Each day I repeated fifteen parts of the Qur'an and in the space of two days managed to repeat the entire Qur'an."

The Maulawi was a loyal and even eager worker. He was given a premium consisting of money, an overcoat, and a diploma for the growth of livestock in his herd. After the war ended, he came back to his native Kokand and again took up a job at the oil and fat plant. Having gone to Tashkent in search of a more appropriate job, he met the mufti of Central Asia, Babakhanov, who, as his adopted son Ubaydulla recalled, gave Muhammadjan an assignment to Dushanbe, Tajikistan. In 1947 the Maulawi settled in Dushanbe, where the Directorate on the Affairs of Religions under the Council of Ministers of the Tajik Republic appointed him *mutawalli* (attendant at a mosque, of lower rank than an imam) at the Mawlana Yaqub-e Charkhi mosque; in another year he became *imam-khatib* in the Haji Yaqub mosque in Dushanbe. But he had only two years to serve in that capacity: his scholarship, exuberantly growing popularity, and unusual past gave him no rest against envious persons and persecutors of religion. He was informed against, rearrested, charged with espionage, sentenced to twenty-five years in a labor camp, and dispatched to serve his sentence in Kazakhstan. From there he wrote petitions to Moscow, proving his innocence of any guilt. A commission that arrived from Moscow, as a result of examination, came to a conclusion that Muhammadjan Rustamov had been wrongfully sentenced, and on serving four and a half years in detention, he returned home (he was to be rehabilitated only at the end of the 1950s).

After he returned to Dushanbe, academician Abdulgani Mirzaev invited Hindustani, who had gained in the republic a reputation as a distinguished expert on the Islamic heritage, to work as a consultant in the Department of Oriental Studies and Written Heritage of the Academy of Sciences of Tajikistan. And again Hindustani's popularity among both scholars and young mullas created problems for him. Mirzaev was pressured by the KGB to fire Hindustani. The Maulawi's eyesight became sharply impaired, and he discontinued any official work forever.

From that time on, Muhammadjan *qari* focused all his efforts on private work with students at home. As testified by his adopted son Ubaydulla, he gave classes either at his home or at other places in various parts of the city. Soon he was recognized by a substantial part of shadow public opinion (which in the Soviet days sometimes was stronger than the official one) as *primus inter pares* among many underground teachers of Islam. But even today Central Asian scholars express diverse and somewhat contradicting opinions about Maulawi's level of scholarly competence. According to Babajanov, Muminov, and Olcott, since Hindustani studied in a number of different institutions, under different teachers, and in different periods, he was not able to gain consistent and systematic knowledge.[27] Also, he had access only to a very limited number of classical Islamic sources. Referring to the view of a former mufti and a well-educated Islamic scholar, Muhammad Sadiq Muhammad Yusuf, these authors also mention that Hindustani excessively followed the lower level of *taqlid*, thus he always made judgments on the basis of consensual opinion (*ijma'*) of local *mujtahids*. This precipitated dogmatism and intolerance of some of his students.

I have met a lot of Hindustani's former students, many of whom are members of the present-day religious class of Central Asia. In 2004 the majority of the imams of mosques in the cities of the Ferghana Valley were former students of Hindustani. They came to Dushanbe and visited the teacher secretly, mostly during the nighttime. All his lessons were individual, and no groups assembled in his house. When another underground Uzbek teacher of Islam, Abdullajan Makhsum *domulla* died in 1985, his students transferred to Hindustani. I asked some of them why the Tajikistan authorities then were so permissive to the informal Uzbek (and non-Uzbek) Islamic teachers and students who would not be able to carry on their activities in Uzbekistan. Ismail khoja, the imam of the Digrizlik mosque in Kokand, told me that the reason probably lay in the fact that the Communist authorities had considered Tajikistan peripheral and of less importance than Uzbekistan, the key republic in Central Asia, and therefore had not put it under such strict control.[28]

In the 1960s Hindustani no longer had to fear persecution. First, he did not call for the overthrow of the Soviet system or the creation of an Islamic state; second, his activity perfectly tallied with the tacit model of Islam in the USSR, where alongside an official, "progovernment" Islam

Imam Ismail qari, Kokand (January 2004).

there existed a parallel, clandestine one, which everyone knew about but often made believe that it did not exist. Hindustani's high reputation as an expert on the Islamic culture, along with the Khrushchev thaw (the very limited liberalization of the political life of Russia under Nikita Khrushchev), also played their roles.

What and how did Hindustani teach his pupils? First and foremost, one cannot regard Hindustani's informal school as divorced from the whole parallel system of Islamic education that existed in Central Asia, and in Uzbekistan and Tajikistan above all. Natives of the Ferghana Valley region made up a significant part of underground teachers of Islam. It was through this network of religious education that the translation of knowledge on Islam was mainly effected. Most likely, the pupils of the home-based *qaris*, *'ulama*, and *fuqaha* were inferior in knowledge to those who received a systematic education (after graduation from the official Mir-i Arab *madrasa* of Bukhara) in one of the Islamic universities of the Middle East (for example, one of the leaders of the Tajik Islamists of the 1990s, qazi kalon Hoji Akbar Turajonzoda, received his education in Jordan). However, they carried the knowledge further, transmitting it to those who could not or did not want to join the ranks of the official clergy. In addition, the informal bearers of Islamic knowledge imparted to their students a supply of independence and critical spirit with regard to the existing order, which, however, did not take the shape of open opposition capable of jeopardizing the existence of the informal network of Islamic education itself.

According to the accounts of Hindustani's pupils, he admitted for study those who already had the requisite minimum of knowledge in Islamic sciences. Those who came to him had, as a rule, studied under other mullas or "informal" preachers, of which there were plenty in Central Asia. Taught in their study groups were Arabic and the Islamic sciences—the latter taught not by individual subject but according to the particular books that the teachers had at their disposal. According to the data obtained by a group of Tajik scholars, Hindustani's pupil Mulla Burhanuddin initially studied *Mukhtasar al-Wiqaya* and *Sharh al-Wiqaya* under his relative Muhammadi *domulla* of Kumsanghir. After that, he moved on to the well-known Abdurrahman-*domulla* Sarfi from the Kuybyshev district of the Kurghanteppa region, who taught him Arabic grammar. Then Burhanuddin for three years studied *Qafiya*, *Sharh al-Mulla*, and other books under Mulla Dodarjan of Kurghanteppa, after which the mulla advised Burhanuddin to turn for study to Hindustani, himself brought Burhanuddin to Dushanbe, and persuaded Muhammadjan *qari* to admit him for study.

Hindustani taught his students Arabic according to *Al-Sarf wal-Nahw* and *al-'Awamil*. They studied Arabic literature, including the *mu'allaqat*, the works of Arabia's pre-Islamic poets, which are among the chefs d'oeuvre of medieval Arabic poetry. It's uncertain why Hindustani taught Arabic according to the *mu'allaqat*; after all, these poems belong to the era of the Jahiliyya, that is, to the Arabs' era of "religious ignorance." He must have used them either because he had little choice in literary works or because the language of pre-Islamic poets was the closest to that of the Qur'an. He also taught the *'ilm al-tafsir*—exegesis, or explication of the Qur'an—particularly from such compilations as *Tafsir al-Jalalayn* and *Tafsir al-Baydawi*. He taught the Hadiths according to *Sahih al-Bukhari*. He paid great attention to the study of logics and taught *fiqh* according to the books *Usul al-fiqh*, *Nur al-anwar*, and *al-Tawdih*, which were used in the Mir-i Arab *madrasa*. Books on the life of the Prophet and the righteous caliphs, and textbooks of rhetoric were studied. The instruction was carried out in Arabic, but Persian literature was taught separately. Hindustani was an expert on Persian poetry. He paid particular attention in the lessons to the works of Saadi. Besides Tajik, Uzbek, Arabic, and Persian, Hindustani was fluent in Pashtu, Urdu, and Hindi. Some of his former students recall that in the beginning he used Urdu as a language of instruction and that he later transferred to Tajik and Uzbek.

Thanks to his lessons, the Maulawi acquired enormous popularity in the republic. These lessons were recorded on audiocassettes, copied, and disseminated. Interest in them was also displayed by the republic's party and state *nomenklatura*. According to Ubaydulla, Hindustani taught classes to the then chairman of Tajikistan's Council of Ministers Abdul Ahad Kahharov and his daughter Naima, who became an Arabist.[29] Intellectuals from every corner of Central Asia came to visit the Maulawi.

Having lived to see the second half of the 1980s, the Maulawi, as he did in his youth, witnessed a sharp struggle between the adherents of various currents in Islam, including that waged between the traditionalists and the so-called Wahhabis. This struggle burst out in the region in the period of Gorbachev's *perestroika*: "Maulawi Hindustani received an anonymous letter which accused him of a deviation from the cause of Islam, of cooperation with the KGB and collaborationism. The letter deeply traumatized the aged scholar. He keenly felt the accusations and wrote a reply in which he challenged the letter-writer to an open discussion."[30]

The Maulawi died in Dushanbe in 1989 at the age of ninety-seven. He was buried in the Yaqub-e Charkhi mosque in Dushanbe. "I am glad," said his grandson, "that people honored him at last. I am also glad that he did not see the wickedness that came after."[31]

HINDUSTANI'S DISCIPLES

Central Asian scholars disagree not only about the level of knowledge achieved by different unofficial teachers of Islam but also about the roles they played in preparing the post-Soviet Islamic revival in Central Asia. Many scholars assert that the main role in this tutorship belonged to Hindustani. Abdujabbar Abduvakhitov, as some others do, argues that Hindustani's importance is exaggerated by those scholars who capitalize on the great interest shown in the academic world to such figures who have remained in the shadow for so long. Abduvakhitov asserts that another Islamic scholar, Mulla Hakimjan *qari* of Margelan, made the most crucial contribution to the formation of a group of new Salafi *'ulama*, some of whom were also the students of Hindustani.[32]

During our conversations in the early 1990s, Shamsuddin Babakhanov told me that it was Mulla Hakimjan *qari* who had begun the dissemination of ideas close to Salafism way back in the early 1950s. If this is the case, then it is this preceptor who played the principal role in the radicalization of the next generation of *'ulama*, though it is unclear from where that *mudarris* could at the time have obtained the literature necessary for teaching pupils in that spirit. It *is* known that travelers to Arab countries began to bring it from their trips later, during the Khrushchev thaw.

Hakimjan seems to be an altogether controversial figure. His brother had received the highest Soviet award, that of the Hero of Socialist Labor. The *qari* brought up quite a few radicals, but he himself later became frightened over what he had done and began to oppose his former "Wahhabi" disciples, such as Hindustani. When I visited Margelan in the beginning of 2004, I found out that Hakimjan *qari*, already in his late nineties, was still alive but recovering from a surgery and not feeling well enough to be interviewed.

I was startled when I learned from a former Uzbek Communist ideologist whom I interviewed in the 1990s that even in the late 1980s the Communist leadership in Tashkent had been ordering the party committees in a secret circular to support the Salafis in order to use them against the influential and therefore dangerous traditional Islam. The Salafis were then viewed as instrumental in splitting the religious class. The informant told me that he had met Hakimjan *qari* when he stayed at Khoja Maghis *mazar*, supposedly in 1988 or near that time, and for the first time heard from him a Salafi criticism of some traditional Central Asian rituals, such as commemorating the fortieth day after the death of a Muslim, which Hakimjan considered an innovation borrowed from the Christians. This ideologist considered it rather funny. "We couldn't have imagined into what a monster this Wahhabi movement here would turn," he told me.

So, many of both Hakimjan's and Hindustani's students later became founders of the "Wahhabi" movement in Central Asia, as well as spiritual fathers of militant Islamic organizations. These included 'Allama Rahmatulla *qari*, who joined the Wahhabis while in Andizhan (he was condemned by Hindustani for doing so). 'Allama Rahmatulla *qari* died in an accident in 1981.

In the words of one of the Tashkent *'ulama*, some people in their circles believed that it was Hakimjan *qari* of Margelan who disposed of 'Allama. Hakimjan had a group of hit men loyal to him; he was not averse to commerce and allegedly in his old days had been a part-time trafficker in gold.[33] Tahir Yuldashev denied the rumors of Hakimjan's role in 'Allama's death, claiming that 'Allama was liquidated on orders from Moscow.

An even more prominent figure was Abduwali *qari* Mirzaev, who, as the imam of the great mosque in Andizhan, was close to professing Hanbali Sunnism, although he cannot be considered a Hanbali theologian because he tried to place himself above all of the four schools, interpreting the main sources of Islam in an independent manner, like a *mujtahid* (a recognized knowledgeable scholar who has a right to issue *ijtihad*, or an independent judgment on a religious matter). Mirzaev inspired others who became leaders of various terrorist organizations. Yet another theologian considered to be a Wahhabi was Obidkhan *qari* Nazarov, a pupil of Rahmatulla *qari*. Other Rahmatulla pupils were Ishaq *qari*, Ismail domla, Ibrahimjan qukandi (in Kokand), Hikmatulla *qari* (in Dushanbe), Muhammad Ali Marginani (in Yazjuwan), Abdullajan Makhsum *domulla* (in Margelan), Abdul Latif Andizhani, and Muhammad Sadiq *qari*. Subsequently, they themselves became teachers of Islam.

It cannot be ruled out that certain teachers (*mudarrises*) lecturing in *hujras* maintained close, possibly even secret relations with government authorities. In the Islamic circles of Uzbekistan, rumors were afoot that Shaykh Makhsum was linked to agencies supervising Islam; if the rumors were not true, it would be hard to explain how he could privately and illegally gather up to 150 students in a large room—which could not remain unnoticed—and suffer no persecution in the process.[34]

Most of these early radicals left behind audiotapes that are still in use among their supporters and continue to be used to recruit new members of radical Islamic movements throughout Central Asia. (Only recently have Central Asian Islamists started to use the Internet for the dissemination of their ideas. Moreover, access to the Internet is still limited in most Central Asian states.)

The students of *mudarrises* who attended clandestine *hujras* in Central Asia had from the 1970s established their circle of scholars (called *dawra*), which was characterized as *mujaddidiyya*, that is, "renovationism." Babajanov and Kamilov mention that by calling themselves *mujaddidiyya*, these radical scholars were making a bridge between themselves and the Naqshbandiyya brotherhood of Ma Wara' al-Nahr in the eighteenth century, who had also used this name. The "renovators" repudiated the principles of the Maturidiyya school of Hanafism prevalent in Central Asian Islam and deemed it necessary to introduce amendments both into the system of current rituals and, in part, into dogmatics by purging the primordial, "true" Islam of later developments and borrowings from pre-Islamic cults and customs. These neo-Salafis stood against any displays of the cult of saints, including the custom of *ziyarat*; against the reading of certain *ayats* of the Qur'an and funeral prayers and prayers for the forgiveness of the deceased or for a person's health; against the dispensation of donations during the funeral (*tokivor*);[35] against the mourning of the dead; against sumptuous weddings; and so forth. They also conducted politicized discussions, for instance, on the question of whether the Islamic *umma* could exist outside of the Islamic state. Moderate Hanafi *'ulama* believed this possible, while adepts of mujaddidiyya believed it impossible. Thus the idea of an Islamic state had already been in the air and was in greater degree engendered by local reality, not completely borrowed from foreign Salafis.

Many researchers speculate about the influence of such ideologists of political Islam as Sayyid Qutb and al-Maududi upon Central Asian radical

Islamists. However, researchers do not always ask whether that influence was manifested in the following of the general spirit of the works of these pillars of radical Islam or in the borrowing of specific ideas and concepts. Without conducting a detailed comparative analysis of the tenets of Qutb, al-Maududi, and Central Asian radicals, I shall make a few key points. I shall make reference to the conclusion drawn by Youssef Choueiri, who writes, "to Qutb and al-Maududi jihad was a total state of war, designed to disarm one's enemy in order to reinstate the Shari'a."[36] Such a constant state of war was the only way to ensure that "God's absolute sovereignty" is the unifying principle for all followers of the Qutbian type of Islamic radicalism in many countries. It is true, as Choueiri assumes, that both Islamic thinkers as well as Khomeini, whose theories he studied, "saw no possibility of coexistence between Islam and other political and social systems."[37]

Although Hindustani was a teacher of these neo-Salafis, he strictly stuck to Hanafism, believing that opinions such as those mentioned above were borrowed from the foreign Wahhabis, whose teachings were unacceptable for Central Asian Muslims.

So, Hindustani himself criticized some of his former students, whom he labeled "Wahhabis." There were three main reasons for his fury: (1) the gradual sliding of these young scholars toward Hanbalism in rituals, the interpretation of sacred texts, and so forth; (2) their quest for bringing Islam into politics; and (3) their criticism of Hindustani. According to Babajanov and Kamilov, Hindustani wanted to stop the Salafi schism among his students, because he considered their views to have been imported from abroad and thus incompatible with Central Asian Hanafi Islam. He even laughed at the strange character of their ideas in a satirical play.[38] During Hindustani's funeral, some of his disciples dispensed donations as a *tokivor* to those present, as if demonstrating their teacher's devotion to traditional Islam. One of his pupils, Mullo Muhammadali Faizmuhammad, asserted that the Maulawi viewed positively the idea of the creation of Islamic political parties and believed that the idea had to be supported.[39] But this statement is not confirmed by any other evidence and contradicts what we know about the Hindustani's views.

The two aforementioned Uzbek scholars, Babajanov and Kamilov, received access from Maulawi students Abdul Latif *qari* Andizhani, Muhammad Sadiq *qari*, and Abduqahhor *qari* to the two *Answers* written by Hindustani to his young Salafi critics in which he defends Hanafism and himself. In the *Answers*, Hindustani considers their appeals to cleanse Islam from innovation to be inappropriate and rejects all accusations against him. Some quotations show what harsh language the teacher used against his former disciples.

It seems to me that you have excused yourselves from many of my discussions, or that evil inclinations have permeated your flesh. It is too bad that you have never met with me face to face or engaged in debate. I would have given you utterly persuasive answers. What are you afraid of? You are like a dog barking from behind a fence. . . .

I am surprised at your stupidity, that you would begin your muddle-headed speech with. . . . Thus, for example, you accuse me of believing in the government and of having friendly relations with the state. But my attendance at that meeting [interrogation by the KGB] was a result of your baseness and your hostility [toward me]. In fact, you even gave evidence that I was the leader of your sect (*firqa*). "I am not a Wahhabi," I told them, making clear the [Hanafite] basis of my beliefs.

And the Maulawi also blamed these Salafis for their wrong interpretation of jihad:

Do you know how many parts does *jihad* for faith consist of? If one part is *jihad* against the unbelievers on the field of battle, then another is to cleanse oneself of evil thoughts and deliver oneself from ignorance. The Lord Prophet of Allah called this second part *jihad-i akbar*, the greatest *jihad*.[40]

Imam Ishaq qari with the author in Kokand (January 2004).

The repercussions of these hot disputes are still vivid in the cities of the Ferghana Valley today. I could feel it while interviewing a number of local imams and 'ulama in the beginning of 2004. Almost all of those I interviewed were disciples of Hindustani, though they also had attended private lessons of other clandestine teachers of Islam (mostly before they went to Hindustani). Among people I met in Kokand, which was home to many famous religious figures who played a crucial role in the post-Soviet Islamic revival, was the aforementioned Ishaq *qari* of Kokand. Ishaq *qari*, who did not descend from a high-born family, spent his childhood in a *kishlak*, began to study privately in 1968 under Muhammadjan *qari* from Kokand, and then was secretly taught in Margelan by Mulla Tashtemir Akhund. Ishak lived at his mosque in a *hujra*, devoting his entire time to the study of religion. After that, in 1969 he moved to Dushanbe, where for about twenty years he was a student of Hindustani. At the end of December 2003, as an old friend informed me, the nobles of Kokand who did not sympathize with the anti-Wahhabi imams (or, better to say, all those who were progovernment) convinced Mufti Bahromov that Ishaq *qari* was sowing discord among Muslims, and the mufti dismissed Ishaq *qari* from his job, although he soon reinstated him (as his opponents said spitefully, at the urgent request of the security services who were backing anti–Wahhabi-minded imams). In a conversation, Ishaq *qari* confirmed to me his anti-Salafi reputation, as I have mentioned already, by criticizing the deceased Mufti Ziyauddin Babakhanov, under whom, he claimed, some local Muslims had even started to pray "in the Hanbali fashion" (without headdress, lifting both hands, etc.), believing that these were the "genuine" rules of Islamic divine service.[41] The imam also sharply criticized one of his colleagues, Ishan Ibrahim *qari*, who is believed to be a Salafi sympathizer, calling him "an ignoramus."

Ibrahim *qari*, forty-five years old, was imam of the Saodat mosque in Kokand. He is of clerical parentage, his father, grandfather, and great-grandfather having all been the well-known 'ulama of Kokand. At first Ibrahim *qari* was taught the Qur'an by his father, 'Abdullah *qari*, who later sent him to study with the eminent expert on Qur'anic sciences Saifuddin *qari* (I have never met him but was informed that he is still alive and is in his late seventies). Then in 1979–1981 Ibrahim *qari* was taught in Dushanbe by Hindustani. In the opinion of Ibrahim *qari*, haji *domulla*, as he calls the teacher, was erudite in all Islamic sciences, was particularly strong in *tafsir*, and especially amazed the students with his knowledge of verses by Bedil by heart. Therefore being taught by him was especially fruitful. Ibrahim *qari* told me that, although he belonged to the clerical estate, his ancestors were ordinary people, not *khojas*. When he wanted to marry a girl from a noble family, her relatives refused to give her away, in spite of the fact that he already had a reputation as a good Islamic scholar by that time. He managed to marry the girl only after Hindustani came from Dushanbe to Kokand at his request and persuaded her relatives to agree to the marriage. The girl's grandfather was the well-known scholar 'Arif Khan *qari*, who had served as *imam-khatib* of the old mosque (where Ishaq *qari* now serves), and his father was also an *'alim*.

An old friend in Kokand privately told me that three years ago Ibrahim *qari* interceded for a Tahriri (see chapter 3) whom the police had caught in the mosque and severely beaten. After that Ibrahim was dismissed. He earned his living for some time working as a taxi driver, then was permitted to work as an assistant to the imam, and only recently has he returned to his former office.

Imam Ibrahim demonstrated his critical attitude toward those imams who adhered to the "Saudi school" of Sunnism inspired by "the Saudi books that are based on the idea of strong link between Islam and power." He stated: "These characters—Rahmatulla 'Allama, 'Abdulla qari and others—wanted power but we resisted them. Allah saved us from this disaster. Arguments we used in our debates with them were given to us by our teacher." Ibrahim *qari* read *Kitab al-Tawhid*, by Muhammad 'Abd al-Wahhab, and he believes that it contradicts *'aqida*. "Money is behind it," he complained. "The people these days think more about this world, not about religion, and this distresses me."

The aforementioned Ismail khoja, who serves in the Kokand mosque of Digrizlik, has pupils and is the son of an Islamic jurisprudent; many generations of ancestors in their family had been *'ulama*. Ismail khoja studied under his father, then under Akhunjan Haydar Khan from Batken (Kyrgyzstan) and 'Abdurashid *qari* of Kokand, who was repeatedly arrested in Uzbekistan just as Hindustani was. Up until 1989, Ismail has been trained and guided by Hindustani. He is deemed to be an opponent of Wahhabism, though not as irreconcilable a one as Ishaq *qari*. Ismail remembers that in the Soviet days the imams and Islamic scholars made a written obligation to the authorities that they would not teach anybody. There are also a lot of other interesting characters in Kokand, such as Jura Khan Tura, who is considered the main religious authority there, a very old man belonging, as can be seen from his name, to the *tura* estate. The nobles of Kokand often gather at his place, discussing the most important questions of local life.

In the early 1990s, the Islamic Revival Party (IRP) of the USSR, which had been established on June 9, 1990, in Astrakhan, became active in Uzbekistan, and some former disciples of Maulawi became its members. However, its leaders held very moderate positions and shied away from calling for the creation of an Islamic state, a platform that would have been natural for an Islamic political party. The IRP was considered too moderate by young Salafi revivalists, who were seeking a more radical organizational framework for their aspirations. On the basis of the pan-Soviet IRP, a separate IRP for Uzbekistan was founded in January 1991. Even this moderate party faced strong opposition from the Uzbekistani government, which was determined not to allow many Islamic political parties to emerge in the republic.

One of the founders of the Islamic political movement in Central Asia, Davlat Usmon (Tajikistan), says that the Islamic movement in Uzbekistan back in the early 1990s had split into several currents and groups, one of which, under the leadership of Abduwali *qari* Mirzaev and Abdulla Utaev, founded the Islamic Revival Party of Uzbekistan. After the destruction of that party, Usmon writes, a group of Muslim youth in Uzbekistan (Usmon is one of the few who mention the existence of this organization) under the leadership of Tahir Yuldashev "joined their coreligionists in Tajikistan."[42]

The Uzbekistani portion of the Ferghana Valley was where Salafis and radical Islamists managed to mobilize popular support. Not only did the Salafis replace the traditional imams who were loyal to the government in Tashkent, but they also channeled the political mobilization that was underway in the region along the course of political Islam. A newly converted Salafi and a follower of Rahmatulla *qari*, Imam Abdul Ahad, who acquired the reputation of being a devoted Wahhabi, preached in the Ata Wali Khan Tura mosque in Namangan, a city that together with Margelan and Andizhan became a stronghold of militant Islamists. For the first time, Muslim preachers began calling for the rule of Shari'a law, which was to solve all the problems and heal all the diseases the Muslims were suffering from, and in particular would end inequality, despotism, and criminal disorder.

The religious-political group Islam Lashkarlari (Warriors of Islam) was also established during the early 1990s. This was followed by the establishment of Adolat (Justice), which, as Muminov argues, was one of the two wings of Islam Lashkarlari.[43] Adolat comprised mostly young men who organized themselves in *mahalla* militias. These militias started patrolling the streets and controlling prices at local markets. In effect, Adolat tried to take over the functions of the local state authorities. Having successfully challenged local law-enforcement agencies, the Adolat militias declared that they had replaced them. Most members of the Adolat militias were strong, well-trained sportsmen (mainly in various types of martial arts). Uzbek scholars have compared the Adolat militias with clandestine associations of craftsmen in the cities of the Abbasid Caliphate such as the *fityan* and *'ayyarun*, associations that performed similar functions and adhered to a certain code of honor.[44]

In other words, initially Adolat was just a team of volunteers desirous to establish order. At that time it was headed by Hakimjan Satimov. The unofficial religious authorities immediately saw for themselves an opportunity to use this force in their interest. A process of Islamization of Adolat teams got underway, but it is still impossible to trace the precise moment when they began to assume Islamist positions and advance the corresponding slogans. Imam Abdul Ahad played a crucial role in the Islamization of Adolat.

The future IMU leader Tahir Yuldashev, as a number of informants claim, then actively assisted the joining of efforts between this voluntary militia and the radical Islamists, hoping to become a key figure in the entire radical Islamist movement.

No wonder that the Islamists swiftly placed such a militarized structure as Adolat under their command, as that group was ready to embrace radical Islamist ideas, while the Islamists themselves sought to establish the fighting units that they lacked. In regard to this, it is pertinent to recall an episode related to me by the Tashkent scholar A., who back in 1990 met in the Gumbaz mosque in Namangan a group of religious activists and Daghestanis then present there, the imam of the mosque Abdul Ahad, and the leader of the secular opposition Birlik party Abdurahim Pulatov. The latter exhorted the Islamists to work actively with the army, and when the Islamists objected that the army personnel were mainly Russians, Pulatov called on the audience "to convert Russians to Islam." It is possible that even then an attempt by secular oppositionists to establish an alliance with the Islamist radicals foreshadowed a subsequent loss of the positions the secularists had started to gain or could gain.

When the merger of Adolat with radical Islam took place, the leaders of the new group came to regard Shari'a as an exclusive legal basis of their activity. They gained broad support in the densely populated cities of the Ferghana Valley, owing to its high level of religiosity. Their contribution to the promotion of the idea of an Islamic state was immense.[45]

They performed all the necessary Islamic rituals and were devoted to Islamic traditions and moral values. In particular, they ordered all women not to appear on the streets unless properly veiled. These injunctions were met with particular admiration by the older generation, which believed that Central Asian youth were disrespectful of tradition and neglected the Islamic code of behavior.

This group of Muslim youth, inspired by the works of such ideologists of Islamic radicalism as Abul Ala Maududi of Pakistan and the sermons of local revivalist Islamic leaders, rallied around the concept of Musulmanabad (The Land of Islam). This paradigm, according to Abduwali *qari*, originally introduced by Rahmatulla 'Allama, was based on the following principles: (1) Central Asia belongs to the Muslim world, which is a homogeneous unified Muslim territory where Islam dominates everywhere; (2) Shari'a governs relations between individuals; (3) all the people in this space believe in Allah, and their society is ruled by the educated *'ulama*.[46] Abduwali explained to Abduvakhitov that Musulman-abad meant "unification of different independent states as one Muslim area in which there would be many states united by Islam."

The idea of Musulman-abad shares some traits with the concept of the Caliphate of Hizb at-Tahrir (see chapter 3). However, it was much more amorphous and could not pretend to be a substantive political concept. Rather it was a common point of reference for the followers of revivalist Islamic scholars in Central Asia at the time.

When I visited the cities of Ferghana in the beginning of 1992, I interviewed several members of Adolat and spoke to local people. By then, the militants had already been in control of most of the mosques in Namangan, as well as many mosques in Margelan, Andizhan, and other cities in the valley. One local resident, Muhammadjan, told me that after months of total chaos, when anybody could be robbed in the streets and have his or her car stolen if it was left unguarded for ten minutes, only Adolat militiamen were able to restore law and order. He also insisted that Adolat militiamen had cut off the hands of one of the thieves in accordance with Shari'a (others said it was not true, but it is interesting that such a myth was circulating). And he claimed that the militiamen were "pure" and honest people who did not take bribes, unlike the officers of the Interior Ministry, and they were serving all citizens. Muhammadjan was therefore eager to vote for the Islamists and not for the "corrupted regime of former atheists."[47]

Certain parallels can be drawn between Adolat in that early period and the Muslim Brotherhood in various Arab countries in the initial stages of the Muslim Brotherhood's development. The new movement in the Ferghana Valley became stronger and more popular with the collapse of the Soviet Union and the emergence of independent Uzbekistan.

SALAFIS VERSUS TRADITIONALISTS

The Uzbekistani Salafis attempted to implant in the republic their own version of Islam, based on Hanbalism and strict monotheism similar to the Wahhabis' version of Islam (see chapter 1). The "popular Islam" incorporating many non-Islamic customs, rites, and festivals became the object of their attack. As an example of a pre-Islamic rite, one may cite the spinning of the bride round the fire during the wedding. The fire is made by men on the part of the bridegroom, and the bride has to walk around it three times counterclockwise. It may well be that in the past this rite had a sacral character and was linked to fire worship (especially considering Zoroastrianism had been widespread in this region). As a parallel, I can cite a dance of women near the fire that I saw in the 1980s in a remote region of Mahrah (a mountain area in the east of Yemen), which generally was then still very superficially Islamized and where local Islam (not yet affected by Salafi sermons) displayed traces of a great number of pre-Islamic tribal customs. The Mahrah women I saw were dancing in the dark with their hair flowing. In those areas, this could hardly be associated with Zoroastrian influence. Among the popular festivals in Uzbekistan that do not form part of canonical Islamic ones are Nouruz, widespread among many peoples, as well as Sayeel and Gul-i Surh.

The cult of local saints and the custom to make a *ziyarat* to the tombs of Sufi shaykhs and other esteemed persons became the object of Salafi attack (as mentioned earlier, the Salafis consider this latter custom as *shirk*, or running counter to *tawhid*, monotheism). However, considering the universal adherence of Central Asian Muslims to that cult, the local Salafis, as far as I can judge, did not oppose it too harshly. In any case, I've never heard any word of the destruction of the *mazars* in these years, as the Wahhabis in Arabia or local Communists in the 1920s and 1930s had been doing.

Although Sufism as the mainstay of traditional Islam in Central Asia was an adversary for Salafi *'ulama* and imams, the technologists of radical Islam made use of the Sufi practice of working with the believers and placing them under the authority of shaykhs. Although Central Asian Sufism is on the whole very tolerant, its experience of handling people has become incorporated into the practice of present-day Islamists and possibly blended with the background against which radical Islam has been developing. Establishing this unquestionable fact, however, does not allow us to give an unambiguous answer to the question of whether the militant Islamic organizations were generated by local tradition or brought in from outside. It is very alluring to give an impeccably convincing answer to this question, namely that both external and internal factors played their role in generating this phenomenon, but the problem of eliciting the "prime mover" of radical Islam thus remains unsolved. Let it be a combination of several factors.

Furthermore, the Salafis became involved in a fierce argument with the Hanafis on questions of creed, championing Hanbali positions and trying to reeducate local Muslims in their own doctrine.[48] To illustrate this phenomenon, I shall cite in translation an excerpt from an unpublished work of the above-mentioned Mufti Muhammad Sadiq Muhammad Yusuf, who from the standpoint of a Hanafi scholar lucidly sets out the history of the battle of ideas in Central Asian Islam.[49]

In the beginning of the excerpt below, the story is of the Muslims during the Soviet regime:

And the fact that among our people there were very few of those who followed religious prescriptions, kept the fast, and offered prayers is a bitter truth. And the fact that even those few with great difficulty taught themselves to offer prayers and keep the fast is also a bitter truth. They were only able to teach themselves these precepts in those forms that had become established among us. These were the precepts of the Hanafiyya *madhhab*. Our people have been following this *madhhab* in rituals and precepts of Shari'a virtually since it came to believe [in Islam]. As centuries elapsed, despite various circumstances, the canons of the Great Qur'an and the Sunna of the Prophet, adapted by our *mujtahid 'ulama* for the ordinary people by dint of resolution of the questions of *fiqh*, have come to be perceived as the foundations of Islam. Especially in the periods when our religion was confronted with an opposition on the part of the unbelievers and the study of the foundations of religion was made difficult, the abridged practical guides on *fiqh* and the lessons based on them were very useful.

For reasons named and others, although our people knew about the existence of the other three recognized *madhhabs*, it knew nothing about their tenets. And this is a natural thing. Anything different could hardly be expected in the field of religion from a people who had come to a point where it did not know even the formula of the confession of faith (*kalima-yi toyyiba*). But be this as it may, the section of our people that retained religion and, like the greater part of Muslims, adhered to the Hanafi *madhhab*, was unanimous and, in proportion to the degree of its knowledge, fulfilled religious prescriptions. In general, our people, like the multitude of Muslims, was perceiving Muslim Shari'a through the medium of Hanafi theses and through them bringing it into their own lives.

As far as the questions of dogmatics ('*aqida*) are concerned, the Muslims of our republic, like the Muslims adhering to the four recognized *madhhabs* in *fiqh*, had likewise always followed the precepts of the Ahl al-Sunna wal-Jama'a [People of the Sunna and Concord, i.e., the Sunnis]. Our *mujtahid* imams unanimously and firmly adhered to those dogmas, which were derived from the Great Qur'an and the Sunna of the Prophet. No one would even think of anything else.

In the field of spiritual education there exist such Sufi *tariqats* as Naqshbandiyya and Qadiriyya. Our people received spiritual education from the shaykhs of these *tariqats*. On these questions there were no contradictions and scandals either. . . .

Some time later, a number of young people began to study the foundations of our religion. They had been growing in peculiar conditions. Insofar as they had been growing at a different time and in different conditions, it was also natural that they possessed a peculiar manner of thinking. They began to mix with certain young Muslims who were studying here and to read the new literature [imported by the latter], which made a great impression on them. These Muslim students were certainly not experts in religion, being just members of various public, ideological, and other movements. They were telling their new friends, the inhabitants of our country, about the foundations of religion, but not from the standpoint of Hanafi *fiqh*, but from that of the organization or tendency to which they themselves belonged. And the books that were being brought by these students were a great novelty for our young people. Usually such books are written for well-known communities and with quite specific aim. But they cannot fit for other conditions, for other countries, and for other peoples. In our country, these delicate questions could not be understood, and nobody tried to understand them. Moreover, those who did understand this situation had no possibility to openly elucidate anything. It was in fact completely forbidden to study Islam, and the teaching was carried on in secret. It is clear to everybody that under such conditions it was impossible [for theologians] to control who was being taught, how, and what.

Thus new ideas and new conversations began to appear among the people. And refutations (*raddiyya*) of these new ideas were quite naturally attempted. Arguments on certain questions and ideas also started to arise between the old generation of the *'ulama* and the youth. The discussions began with the following questions: Is it possible by reading the Qur'an to consecrate somebody into the godliness (*sawob*) of this activity? May one meet an [esteemed] person who enters the room standing, or may one be seated while greeting him? Gradually the scope of questions under discussion broadened. Later scandalous disputes and mutual accusations—"You are a fanatic!" "And you are so-and-so!"—emerged and began to grow. The leaders of opposing groups began to be joined by their students. The following rumors spread: "This man has read such and such book and become a mulla, while that man has read another book and become a mulla."

The theological community of our people, small as it was, split into three groups. The first group was made up of those theologians who firmly stuck to the old-time traditions in ritual. The second group was called *Yosh mullavachalar* (i.e., the young *mullavacha*—from the Tajik *mulla-bacha*, "young mulla"). The third group consisted of those theologians who carried on their activity on the basis of an official authorization. These latter were also called *Davlat mullalari* ("state mullas"). All three groups had their peculiarities. . . .

Then the years of the *perestroika* had set in. Such issues as the freedom of conscience and the freedom of religious confession were raised. Gradually the possibilities appeared to build mosques, legalize religious education, publish religious literature, and so forth. Muslims from abroad began to visit us. Similarly, some Muslims from our countries began to visit other Muslim countries. The most important thing is that our people started to study the foundations of religion on a massive scale. But all this teaching went on in an irregular, haphazard, and unprepared manner. There was no other way to proceed, though.

This resulted in a very unseemly situation. There were people wishing to learn, but not enough teachers. The people wishing to learn were many, but there were not enough textbooks. There were mosques, but not enough imams. Such a situation reached a point where those who had no appropriate knowledge became teachers, books that could not serve as textbooks were being used as such, while people unworthy of such a title were becoming imams. Very soon it turned out that such a situation would lead to no good. "Teachers" with a low level of knowledge drawn from the corresponding inferior literature began discussing issues with their opponents, basing themselves on ideas borrowed from the same books. Failing to understand that the circle of those taking part in the discussion must be confined only to knowledgeable experts, they began to get their pupils involved in arguments and scandals. Thus the most insignificant questions were the cause of a huge and monumental scandal. Those imams whose knowledge was of questionable quality failed to keep out of this affair, either. They, too, meddled in the conflict with great relish.

The Muslims coming from abroad seemed to rub salt into the wound. Not all of them, of course. To be fair, among the foreign Muslims who were visiting us there were sometimes good and scholarly theologians. They understood our situation well and gave us very useful advice. But such people were few and far between and they, having a lot of things to do in their countries, would quickly return home. Those who remained here were those gentlemen who, taking a good opportunity, sought easy money by becoming representatives of various societies and organizations. Among them were also many of those who had earlier studied in the former USSR. In their own countries, all these gentlemen were the possessors of very mediocre knowledge, but after coming to us they were becoming "outstanding" scholars who acted as if they knew everything [in advance] right up to judgment day. These gentlemen, having become eminent professors in the twinkling of an eye, were trying to amaze the receptive and inexperienced youth with their foreign manners, clothes, and above all, religious views of their home country. These were the people who did not care about the doctrines of the *madhhab*, rituals, history, and other customs of the country they were guests in. Even if they served religion, they naturally promoted the religious views of a group or community to which they belonged and on whose money they subsisted. Thus those who were coming to us from abroad brought with them [new] divisions and scandals. These semi-literate representatives of foreign countries tried very hard to intensify the old scandals mentioned above.

In contradiction with local customs and rituals, they began to offer prayers in a different way, loudly pronouncing *Amin* after reading the *sura* Fatiha [Qur'an, 1], raising their hands high and whispering something while standing behind the imam before and after the performance of the ritual bow (*ruqu'*). Local Muslims asked them about these deviations from the norms customary to them. These pseudoteachers replied: "We are following the Sunna of our Prophet (let Allah bless and welcome him!). These prescriptions you are asking about are mentioned in such and such Hadiths. Unfortunately, you do not follow the Sunna of the Prophet—let Allah bless and welcome him! You are performing what was told by Abu Hanifa."

While saying this, they continued to instruct people in the same vein, trying to explain what Sunna was and that one had to observe it. Then they said that the Hanafi *madhhab* was pernicious. To people around them, these speeches were a novelty and therefore seemed attractive. Gradually some local Muslims followed them. The rest of the Muslims of advanced age were displeased with this state of affairs. For them, it was unacceptable to renounce the method of prayer that had been followed by their forebears and comply with what these gentlemen with long beards and long white robes were saying. At the same time, most of our Muslims were unable to give a sufficiently reasoned explanation that their method of offering prayers was precisely the Sunna of our Prophet (let Allah bless and welcome him!). They had not been taught to do this. As a result, it began to seem to everyone that to follow the *madhhab* was one thing and to follow the Qur'an and the Sunna was something different. Mutual grudges were turning into stormy disputes and disputes into scandals. In the end, the opponents developed such an enmity that I have no wish even to speak about it.

As mentioned above, we wish neither to look for a culprit nor to describe the events that took place, nor even to analyze them fully, naming their reasons. We have only one aim: as far as possible to show that divisions, scandals, and enmity among Muslims are an inadmissible phenomenon. However, such a position does not relieve us of the need to ask ourselves: Who benefited from these misplaced antagonisms, after all?

Let us think about this without bias. Who gained profit from the fact that hostility arose among Muslims? The enemies of Islam! But Muslims themselves only suffered damage from these antagonisms.

Was it news that divisions arose among our Muslims? No! There was nothing new about it! The same kind of divisions appeared before. Then the theologians of the Muslim community, on coming to an agreement, decided that with a view to preventing divisions one had to follow the precepts of the *madhhab* that was espoused by the bulk of the people. And the people, tired of various kinds of contradictions, accepted this decision with joy and then the Community of Concord emerged. If it were so, why again repeat the same mistake?!

Formerly all the said problems led to a point where divisions and enmity among Muslims even caused armed collisions. The theologians were compelled to engage themselves in these questions very seriously, to such an extent that they are included in our books on dogmatics.

Not only Hindustani, but also many other teachers distanced themselves from the rising Central Asian Salafis, although there were cases when traditionalists who did not support Salafi in their religious thinking became enmeshed in politics.[50] These traditionalists became very active in the late 1980s, after the launching of the Gorbachev reforms. They were allowed to start mobilizing support, although not directly under the banner of political Islam. Rather, they focused on issues such as the return of mosques that had been seized by the state and the establishment of new Muslim communities.

A NEW WAVE OF ISLAMIST ACTIVISM

The Islamic radicals started to show muscle in relations with the authorities, resorting not only to acts of open disobedience, but also to the forcible seizure of premises. In December 1991 Muslim youths took over the building of the former Communist Party (now National Democratic Party) Committee headquarters in Namangan and urged that the president listen to their fifteen demands. Among other things, they demanded that the government (1) proclaim the establishment of an Islamic state in Uzbekistan; (2) use Shari'a as the only legal system; (3) cease to orient themselves toward Turkey; (4) turn all schools into separate ones for boys and girls; and (5) give local Muslims one of the administrative buildings in Namangan.[51] The building in question was the so-called House of Political Education, which had been used by the Communists for atheistic propaganda. Islam Karimov agreed to consider these demands but said that he had to discuss them in the Supreme Soviet (parliament) of Uzbekistan. Only then was the party headquarters restored to the local authorities.

After the former House of Political Education was given to the believers, various militant groups launched a competition for control over it, but they could not agree among themselves on its partition. After the Friday prayer in the spring of 1992, an angry group of members of Tawba in Namangan, having left the Jami mosque, seized several hostages, including representatives of the regional authorities, and destroyed some public property. Negotiations did not help to solve the problem, and the authorities had to resort to the Interior Ministry troops in order to compel the militants to release the hostages. Several senior members of Tawba were arrested, then sentenced to imprisonment, but their leader, Tahir, managed to escape.[52] It is unclear to what extent these actions could have been orchestrated by foreign missionaries who had been intensively instructing the first Ferghana militants, but some of my contacts among the militants in the early 1990s admitted this had been the case.

The political mobilization of Uzbekistan's militant Islamists was supported by foreign missionaries and teachers of Islam and Arabic from Saudi Arabia, Egypt, Turkey, Pakistan, Afghanistan, and other Muslim countries. Most supported the idea of an Islamic state and were hostile to the Karimov regime in Tashkent. Muminov believes that the second wing of Islam Lashkarlari (the first being Adolat) was comprised of Wahhabis who "concentrated on religious questions under the leadership of Tahir Yuldashev." They formed groups of twenty to fifty people, and there were some sixty groups in total.[53] If this information is accurate, then a united movement had already formed with its own military and political-ideological wings, international support, and local political allies. Ahmed

Rashid asserts that local Wahhabis had been receiving massive aid from abroad by then, especially from Saudi Arabia.[54] But my own impression in those days was that this aid had not yet reached the level claimed by the militants. The imam of a Margelan mosque at the end of 1991, for example, asked me to help procure religious literature from the Gulf states, despite his own wide connections in the Arab world.

As I was told in November 1991 in Namangan by a local citizen named Tashpulat, the representatives of the "new" local clergy oriented toward various external sources of aid then competed with each other for influence over the believers. "In some places in the corners of one and the same *mahalla*," said Tashpulat, "stand different mosques: one is controlled by one's own people, the second by Saudi Wahhabis, the third by Pakistanis from Tabligh, the fourth by the Afghan Salafis, and each one is pulling in his own direction."[55]

In the same years, as I saw for myself during my trips to the Ferghana Valley, a great many emissaries from various countries of the Islamic world, emissaries who regarded that region as a sort of testing area, were staying there.[56] Cunning, well equipped for such work, and possessing great financial resources, they openly supported local extremists, pursuing agitation for building an Islamic state and implanting extremist ideas through lessons and admonitions under cover of charitable activities. I recall how a Sudanese preacher confidently spoke that the proclamation of an Islamic state in Uzbekistan was just around the corner.

It was in those years, as testified by the local Islamists, that Arabs from the al-Qa'ida circles began to appear in Ferghana, although that organization had not gained notoriety.

It should be noted that a lot of researchers of political Islam in this region emphasize the absence of a unifying platform among radical Islamists, the constantly progressing process of fragmentation, regrouping of forces, breaking off of relations, and joining of hands. However, this paradigm is generally characteristic of any radical movement, including national liberation, radical left, and religious ones. Only when leaders of a movement manage to build their activities on the basis of strict discipline, subordination, and a well-organized conspiratorial network can these movements continue to exist, even in the absence of a clear-cut ideological basis, though the unifying significance of the latter is beyond doubt.

As far as the period under review in Uzbekistan is concerned, Abduvakhitov writes of "a split among the Wahhabis" in the Ferghana Valley in late 1991, when a group of youths loyal to Abdul Ahad, imam of Namangan's Gumbaz mosque, failed to support the radicals headed by the above-mentioned Tahir and refused to take part in "active political struggle."[57]

Despite all the internal conflicts, Adolat also tried to extend its activities to the capital, Tashkent. Although the Uzbekistani government of those days was cautious about direct confrontation with the domestic Islamic opposition, it prevented this penetration, keeping Tashkent under the firm control of its security forces. The state also in some degree retained control over the Directorate for the Muslims of Uzbekistan (DMU, formerly SADUM).

Although Muhammad Sadiq Muhammad Yusuf in 1989 replaced Shamsuddin Babakhanov as representative of the new, nonconformist generation of the clergy, with respect to political Islam he in principle continued the line of his predecessor, conveniently enough for the authorities. This can probably be explained not so much by the mufti's servility—his wish to oblige the powers that be—as by his sincere position, most likely dictated by the fact that in the person of the young leaders of the rising Salafism he saw competitors. The new mufti categorically refused to support the appeals made by a section of believers to set up an Islamic Revival Party and also took an explicitly critical position vis-à-vis the Salafis. This, however, did not mean that Muhammad Sadiq in all matters acted in a way likely to please the authorities. On the contrary, his growing independence and popularity aroused an ever greater resentment on their part. One example is cited by Abduvakhitov, who claims that Sadiq was orienting the DMU toward Libya (where he had received his education), which contravened the official position of the Uzbekistani government. Furthermore, it allegedly became known that in the early 1980s Muhammad Sadiq had been involved in the activities of the early Islamist activist groups in the Ferghana Valley, though later as mufti he dissociated himself from them. Apart from that, as asserted by Abduvakhitov, a part of the large sums of money that began to be accumulated by the DMU as a result of increasing financial assistance from abroad might have been funneled to Islamic fighters in Tajikistan in the early 1990s.[58] All this exacerbated tensions between the DMU and the government.

Now the Islamists were led by Tahir Yuldashev, who already regarded himself as a ruler of the Ferghana Valley. Under his leadership, the Islamists believed they were capable of launching a war to overthrow Karimov. Yuldashev, born in 1967 and an underground imam at the beginning of the 1990s, was a talented and energetic speaker and organizer. Another prominent young figure was a former Soviet paratrooper, Juma Hojiev (Namangani), born in 1969, who returned from Afghanistan in 1988 after serving in the Soviet military contingent. He, too, became engaged in the activities of radical Islamists. The militants began to openly criticize Karimov, whom they characterized as an infidel, and they began to accumulate weapons in their houses in order to arm a popular rebellion. They also took steps to prepare for the creation of an Islamic state in Uzbekistan and were completely confident that they would be supported by a majority of the people and win the forthcoming conflict easily. As one Tashkent analyst later told me, in those days many people in Uzbekistan considered Karimov to be half Uzbek and half Tajik (or maybe even pure Tajik). He was also married to a Slav woman, represented the Samarqandi clan, and was allied with the Jizak clan (not the strongest one in the republic). He was therefore viewed initially as a weak politician who would be unable to defeat the opposition, which by that time had already consisted of radical Islamists as well as "democrats" (the Erk and Birlik political parties). But Karimov, despite the fact that he was not supported by any strong Uzbek political clans (for instance, the Tashkent and Ferghana clans), managed to consolidate his grip on power in the critical period following the Soviet collapse.

Indeed, it seems clear that the Islamists underestimated Karimov, who had strong "administrative resources," a critical factor in Uzbekistan's sociopolitical environment. Yet they were encouraged by the fact that the democrats decided to build an alliance with them, as also happened in Tajikistan, although their agendas were quite different. This alliance of convenience was based on their common goal—toppling Karimov and his regime.

Adolat's devotion to the ideals of equality and justice proclaimed by that group did not stand the test of time. Abduvakhitov asserts that Adolat was soon "transformed into a new structure interested in the distribution of wealth for the benefit of its leaders."[59] True, there are an insufficient number of arguments in favor of this assertion, and we cannot say with certainty to what extent Adolat activists were afflicted with the universal disease of corruption. Be that as it may, when Adolat was banned, some of its members were sentenced to prison for financial offenses.

There is nothing unusual in the fact that the Ferghana fighters for justice engaged in robberies. Their expropriation of property was for them as morally justified as the same act had been for the Bolsheviks (one cannot help recalling the young Stalin, who robbed banks). But the local Robin Hoods used to link up with real bandits who made use of Islam to put a noble face on their criminal activity. Shukhrat, a man notorious in Tashkent in 1992–1993 for his carjackings and kidnappings, went on a pilgrimage to Arabia and donated part of the profits he gained from his business as a criminal to the construction of mosques (later he was sentenced to twenty years in a penal colony).

The radical Ferghana imams at that time enriched themselves at the expense of the financial aid coming to the region from the Islamic foundations. A Tashkent businessman, A., related to me that in 1992–1993 Abdulwali *qari* of Namangan asked him to render assistance in the acquisition of a used TU-154 passenger plane.

In February 1992, Adolat, Birlik, Erk, and the IRP asked Karimov to start negotiations in Namangan. It seemed to me at the time that Adolat leaders were hoping that Karimov would refuse to negotiate, which would help them mobilize supporters for a planned uprising. Yuldashev and certain other militant Salafi leaders intensified their contacts abroad at the same time. A representative of a charity organization from Saudi Arabia who visited Russia in March 1992 told me that he hoped Karimov would have to declare Uzbekistan an Islamic state in the near future. Yuldashev and his comrades apparently hoped the same.

But Karimov, after being directly challenged by the Islamists, severely cracked down on the Ferghana militants with the help of his loyal law-enforcement agencies. All foreign "missionaries" were immediately expelled from the country, and many supporters of the Islamic and democratic opposition were arrested. The leaders of the opposition groups fled from the country, and these groups were declared illegal. The leader of the IRP, Abdulla Utaev, was arrested in December, even though his small party had not been directly involved in violence. Only one insignificant radical Islamic political group, Tawba (Repentance), continued to operate in the republic. In 1995, however, it disappeared as its predecessors had.

As far as Muhammad Sadiq is concerned, in February 1993 the All-Muslim Kurultai (Congress) of Uzbekistan ousted him from the post of mufti in connection with the authorities' suspicions of his sympathies for Tajik Islamists and elected to that office a more loyal man—Mukhtar Abdullaev. This signaled the imposition of a tighter government control over the DMU.

After the expulsion of foreign emissaries, the toughening of the rules of entry by such people into the republic, and other measures, outside influence on the affairs of Islam in Uzbekistan was sharply curtailed. In situations similar to the one described above, when several mosques competing over the minds of Muslims were active in one and the same *mahalla*, "surplus" mosques whose construction had been dictated exclusively by the desire of a foreign sponsor to implant his own understanding of Islam in the Ferghana Valley were being closed.[60]

UZBEK MILITANTS ABROAD

In April 1992, when the situation in Tajikistan proved most favorable for activity by Islamists of all types (in May that year a government of national reconciliation was established in which the Islamists tried to play the dominant role), the majority of Islamic radicals and extremists from Uzbekistan fled to Tajikistan after President Karimov dealt a shattering blow to their positions. During the short-lived civil war in Tajikistan, the

"Namangani battalion" was formed by these Uzbek radicals. The battalion fought as part of the forces of the Tajik Islamic opposition. After the opposition's defeat in December 1992, the Uzbeks together with the Tajik Islamic opposition left for Afghanistan, where they formed their main base.

The leaders of Uzbek Islamic extremists, Tahir Yuldashev and Juma Hojiev, remained active. Rashid recalls that after the war broke out, Yuldashev went to Afghanistan with the leaders of the IRPT. In Taloqan, he helped to spread IRPT propaganda and newsletters. He also began traveling to Pakistan and Saudi Arabia, and later began traveling to Iran, the United Arab Emirates, and Turkey, where he established contacts, not only with other Islamic parties and movements, but also with the intelligence agencies of these states, from whom he requested support. Pakistan's Interservices Intelligence provided funds and a sanctuary. Between 1995 and 1998, Yuldashev was based in Peshawar, "the center not only of Pakistani and Afghan Islamic activism, but also of pan-Islamic *jihadi* groups."[61]

One of the most important sources of support for the IMU in Pakistan was the Jami'at-i-Ulema-i-Islami, a future supporter of the Taliban. Funds were raised by this party to cover the costs of enlisting young Uzbek Islamists in their *madrasas*. Rashid writes that, in these *madrasas*, he saw hundreds of students of Islam from Central Asia, the majority of whom were Uzbeks and Tajiks, "although there were also a few Kazakhs, Kyrgyz, and Uighurs from China."[62]

Meanwhile, the Tashkent government was purging the country of all radical Islamists. In August 1995, Abduwali *qari* Mirzaev, after flying from Tashkent to Moscow with his assistant, suddenly vanished. Soon thereafter another of his assistants disappeared as well. It was rumored that all had been seized by the Uzbekistani special services. Also, unexpectedly, the imam of the Tukhtaboi mosque in Tashkent, Obidkhan Nazarov, vanished together with his thirteen-year-old son in March 1998. In this case also, many people believed that the family had been destroyed by the Uzbekistani security forces, although official sources denied this. Amnesty International reported in 2001 that Abduwali *qari* was held in an underground cell in Tashkent for several years, where he was constantly tortured.[63] The authorities hated Abduwali *qari* so much that his name was always mentioned later on when any extremists or terrorists were put on trial. In September 1995, after the mysterious disappearance of Abduwali, his former bodyguard, Negmat Parpiev, also disappeared. Strangely, rumors are still circulating among some residents of the Ferghana Valley that Abduwali *qari* has miraculously escaped and found a secret hideaway in the mountainous part of Tajikistan. Similar legends rooted in the story of the "hidden imam" about other popular religious authorities who were kidnapped and murdered by their foes, stories that turn them into escapees or predict that they will miraculously return one day, can be heard all over the Islamic world. Recently I heard a version of the story about Obidkhan Nazarov.

In December 1995, masked men in Namangan captured a police officer who was notorious for his brutality and decapitated him. A journalist who reported the news believed that the beheading was the Islamist response to the earlier disappearance of Abduwali *qari* and Negmat Parpiev. In a gun battle that followed, the masked men, one of whom was killed, shot and killed three more policemen. The authorities reported that the gunman who had been killed was a Wahhabi. This was used by the government as a pretext to impose curfews in the cities of the Ferghana Valley and to detain large numbers of local residents accused of religious extremism.[64] The first trials of suspected Islamists were held behind closed doors, but later, in 1998, the authorities decided to give them wide publicity.

As a result of these repressive measures, the Islamists were forced to change tactics. In 1996, they announced the creation of the Islamic Movement of Uzbekistan (IMU). The IMU declared that its ultimate goal was the removal of the Karimov regime by force and the establishment of Islamic rule in Uzbekistan.

THE RISE AND FIRST ACTIONS OF THE IMU

In the opinion of a Tajik journalist then in Afghanistan and familiar with the opposition forces, the IMU was created by Tahir Yuldashev once it became clear that the Tajik oppositionists were going to negotiate a peace settlement with the government.[65] It is hard to say whether "the Tajik factor" was in fact critical to the formation of the IMU, however, because Uzbek extremists still had the opportunity to carry on armed struggle on the side of the United Tajik Opposition (UTO), which was based in the Tavildara district of Tajikistan. From the very beginning, the IMU oriented itself toward support for the Taliban, which probably accounted for their increasing divergence from the Islamic Revival Party of Tajikistan, which was firmly resolved to support the anti-Taliban Northern Alliance and its leader Ahmad Shah Masoud.

A British observer asserts that "the IMU and its leader have resembled little more than a network of militants primarily motivated by economic interests." In other words, the organization "resembles a gang of guerrillas more than a group of terrorists."[66] This observer supports her argument by noting that the IMU's activities have largely focused on transporting drugs from Afghanistan to Tajikistan and Kyrgyzstan, drugs that are destined for Russia and Europe. She also notes that the IMU has been active in making money from taking hostages. Strangely enough, this observer claims that Namangani "has never been driven solely by Islamic ideology." And in Rashid's words, Namangani "is a guerrilla leader, not an Islamic scholar." In fact, leaders of militant movements at the head of armed struggles are very rarely scholars. However, this hardly means they are not terrorists. Davlat Usmon draws a distinction between political Islam and the military wing of the Islamic Movement of Uzbekistan (the military wing came to be headed by Juma Namangani), while "the government of the Republic of Tajikistan," as he put it, "forced the IRPT to break any ties with the IMU." Even in 2003, Usmon continued to consider IMU members unjustly treated and deprived of the right to return home, noting in the process "a serious mistake of the IMU military wing, which took part in the intra-Afghan conflict [Usmon does not say "on the side of the Taliban"] and which later gave occasion for it to be put on the list of terrorist groups on the part of the US administration."[67]

As noted earlier, the government of Tajikistan, with active mediation by the UN and a number of neighboring states, signed a peace agreement with the UTO in 1997. Under the terms of the General Agreement on the Establishment of Peace and National Accord, the UTO obtained a 30 percent quota of seats in governmental bodies. UTO fighters, including the Uzbek militants, were to be integrated into the power structures of the republic after being certified in commissions expressly created for the purpose.

The Tashkent government regarded this process as unacceptable and accused Dushanbe of using the Uzbek Islamic militants as leverage to exert political pressure on Uzbekistan. In its turn, Dushanbe accused Tashkent of supporting a rebel colonel from the Tajik military, Mahmud Khudoiberdiev. A native of Kurghanteppa, Khudoiberdiev on several occasions in the 1990s attempted to use forces under his command to force Tajik president Emomali Rahmonov to remove the colonel's rivals, among whom were the president's fellow countryman, Mahmadsaid Ubaidullaev, who was the speaker of the upper chamber of parliament and mayor of Dushanbe (known as "the strong man of Kulyab"), and Gaffur Mirzoev "Sedoi" (the gray haired), commander of the presidential National Guard until 2004. During the civil war, Khudoiberdiev had courageously fought on the side of the Popular Front (to which the Kulyabi clan owed its victory), and he believed that he had been insufficiently rewarded by the Kulyabis for his efforts. A military operation in the town of Tursunzade in 1996 by Khudoiberdiev's regiment had become one of his best-known campaigns. His regiment forced Mirzoev's men back from Tursunzade and reasserted its claim to the Tajik Aluminum Plant. As the winner of the engagement, Khudoiberdiev demanded that Vice Premier Ubaidullaev be ousted from his post. Rahmonov met this condition. A year later, the colonel instigated another mutiny, this time without success. As a result, he was compelled with some of his fighters to take refuge in Uzbekistan.

After another of the colonel's mutinies was suppressed in the fall of 1998 and he again hid in Uzbekistan, Rahmonov convened a secret conference. As Sanobar Shermatova, a Moscow journalist of Uzbek origins, asserts, the president did not hide his feelings and spoke of Uzbekistan's Karimov in a very uncomplimentary fashion. He asked a question of the audience: How could one take revenge on a neighbor who continued to destabilize the situation in Tajikistan? Shermatova says: "And then Ubaidullaev reminded those present that Juma Namangani and his fighters, whom the Uzbekistani authorities wanted expelled, were based in Tavildara. Thus the Uzbek militants were again revived on the political scene."[68]

The journalist repeats here the widespread theory about how the Tajik authorities, supported by the Russians, who wanted to keep Karimov within their sphere of influence, not only tolerated Uzbek extremists but even helped them survive. But this theory may be too sophisticated to be true. In any case, in the summer of 1998 Khudoiberdiev again staged an abortive revolt in the north of Tajikistan. He mounted his attack from Uzbek territory, where he was hiding from the Tajik authorities. He was not supported by the local population, however, and was therefore forced to pull back.

The IMU leadership characterized its organization as "an Islamic popular movement." Declaring that it derived programmatic ideas exclusively from the Qur'an and the Sunna, IMU leaders proclaimed themselves adherents to the Hanafi *madhhab*. Indicative of the IMU's general conception is a document I obtained in Tashkent dating from 1999 (it mentioned the explosions in Tashkent in February 1999, which I will discuss later). Below is an abridged translation from Uzbek of this document:

A CHARACTERISTIC OF THE IMU

(Begins from the 138th *ayat* of the *sura* Al-'Imran from the Qur'an)

The IMU is an Islamic popular movement seeking on the fullest scale and in the fullest content to realize the requirements of Shari'a with reference to the personality, society, and the state.

The aim of the IMU is a broad diffusion of Islamic science and culture among the broadest possible strata of the population by elucidating Islamic rights for the upbringing of the personality, family, and also greater knowledge, bringing the beauty of Islam into everyday life, directing toward good deeds and averting the bad ones.

The movement is striving against discords, arguments, seeking to expel coldness and the division into parties that debilitates the Muslims. The movement, believing that the Book of Allah and the Sunna of the Prophet contain all the solutions to problems for the Muslims, acknowledges for itself as an Islamic theological source—with full respect for other authoritative Islamic *madhhabs*—the *madhhab* of the great Imam Abu Hanifa. This is so because in the science on the laws of Shari'a (*fiqh*) on questions of principle the heads of *madhhabs* have a solidified position, while on minor problems each head of a *madhhab* has his independent views. The movement urges any Muslim, the public, and the Muslim authorities to fulfill without fail and accord the proper respect for Islamic norms, laws, and rights. The fulfillment of Shari'a is a duty of each person wielding authority—more than that, his only way to confirm his power prerogatives. The Maker of Humanity does not submit to man born in sin.

With a view to create a real Islamic movement, it is necessary to understand the importance of unity, which can be reached on condition of the creation of governing bodies leaning on a solid collective, while the enrollment of new members on these principles does not mean a separation from one's people, but simply a service to the Muslims and Islam, keeping body and soul in harmony with Allah, a sincere wish and desire to serve one's people.

THE IMU'S VIEW ON THE SITUATION IN UZBEKISTAN

The movement considers the Uzbek people to be one who had given preference to the Islamic thought, who had defended Islam in extremely difficult situations, as one of the peoples having a long Islamic history. Uzbekistan had from the earliest times been considered as one of the Islamic centers.

Presently, the age of the rule and oppression of these lands on the part of the Russian conquerors, Bolsheviks, has ended.

Having attained freedom, instead of bringing back Islamic life, which had been here for centuries, we have allowed tyrannical apostates to seize power. They had been fighting against Islam; their preceptors had shed more Muslim blood than the Bolsheviks; they had jailed, deported, and killed the *'ulama*. They had been oppressing young Muslims with particular cruelty. They had closed the mosques of Allah, forbidding the mentioning of Allah's name. In former times, they had been serving Communist interests in Uzbekistan. History knows that on the territory of Uzbekistan they are pursuing the policies of Israeli Jews and enemies of Islam in America. All that runs counter to religion, Shari'a, and Muslim prayer, all the criminal encroachments give our people the right to change the existing state of affairs by force. But along with that we do not lose hopes that we shall be able to overcome the tragedy generated by these criminals in peaceful ways. In our view, the final upshot consists of the following:

–the president and his government must immediately resign; the state, for a term not exceeding six months, must be ruled by a neutral government. In this

(continued)

period, the following actions must be carried out: (a) every single prisoner, as well as 'ulama, must be released; (b) all 'ulama who had suffered religious persecution or emigrated from their countries, as well as all those whom the present government had forced to leave the territory of their state, must be invited to come back; (c) a council of top-level 'ulama must be set up, to draft and pass laws in conformity with Shari'a, and also to select people who will perform the political and executive functions; (d) it is out of the people thus selected that the leadership of the state and members of the supreme Shura will be chosen;

–after the structural renovation of the state, to hold an investigation into the cases of those who suffered innocently and bring the cases of those guilty of crimes before Shari'a courts so that the norms of Shari'a can be applied toward them;

–to annul all inequitable treaties concluded by the present government with tyrannical forces around the world. Now foreign policy will be built on the principles of justice, equality, and noncontravention of the norms of Shari'a. The Islamic State of Uzbekistan will never have friendly relations with states that are enemies of Islam, Muslims, or conquered their lands, or assisted these crimes. An attack against a Muslim individual is an attack against the entire Muslim people. (Each Muslim is obliged to fulfill the precepts of our Prophet: Muslims must treat each other cordially and lovingly, feeling concern over one another.) Since, for example, if one member of the community has fallen sick, then others, being a part of the same body, react to this with insomnia and high temperature;

–the IMU reminds the present regime on the still existing possibility to resolve the problem peacefully, without bloodshed. However, the government's continued aggressive policy in relation to the Muslim people may lead to events similar to the explosions in Tashkent, the present regime being the only party to blame for them;

–therefore the IMU, calling on the government to accept the above proposals, asks it to examine and study them, because the patience of our Muslim people also has limits. In the nearest future the tyrants will learn to what result they are drawing close.

The IMU leadership

THE FEBRUARY 1999 TERRORIST BOMBINGS

On February 16, 1999, militants detonated a series of bombs in Tashkent. They had hoped to kill the Uzbek president, but he escaped. Sixteen innocent civilians were killed and more than one hundred were wounded. Until then, the regime had claimed that stability under Karimov was their main achievement, pointing to the catastrophic consequences that resulted from the legalization of opposition parties in neighboring Tajikistan in the beginning of the 1990s. The country had managed to avoid political murders, conflicts in the criminal world, and the redistribution of spheres of influence. The explosions in the compound of government buildings in Tashkent were therefore a shock.

The Uzbekistani authorities accused the IMU of perpetrating this act of terrorism and started a broad wave of repression. Later, when the terrorists who had allegedly performed this act were captured, their indictments in the Supreme Court of Uzbekistan read:

> The main task was assigned to Z. Hasanov, who was to drive a Kamaz truck laden with explosives to the territory of the Olii Majlis (Supreme Council) and blow it up. He was to finish his life as a *shahid* [martyr]. There were also other plans, [each] one more fantastic than the other: to blow up the president's residence in Durmeni; to stage a collision of the president's automobile with a Kamaz filled with explosives; and to take the president's daughter and diplomats of foreign states hostage.
>
> The explosion at the . . . Interior Ministry was timed for 10:50; in the building of the Nodirabegim Cinema for 10:55; at the cabinet for 10:57; in the building of the National Bank for Foreign Trade Activity for 11:20; and at the house rented at Kahhar Street #22 for 12:05. Work for the preparation of sabotage in the republic was carried out in parallel. A. Alimov and A. Mamajonov were to buy ten Kamaz trucks to bring the Namangani militants from Tajikistan to Osh, Kyrgyzstan, and to prepare medicines that would "keep them from freezing in cold weather" and medicines that would remove the "feeling of hunger."[69]

Given that Uzbekistani security agencies were known to have the used torture against the detainees, one should not trust these allegations without thorough, critical review and comparison with sources other than official ones. Furthermore, there was a general impression that the trial of the suspected Islamic terrorists was not fair because it was closed to the public and mass media. Still, because the access of scholars to any materials on these explosions is very limited and the range of sources in general is extremely narrow, it is a chance to be able to critically read at least some of them. A total of twenty-two people appeared before the court on charges of attempting to assassinate Karimov and overthrow the government. All twenty-two were found guilty. The material damage from the explosions amounted to more than 690 million soms (about $5,480,000). The court's verdict asserted that bombings were aimed at the physical elimination not only of Karimov but of other members of the government as well. Given the closed, secretive character of the procedure, the general impression was that the trial was not fair.

The Supreme Court sentenced six defendants to the maximum penalty—execution by firing squad. The others received sentences of ten to twenty years, to be served in maximum-security prisons. The verdict claimed that the defendants were connected with foreign extremist groups whose purpose was to overthrow the constitutional system in the republic, seize power, and establish an Islamic state. Some were accused of having received military training at terrorist camps in Afghanistan, Tajikistan, and Chechnya. The defendants were also convicted of other crimes from earlier years, including robbery, the organization of a criminal community, and smuggling and illegal storage of firearms.

The court's verdict asserted: "Wearing a mask of Islamic religion, the criminals created a special fund in the Ferghana Valley, whose purpose was the collection of money for the conduct of jihad, the seizure of power, and the creation of an Islamic state in Uzbekistan. In order to accumulate financial resources in this fund, the criminals attacked the houses of citizens and plundered businessmen." The verdict also listed the names of "plotters" who had been active in two regions of the Ferghana Valley and cited details of the preparation of the coup. In particular, it stated that as a result of the activity of two criminal groups during 1992–1998 in the Andizhan and Namangan regions, twelve people were killed and thirty-eight were injured. It also asserted that over 5.5 million soms of valuables and property had been stolen by the accused.

The entire set of people connected with the Salafi radical imams became the object of repression. A report by the U.S. Department of State read that Obidkhon *qari* Nazarov had been missing "since March 5, 1998, when dozens of police and security agents raided and searched his home. Although his family claims that the security services abducted him, the Government and many observers believe that he fled to avoid arrest." The report mentioned also that, since then, the government "had persecuted his family harshly." After the terrorist bombing in Tashkent in February 1999, the authorities detained Nazarov's wife, Minnura Nasretdinova, "for ten days on charges of hooliganism"; Nazarov's associate, Mukhtabar Akhmedova, was arrested and on March 4 was sentenced to ten days' imprisonment.[70] The sentences for the women were extremely mild, but that was not the case for the men. Nazarov's brother Umarkhon, his uncle Akhmadali Salomov, and his brother-in-law Abdurashid Nasretdinov were charged with planning a coup d'état and sentenced to four to eleven years in prison. A lot of other associates of Nazarov were arrested and sentenced to years in prison as part of the government's campaign "to rid the country of the so-called Wahhabists."[71]

Some Central Asian dissidents living abroad later put forward their own version of the February events in Tashkent. According to them, the IMU was indeed preparing a terrorist act, but the explosions were a provocation carried out by the authorities themselves. Political scientist and Munich resident Anvar Usmanov, for example, declared in an interview with *Die Deutsche Welle*: "The Islamic Movement of Uzbekistan was undoubtedly preparing an attempt on the life of President Karimov. But there were SNB (political police) agents within that organization, who preempted it and provoked the notorious explosions. They served as an occasion for the opening of a real 'witch hunt' in Uzbekistan. A frenzied campaign started against all those who were a little bit out of the ordinary—for example, people who attended the mosque or voiced their own opinions. Anyway, Karimov tightened up on everyone."[72] Usmanov and other dissidents are thus convinced that the Uzbekistani secret services manipulated the Islamists into attempting the assassination of Karimov for their own or their master's political purposes.

This explanation, in Usmanov's view, is supported by a later event when the Uzbekistani secret services were supposedly involved in another assassination attempt. This time, however, it was Saparmurad Niyazov, the president of Turkmenistan, who was the target of the operation. The incident took place three years after the 1999 Tashkent explosions, on November 25, 2002. Though Usmanov saw a link between the two, in the second case the scenario was different:

> Some political groups in Russia and Uzbekistan, in my view, clearly helped Boris Shikhmuradov [a former deputy prime minister of Turkmenistan turned dissident, who was accused of having orchestrated the assassination attempt]. One may even speak about a certain Russo-Uzbek scenario. Naturally, Shikhmuradov had secured the support of these circles and leaned on them. In the process, he overplayed his hand, as well as that of his supporters and the circles named above. I do not believe that Shikhmuradov found support at the highest level in Russia and Uzbekistan, but nevertheless forces were found in these countries that pushed Shikhmuradov to take active steps. And then his patrons simply stepped aside, leaving him to the mercy of fate.[73]

Is there any truth in the statements of a dissident who, without whitewashing the Islamists, wants at the same time to accuse Karimov of the worst of sins? Knowing the clan-based character of Uzbek society, the low professionalism of most of the personnel in local security agencies, and the widespread corruption, it is hard to believe that, had the Uzbekistani special services organized a "provocation" that caused so many victims among the population, they could have prevented a leak of information from their ranks.

There is yet another version of these events. A British expert believes that although the IMU was blamed for the Tashkent explosions in 1999, "the evidence has never been conclusive. In fact, there are strong indications that the Tashkent bombings were perpetrated by one of Karimov's political opponents who had ties to powerful criminal organizations."[74]

In March 1999, Karimov appealed to Uzbek citizens who had joined the terrorists to lay down their arms in return for pardon. According to official data (which is difficult to verify), about eleven hundred people returned to their *kishlaks*. Abduwali Yuldashev, who had headed one of the camps located in the Tavildara zone of Tajikistan (according to Uzbekistani authorities), seized some young residents of the Khorezm region of Uzbekistan who had fled the camp in hopes of giving themselves up to the authorities. Some were shot to death on the spot, while others were beheaded personally by Yuldashev in front of a line of his fighters.

Many notorious participants in the events in Uzbekistan in the early 1990s have reappeared on the political scene in the period since. Investigating their origin and entrance into political life will help us better understand the role of terrorist networks in the region.

TERRORIST NETWORKS

Abduwali Yuldashev has been one of the most notorious IMU terrorist leaders. Having visited Tajikistan in the early 1990s, he left for Afghanistan, where he underwent combat training at one of the camps of Islamic extremists. Afterward he returned to Uzbekistan and engaged in robberies in the Ferghana Valley, which replenished the *bayt al-mal*—the treasury of Islamic terrorists.[75] His group killed a major of the Namangani traffic police, as well as a number of policemen at the Chartak customs post, and carried out a series of robberies in Andizhan, during which several well-known entrepreneurs were killed. Among Yuldashev's group there were two gunmen, Zahid Dehkanov and Kazimbek Zakirov, who were later put on trial for various crimes, including an attempt to take the life of Karimov in February 1999. According to a memo of the investigation group of the office of the attorney general of Uzbekistan (I am not sure that we can fully rely upon the data this memo contains, especially given the absence of other sources but, nevertheless, we can take it into account), Dehkanov (alias "Said") started to attend the main mosque of the city of Andizhan in 1992, where Abduwali *qari* (Mirzaev) then preached. Under the influence of Zafar Mahmudov, he embraced Wahhabism and began to engage in robbery in search of funds. In October 1996, under the instructions of Kazimbek Zakirov, he left for Almaty, where he recruited Islamic extremists who were to be sent to fighting camps in Chechnya, Tajikistan, and Afghanistan. He himself underwent training in Chechnya in 1997. In October 1998, as an adviser to Tahir Yuldashev, he was sent, together with Bahrom Abdullaev, to Turkmenistan to set up an Islamist political center there. He was detained, however, and handed over to Uzbekistan.

The memo also mentioned that Bahrom Abdullaev (known by the aliases "Nurlan" and "Abdulla") was also a student of Abduwali *qari* and himself a *qari* from 1991 on. In 1997, he allegedly underwent training in the camp of the Arab jihadist Khattab in Chechnya, to which he personally sent 150 persons from Uzbekistan, among whom were accomplices in the Tashkent explosions. He likewise coordinated his activities with Kazimbek Zakirov (alias "Palvan"), mentioned above. According to the investigation group, in September 1998 Bahrom Abdullaev allegedly was appointed by Tahir Yuldashev to be his representative (*amir*) in Uzbekistan.[76] Together with Dehkanov, Abdullaev was extradited to Uzbekistan by the Turkmen authorities.

In the early 1990s, "Palvan" was also an active partner in robberies and murders in Andizhan. Then, having moved to Almaty, he coordinated the plotters' activities in Tashkent, acting as one of the group's leaders. After the explosions, he was apprehended in Taldy-Kurgan, Kazakhstan, where there was no tight control over Islamist activity. The city served as a transit base for terrorists, who, as shown by the materials of the investigation, in May 1997 devised a plan for a violent seizure of power under the slogans of jihad. According to the Israeli journalist Oleg Yaqubov, a native of Uzbekistan who carried out a journalistic investigation of the 1999 events in Tashkent and interviewed many people, including the arrested conspirators, more than three hundred people were trained in the use of various kinds of weapons, combat skills, working with explosives, and reconnaissance, in special camps in the villages of Shali, Serzhen-Yurt, and Aftori-Yurt beginning in 1997. All of this took place pursuant to an arrangement with Khattab, who had by then settled down in Chechnya. Yaqubov claims that, altogether, more than five thousand Uzbek citizens were trained in fighting camps in Chechnya, Afghanistan, and Tajikistan.[77] A base disguised as a private firm in Almaty supplied the militants with money, temporary lodgings, and false passports made in Kyrgyzstan.

Regardless of how murky the story of the February 1999 Tashkent bombings is, it is clear that IMU militants were involved and that many of them were cold-blooded killers who were closely linked to transnational terrorist networks. This does not mean that some were not sincere believers who were mobilized through effective indoctrination. An example was Mahamadsobir Mamatov, who was born in Andizhan in 1973, received his secondary school education, and beginning in 1995, attended the Jum'a mosque in Andizhan together with his neighbor, Z. Mahmudov. There he became acquainted with K. Nazarov, T. Nuraliev, and Z. Dehkanov. At the end of 1995, together with M. Ashurov, he guarded the house and family members of Abduwali *qari*. After the disappearance of Abduwali *qari*, he ceased to attend the mosque. He took the following oath: "I shall serve Allah, I shall not swerve from the path of Allah, I am ready to do everything for the sake of Allah, and I agree that I shall be punished in case I violate the oath." He committed marauding raids and contributed one-fifth of the plundered property as *zakat* to the *bayt al-mal* foundation. He was arrested on April 16, 1999, and a military court sentenced him to nineteen years in a maximum-security prison.

The IMU leaders did not take responsibility for the explosions in Tashkent. A leaflet specially distributed for the purpose (a copy of which was given to me by Sabir, an Islamist sympathizer, soon after the bombing attack) said that none of the defendants had even been implicated in those events, but the action had been performed by "the people" protesting against despotism. The leaflet was signed by Tahir Yuldashev, who used his party pseudonym "Faruq."

STATEMENT OF THE IMU POLITICAL DEPARTMENT

The IMU holds the ruling despotic regime fully responsible for the explosions that took place in Tashkent, the capital of Uzbekistan, as these explosions are a logical outcome of the manifestly brutal and violent policy of the Uzbek government toward its own people. The people, having no way to communicate with its government in peaceful language, had been forced to use a language that government could understand. The IMU believes that the events that have fallen completely at the feet of the whole Uzbek people and especially the tyrannized youth are the manifestation of deep-seated inner perceptions and therefore went completely out of control. It is also to be recalled that, aside from this, life inside the country is in absolute decline, while the despotic government in the prosecution of its policy finds itself in complete subservience to the dark forces of the world. In this connection, the IMU declares that there is no link whatsoever between the explosions in Tashkent and the Movement as a whole, nor with a single participant in that Movement. Still, the Movement does not exclude objective reasons for what happened and makes the totalitarian regime responsible for the explosions, and draws attention to its fruitless activity in domestic and foreign policy.

The IMU believes that such events can be eradicated only in conditions of an independent Islamic regime after the overthrow of the cruel government that has fallen under the influence of outside imperialist forces.

IMU Commander-in-Chief
Muhammad Tahir "Faruq"

In another leaflet that I have at my disposal, "Faruq" also claims that Erk was not implicated in the February explosions in Tashkent.

Besides the statement cited above, presumably addressed to the public, the IMU appealed in a leaflet to all the Muslims in the republic. Here is the text of that leaflet, which I obtained in Tashkent and translated from Uzbek.

AN OPEN LETTER TO EVERY MUSLIM

My Muslim brother!
This is an open letter from the IMU leader Muhammad Tahir Faruq; this open letter, expressing the IMU's attitude to the explosions of February 16, 1999, in Tashkent, explains their cause and consequences. Let the Muslims and the global community learn the truth about that incident. Let them know those who received advice and assistance from the external anti-Islamic forces, who oblige our ancient Muslim people to live according to the law of the infidels, who slanderously attack Islam, who are the enemies of Islam.

Indeed, the condition of our country's Muslims has worsened. The changes that barely started in the 1970s–1980s proved to be not very deep. Atheists again reared their head, mosques were closed, the morning prayers were silenced, the freedom to offer prayers became restricted, the call to follow the path of Allah was forbidden, the sufferings of the *'ulama* became even worse than before, they are being tortured with electrical appliances, arrested as drug addicts, and for possession of arms, while their corpses alone emerge from prisons.

Needless to say, these explosions are the expected result of oppression, the invalidation of legitimate human rights, terrorism, and dictatorial policies. This event is a reaction to persecution; it is the doing of people gone out of control. It is important to stress that the idea of replacement of the existing authority with an Islamic one is held universally. Islam grants us the freedom of personality, directs us along the rightful path, and endows us with natural rights. People have lost the ability to think in the right way and act deliberately as a result of a policy of intolerable oppression.

The Creator will reward the Muslims for these torments in the afterlife, but the new generation is moving away from its faith and veneration of Allah, being imbued with Western culture. This is where the real trouble lies.

Therefore we ask you, dear brothers and Muslims of the whole world, in these hard times to be side by side with us, so that we could come through this ordeal with humility, following the Creator and returning to the righteous path—thus shall we find our religious rights, peace of mind, and be praised.

LEADERS OF ERK CONVICTED

The names of those who guided the perpetrators of the terrorist acts in Tashkent were announced at the trial as organizers. Blame was placed on "Islamic fundamentalists" and their "ringleaders." According to the investigation, one of them, Tahir Yuldashev, financed the acts, providing about $500,000 for the purchase of explosives, weapons, and vehicles. The prosecution noted that in the event that they achieved their goal—the physical liquidation of Karimov and other government leaders—the terrorists would follow up with a series of acts of sabotage in various regions of the republic with a view to completely destabilize the country. After that, evidence gathered by the office of the attorney general indicates that the fighting groups of Islamic fundamentalists Yuldashev and Juma Namangani were to penetrate the territory of the republic and seize power. With the seizure of power, a secular oppositionist to Karimov's rule, Muhammad Salih, was presumably to become head of state. Salih had run for president in 1991 but lost to Karimov and was then forced to emigrate.[78] A writer and poet, Salih had been the founder of Erk, a nationwide liberal and secular party with strong elements of Turkic nationalism in its ideology. Salih received 12 percent of the vote in the election. In late 1993, the party was banned, and he emigrated to Turkey. Most observers did not believe that Salih could have been involved in the conspiracy, although some political émigrés argued that the obligations that Salih had taken toward his Islamist partners in exchange for their support might have led him to fully support their attempt to assassinate Karimov (as was the case with the former deputy prime minister of Turkmenistan, Boris Shikhmuradov).

To what extent were the allegations against Salih supported by facts? An interview with an Uzbekistani official sheds light on the measure of the government's hostility toward the poet at large but cannot convince us that the Erk leader had participated in the conspiracy.

Question: Officials in Tashkent asserted that it was Muhammad Salih who stood behind the explosions in February 1999, and he was convicted *in absentia*. [Was] there concrete proof of his guilt?

Answer: We received information from intelligence sources that in May 1997 Salih met with Tahir Yuldashev and Juma Hojiev [Namangani] in Istanbul. They declared their intention to proclaim a so-called movement for the revival of Islam in Uzbekistan. As we know, they found common language and agreed on joint action. They had one objective—the overthrow of the present system in Uzbekistan. More than a year passed. At the end of September 1998, Yuldashev, Namangani, Zakirov, and Bahrom Abdullaev met in Kabul. Yuldashev was proclaimed the amir of the movement, Namangani became his assistant for military affairs, and Bahrom Abdullaev the amir of the jihad organizations carrying on their activity in the territory of Uzbekistan. In early December 1998, a meeting of Yuldashev, Namangani, and Muhammad Salih was held in Kabul. It was long, and for ten days the plotters were busy drawing up a plan of the jihad movement in the republic, which was to begin in the spring of 1999. According to that plan, the president and members of the government were to be liquidated in Tashkent. Chaos would ensue in the republic, and it was at that time that Yuldashev with his militants was to break through into the republic from the south. And the Namangani militants were to enter the Ferghana Valley aboard twenty Kamaz trucks. The plotters' arrangements boiled down to the following: amid chaos and fighting, Muhammad Salih was to assume leadership in the republic, while Yuldashev was assigned the role of war minister in the new state. Salih pledged to give $1,600,000 for this affair.

Question: How can a dissident living in Norway have such money? Did he really give it for the takeover?

Answer: We know that Salih handed over part of the money for the organization of explosions in Tashkent. But, fortunately, their plans failed. There is evidence that part of the money promised by Salih was to be allocated by Arab foundations. He was also connected with the Taliban. But Salih had some additional shady ties, which we were unable to uncover.[79]

The conviction of Salih left no hope that Karimov would ever reopen a dialogue with Salih and his supporters.

REGIONAL AND CLAN RIVALRIES

Although many Russian and Western observers expressed strong suspicions that the accusations against Muhammad Salih were fabricated, versions appeared in the Russian press trying to link the Islamist radical plotters not only to the leader of Erk but also to other regional groups and personalities, as well as to clans that were interested in toppling Karimov. One of these versions named someone close to Karimov, Ismail Jurabekov, who had for many years stood behind Karimov before and after his ascent to power and who reportedly had for many years been the president's "purse."[80] Jurabekov has always been considered the unofficial leader of the so-called Samarqandi clan, to which Karimov belongs.[81] For many years he occupied the post of vice premier. However, in the secret hierarchy of the political elite, he had long remained *de facto* second in command, and in the president's absence he decided many important questions. About a year before the explosions, Jurabekov was unexpectedly forced to retire. Rumors circulated in Tashkent that the resignation was connected to drug dealing. Afterward, pressure began to build on Jurabekov's son, who had close links with one of the two wealthiest businessmen in Uzbekistan from the Ferghana Valley, Salim Abdullaev, who, according to rumors, is a mafia boss. Abdullaev is known in Moscow as a successful businessman who owns a complex of commercial buildings and restaurants on Moscow's Novy Arbat Street and is believed to be well connected in Russian business and political circles. Salim and Jurabekov's son together supervised a network of supermarkets in Tashkent.

Information from Uzbekistan was supplemented by a confession from one of the most senior officers of the Russian Interior Ministry, who, in a private conversation with Shermatova, stated that Russian mafia rings were somehow involved in the Tashkent coup attempt. He claimed that Karimov had thrown an iron curtain around Uzbekistan, preventing the penetration of so-called shadow structures. In the Soviet period, Uzbekistan had been one of the main bases of shadow operators. Today, however, unlike other CIS republics, Uzbekistan does not participate in the laundering of big capital. The Russian shadow operators were therefore allegedly interested in a regime change in Uzbekistan and supported the radicals accordingly. A strange chain of links that related to the events in Tashkent was drawn: Russian shadow business circles–Abdullaev–Jurabekov–Salih–the Islamists. Shermatova believed that if this version was correct, the origin of the sums promised by Salih to the Islamists (Yuldashev) to stage a coup could be explained.

On April 2, 1999, soon after the explosions, Jurabekov was appointed to a post specially created for him as head of state inspection on control and supervision of the technical condition and safety of irrigation facilities.[82] In light of the agrarian base of the country, where the artificial water supply is well developed, the head of state inspection is considered an influential figure. One year later, Karimov created yet another post, of state councilor for supervising reforms in agriculture and water facilities, and he appointed Jurabekov to this post.[83]

It therefore is difficult to accept a *Moscow News* version of the involvement of Jurabekov and the Uzbek/Russian mafia in the Islamists' plot against Karimov. It is worth noting that in the fragile balance of regional, clan, and interest groups in present-day Uzbekistan, Jurabekov is supported by the minister of interior, Zakir Almatov, and Jurabekov and Almatov, who are members of the Samarqand clan, are in turn allied with the Jizak clan. This clan was represented by one of the most skillful Uzbek diplomats (and the son-in-law of Rashidov—a late Communist Party leader of Uzbekistan); the former minister of foreign affairs, Abdulaziz Kamilov (in March 2003 Kamilov became the president's adviser for foreign affairs, then he was appointed ambassador of Uzbekistan in Washington); and some other influential officials. Members of the allied Tashkent and Ferghana clans (including the minister of defense, Qadir Ghulamov, as well as others) believed that their representation in the government was insufficient, and the underground rivalry between these alliances, as well as some other interest groups, may have been related to the Islamists' activities.

Special attention should be paid to the fact that the Ferghana Valley has always been the main base of support for the Uzbek Islamists. Many secular personalities from business, the mafia, and the political sections of the Ferghana clan maintain relations with the radical Islamists. Olivier Roy has suggested that "the Islamists' implantation in Uzbekistan corresponded broadly to a regionalist identity—that of Ferghana, which was not well represented in the central government."[84] This is, however, only part of the truth. The struggle for power and resources among regional elites and clans helps shape the activities of *all* political movements, not only Islamist ones. Moreover, the IMU has been intensively engaged in drug trafficking, which deepens its already close relations with different mafia-type and patronage networks. Representatives of different regional clans sometimes cooperate with shadow and mafia-like groups that are engaged in illegal and criminal business. However, this does not preclude politicians from appealing to these groups for support and the promotion of the interests of their regional clans.

We can summarize all various accounts of the events of February 1999 in Tashkent as follows: (1) they were organized by local Islamists (the IMU); (2) they were carried out by Islamists but masterminded by some foreign or international networks; (3) they were organized by the Uzbekistani secret services on orders of Karimov, who wanted to carry out a campaign of repression against all opposition forces; (4) they were organized by these services in order to scare Karimov and raise their own status; (5) they were organized by one of Uzbekistan's rival political clans (or one of their leaders) to force Karimov to make concessions in their favor; (6) they were organized by the local mafia; or (7) they were planned and carried out by some external actors. None of these explanations, nor any combination of them, can either be confirmed or refuted by the available evidence, so many experts remain open-minded about which is closest to the truth. Still, the first scenario seems to me to be the most convincing of all (the second scenario is the next most probable).

THE FIGHTING CONTINUES

Keeping on its course toward antiregime armed struggle using all methods, terrorist ones included, after the February events of 1999, the IMU found itself under strong pressure from the government, which took drastic measures to combat the Islamists. Nonetheless, the IMU kept trying to mobilize the population for jihad. The appeals to take part in jihad were addressed to both men and women. Here is the text of an oath, translated from Uzbek, that anyone joining the tanks of the mujahedeen had to take (I received the text from a resident of Margelan).

OATH OF THE ISLAMIC MOVEMENT OF UZBEKISTAN

A certificate of an oath performed during the passage of the IMU onto the path of jihad, in which the host of Allah demonstrates its physical and spiritual readiness to pick up the broken banner of Islam, as well as the understanding of responsibility for the liberation of Muslim men and women from under the yoke:

I, mujahed _____, have acquainted myself with the IMU statute and support it.

In this struggle the IMU is in the forefront; as an active participant in the movement I undertake to obey the orders of Allah, his Prophet, IMU Commander-in-Chief Muhammad Tahir, and the commanders appointed by him without question.

I swear, calling Allah and you to witness, to endure in the cause of jihad all the hardships, to fight to the last drop of blood; for the sake of reaching a lofty goal I am also prepared to become a *shahid*.

The February 1999 bombings in Uzbekistan affected the situation in Tajikistan. As a result of the broad campaign launched by Tashkent to ferret out members and supporters of Islamic organizations, many of those who sympathized with political Islam, as well as many others who simply had a spiritual education or orientation, were arrested, while others fled to Tajikistan, where they received the protection of IMU commanders in the Tavildara district. It appears from press reports that Juma Namangani's detachments received as many as several thousand reinforcements (which confirms that the Uzbek militants had decided not to respect the disarmament provisions in the General Agreement). At the time, Namangani was deciding whether he should keep his promise to the new Tajik government (which now included some of his former comrades in arms) that he would not take up arms against them. He was under pressure from some of his supporters to break his promise and launch a war against all regimes in Central Asia. As Zahid, one of the Uzbek militants in Tajikistan, told me, even though Islamists had been included in the Tajik government, it was in fact no better than Karimov's government in Uzbekistan. Rahmonov, he asserted, was as much a *kafir* as Karimov.[85]

Namangani did not want to quarrel with the leaders of the Islamic Revival Party of Tajikistan, however. He also understood that he should not disperse his forces. Instead, as Rashid has written, "he only asked to be given transit rights to cross the Tajikistan–Kyrgyzstan border into the Ferghana Valley, where he was continuing his war against Uzbekistan."[86] At the same time, the IRPT was in the midst of difficult negotiations with its former allies in the United Tajik Opposition and the government in

Dushanbe on the implementation of the General Agreement, and the parties preferred not enter into open conflict with Namangani, which might have meant a new round of violence for the country. The unwillingness of the Tajik government to confront Namangani, however, led authorities in Uzbekistan to conclude that the leaders of the UTO were deliberately helping Namangani and his guerillas to leave Tajikistan.

A fragment of an IMU dossier compiled by an Uzbekistani officer was confidentially passed on to me by a journalist. The document clearly demonstrates the enmity the Uzbekistani authorities felt for the UTO leaders at the time. While some of the facts that the dossier contains can be confirmed by Tajik sources, others are doubtful. The document reads:

> At a period of sharp escalation of the situation in May 1999, which threatened to grow into open violent confrontation in view of serious divisions between the official Dushanbe and the opposition, IMU detachments commanded by Juma Hojiev and UTO forces were preparing for the resumption of joint military actions against government troops.
>
> Meetings and consultations between Said Abdullo Nuri [the leader of UTO], Tahir Yuldashev, Juma Hojiev, and their plenipotentiaries have continually been held in the territory of Tajikistan, Afghanistan, Pakistan, and Iran. These sessions adopted decisions on general and coordinated tactics of action in case of resumption of armed conflict in Tajikistan and also worked out long-term plans for unleashing jihad on the territory of Uzbekistan.
>
> On May 12, 1999, Nuri met Yuldashev in Tehran, where they discussed plans to organize further action by IMU militants to destabilize the situation in Uzbekistan and other states in the region. The high-ranking functionaries of the Tajik opposition frequently met Hojiev, who resided in Republic of Tajikistan territory and directly administered the IMU headquarters in the Khoit settlement. These conferences continued up to August 12, 1999, when Hojiev (before the start of the action in the Batken district of Kyrgyzstan) met Nuri as usual and discussed with him the question of further stay of the IMU militants in the opposition-controlled territories of Tajikistan.[87]

HOSTAGE TAKING IN KYRGYZSTAN

A network of IMU members and sympathizers was established in one of Kyrgyzstan's southern regions, Batken, where militants in the summer of 1999 began to plan a move from Tajikistan. It is here, in the south of Kyrgyzstan, that two enclaves are located—an Uzbek one in Sukh and a Tajik one in Vorukh. Both regions have traditionally been considered as mainstays of Islamic radicalism—Rashid calls them "hotbeds of IMU support."[88]

In August 1999, a group of twenty militants took a mayor and three of his employees hostage in a small village in the Osh region of Kyrgyzstan.

The Kyrgyz authorities gave in to the terrorists' demands, paid ransom for the hostages' release, and gave the terrorists a helicopter to fly to Afghanistan. This caused a sharp reaction in Uzbekistan, whose authorities regarded the behavior of the Kyrgyz authorities as a manifestation of extreme weakness and even treachery in relation to Uzbekistan. One of the leading officials of Uzbekistan's Foreign Ministry told me at the time that Bishkek's orientation toward "pseudoliberalism" and actual demobilization of its power agencies undermined the interests of Kyrgyzstan and showed other leaders in Central Asia how reforms should not be carried out. My interlocutor also asserted that Kyrgyzstan was poorly served by the "appeasement" of Islamists, who, in reality, "must be crushed like harmful insects."[89] It was no surprise, therefore, when Uzbekistani planes decided to bomb presumed terrorist bases in Tajikistan the same month, which naturally drew a sharp reaction from the authorities in Dushanbe.

Soon thereafter, the IMU entered three Kyrgyz *kishlaks* and took a general of the Interior Ministry of Kyrgyzstan hostage. During the night of August 21, an armed detachment of fifty people captured a meteorological station of the Uzbekistan Meteorological Committee at the Abramov Glacier in Kyrgyzstan. Ten people working there were taken hostage. In addition, an entire group of mountain climbers was taken hostage, together with the personnel from the meteorological station. Before that, in the beginning of August, these fifty militants, among whom were Uzbeks, Tajiks, Arabs, Afghans, Pakistanis, and others, had captured a mountain village known as Zardaly in the Batken region.

The terrorists called themselves mujahedeen. They were well armed and had modern communication equipment. Soon they appeared in the territory of Tajikistan, and new hostages—nine policemen from Kyrgyzstan and two local inhabitants—were added to the old ones. The hostage takers reportedly boasted that they had an additional five hundred to six hundred militants in Tajik territory. They also told the hostages that they were responsible for the February explosions in Tashkent. On August 25, law enforcement agencies in Uzbekistan and Kyrgyzstan received a statement by fax from Tahir Yuldashev declaring that, if the Kyrgyzstan authorities showed leniency to his people, his forces would simply pass through the territory of Kyrgyzstan into Uzbekistan. The overall objective of the militants, according to the politicians, was the destabilization of the situation in Uzbekistan and the creation of an Islamic state in the Ferghana Valley.[90]

According to an agent in Kyrgyzstan's National Security Ministry, one of the leaders of the militants was a certain Azizkhan, a former citizen of Uzbekistan and "the right hand" of Namangani.[91] In the early 1990s, he had left Uzbekistan for Tajikistan and joined the armed Tajik opposition.

He completed combat training in an Afghan camp in the town of Tahor, and, upon returning to Tajikistan, headed one of the groups of the intransigent oppositionists who refused to lay down their arms. The first hostages were released, but soon new ones—four Japanese geologists and an interpreter—fell into terrorist hands. At first, the terrorists demanded a ransom of two million dollars for their release, but later the ransom was raised to five million dollars. Despite the Kyrgyz power agencies' inability to prevent these hostage-taking incidents, they refused to allow the militants to pass into the Uzbek part of the Ferghana Valley; instead, Kyrgyz troops launched a military operation that forced the militants back into Tajikistan.

Prior to this, the defense force ministries of Kyrgyzstan, Tajikistan, Uzbekistan, and Kazakhstan had decided to form a joint operational headquarters in the town of Osh at a meeting of the foreign and defense ministers along with the heads of the four countries' intelligence services. But these meetings, as well as the establishment of the joint operations center, proved of little effect: they did not lead to the liberation of the hostages or the departure of the militants, which took place in early October. Nevertheless, Kyrgyz officials claimed that the militants had left Kyrgyz territory because they were "unable to endure constant strikes of the united grouping of government troops."[92]

The confusion that reigned among the military leadership of the three countries, and the quarrels between the generals involved, only became public knowledge much later.[93] Here is how one of the Kyrgyz officers recalls the events of those days.

> Only we and the police special force were left. Two generals commanded them, Isakov and Sadiev. The operation led to nothing. In approaching the place, a militant fired a shot from a sniper rifle and hit a soldier in the leg. After that the detachment waited a little more and left empty-handed. And what we were dealing with was only a band numbering 25–30 rifles! Then they began to rub the militants out, gathering three special-forces groups from each power agency. . . . Now there's no use lying any more, the time has passed. . . . Certainly everything was so unexpected that we lost our bearings. To speak honestly, the army was not ready to fight. Fables are being told that our army closed the road to Uzbekistan for IMU gunmen and therefore the war began. A fat lot we care for them; they could quietly go to their Ferghana, we did not even notice them.[94]

The head of Kyrgyzstan's National Security Ministry, Misir Ashirkulov, described the situation in an interview in a similar vein, arguing that the Uzbek militants could have easily penetrated into Uzbekistan using mountain tracks.[95] However, for some reason they stopped halfway and remained in Kyrgyz mountain *kishlaks* for almost two months, contacting members of the Kyrgyz and foreign mass media through a Kyrgyz parliamentary deputy, Tursunbai Bakir-Uulu. During this time, they staked out their claims, set out the aims and the tasks of the movement, and hurled threats against the Uzbekistani authorities. The impression was that this was their real mission.

Why did they do this? Some observers believed that they wanted to force the Uzbekistani leadership to recognize them as political opponents and negotiate with them. However, a former Tajik fighter informed us that during the standoff in the Kyrgyz mountains, a split occurred in the IMU leadership. Yuldashev believed that the Japanese hostages had to be given back in exchange for political concessions on the part of official Tashkent, but Namangani wanted a ransom for them. Most of the hostages (including all the Japanese) were released, and although it was not officially reported, there is no doubt that a ransom was paid for them.

During the operation against the terrorists, Uzbekistani aircraft bombed Kyrgyz territory. Later there were reports that the incursions had actually been approved by the Kyrgyz side. As an officer of Uzbekistan's law-enforcement agencies told me, Uzbekistani authorities were convinced that Kyrgyzstan alone was unable to cope with the terrorists. Officials in Tashkent had a very low opinion of the fighting ability and potential of the Kyrgyz army and law-enforcement bodies, and they also doubted the political will of the Bishkek authorities to resist terrorists. To this day, the Kyrgyz grumble that the Uzbeks had accidentally or intentionally dropped bombs on a Kyrgyz village, killing twelve villagers and damaging dozens of houses.[96]

During the terrorist operation in Kyrgyzstan, the Islamists attacked one of the guard posts, and in the course of the ensuing battle, the militants lost a few dozen people, including Abduwali Yuldashev.[97] Again, many voices accused the IRPT of links with the IMU terrorists, although Nuri had used all his influence to effect the release of the hostage. Still, a Russian website reads as follows:

> For his part, Juma Hojiev, who coordinated the actions of the militants, invaded the Batken district of Kyrgyzstan. He reported by radio on the course of fighting and the actions taken not only to the IMU headquarters in Kabul and Kandahar, but also to Mirzo Ziyoev's headquarters in Tajikistan. Communication between the leadership of the Tajik opposition and Hojiev was maintained by couriers constantly traveling back and forth along the route from the UTO headquarters. Nuri and Ziyoev handled instruction and advice bearing on the most confidential [matters]. Thus on August 26, 1999, UTO leader Said Abdulla Nuri sent a message through a courier to Juma Hojiev in which he recommended the release of the Japanese hostages in order to prevent an international outcry. However, this recommendation ran counter to Yuldashev's instruction, which demanded that the foreigners

taken hostage not be released in exchange for money and should be detained until the end of jihad.[98]

Several people later privately claimed that they had played a role in the release of the prisoners. One was a Tajik poet, Gulrukhsor Safieva, who is a close friend of President Akaev and someone who carries a great deal of authority among the Tajik opposition. In a private conversation with a journalist, she asserted that she had made a major contribution to the hostage release by persuading two people with influence over Namangani—the aforementioned IRPT leader Nuri and Minister for Emergency Situations Ziyoev—of the need to release the captives.[99] But again, the truth about the details of 1999 is still unknown. What is clear is that, pursuant to negotiations with the militants who had by then been driven into Tajikistan, the Japanese hostages were released in October 1999. According to rumors that were denied by the authorities, the release came after a substantial ransom was paid by the Japanese government.

THE IMU'S ADVENTURES IN TAJIKISTAN AND AFGHANISTAN

In the wake of the 1999 incursions, Tajikistan found itself in an extremely difficult situation because the Uzbekistani government stepped up pressure on Dushanbe to take resolute measures against the Islamists. The Uzbek mass media, supported by some of their counterparts in Russia, Kazakhstan, and elsewhere, blamed the IRPT for what had happened. Tashkent probably expected that the alliance between "the party of power" and the opposition in Tajikistan, an alliance whose supporters hoped would successfully provide a case of integration of moderate political Islam with government structures, would in fact collapse.

A moment of truth ensued in relations between Rahmonov and the IRPT leaders. The leaders of the IRPT did everything they could to resolve the hostage crisis peacefully, and in addition, Nuri and a number of UTO commanders who had fought alongside Namangani managed to convince the latter to agree to the expulsion of the IMU fighters to Afghanistan in November 1999. This action was approved not only by the Tajik leadership but also by the Russian troops guarding the Tajik–Afghan border. As a result, Uzbek political figures accused Moscow of abetting the terrorists, arguing that Russia wanted to use the IMU to pressure Karimov. Namangani thus managed to create tensions not only in relations among the three Central Asian republics but also between Uzbekistan and Russia.

Only a few months later, however, IMU gunmen reappeared in the mountains of Tajikistan. In May 2000, the mass media reported another expulsion of IMU militants led by Namangani into Taliban-controlled parts of Afghanistan. In August, Namangani and his detachment managed to return once again to the Tavildara district, and again Uzbekistani officials accused the Tajik authorities and the Russian border guards of aiding the Islamists. According to one Tajik official, the Tajik leadership wanted to avoid renewed fighting on its territory because the Tajik people were tired of civil war. In addition, the leadership was afraid of aggravating relations between "the party of power" in Dushanbe and the IRPT. However, experience showed that it was impossible to neutralize the extremists merely by expelling them to Afghanistan. They had been waging guerrilla war in the mountains for five years, and they therefore knew all the vulnerable places of the Tajik–Afghan border. It was therefore impossible to prevent them from crossing the border as long as they had complete freedom of movement and support on the Afghan side.

Although Uzbekistani law-enforcement agencies are not unbiased, their information deserves to be analyzed in regard to the possibility of some degree of cooperation between Tajik authorities and the IMU. The document below also demonstrates the desire of these services to describe the leaders of the IRPT as terrorists.

After the signing, on 17 June 2000, of a conciliatory protocol on the dissolution and disarmament of illegal armed formations between the government of Tajikistan and the United Tajik Opposition, Nuri, Ziyoev, and [other] well-known field commanders of the Tajik Islamists, . . . considering the authority carried by Juma Hojiev among his militants and the part he had played in fighting on the UTO side, actively responded to the requests of IMU leaders and offered every kind of assistance in transporting the Movement's detachments into the areas of the region of Karategin controlled by the Tajik opposition. . . . [They] stayed [there] until the start of the operation for penetration into the territory of Uzbekistan and Kyrgyzstan.

Similar aid and assistance was rendered to the IMU by the UTO after the government of Tajikistan decided to expel the so-called Uzbek refugees. In particular, a redeployment of militants and members of their families to other localities of Tajikistan was organized. These localities were situated in far away mountain regions. In view of the fact that pressure and demands to deport IMU militants and "refugees" from Tajikistan began to mount, Tahir Yuldashev came to an agreement with Said Abdullo Nuri and Mirzo Ziyoev on the question of transporting members of the families of the Movement's functionaries and militants to Afghanistan. In the process, the UTO leadership promised to arrange "a corridor" through the territory of Tajikistan for the withdrawal of the above-mentioned persons to the Islamic State of Afghanistan. The "refugees" were withdrawing to the regions of Afghanistan controlled by the Taliban. The safety of their passage through Tajik territory to the border with Afghanistan was ensured by the units of UTO field commanders—Bobo Nemat, Sarabek, Dodi Khudo, and "the Shaykh," confidants of Ziyoev, also actively cooperating with Hojiev and other IMU functionaries in Tajikistan.

After the Tajikistan government made a decision to expel the so-called Uzbek refugees from the territory of Tajikistan, the IMU leadership instructed the militants deployed in the area of the Khoit settlement to bring their family members only to the territory of the Islamic State of Afghanistan controlled by the Taliban Movement, as the Kandahar administration undertook to accommodate them. In the opinion of the Taliban leader Mullo Omar, the opposition forces (the Anti-Taliban Coalition), including senior commanders, were traitors to their nation, and it was necessary to be on guard against them. In this connection, the Taliban leader was given lists containing 431 militant family members, who were transported to the territory of Afghanistan by cars supplied by UTO leaders Nuri and Ziyoev.

Having regard to the evolving situation concerning the refugees, Tahir Yuldashev sought an opportunity to discuss this question with Said Abdullo Nuri and Mirzo Ziyoev, so as to organize the corresponding "corridor" and obtain a security guarantee when crossing the Tajik–Afghan border. Furthermore, the Tajik and Uzbek Islamist leaders reached an agreement on continued activity of the IMU headquarters in Tajikistan in the form of the preservation of the established material and technical base, as well as camps for training militants. They decided to leave some representatives of the movement in the localities where its main forces were to be deployed. Mullo Safar, the UTO commander of the Jirgatal sector, who had long since been linked to Juma Hojiev, was appointed to be in charge of work with IMU functionaries left behind in the territory of Tajikistan. IMU leaders Yuldashev and Hojiev, as before, coordinate all their actions with Nuri. At the same time, the latter renders both material aid to the militants and assistance in replenishing their ranks with effectiveness. Nuri's supporters from among UTO militants, in particular from among the formations of Mirzo Ziyoev "Jaga" and Abdullo "the Shaykh," are direct associates of IMU militants. However, in June 2000, Nuri officially placed his office in Meshhed at the disposal of Yuldashev.[100]

In August and September 2000, IMU units fought government troops in the south of Kyrgyzstan and in the Surkhan Darya region of Uzbekistan. Having penetrated the area north of Tashkent, the militants attacked Uzbekistani units in the area of Janjiabad and Bostanlyk, near Tashkent (earlier the Bostanlyk region had been part of Kazakhstan). Uzbekistan's army managed to repulse the IMU gunmen, but suffered considerable losses. As one of the participants in the fighting told me, the militants demonstrated unprecedented tenacity. When the Uzbek soldiers approached the corpses of the slain militants to remove them, the corpses, which had been mined, blew up.

The fighting led to a further deterioration of relations between Uzbekistan and Tajikistan. During the operation, Uzbekistani government forces drove more than two thousand ethnic Tajik peasants from the Surkhan Darya region into the mountains. They were accused of supporting the militants who, as it turned out, had established a fortified camp in that region. In Rashid's opinion, it was "a sorry example of Uzbekistan's ability to alienate and traumatize its own people whilst trying to deal with the IMU."[101]

A Tajik journalist who had earlier been in Afghanistan with the UTO and is now the press secretary of the IRPT chairman stated that the armed actions by the IMU in the south of Kyrgyzstan and the Surkhan Darya region of Uzbekistan in 1999–2000 were not an end in themselves.[102] In part, they were designed to destabilize the situation in Central Asia, but their main purpose was to ensure the Taliban's complete victory in Afghanistan and the liquidation of the Northern Alliance troops led by Ahmad Shah Masoud. However, it is not clear why, if this was indeed the purpose of the operations, Kyrgyzstan and Uzbekistan were objects of destabilization and not Tajikistan, which was providing considerable political and military assistance to Masoud. Moreover, such a destabilization would have weakened the positions of the Islamists in Tajikistan, who had gravitated toward an alliance with the Taliban and would have liked the support for Masoud to cease.

Nevertheless, it was during that period that the links between the IMU and the Taliban movement became clear. The international media reported that Namangani had been appointed deputy defense minister by the Taliban government, a report that was not denied by the Taliban. With reference to Masoud's intelligence, it was also reported that during the battle for Taloqan in October 2000, IMU militants, as well as those from the ranks of Uighur and Chechen separatist groups, were airlifted out of the international terrorist base at Rishkhor near Kabul.[103]

THE IMU IDEOLOGY

Many analysts have argued that the IMU is not guided by programmatic principles but instead has a purely practical political and economic agenda and thus pays scant attention to ideology. To assess this argument, we need to begin by reviewing the roots of the movement, focusing in particular on the radical Islamic organizations in the Ferghana Valley that predated the IMU—Adolat, Tawba, and Islam Lashkarlari—each of which was headed by future IMU leaders.

Unfortunately, there is a dearth of material on the ideology of Adolat. In part, this can be compensated for by tracing the nature of Adolat's practical actions. Doing so reveals four dimensions to Adolat ideology. First, it practiced Islamic puritanism, directing its efforts at ensuring the strict observance of the ordinances, rituals, and norms of Islamic morality, as well as devotion and piety. In this sense, Adolat was a Salafi organization. Second, it attempted to assume responsibility for maintaining public order and eradicating larceny, theft, corruption, and so on. Third, it called for social justice and equality. And fourth, it advocated Islamic governance and the creation of a state ruled by Shari'a law.

It is therefore wrong to characterize the organization (as a number of observers have done) as merely a gang of murderers and drug dealers. Above all, it is important to stress that there was a law enforcement component in the program of the Ferghana Islamists from the very beginning. This can be seen in three important trends. First, they attempted to enforce Islamic norms and punish lawbreakers in keeping with the spirit and letter of Shari'a (again, they are similar in this regard to the Middle Eastern Salafis). Second, members of special "patrol squads" were trained in policing and martial arts.[104] And third, arms were stockpiled and youths were trained in using them.[105] After the beginning of open confrontation between the Karimov regime and the Ferghana Islamists, two more violence-oriented points appeared in their program—the advocacy of overthrowing the secular "anti-Islamic" regime by force and intimidation in the form of terror directed against government representatives.

These five trajectories allow us to classify the early Ferghana Islamists not only as Salafis but also as jihadists—they were committed to violent struggle against a secular regime in the name of Islam. They subsequently received practical combat training during the civil war in Tajikistan and again during their military actions in Afghanistan and Chechnya. As a result, the armed wing of the Uzbek Salafi movement gradually came to dominate. Repression drove the militants out of Uzbekistan, and events unfolding in neighboring countries made it easier for terrorists and extremists in the movement to gain the upper hand. The "theoretical" or ideological wing of the movement—the Wahhabis—was relegated to the background. Moreover, the activity of the Salafi mullas in the mosques and *madrasas*, which had been centers of Salafi indoctrination and recruitment in the early 1990s, was discontinued.[106]

Thus, the Islamists lost their ability to influence simply and reliably the minds and sentiments of Muslims in the region. Having been routed politically, they could only work illegally by recruiting supporters through underground circles, by training candidates for Islamic radicalism by means of audio recordings of sermons of Salafi mullas and imams, and by circulating printed materials. The extremists also lost their theoreticians in the persons of the acting Wahhabi mullas. Mosques now were becoming more and more tightly controlled by the authorities. Any attempt by the militants to openly propagate their ideas inside the country was now doomed to failure, apart from being very dangerous, and it also became less of a priority for them. Yuldashev and Namangani focused instead on sending the Uzbek youth abroad for training in the *madrasas* of Pakistan, while they themselves were preoccupied by the fighting in Tajikistan and Afghanistan.

It is for these reasons that many observers have come to the conclusion that the IMU is completely without doctrinal underpinnings. In fact, however, as noted earlier, they were committed to Salafism and were also jihadists. This was true even before the creation of the IMU, as is shown by leaflets, booklets, and audio- and videocassettes collected by an Uzbek researcher, Babajanov. One of these, entitled *Lessons of Jihad* (*Zhihod Darsliklari*), is particularly instructive.[107]

Before turning to the text of this document, I should emphasize that the use of illegal materials as sources for scholarly research has risks. It is not always clear where these materials come from, who the authors were, or who disseminated them. In this instance, there is also an inconsistency in the substance of the material. Babajanov reports that the *Lessons* were intended for mujahedeen from both the IMU and an organization called the Movement of Islamic Revival of Uzbekistan (MIRU). He also argues that references to certain events in the text indicate that the booklet was written around 1999–2000. However, he also reports that the MIRU was formed "in about 1994–95," and that "in 1998 [it] was transformed into the IMU." Could this material really have been prepared in 1999–2000 for an organization that no longer existed?

Nor can we assume that the IMU was the document's author. One can assume, for example, that it was forged by Uzbekistani intelligence services to discredit the IMU. Ideally, we could compare the content of these materials with public statements by IMU leaders to assess their validity, but such statements are unfortunately extremely rare.

Nevertheless, Babajanov and Martha Brill Olcott argue that the materials collected by Babajanov provide "a fuller and, what is most important, more objective idea of the plans and objectives of the Movement inside Uzbekistan." They note that, in contrast, the IMU's leaders are reluctant to publicize the details of their program and that they merely assert that their ultimate goal is "the overthrow of Islam Karimov's regime," "the release of brother Muslims from prisons," and so on.

With these reservations in mind, let us turn to the substance of the *Lessons*. To begin with, they describe four "stages of jihad" (*zhihod urinlari*): (1) a political stage (*siyosiy urin*); (2) a military stage (*askariy urin*); (3) an economic stage (*iktisodiy urin*); and (4) a stage of struggle against the believer's profane desires (*nafsiy urin*). The IMU strategists accordingly combine military, power, moral–religious, and political dimensions in their approach to jihad.

The passage below from the *Lessons* begins by stating the objective:

To destroy the [state] system of infidels and construct the Islamic Order. *Comment*: When speaking of the system of infidels, what was meant was the *Sovetniklari* (advisers),[108] plants, factories, slavery [the translators noted that in the radical view of the IMU, all Central Asian Muslims were in slavery to the Jews and America], schools, kindergartens, maternity houses, the TV, hospitals, collective farmers and even their houses, and so forth. . . .

But how is constructing "the Islamic Order" to be accomplished?
Our people are meek as sheep. But if one takes power over us, all of them will follow you. But we had been pursuing jihad in the mountains for about 30 years.
And still it is necessary to find out whether the group of people among whom you find yourself is inclined toward Islam, or if they are inclined as Jews or Christians. For example, if our people call themselves the followers of *Imam-i a'dham* [a reference to the followers of the founder of the *madhhab* prevailing in Central Asia, the Sunni school of Abu Hanifa (*al-Imam al-a'dham*)], it means that they should be called this way. [Their outlook] should not be changed at once; this can be done afterward. When you are among them, they must perceive you as one of their own. . . .[109]

Thus the text mentions the followers of the Hanafi *madhhab*. In doing so, it appears that the authors are claiming that some recruits who call themselves Hanafis may not be "bad Muslims" altogether, though some may be. The goal, then, is to transform recruits into "good" Muslims who are still adherents of Hanafism. If so, the authors could be characterized as "strict Hanafis," which would make sense tactically, given that Hanafi Islam is very popular in Central Asia. But a different interpretation is also possible. It may be that the authors envisage the replacement of Hanafism with a different and more suitable *madhhab*. For the Arabian Wahhabis, this would be Hanbalism. If so, the authors are in effect rejecting the traditional form of Islam practiced in the region.

The text does not allow us to reach a conclusion on this question. Indeed, some parts leave the reader with the impression that it was written by semiliterates. It continues:

1. Military forces of the state. *Comment*: This can be compared to a man who has hands and legs. In precisely this way, an army is a hand of the state. If it has opponents, it catches them by the hands. It is very difficult to learn something about the military force of infidels, that is, about the amount of weapons, tanks, planes, and other things. But know that a boxer at the ring works with his hands, and if his leg is broken, he can do nothing. . . .
But how can we learn about the degree of enemy readiness? For this purpose, one should strike a blow at one small part [of the military] and quickly retreat, watching them. How and in what time will they construct a roadblock,

who and in what strength will come to their rescue? Police will not interfere here; this means that military experts will have to come to their aid. For example, if in Palestine one bus blows up, Jews quickly cordon that place off and detain everybody. And it is in no way possible to bring in arms there. It means that this army is strong. To capture Palestinian cities and strengthen military force, the Jews improve their tactics, which raises their power and fighting capacity. They are trying to prove that they have a strong army. It is extremely hard to struggle against such a country. But this may be compared to a dog. If a flea bites it, what a huge part of the body it begins to bite. And if we strike at a small part of these infidels, what a large territory they will be forced to cordon off. It is important to know the following. If we strike at the Hamza district [one of the districts of Tashkent], what shall they do, cordon off the whole city or only this Hamza district?

Goal is paramount to any cause. *Comment*: The only goal of the Muslims is for Allah to be pleased with us. This means to carry out all Allah's commands and to struggle. For the word of Allah to be above everything, for everything to be accomplished as Islam commands, so as to implement Allah's commands worldwide.

Idea. Any command except for Allah's commands is oppression, no matter what its forms are. We shall strive until it disappears completely.

Slogan. It is necessary to build such a political and military system that would never change, that would never come to an agreement with infidels, by rejecting their political system, their culture, to discharge them from all posts and establish such an Islamic order. This is our slogan. That is: *"La ilaha illa Allah, Muhammadu Rasulullah"* (There is no God but Allah, Muhammad the Envoy of Allah).

Comment: There should be no exceptions! Whether it be TV, radio, bazaar, even the church. Let everything even become expensive! The slogan must be realized, come what may! All foreign ties are to be severed and built on the Islamic order alone. Will it be a bank? It will only be in the order laid down by Islam. In the Islamic state there will be no foreign ministry. All of them will be liquidated.

The founding of special organizations in the workplace is needed, to educate people in the spirit of true faith and world outlook. *Comment*: Many people understand Islam, but they do not understand its ultimate goals. They do not understand that Islam is a life, a thing (*narsa*) reviving man. They think that it is only one of the parts of their life. . . . There is no such nation— "infidels." Allah had created all His creatures so that He be worshipped. We shall call on them to embrace Islam. If they do not accept—they must be killed, turned into slaves, and valued no more than cattle! Jews, Christians, and polytheists—every one of them will turn into a thing. They will be divided as things. Man must not have a notion of what is true. One should not regard them with indulgence, saying: "They are humans, too." No, for they have become infidels to Allah!

One should know precisely—what is the condition of Islam, what are its assignments, what do infidels have in store against Islam, or what do they do in general? All this should be known. People with correct understanding are necessary to us for this purpose. Now one should be able to make *ijtihad*. There should be a correct understanding of the situation. Plenty of fatwas have now been issued, proceeding from the situation in the Islamic state. For example, the rules of prayer, the wearing of a beard, and so forth. These are immutable things. But one cannot lag behind in the military field, armament, transportation, and other similar things. . . .

These passages clearly demonstrate the Salafi spirit of the document.[110] Above all, there is an unequivocal rejection of an "infidel" political system and culture. But it is unclear whether it is calling for a complete rejection of, for example, television and radio, or whether its authors only want to let them "become expensive." Also unclear is the mention of the church, especially in the sentence that includes the mention of television and radio. The claim that an Islamic state will have no foreign ministry is pure demagogy—Islamists cannot do without one even if they give it a different name.

On the whole, these passages have a certain flavor of anarchism. Themes of strict and puritanical observance of Shari'a, together with a vague, anarchistic, and poorly articulated political model, appear alongside themes that are clearly unacceptable to Wahhabi theologians today. For example, the defense of *ijtihad* suggests that the authors do not understand the details of the theological disputes over *ijtihad*. They even erroneously associate it with the process of issuing fatwas. In the process, they clearly support such Salafi fatwas as those obliging men to wear a beard.

There are other deviations from classical Salafi revivalism as well—in particular, the claim that issuing fatwas according to the spirit of the era of the Caliphate is unreasonable and that one should adjust to the dictates of time. This, however, does not suggest "a certain tendency toward modernization."[111] Instead, it implies an understanding that the Uzbeks are accustomed to the reverence of saints and other practices that are categorically unacceptable to the Wahhabis and that atavistic fundamentalist appeals will be rejected in the region. Certain adjustments, then, are necessary to ensure the appeal of the Salafi *da'wa* (appeal or call to Islam).

The irreconcilable attitude toward infidels—Christians and Jews, who must turn into "things" to be owned by Muslims—also testifies to the extremist quality of the *Lessons*. Here again somewhat contradictory elements are discernible. If the goal is the establishment of an Islamic state within Uzbekistan, it will not be necessary to make an issue out of the insignificant number of non-Muslims living in the republic, particularly because the "infidels" do not occupy command positions in the Uzbekistani state. If, however, the goal is a state that extends beyond the geographical limits of today's Uzbekistan, which the reference to infidels might suggest, other parts of the document imply that the objective is something different from Islamic rule in Uzbekistan. Were Christians and Jews not specifically mentioned, one might conclude that "infidels" refers to Uzbekistan's rulers, people whom the Salafis do not consider Muslims. If so, it follows that the Salafis should subject these false Muslims to *takfir* (an accusation of godlessness), but there is no evidence that they have.

The following passage describes what will happen to Uzbekistan under its "state of infidels":

> As a result of your [subversive] actions, anarchy and disorder are appearing in the state; corruption, larceny, and murders are escalating; and order among government officials has been upset and they will begin to devour each other. The SNB [National Security Service] will begin to devour the Interior Ministry and so on. If disorder is not stopped, the SNB will begin to permanently check the work of the Interior Ministry. So they will start killing each other and themselves.
>
> The state will impose a curfew. It will begin to strongly torment the people. This is to your advantage. *Comment*: Forces opposed to the state will appear.
>
> Whatever the troop strength the state would muster, it will collapse, as the internal order in it will be broken. This means that immunity will be gone [and] its fatal outcome will be there for all to see. You should carefully analyze and get to know this time. *Comment*: This is similar to a stomach cold.
>
> The same happens to the state of infidels. They will start to devour each other, and there will be no force that can resist you. The army will be able to protect itself only.
>
> You should take advantage of such a moment. From now on you have to learn such fine policy—that is, help the people financially and with kindly words, and so on. *Comment*: What did Lenin do? He was with the people all the time. The one who is going to topple a state should always be with the people.
>
> For example, the Decembrists all came from the intellectual milieu. They lost their struggle. The revolution was made by the Jews on Lenin's behalf. But the people do not understand anything. Like sheep, [they] can only eat. [They] will not even ask: "Where are you leading me?" The Americans are also like sheep, as they have no faith and ultimate goal.

These passages are obviously addressed to an older generation, not to the fifteen to twenty year olds who are usually the main target of Islamist propaganda. Although it appears that the document dates from 1999 to 2000, it might also include passages that date from earlier periods—we know that it is common for texts to wander from one Islamist document to another. People born in 1980–1985, whose political identity was formed during the early years of Uzbekistan's independence, almost certainly do not know who the Decembrists were. In fact, they do not even know who Lenin was, and so the claim that Lenin was "with the people" is hardly likely to be convincing for them. Nor do Uzbek youths have a clear idea of what the Bolshevik revolution was about. The claim that it was brought about by the Jews on Lenin's behalf thus has little meaning to them.

Perhaps, then, the *Lessons* were written by former Communist propagandists who had become Islamists. For them, it is difficult to write anything without mentioning Lenin. Another clue here is Babajanov's remark that the description of many "secrets" and tactics of guerrilla warfare were borrowed from secular films about guerrillas during World War II.[112] Again, this would suggest that they have a memory of the war. The strategy of a campaign of sabotage is also explained by drawing on examples from daily life ("a flea on a dog") and also with reference to the models of diversionary guerrilla tactics elsewhere (Vietnam, Afghanistan, Chechnya).

The uncertainty and vagueness of the ideological platform of Islamic extremists, the fluidity and changeability of their positions on the one hand and the simplicity and even primitivism of their main principles on the other, perform an important practical function. It consists in the need to facilitate recruitment of a maximum number of people as members and sympathizers, including people from various social strata and with different educational levels.

The obsessive and shoddy eclecticism of the *Lessons* is evident in its treatment of "the people." On the one hand, the people are supposed to be with the militants, who are going "to topple the state." On the other hand, they are treated as utterly stupid and like sheep that crave to fill their bellies. Americans, too, are sheep-like because they lack faith. Are the people who have faith, then, not sheep? It is therefore evident that the *Lessons* are written in the voice of an elite that stands above the people. Babajanov and Olcott's assertion that the treatise is in essence egalitarian is in my opinion incorrect. Rather, the *Lessons* are like the doctrine of *'amma* (the common herd) and *khassa* (the selected ones), which was advanced by esoteric Islamic sects in the Middle Ages, such as the Ismailite Batinites. The intent is to instill in the minds of the future mujahedeen a feeling of "chosenness." The people, the common herd, are merely instruments in the hands of the revolutionaries who will bring down the state, just as Lenin and the Bolsheviks brought down the Provisional Government.

At the same time, however, the "people" play a role in the action program of the militants:

> Let the people always be with you, as otherwise you will start to be superseded by the infidel armed force. It is then that they will be necessary [to]

you. They will work for you: in collecting information, or distributing the information you need, and will help secretly to spoil the machinery of the infidels, to prepare explosives for you beforehand in the villages and at small enterprises, which should always be linked to our center.

We have to study the possibility of manufacturing explosives in the countryside. There we have to attract those who are not enlisted into the army—invalids, patients who can be trained to produce explosives. For example, we will have to blow up some bridge. And we have only antitank mines. They can destroy the bridge only partially. Therefore we need an expert in the manufacture of explosives. We also need experts on weapons that are hard to import. Then we have to organize its production in the countryside as well. . . .

Thus the weakest part of society is called upon to help with the manufacturing of explosives, despite the fact that the rural population does not fit the authorities' profile of those who are inclined to engage in terrorism. According to Babajanov, the *Lessons* also addresses subjects such as the chemistry of explosive substances, the tactics of fighting in mountain areas and in urban surroundings, the tactics of underground work in cities and in villages, and so on.

Babajanov also notes that the propaganda, or the *da'wa*, of the Ferghana extremists does not fit with traditional Islamic teaching. In particular, it is heavily politicized. It is in the first stage that politics and *da'wa* (*siyesat wa da'wat*) are joined together closely. Moreover, *da'wa* must be directed mainly at rural inhabitants because they "are far from sumptuous and parasitic life and their hearts are full of resentment." The appeal, then, is to the discontent of rural inhabitants over low salaries, delays in their payment, and so forth.

Significantly, *da'wa* must be combined with active misinformation through portable radio stations, newspapers, and leaflets.[113] According to Babajanov, this misinformation includes denying that Islamists participate in the terrorist acts they commit. One of the purposes of terrorism is to undermine the economy, which will in turn promote the growth of discontent on the part of the people and lead them to support the Islamists. It is not clear, however, just how they expect to convince the public that the state is responsible for the terrorist acts the Islamists commit.

The *Lessons'* authors probably took it into account that the mujahedeen, most of whom are young, are trying to mobilize older Uzbeks who were raised under Soviet socialism and still feel a certain nostalgia for Soviet-era egalitarianism, one that provided everyone with stable, albeit meager, wages and a secure tomorrow. These people, the "invalids and patients" who will have to produce explosives for the militants in their homes, still respect Lenin, who symbolizes for them that mysterious "radiant Communist tomorrow," alluring in its affluence, but which never quite came to pass. This is the reason why the shepherds of these "silly rams" allude to the leader of the Bolshevik revolution, and why they refer to the war of Soviet guerrillas against the fascists, references that are entirely familiar to the senior generation and that for them are still a matter of great pride.

In sum, we can discern a very cynical three-part hierarchical scheme in the *Lessons*. At the top are the leaders (including the authors of the text). Below them are the active militants who tower above the ordinary people (it is to them that the sermons and instructions of the leaders are addressed). And, finally, at the bottom is the general population, which is supposed to support the Islamists' program for changing the existing order. So the program is elitist in its nature, rather than egalitarian.

The leaflets issued on behalf of IMU leaders also provide material that helps reveal the movement's political platform. As after the events of February 1999, the movement was deprived of the possibility of active operation inside the country, and while the forced departure from Tajikistan dealt an even greater blow to the IMU's potential, foreign Islamic extremists started to reproach it for "postponing" jihad for too long. Replying to critics, IMU leaders confirmed their adherence to jihad, as attested by the following document I received in Margelan and translated from Uzbek:

THE IMU'S MESSAGE OF JIHAD TO ALL UZBEKISTANI BRETHREN, ÉMIGRÉS, AND FIGHTERS FOR THE FAITH IN CHECHNYA

I think I have to begin with the 20th *ayat* of the *sura* Tawba.

I call on all brother émigrés and fighters for the faith to fear Allah alone and only with his blessing to take a firm decision on the furtherance of righteous causes, especially the cause of jihad. The Prophet Muhammad indicates: he who strives for the word of Allah to be above all is the only genuine follower of Allah.

'Umar b. al-Khattab said the following parting words to Sa'ad al-Waqqas, head of the mujahedeen for fighting in Iran: "I order you and your subordinate mujahedeen under any circumstances to fear Allah alone. Because the fear of Allah is the strongest means during the fight against enemies."

Honorable brothers in faith. Let there be an endless amount of gratitude to Allah: it was He who taught us to take the path of holy jihad. On this occasion the Prophet gives such parting words: by following the path of Allah, you may join jihad. Because this is one of the doors to paradise. Thus Allah purifies one from woes and sorrows.

In the system of fiqh there is one principle: "Each thing for perfect fulfillment must have its instrument." In keeping with this, pursuing jihad without society is a futile affair. The enemies of Islam in the world are struggling after having become united and in a disciplined way. The Muslims of the resistance must likewise marshal their ranks and struggle after having coalesced into society.

(continued)

Allah had spoken about this in the 4th ayat of the sura Sof. 'Umar b. al-Khattab said very clearly about this: "Islam without society cannot exist. Society cannot be without its sovereign. And a sovereign does not exist without obedience."

In keeping with this, we demand from all mujahedeen in our ranks to submit to their military leaders if these have not fallen into sin, to fulfill with obedience even that work which is not to one's liking.

In the history of Islam there are too many examples of so much harm that was done by deeds performed without obedience. A graphic example of this are the events of February 16, 1999, in Tashkent. Willfulness in performing this deed did enormous harm to jihad in Uzbekistan; thousands of Muslims landed in jails of the infidel regime. We, of course, recognize their conformity to Shari'a. However, each action must conform to three criteria, and only after this can one embark on it: (1) conformity to Shari'a; (2) resources for fulfillment; (3) harm that does not outweigh benefits.

The argument, ascribed to the IMU, that "jihad must be postponed" is absolutely deniable. We understand perfectly well that it is impossible to defeat the infidels without arms. However, the launching of such a large-scale undertaking without a corresponding political, economic, and military preparation will inevitably cause unfounded losses. The infidel regime understands this quite well, too. Therefore, it is trying to create a political situation that could draw the Muslims into a premature struggle. The IMU is starting the armed struggle without hesitation. However, only its supreme leadership will determine the date and place.

Brother mujahedeen, let us draw conclusions from the events that passed. Let us not repeat our past mistakes and let Allah give us the power to elevate the word of Allah not only in Uzbekistan but also the world over; let Him strengthen our determination to build our Islamic Caliphate anew. *Amin.*

IMU Commander-in-Chief
Muhammad Tahir "Faruq"

THE IMU AFTER SEPTEMBER 11

During the antiterrorist operation in Afghanistan after September 11, some IMU militants (the exact number is unclear) fought alongside the Taliban. As the tide of battle turned against the Taliban and its allies, there were intermittent media reports that IMU fighters had fled the bombing and returned to Central Asia. The Kyrgyz press reported in 2002 that Tajikistan's Ministry of Security, supported by the CIA, had conducted a search for IMU forces in the mountains of Tajikistan but had failed to find any evidence of an IMU presence.[114] The American administration, however, felt differently. The State Department claimed that the IMU was continuing to plan terrorist acts.[115] It also asserted that the IMU still represented a serious danger to Uzbekistan and the region. But had the IMU been demoralized or had it retained its potential? And if the latter, where were its militants?

Again, according to reports from Uzbekistan, IMU militants were allegedly using their former bases in Tajikistan and being assisted by their former Tajik Islamic allies.[116] But IMU members who had fallen into the hands of Uzbekistani special services reported that the IMU military leadership was for the time being hiding in Pakistan. And a British observer claimed in November 2002 that Yuldashev had fled either to Iran or Pakistan.[117]

As far as Namangani is concerned, there have been many contradictory reports that he was killed in a battle between the Taliban and the Northern Alliance. General Abdurashid Dustum, who became deputy defense minister in the government of Hamid Karzai, was the first to report Namangani's death. He asserted that Namangani had been killed in the fighting around Kunduz. The Taliban also confirmed his death, but said that he had been killed near Kabul after being summoned to attend a military conference of the Taliban leadership. Since then, the deceased has repeatedly, and mysteriously, been resurrected, only to die once again. There were claims that he had been seen alive and unharmed in Kunduz during the bombings. But in March 2002, there was a new acknowledgment of his death. When the Northern Alliance, with American support, took control of the Balkh province, they captured Taliban fighters who revealed under interrogation that Namangani had been killed during the assault against Mazar-i Sharif. Later, the son of Uzbek militant Husain Alimov claimed to have participated in Namangani's funeral in November 2001 in Afghanistan's Tahor province.[118] Supposedly, only Yuldashev, Namangani's nephew Abdurahman, Alimov's son, and a bodyguard were present. Alimov's son reiterated the story that Namangani had died on his way from Tahor to Mazar-i-Sharif after an American bomb hit his car. Nevertheless, in July 2002, the secretary of Kyrgyzstan's Security Council, Misir Ashirkulov, claimed that Namangani was still alive and once again preparing attacks on the Ferghana Valley. And Ashirkulov also resurrected the charge that Namangani's fighters were regrouping at bases in the Tajik region of Gorno-Badakhshan. The Tajik authorities and then the Foreign Ministry of Kyrgyzstan vigorously denied these claims, however.

In August 2002, a Russian website asserted that IMU militants were planning an operation to shoot down American and Russian military aircraft.[119] The website identified the individuals who had been charged with carrying out the operation, including their surnames and aliases, and it also identified those who had given the orders. The aircraft were to be downed by portable antiaircraft missiles, and supposedly the orders to carry out the mission had come from Kunduz and had been given to a commander who was based in the Sogd region of Northern Tajikistan. The attacks themselves were to be mounted from Tajik territory. In all likelihood, however, this report was spurious.[120] It was apparently based on information from an intelligence report that was written in a clumsy bureaucratic style with an obviously false surname for a signature—*qazi* Nizametdin. The report, which was reproduced in a Russian newspaper, reads in part:

> In October 2001, Juma Hojiev (Namangani) from Kunduz gave an instruction to Ilhom Hojiev, then residing in the Tavildara district of Tajikistan, and to Rasul Okhunov, a native of Uzbekistan, alias "Bakhtiyar," "Lieutenant," residing in that period in the RT Sogdian region, to commit terrorist attacks on U.S. and Russian aircraft with the use of portable rocket launchers. Responsibility for committing this terrorist act was placed on Ilhom Hojiev.
>
> Russia was not accidentally targeted by the IMU bandits for this action, as that country stepped up military and humanitarian aid to the anti-Taliban coalition in Afghanistan through the territory of Tajikistan. The bandits planned to commit attacks against U.S. military aircraft in Tajikistan and Uzbekistan in connection with the starting of the antiterrorist operation in Afghanistan. *Wallahu bi-s-sawob. Qazi* Mir Nizametdin.[121]

There was renewed speculation about impending IMU operations at the end of 2002. Ahmed Rashid, writing in October of that year, suggested that "scattered militants" from the IMU might soon unite with other regional radical groups under one leader, although that leader would possibly not be Yuldashev. The real danger, he asserted, was that "some of the elements" of the Central Asian Islamists might "try to link up with Gulbuddin Hekmatiar."[122] In addition, the head of the Kyrgyz National Security Service, Kalyk Imankulov, stated that he had obtained information that indicated that members of different radical groups might be "attempting to join forces in a single organization." The IMU, HTI, Uighur separatists, and Tajik and Kyrgyz Islamists were, he claimed, joining together in an organization called the Islamic Movement of Central Asia (IMCA).

It is doubtful, however, that these diverse movements and organizations, which have quite different agendas, could ever be united. As Abduljelil Karkash, president of the Munich-based East Turkistan Information Center, has noted, the goal of the Uighurs, for example, is to achieve independence from Beijing, "an aim that has little in common with the IMU's agenda."[123] Nor would there be any clear benefit from such an alliance. Some observers believe that Imankulov was deliberately spreading misinformation in order to heighten anxiety over the terrorist threat in Central Asia and thus secure additional support for Kyrgyzstan from the West. Still, reports persist that the IMCA is preparing attacks on

Western targets in Central Asia. Uzbek sources, however, have so far reported little "visible change in the pace or volume of IMU recruiting," although one consultant in October 2002 expressed the expectation of "a series of sabotage incidents targeting domestic and international military bases" in Uzbekistan and Kyrgyzstan "in the immediate future."[124] Others shared these fears, suspecting, like Rashid, that the IMU or some successor organization would target foreigners in Central Asian countries in order to "show the regimes to be vulnerable and unable to protect foreigners."[125]

There has also been much speculation about possible cooperation between the IMU and al-Qa'ida. With its leaders and operatives now in hiding, it was not clear whether al-Qa'ida could mount an operation in Central Asia, even if it wanted to. Nor was it clear if such a dangerous alliance would benefit the IMU. However, it is clear that IMU militants who had been fighting alongside the Taliban in 2001 escaped to Pakistan together with al-Qa'ida members. Moreover, the Islamic parties that later formed the government of the Northwest Frontier Province of Pakistan had traditional links to the IMU and, in the words of Rashid, these parties "could sustain the IMU in the future."[126]

To determine whether there is any reason why these groups could come together in such alliances, one should grasp the political objectives of the IMU jihadists. Are they focused on the local situation, do they have a broader regional scope, or are they oriented toward global projection? Thorough examination of the insufficient written sources and scarce evidence obtained in the field suggests the IMU leaders are primarily motivated by an Uzbekistan-oriented agenda. To topple Karimov's regime and to replace it by an Islamic state ruled by the Shari'a law is their main goal. But this does not mean that they would not side with those who support them outside their country, as they have already done more than once. Moreover, because the IMU militants for many years have been conducting their activities and mobilizing support abroad, international projection would help them acquire growing significance. The events that unfolded in the region after the 2001 battles in Afghanistan confirm this judgment.

THE STRUGGLE AGAINST ISLAMIC
TERRORISM IN UZBEKISTAN

After the events of February 1999 and the ensuing terrorist attacks of the extremists, the Uzbekistani authorities cracked down on a massive scale against all those suspected of complicity with, or the slightest sympathies toward, the Islamists. In the opinion of many foreign analysts, Karimov's harsh repression not only of Islamists but also of ordinary believers in Uzbekistan has been counterproductive, feeding radical sentiments and widening the IMU's base of support.[127] While Karimov has been strongly criticized by the international community for violating human rights,[128] he has seemed to remain convinced that ruling with an iron fist is the best way to protect the stability and security of Uzbekistan and to secure his position politically. Arrests and repression continue accordingly, despite the fact that the defeat of the Taliban has improved Uzbekistan's security and deprived Karimov of one of his excuses for a strong reaction at any hint of liberalization. The U.S. State Department has concluded that "there were about 300 arrests in the first seven months of 2002 on religious or political grounds, compared with 1,500 on average in any seven month period in 1999–2001."[129] U.S. officials had hoped that, by the end of 2002, the figure would be five hundred to six hundred.[130] The Independent Human Rights Organization of Uzbekistan (IHROU) estimated that in December 2002, about 6,400 people remained imprisoned on political and religious grounds in the country. "Of those arrested on grounds of religious activism, about 1,200 to 1,700 are considered 'Wahhabis' (i.e., members of radical Sunni Islamic groups), 4,200 to 4,300 members of Hizb at-Tahrir, and 600 to 700 are pious Muslims not belonging to any political religious organization."[131] Yet another human rights group offers an even higher estimate, claiming that there were "up to 30,000 political and religious prisoners" in Uzbekistan in 2002.[132]

As David Isby, a Washington-based expert, believes, "Governments in Central Asia continue to be criticized for using the terrorist threat to justify repressive policies. But this sort of invocation of the terrorist threat does not diminish the continued danger that the terrorist threat poses."[133]

Still, the counteraction to Islamic extremism even in Uzbekistan was not limited to punitive measures. Right after the February 1999 events the authorities in Uzbekistan decided that it was impossible to manage the Islamic extremists with harsh police measures alone. It was resolved to develop and actively utilize the institution of municipal neighborhood communities—the *mahallas*. Everywhere in these, the councils of elders—*aqsaqals*—began to form; these councils received support from the state and channeled financial assistance to the *mahallas* (one *mahalla* may comprise up to several hundred households, the number of residents usually totaling no more than five thousand; a council of elders, as a rule, consists of six to eight persons). The *mahalla* councils make it possible to control the situation in residential areas, while government agencies may obtain information on the situation in the neighborhood and prevent mobilization actions by the Islamists. Furthermore, the development of these councils, consisting in the transfer of certain governing functions to them, is viewed as a step toward the development of local self-government, along with the observance of local customs.

As A., one of the high-ranking officials in the government of Uzbekistan, reported to me in a confidential interview, in her opinion, the republican leadership's support of the *mahalla* in the hope of helping it to control the sociopolitical situation is misguided.[134] On the one hand, authorities' support of the *mahalla* and the daily contact of government representatives (including those of the law enforcement agencies) with the *mahalla* councils indeed help in monitoring the situation in the localities, revealing undesirable tendencies and counteracting them, while exerting an influence on the population.

In particular, it was to a certain extent with the help of the *mahalla* that it became possible to counteract the spread of radical Islam. The government, according to A., wishes to represent the growth of the *mahalla*'s influence as a trend toward the development of civic society, and it is partly succeeding in this—many Western partners of Uzbekistan and representatives of international institutions see in this the sprouting of local self-government, the formation of which is important for Uzbekistan's transition toward democracy, while keeping its own identity and cultural traditions intact.

However, on the other hand, A. suggested, the *mahallization* leads to a retraditionalization of society, undermining modernization. Moreover, it bears in itself an antisecular potential and paradoxically promotes the realization of the Islamists' objectives. This is manifest, in particular, in the sharp strengthening of the positions of local mullas, without whose sanctions no question can be decided in the *mahallas*. Today a mulla is loyal to the authorities, and tomorrow he can go over to the side of the radicals, A. believes. This viewpoint has a significant number of exponents in the modernized Uzbek intelligentsia.

Be this as it may, *mahallization* helps the government to oppose the Salafi influence. It is the desire to cut the ground from under their feet that explains the campaign against certain popular customs incorporated into local Islam, resumed by the official clergy of Uzbekistan loyal to the regime and controlled by it. The Salafis successfully capitalize on the fact that the observance of these customs is costly and wasteful for ordinary people; therefore their calls to repudiate them as running counter to genuine Islam fall on fertile soil. Continuing the tradition of Mufti Ziyauddin Khan Babakhanov, the current leadership of the Directorate for the Muslims of Uzbekistan also argues against feasts into which funeral repasts turn on the twentieth day, the fortieth day, and a year after death, against the appearance of new places of mass pilgrimage, against quackery, and so forth. Below is a translation from Uzbek of an excerpt from a fatwa by Mufti Bahromov on December 28, 2002.

FATWA ON THE STANDARDS OF HOLDING WEDDINGS, FESTIVE OCCASIONS, AND FUNERAL REPASTS

Fatwa Requirements

1. The *imam-khatibs* of all official institutions of our Republic should in their appeals during Friday prayers, basing themselves on the basic principles and living examples, carry on a broad explanatory work on the material and spiritual damage wrought by luxuries, vanity, and pompousness, and at the same time on the benefits of moderation and modesty in the holding of weddings, celebrations on occasion of the birth of a child, and other public events.

2. The *imam-khatibs*, jointly with the *mahalla aqsaqals* and activists, should submit their proposals and recommendations on how to successfully hold festive occasions with due regard for national and religious traditions.

In the course of realization of these tasks, each *viloyat* (region) and *tuman* (district) must take into consideration the customs peculiar to each *mahalla*.

3. It should be explained that the holding of funeral repasts, made customary on the seventh, twentieth, and fortieth day, as well as on the first anniversary of death and during the *khaits*, does not conform to Shari'a. It should also be explained that after a man's death [only] three days are considered to be the days of mourning.

4. Instead of great costs required in holding *khudoi* and funeral repasts, it is better to render homage to the deceased by offering material aid to the needy families, orphanages, residential and old people's homes, or to allocate funds for municipal improvements.

5. In view of the negative consequences of the organization of morning pilaus [traditional local meal made of rice and meat], especially in Tashkent, on occasion of weddings, births, and jubilees [steps should be taken], jointly with the *mahalla aqsaqals*, for such ceremonies to be held at 7 or 8 a.m. or at dinner time. The *imam-khatibs*, jointly with the *mahalla aqsaqals* and representatives of women's committees, should carry on explanatory work on the negative impact on our Oriental culture [caused by] luxuries and throwing money [at the guests] during nighttime wedding festivities.

6. Not to hold pompous celebrations before, during, and after the weddings with the participation of women. Ceremonies during the *khaits* in the houses where a new daughter-in-law has appeared should be held for one day within a circle of relatives, after having arranged all questions with the *mahalla* and women's committees.

7. Considering that the Ramadan and the Kurban-khait are sacred holidays, all the families should commemorate them with joy. In other words, it should also be explained that one does not have to go to a public prayer in groups, nor should we turn these days into a time for play.

8. The *imam-khatibs* are instructed to submit without fail to the Directorate for the Muslims of Uzbekistan evidence on how the requirements of this fatwa are being observed. All the rites prescribed by Shari'a must be performed by the official *imam-khatibs*.

9. Those *imam-khatibs* who will be lazy and fulfill their duties negligently have to bear in mind that appropriate measures will be taken toward them. Let

Allah help us in all our good deeds [intended] for the purity of our religion, comfort of our motherland, and well-being of our people!

Chairman of the Directorate for the Muslims of Uzbekistan
Mufti Abdurashid *qari* Bahromov
December 28, 2002[135]

The Directorate for the Muslims of Uzbekistan (DMU) and the Islamic University (set up under government auspices) likewise oppose extremists by publishing pamphlets and books, including those devoted to very delicate questions of Islamic doctrine and practice: democracy and Shari'a, women in Islam, the HTI, and so forth. The Islamic University is playing a growing positive role in the religious life of the republic.

The return to the country of young people who have received their schooling in religious educational institutions in the Middle and Near East creates difficulties for Uzbekistan's official clergy. Many of these people have become adepts of radical Islamist doctrines. However, as Chairman of the Uzbekistan Committee on the Affairs of Religion Minavvarov told me in a conversation, they are not being thrown out on the street (as is done in Tajikistan, where such people are not appointed imams of mosques), but assisted in employment, and thanks to this environment they return to the fold of tolerant, moderate Islam.[136] Officials of the Committee on the Affairs of Religion and the Directorate for the Muslims of Uzbekistan believe that stability in the republic is jeopardized, not only by emissaries of the Saudi Wahhabis or Afghan extremists, but also by emissaries of those groups experts view as having peaceful tendencies, such as the Pakistani Tabligh. The Tablighis, in the opinion of the local official clergy, in their activity in the early 1990s were "among the instigators of the disturbances." Members of the official clergy also told me that they did not think the entrenchment of Sufism, as opposed to fundamentalism, to be the way to stabilize the situation in the republic. As I was told in a conversation at the Islamic University with one of the high-ranking DMU leaders, Shaykh Qabbani of the United States, during his visits to Uzbekistan, praised moderation, but "in fact wanted to turn Uzbekistan into a branch of his brotherhood," something he was not allowed to do.

Thus the policy of the authorities and the official Islamic institution in Uzbekistan, if one is to believe these claims, differs radically from, for example, that of the leadership of one of the North Caucasian republics of Russia, Daghestan, which has also been confronted with the threat of Salafi expansion, but relies upon local Sufi brotherhoods, whose shaykhs have acquired an enormous influence. As claimed by one of the members of the Council of *Ulama* who was present at the session I attended, the positions of the Sufi brotherhoods are the strongest in the Surkhan Darya and Bukhara regions, as well as in a portion of the Ferghana Valley (where the Naqshbandiyya shaykh Ibrahim Hazrat of Kokand is especially well known).

Independent students of Sufism also acknowledge the growth of Sufism, but they don't tend to exaggerate the influence of shaykhs. B. Babajanov writes: "The revival of Sufism is proceeding apace. Even now one may speak about forming the basis of an organizational structure—the *tariqa*—of that brotherhood [Naqshbandiyya], with a classic hierarchy and regional branches in the cities of Uzbekistan, the neighboring republics, and even Russia."[137] Babajanov even writes of such a new phenomena as the appearance along with the shaykhs of the "traditional *silsila*" of a multitude of impostors recruiting pupils and founding their circles (*halaqa*), which are particularly numerous in the Samarqand and Jizak regions.[138] Representatives of official religious institutions who have no Sufi background express an even more skeptical view, which probably reflects their envy of the easy popularity of the Sufi shaykhs. They stress that most of the Sufi shaykhs inherit their position without having acquired any religious education or culture. As Sabir *qari* Eminov, *imam-khatib* of the *vilayet* (province) of Ferghana, told me, "There is no mass rush for Sufism; *zikr* gatherings do not bring together more than a thousand people."[139]

But a fall in the Salafis' popularity naturally leads to the growth of Sufi influence. Contrary to the statements of the leaders of the Committee on the Affairs of Religion and the DMU, the authorities in Uzbekistan, like authorities in other republics (and also in Russia's North Caucasian regions), see in Sufism a counterbalance to Salafism, one controlled by the government and loyal to it, laying no claim to power. The growth of Sufi influence is also noticeable in the capital. As has been mentioned above, the Sufi orders are transborder institutions, with the same shaykhs extending their influence simultaneously to the inhabitants of the regions of Uzbekistan and South Kazakhstan. On evidence obtained from women's nongovernmental organizations, a vigorous inflow of women into Sufism is observable, with women visiting *mazars* on an especially massive scale.

Incidentally, it is possible that in the right situation the experience of Sufi brotherhoods can again be called for by the technologists of radical Islam, as has happened in the past.

MARCH 2004: VIOLENCE AGAIN

In March 2004, after a massive offensive in the tribal areas near the Pakistani border with Afghanistan, Pakistan's authorities asserted that it was IMU militants who had constituted the core group of fighters surrounded by Pakistani troops. The Pakistani military targeted Tahir Yuldashev, who was allegedly in command of the militants. Later they suggested that he had been wounded during the Pakistani offensive and had narrowly escaped capture. The Pakistani generals assessed that roughly five hundred militants in the village of Kaloosha in this region were mostly Uzbeks and Chechens, with the remainder thought to be local tribesmen. Sevdar Husain, the Pakistani commander of the counterinsurgency operation, reported that military communications experts had intercepted radio transmissions in both Chechen and Uzbek.[140] It remained unclear, however, to what extent the Pakistani crackdown on Islamic militants diminished the IMU's capabilities.

On March 28, five years after the February 1999 events in Tashkent, a new wave of violence began that lasted for several days and swept not only Tashkent but also Bukhara. Uzbekistani officials swiftly declared that the insurgents had been preparing a series of large-scale terrorist attacks in the republic but were forced to expose themselves prematurely because of the successful work of the law enforcement bodies, then carried out some explosions and attacked police checkpoints, and only authorities' alleged awareness of the planned acts of violence averted great loss of life among the population. Nevertheless, during the bombings and gunfire of March 28 to 31, based on government data, no less than forty-seven persons, including four civilians, thirty-three militants, and ten police officers (but probably many more) lost their lives.

Just as in 1999, the authorities hastened to shift the blame for the terrorist attacks on the Islamists, at first identifying HTI and then the IMU as organizations suspected of having perpetrated the terrorist attacks. The insurgent activities were proclaimed to be the result of conspiracy of international terrorist organizations. The HTI immediately reacted by protesting. It has not gone unnoticed by observers that the new flare-up of violence took place in Uzbekistan shortly after the Pakistani army had struck a blow against IMU militants led by Yuldashev. According to a version based on the assumption that there was a direct link between the events in Pakistan and Uzbekistan, the surviving part of the militants had been forced out of Pakistan, possibly to the Central Asian republics. Authors of another version linked the events with revenge meted out by the "Islamist International" upon Uzbekistan as a country in which American troops are based. Certain exiled Uzbek oppositionists, just as in 1999, suggested that the events were a settling of scores between competing clans or government agencies.

Most Western and Russian political scientists dismissed these speculations as preposterous and not supported by evidence, but at the same time they stuck to a dominant belief that the March events in Uzbekistan had purely internal underlying reasons and could hardly be considered to have been the mere result of conspiracy by external forces. (Incidentally, violence in Tashkent started almost immediately after an old man was brutally killed at a Tashkent market by police.) Government repression fosters further Islamist radicalization, violent actions by Islamic radicals prompt the government to intensify repression, and it is becoming harder and harder to break this vicious circle of violence. Uzbekistani officials, for their part, continue to insist that their country has been confronted with a terrorist conspiracy from the outside for the purpose of destabilizing the situation inside. "To think that what has happened was caused solely by socioeconomic reasons, would mean to oversimplify matters a great deal," Uzbekistan foreign minister Sadyk Safaev was quoted as saying by the Interfax agency in April. "Poverty is not the reason for extremism and terrorism, just as wealth does not offer an immunity from these phenomena."[141] In the view of official spokesmen, the fact that for the first time in Uzbekistan female suicide bombers participated in the events attests to the existence of links between the perpetrators and al-Qa'ida. But the Central Asian society was already familiar with women suiciders, as long before the appearance of radical Islamic insurgency some women burned themselves protesting cruel and unfair treatment of women by their relatives. We also cannot disagree with O. Roy, who commented, "As far as we know, most of the female suicide bombers were just members of families whose members are in jail, and it was some sort of a protest against the police in Uzbekistan."[142] Roy also said that the Uzbek events "bore all the hallmarks of an indigenous revolt."[143]

After the March events, the government of Uzbekistan unleashed a sweeping campaign of arrests of persons suspected of participating in Islamist activity and organizing conspiracy with the aim of overthrowing the legal authority in the country. Reports have appeared that about four hundred people were arrested and that "a tightening of basic liberties was in the offing, possibly including new restrictions placed on access to foreign-based media."[144]

Human rights organizations expressed increased concern over the possibility of new, more severe persecutions of believers. Even before the March events, Human Rights Watch reported, "Despite the government's assertion that these persecutions are a response to terrorism, in fact in the vast majority of cases we researched, those imprisoned were not charged with terrorism, or even with committing any act of violence."[145] Many Western think tanks also severely criticized Karimov's policy toward believers. A report issued in February 2004 by the Institute for Foreign Policy Analysis insisted that "the combination of economic hardship and political repression provides ample breeding ground for extremist Islamic movements."[146] The report criticized President Karimov's reluctance to implement reforms and his repression of all opposition forces. The authors of the report believed that the strategic alliance with Uzbekistan undermined U.S. regional security interests, "potentially lending credence to Islamic extremist characterizations of the United States as a cynical, self-serving power."[147] Considering U.S. military presence in Uzbekistan as a reward to its leader, the authors of this report called for diversifying the military presence and particularly relying upon Kazakhstan instead of Uzbekistan.

This view was not supported by those political scientists and governments who took a more cautious position toward Tashkent and expressed their solidarity with the Uzbekistani authorities, especially after a heretofore unknown organization, Islamic Jihad Group (Jama'at), claimed responsibility for the violence. This group asserted that in the future it would resort to wider and more violent attacks on Karimov's regime. Surprisingly, Kazakhstan said there was a link between Jama'at and a similar group in Kazakhstan, and Vyacheslav Kasymov, who heads the Shanghai Cooperation Organization's antiterrorist center in Tashkent, reported that mobile phones found at the homes of suspects in Uzbekistan showed they had called phone numbers in Kazakhstan.[148] It was unclear, however, whether this group was an offspring of the Uzbek organization (and consisted of ethnic Uzbeks) and possessed the same Uzbek agenda or was a local group that had its own goals inside Kazakhstan.

"We need to support Karimov's efforts to crack down on terrorism, then move to democracy," said a veteran U.S. policy maker to *EurasiaNet*.[149] Intelligence analysts in both Washington and Moscow, as well as in some European capitals, saw a connection between terrorist acts in Uzbekistan, Spain, and Great Britain. Some U.S. officials even characterized criticism of Karimov under the existing circumstances as inaccurate and damaging to the U.S.–Uzbek strategic partnership, and a senior Bush administration official told EurasiaNet on condition of anonymity: "The human rights community and many in the media do not accept or understand what global Islamic threat is, and do not know what is really going on in Uzbekistan."[150]

The Russian authorities have also expressed full support to the government of Uzbekistan in connection with the violence and threat of destabilization. Supporters of Karimov point out that in conditions of terrorist threat on the part of radical Islamic groups supported from the outside, it would be shortsighted to expect President Karimov to effect measures for the democratization of the country's political life. By way of comparison, some Western commentators mention the experience of such states as Taiwan, Turkey, and South Korea, whose journeys to more democratic governments lasted for decades.

Speaking at a press conference on April 29, 2004, President Karimov again mentioned the IMU, saying that the origins of the March attacks in

Tashkent and Bukhara are now clearer and that remnants of the IMU were responsible for them. He also said "that evidence from people arrested in connection with the attacks—particularly maps allegedly in their possession—showed they came from Pakistan."[151] Karimov said that the trials of the forty-five suspects would be fair and open to the media.

On July 30, 2004, three (based on other evidence, two) suicide bombers blew themselves up near the U.S. and Israeli embassies in Tashkent. The Uzbekistani authorities identified one of the bombers as a citizen of Kazakhstan, an ethnic Uzbek named Avaz Shoyusupov (all the perpetrators of the spring terrorist attacks also had supposedly been Uzbeks).[152] Almost simultaneously with the explosions near the embassies came the blast in the main building of the State Office of the Public Prosecutor-General in Uzbekistan. There, too, it had been the work of a suicide bomber. The responsibility for the terrorist attacks was claimed by a little-known Islamic Jihad group in Uzbekistan, but the official Tashkent authorities (as well as the Israelis) suspect the complicity of al-Qa'ida and the IMU in this terrorist attack.[153]

The July terrorist attacks coincided with the trial being held in the Uzbek capital of fifteen Islamists suspected of organizing a series of explosions in March–April in Tashkent and Bukhara.[154] It is impossible to definitively determine whether the IMU can reemerge or has already reemerged as an active player in Central Asia and is again capable of mobilizing supporters for violence. Also, it is possible that the IMU has been or will be reborn under a different name. What is clear is that opportunities for launching new operations in Uzbekistan under the auspices of the IMU are much more limited now than they were before September 11, 2001, because of the tremendous risks for the regime's opponents of associating with an organization that the international community has designated a terrorist group. As a result, political opposition is much more likely to gravitate today toward the nonviolent but clandestine radical Hizb at-Tahrir al-Islami.

NOTES

1. See Bakhtiyar Babajanov, "O fetvakh SADUM protiv 'neislamskikh oby-chaev'" (On the fatwas of the Spiritual Board of the Muslims of Central Asia against "non-Islamic rituals"), in *Islam na postsovetskom prostranstve: vzglyad iznu-tri* (Islam in the post-Soviet space: a view from inside), ed. Alexei Malashenko and Martha Brill Olcott (Moscow: Moscow Carnegie Center, 2001), 180.

2. Shamsuddin Babakhanov, *Mufti Ziyauddin Khan bin Ishan Babakhan* (Tashkent: Uzbekiston milliy encyclopedia, 1999), 12.

3. According to Babakhanov, these shaykhs lived in the vicinity of medieval Sayram, sixty to seventy kilometers from present-day Chimkent. (See Bakhtiyar

Babajanov, "Vozrozhdenie deyatel'nosti sufiiskikh grupp" [The revival of the activity of Sufi groups], in *Sufizm v Tsentral'noi Azii* [Sufism in Central Asia], ed. A. Hismatullin, St. Petersburg: St. Petersburg University, Philological Faculty Publishers, 2001, 336.) This researcher tells us that the fact in question had been discovered by another Tashkent scholar, Ashirbek Muminov, on the basis of a study of a number of Yasaviyya family trees, including that of the Babakhanov family. In a conversation with me on August 3, 2003, Muminov confirmed that according to his evidence, the ancestors of the Babakhans had been Yasaviyyah shaykhs. This did not exclude the possibility that they might simultaneously have been (or later became) Naqshbandiyyah ishans, given that both Sufi orders were always intertwined.

4. M. B. Olcott, "Islam and Fundamentalism in Independent Central Asia," in *Muslim Eurasia: Conflicting Legacies* (London: Frank Cass, 1995), 234–35.

5. Shamsuddin became mufti after the death of his father, Ziyauddin Khan, in 1982. He was likewise a highly educated man, an expert in Islam, but was deposed from his post by the radically minded believers in 1989 as a result of incitement on the part of the "new" clergy, who accused him of being loyal to the Communist regime and of failing to observe the norms of Islam in everyday life. I had for a long time entertained friendly relations with Shamsuddin; he warmly supported the idea of this book, which I shared with him, and promised every kind of assistance (in recent years, after returning from Saudi Arabia, where he was Uzbekistan's ambassador, Shamsuddin had been working in the Foreign Ministry of the republic), but unfortunately he died an untimely death in 2003.

6. One may hope that the efforts of Uzbek researchers in studying the legacy of the teachers and scholars of twentieth-century Central Asian Islam will rescue from oblivion the names of both al-Tarabulsi and many other Islamic scholars who had played an invaluable role in preserving Central Asian Islam.

7. Significantly, the first Soviet diplomats who came to Hijaz in the mid-1920s regarded Wahhabism with sufficient sympathy, seeing in it an "anti-imperialist potential." This can be traced through the correspondence of the first Soviet ambassador in Saudi Arabia, Karim Hakimov, an ethnic Bashkir, and even later through the letters of the second Soviet ambassador, Nazir Tyuryakulov, an ethnic Kazakh, both Muslims.

8. Bakhtiyar Babajanov, Ashirbek Muminov, and Martha Brill Olcott, "Muhammadjon Hindustani i religioznaya sreda yego epokhi" (Muhammadjan Hindustani and the religious environment of his epoch). Article submitted for publication in *Vostok-Oriens* (Moscow), 9.

9. Babakhanov, *Mufti*, 17.

10. See chapter 1 for differences between the *madhhabs*.

11. See, in particular, Babajanov, "O fetvakh."

12. Al-Qiziljari, whose full name was Hasan *khazrat* Ponomaryov al-Qiziljari, was a deportee from Petropavlovsk. Babajanov, Muminov, and Olcott assert that he was active in 1933–1937 and died in 1937. They also mention that, among those who influenced Islamic education in Central Asia in the spirit of strict adherence to the Qur'an and the Hadiths, there was also a Turkish immigrant. Turk *domulla* had arrived in the region from a part of Ottoman Empire; he was active in 1920–1930 (Babajanov, Muminov, and Olcott, "Hindustani," 9).

13. Being a young Russian Arabist at the end of the 1960s, I repeatedly interpreted at official meetings between Mufti Babakhanov and representatives of upper Islamic circles from the Arab countries and noted that they treated him with invariable esteem, not only as a representative of a superpower, but also as a religious authority, despite the fact that they viewed the SADUM as an organization controlled by the Communist Party and the KGB.

14. Meeting in Kokand on January 10, 2004.

15. Babakhanov, *Mufti*, 193.

16. Babakhanov, *Mufti*, 194.

17. Babakhanov, *Mufti*, 197.

18. Babakhanov, *Mufti*, 204.

19. Babakhanov, *Mufti*, 207.

20. Babakhanov, *Mufti*, 206.

21. Babakhanov, *Mufti*, 209.

22. See Babajanov, Muminov, and Olcott, "Hindustani."

23. This retelling of Hindustani's life is based on Bakhtiyar Babajanov and Muzaffar Kamilov, "Muhammadjan Hindustani (1892–1989) and the Beginning of the 'Great Schism' among the Muslims of Uzbekistan," in *Islam and Politics in Russia and Central Asia (Early Eighteenth to Late Twentieth Centuries)*, ed. Stéphane Dudoignon and Komatsu Hisao (London: Kegan Paul, 2001), 195–219 (Babajanov and Kamilov's work is based on autobiographical materials from the Hindustani family archive), and Muzaffar Olimov and Saidnazar Shokhumorov, "Islamskie intellektualy v Tsentral'noi Azii XX v. Zhizn' i bor'ba Mavlavi Hindustani" (Islamic intellectuals in twentieth-century Central Asia: the life and struggle of Maulawi Hindustani), *Vostok-Oriens*, no. 6 (November–December 2003). See also a detailed biography of Hindustani by Monica Whitlock, *Beyond the Oxus: The Central Asians* (London: John Murray, 2002).

24. Some other influential underground Islamic teachers of the Soviet period also came from Kokand, for example, Abdurashid *qari* (who is less known than Hindustani but also played an important role in the transfer of Islamic knowledge).

25. Olimov and Shokhumorov, "Islamskie intellektualy."

26. Olimov and Shokhumorov, "Islamskie intellektualy."

27. Babajanov, Muminov, and Olcott, "Hindustani," 7.

28. Ismail khoja, interview with the author on January 11, 2004, in his house in Kokand.

29. In 1966–1967, when I studied at Cairo University, Naima Kahharova was also taking training courses in Arabic there. She seemed to be interested in Islamic heritage.

30. Olimov and Shokhumorov, "Islamskie intellektualy."

31. Whitlock, *Beyond the Oxus*, 147.

32. Author conversation in Tashkent, September 3, 2003. See also Abdujabbar Abduvakhitov, "Islamic Revivalism in Uzbekistan," in *Russia's Muslim Frontiers*, ed. Dale F. Eickelman (Bloomington: Indiana University Press, 1993), 79–100.

33. It is said that once he was supposedly detained by the police for being in possession of a consignment of gold.

34. See Ashirbek Muminov, "Traditional and Modern Religious Theological Schools in Central Asia," in *Political Islam and Conflicts in Russia and Central Asia*,

ed. Lena Jonson and Murad Esenov, Conference Paper no. 24 (Stockholm: Swedish Institute of International Affairs, 1999), 109.

35. There are various occasions on which it has been customary to make presents or donations. For instance, when a student of a shaykh completed his study of a certain Islamic source, he made a present to his shaykh. This custom was called *maftana*.

36. Youssef Choueiri, "The Political Discourse of Contemporary Islamist Movements," in *Islamic Fundamentalism*, ed. Abdel Salam Sidahmed and Anoushiravan Ehteshami (Boulder, CO: Westview, 1996), 29.

37. Choueiri, "Political Discourse," 32.

38. Babajanov and Kamilov, "Muhammadjan Hindustani," 203–204.

39. Interview quoted in Olimov and Shokhumorov, "Islamskie intellektualy."

40. Babajanov and Kamilov, "Muhammadjan Hindustani," 214–15.

41. Conversation at Ishaq *qari*'s home on January 10, 2004.

42. Davlat Usmon, "Mirnyi protsess v Afganistane i yego vliyaniye na razvitie Islama i islamskikh tsennostei v stranakh Tsentral'noi Azii" (The peace process in Afghanistan and its influence on the development of Islamic movements in the Central Asian states), in *O sovmestimosti politicheskogo Islama i bezopasnosti v prostaranstve OBSE* (On the compatibility of political Islam and security in the OSCE space), ed. Arne Seifert and Anna Kreikemeyer (Dushanbe: Sharqi Ozod, 2003), 85.

43. Almost all those who have written about these organizations describe them as separate. This is inaccurate. For example, Ahmed Rashid, who focused on Adolat, argued that "other underground militant groups, including *Tawba* (Repentance), Islam Lashkarlary (Fighters for Islam), and Hizb-i-Islami (Party of Islam), also arose in Ferghana Valley" (See Ahmed Rashid, *Jihad: The Rise of Militant Islam in Central Asia*, New Haven, CT: Yale University Press, 2002, 139). Rashid also claims that Adolat was created by radical members of the recently formed Islamic Revival Party (IRP) of Uzbekistan, who were disappointed by the party's refusal to demand an Islamic state. As the imam of the Namangan mosque, Abdul Ahad told Rashid at the time: "The IRP is in the pay of the government, they want to be in parliament. We have no desire to be in parliament. We want an Islamic revolution here and now—we have no time for constitutional games (139).

44. See Muminov, "Theological Schools," 110.

45. Babajanov, Muminov, and Olcott assert that Tahir Yuldashev, with his religious group under the name Islam Adolati (Islamic Justice), broke off from the mainstream Adolat ("Hindustani," 15, note 9). This statement clearly contradicts the statements of some actors whom I interviewed, as well as some witnesses who spoke of a merger, not a split, and I have found no evidence of such a split in this group through my interviews.

46. Abdujabbar Abduvakhitov, "The Jadid Movement and Its Impact on Contemporary Central Asia," in *Central Asia: Its Strategic Importance and Future Prospects*, ed. Hafeez Malik (Basingstoke, England: Macmillan, 1994), 73.

47. Muhammadjan K., author interview, January 13, 1992.

48. Some religious and secular scholars use the term *Ahl al-Qur'an*, or *Uzun sakollilar* (Long-bearded), to identify a group of imams and religious scholars in Uzbekistan who until the beginning of the 1990s called on believers to rely almost

exclusively on the Qur'an and attacked Sufism, although I don't think that this group could have been attested as an organization (see Babajanov, Muminov, and Olcott, "Hindustani," 11). Former Mufti Muhammad Sadiq Muhammad Yusuf, according to these authors, considered as part of this group scholars who, according to my information, diverged in views on many matters, for instance, not only such well-known partisans of Salafism as Abduwali *qari* and Rahmatulla 'Allama from Andizhan and Abdullajan Makhsum *domulla* and Hakimjan *qari* from Margelan, but also Muhammadsharif Himmatzoda from Tajikistan and Tajibai *domulla*, Turdybai *domulla*, and Abu Turab Yunusov from Tashkent.

49. The manuscript is quoted with kind permission of the author (and translated from Uzbek).

50. Babajanov, Muminov, and Olcott mention several conservative mullas from Namangan ('Umar Khan *qari*, Abid Khan *qari*, Dawud Khan *qari*) who demanded the establishment of an Islamic state in Uzbekistan ("Hindustani," 17, note 42).

51. Abduvakhitov, "Jadid Movement," 74.

52. Abdujabbar Abduvakhitov, "Independent Uzbekistan: A Muslim Community in Development," in *The Politics of Religion in Russia and the New States of Eurasia*, ed. Michael Bordeaux (Armonk, NY: Sharpe, 1995), 297–98.

53. Muminov, "Theological Schools," 110.

54. Rashid, *Jihad*, 138.

55. Tashpulat, conversation with the author, November 19, 1991.

56. Like revolutionary Marxists and pan-Arab nationalists (especially Ba'th and the Movement of Arab Nationalists), Islamists also had an idea of "the weak link in the chain"—a country into which they rushed financial, manpower, and military resources, so as to ensure the establishment of an Islamic state there.

57. Abduvakhitov, "Independent Uzbekistan," 298.

58. Abduvakhitov, "Independent Uzbekistan," 296–97.

59. Abduvakhitov, "Independent Uzbekistan," 298.

60. However, to this day in Uzbekistan, unlike in Tajikistan, there is no special legislative act regulating the construction of mosques strictly in conformity with the number of believers in a community who wish to open the mosque.

61. Rashid, *Jihad*, 140.

62. Rashid, *Jihad*, 140–41.

63. Rashid, *Jihad*, 146 and 256–57, note 11.

64. Dilip Hiro, "Politics-Uzbekistan: Karimov Keeps His Gun Ready for Islamists," *World News*, Inter-Press Service, IPC/DH/RJ/98: 2.

65. Sulton Khamadov, "Mezhdunarodnyi kontekst—afganskii faktor (International context—the Afghan factor), in *Religioznyi extremizm v Tzentralnoi Azii: problemy i perspectivy* (Religious extremism in Central Asia: problems and perspectives) (Dushanbe: Organization for Security and Cooperation in Europe, 2002), 130–50.

66. Tamara Makarenko, "The Changing Dynamics of Central Asian Terrorism," *Jane's Intelligence Review*, February 2002, 1–2, at www.cornellcaspian.com/briefs/020201_CA_Terrorism.html.

67. Usmon, "Mirnyi protsess," 86.

68. Information passed on by Sanobar Shermatova to the author by e-mail in November 2002.

69. Materials provided by the Ministry of Internal Affairs of Uzbekistan, 1999.

70. U.S. Department of State, Uzbekistan, Country Reports on Human Rights Practices, 1999. Released by the Bureau of Democracy, Human Rights, and Labor, February 23, 2000, at www.state.gov/g/drl/rls/hrrpt/1999/369.htm, 11–12.

71. Department of State, Uzbekistan, 12.

72. Interview with Anvar Usmanov, conducted by Ludvig Gibelhaus, DW correspondent *Deutsche Welle*, January 24, 2003.

73. Usmanov, "Interview."

74. Makarenko, "Central Asian Terrorism," 3.

75. Oleg Yakubov, *Volchya Staya* (A pack of wolves) (Moscow: Veche, 1999), 224.

76. Yakubov, *Volchya staya*, 217ff.

77. Yakubov, *Volchya staya*, 224.

78. Interfax: 06-09b-1992, 17:22 (Uzbekistan/terrorists/trail).

79. Interview by Sanobar Shermatova on behalf of the author, December 13, 2002.

80. *Moscow News*, June 22–28, July 6–12, 1999.

81. By "clan" I do not necessarily mean a kinship, strictly speaking.

82. Interfax: 04-02–1999, 17:40 (Uzbekistan/appointment).

83. Interfax: 03-15-2002, 17:58 (Uzbekistan/president/councilor/appointment).

84. Olivier Roy, *The New Central Asia: The Creation of Nations* (London: Tauris, 2000), 156.

85. Zahid, author interview in Dushanbe, May 14, 1999.

86. Rashid, *Jihad*, 159.

87. Untitled document in the author's possession, 2002.

88. Rashid, *Jihad*, 160.

89. This official asked that his name not to be disclosed. Author interview in Tashkent, September 12, 1999.

90. Interfax: 08-24-1999, 18:40 (Kyrgyzstan/Uzbekistan/militants/expert).

91. TASS: 08-24-1999, 16:18 (Kyrgyzstan/terrorism/Azizkhan).

92. TASS: 10-11-1999, 10:26 (Kyrgyzstan/terrorism/militants).

93. *Vecherni Bishkek* (Bishkek), no. 163, August 23, 2002.

94. *Moya stolitsa* (Bishkek), August 30, 2002.

95. Misir Ashirkulov, interview by Sanobar Shermatova in Bishkek on behalf of the author in October 2002.

96. *Economist*, January 27, 2001.

97. Yakubov, *Volchya Staya*, 301.

98. See the IMU dossier at www.centrasia.ru.

99. Information provided by Sanobar Shermatova to the author.

100. Untitled internal document of an Uzbek law enforcement agency in author's possession, 2002.

101. Rashid, *Jihad*, 168.

102. Khamadov, "Afganskii factor," 147.

103. Khamadov, "Afganskii factor," 147.

104. This feature, as already mentioned, is characteristic of the greater part of radical and even moderate Islamic movements in the post-Soviet space. For example, all young men recruited by the local Wahhabis in Dagestan were engaged in contact sports training, in particular in various kinds of wrestling. There were

many sportsmen of the highest qualification among them, and all of them took shooting lessons. The youths who were studying Islam at a *madrasa* in Makhachkala were also actively engaged in karate, as I witnessed on several occasions.

105. The scope of the Islamists' combat training from the beginning of the 1990s until the first wave of arrests is not precisely known, but there surely was training. Nevertheless, during this early stage, Adolat does not appear to have planned a violent seizure of power, possibly because it was prepared to gamble on the weakness of the Karimov regime and believed (erroneously) that Karimov would eventually make concessions. Indeed, Karimov's invitation to dialogue with the Islamists in Namangan suggests that the latter hoped to represent themselves as a legal political force that could negotiate with the authorities, despite the fact that the authorities were doing so from a position of diktat.

106. Muminov, "Theological Schools," 110. The "Mullo Kyrgyz" *madrasa* in Namangan was believed to be the center of a network for training Islamic radicals. As has already been mentioned, in the beginning of the 1990s the Salafi mullas gained control over most of the mosques in the cities of the Ferghana Valley. This group of mullas, natives of the same region, came to serve in a number of mosques in Tashkent.

107. Bakhtiyar Babajanov, "Teologicheskoye obosnovaniye i etapy jihada v dokumentah islamskogo dvizheniya Uzbekistana, perevod i kommentarii Babajanova B.S. i Olcott M. B." (Theological justification and stages of jihad in the documents of the Islamic Movement of Uzbekistan, translation and commentaries by Bakhtiyar Babajanov and Martha Brill Olcott), *Kazakhstan-Spektr*, Almaty 3 (2002): 15–21. (The article is by Babajanov, while the commentary and translation are by Babajanov and Martha B. Olcott).

108. The Uzbek *Sovetniklari* is borrowed from Russian. Having a semantic association with the word "Soviet," the term was probably used by the authors of the document to emphasize how alien Uzbekistan government officials are to the national soil.

109. The Russian text by Babajanov and Olcott was translated by the author into English.

110. I am deliberately avoiding a claim that it was drafted by IMU ideologists.

111. Babajanov, "Teologicheskoye obosnovaniye," 19.

112. Babajanov, "Teologicheskoye obosnovaniye," 18.

113. Babajanov, "Teologicheskoye obosnovaniye," 18.

114. *Slovo Kyrgyzstana* (Bishkek), June 25, 2002.

115. Interfax: 10-02-2002, 10:42 (Uzbekistan/USA/terrorism).

116. Their locations were reported as follows: the *kishlak* of Khoit; the town of Garash, located three kilometers from Khoit; Chusal, located between Tavildara and Khoit, in the area of the Nazarailok coal mines of the Devanasu gorge (fifty kilometers north of Khoit); the *kishlaks* of Jirgatal and Takob (twenty-five kilometers north of the city of Dushanbe); the settlement of Akademgorodok, located between Kofarnihon and Dushanbe; Eski-matchi, Penjikent district; the settlement of Khovolang; the gold mine of Sovkhoz-2, in the *kishlak* of Childara; the Russia and Leningrad collective farms near Dushanbe, in the *kishlak* of Sari-Chinor, Kofarnihon district (the former sanatorium "House of the Cinema"); and the *kishlaks* of Chorku and Vorukh (the latter being an enclave in Kyrgyzstan).

117. Makarenko, "Central Asian Terrorism," 2.
118. Kto yest' kto v uzbekskoi oppozitsii. Doklad kazakhstanskikh spetsialistov (Who is who in the Uzbek opposition. Report of Kazakhstani specialists), October 24, 2002, at www.centrasia.ru/news2.php4?st=1035407100.
119. The document appeared on Russian websites, as stated in *Moskovskiye Novosti*, where it was published on August 18, 2002.
120. If we suppose for a moment that this information can be trusted, attacks had been planned for October 2001. In fact, after the start of the antiterrorist operation in Afghanistan, there was evidence that the militants were preparing actions against American forces in Uzbekistan. However, Russian military planes based in Tajikistan were never mentioned as targets by Islamic militants. Who felt the need to disseminate this information (or misinformation) nine months after a possible event, and why did they do so?
121. The document calls to mind one of the events of the summer of 2000, when there was a surge of dubious information about Tajik officials on the Internet, information that supposedly showed how, with the help of specific Tajik officials, IMU militants were able to organize their summer offensive in Kyrgyzstan and Uzbekistan.
122. Zamira Eshanova, "Central Asia: Are Radical Groups Joining Forces?" *EurasiaNet*, October 11, 2002, 2, at www.eurasianet.org.
123. Eshanova, "Central Asia."
124. Ibragim Alibekov, "IMU Reportedly Expands, Prepares to Strike Western Targets," *EurasiaNet: Uzbekistan*, October 29, 2002, 1, at www.eurasianet.org.
125. Alibekov, "IMU Reportedly Expands," 2.
126. Alibekov, "IMU Reportedly Expands," 2.
127. Most notably, the repressive measures carried out at the end of the 1990s forced many young religious Uzbeks to go underground or to flee to Tajikistan and Afghanistan, where they were recruited by the IMU.
128. For example, the first deputy assistant secretary of state told the House of Representatives: "We have repeatedly expressed our view to Uzbekistan's President Karimov that his persecution and repression of legitimate, peaceful practitioners of Islam is counterproductive. Rather than lessening the threat, he is actually radicalizing Uzbekistan's disaffected and disenfranchised youth and driving them into the Islamic Movement of Uzbekistan and its radical allies." See Michael E. Parmly, Testimony at the Joint Hearing of the Subcommittee on the Middle East and South Asia, "Silencing Central Asia: The Voice of Dissidents," U.S. Congress, Washington, DC, July 18, 2001.
129. "International Religious Freedom Report: Uzbekistan" (Washington, DC: Bureau of Democracy, Human Rights, and Labor, 2002), at www.state.gov/g/drl/rls/irf/2002/13990.htm.
130. "Uzbekistan's Reform Program: Illusion or Reality?" *International Crisis Group Asia Report*, no. 46, February 18, 2003, 5 (Osh/Brussels).
131. Interview with Mikhail Ardzinov, IHROU Chairman, Tashkent, December 9, 2002, quoted in *International Conflict Group Asia Report*, no. 46, February 18, 2003, 6.
132. Interview with Tolib Yakubov, HRSU Chairman, December 14, 2002, quoted in *International Conflict Group Asia Report*, no. 46, 6.
133. David Isby, "The Terrorist Threat in Central Asia: Resurgence and Adaptation," *Terrorism Monitor* 1, no. 13 (2004): 7.

134. A., interview with the author, August 16, 2003.

135. Uzbekiston musulmanlari idorasi raisi, Mufti Abdurashid *qari* Bahromov, *Tui, marosim va ma'rakalarni me'yorida utkazish haqida Fatvo,* December 28, 2002.

136. Shaazim Minnavarov, conversation with the author, September 2, 2003, at Islamic University, Tashkent. Minavvarov belongs to the family of Munavvar *qari,* a spiritual leader highly renowned in the past, and has served in the Uzbek Foreign Ministry since 1996. Munavvar *qari* was one of the leading Central Asian Jadids who after the Bolshevik revolution joined the Communist Party, though later he accused them of continuing old colonial policy.

137. Babajanov, "Vozrozhdenie deyatel'nosti," 333.

138. Babajanov, "Vozrozhdenie deyatel'nosti," 340.

139. Sabir *qari* Eminov, interview with the author, January 11, 2004.

140. Mike Redman, "Central Asian Militant Group Remains Active in Pakistan," *EurasiaNet: Eurasia Insight,* March 24, 2004, 1–2, at www.eurasianet.org/departments/insight/articles/eav032404_pr.shtm.

141. Interfax Agency, Moscow, April 4, 2004.

142. Bruce Pannier, "Uzbekistan: Karimov Elaborates on Recent Attacks, Criticizes West," *Radio Free Europe/Radio Liberty,* April 30, 2004, 2, at www.rferl.org/featuresartocleprint/2004/04/f9c2f480-2764-4463-ae16-0d3c7b99.

143. "US Failure," *Expert,* Moscow, June 24, 2004, 2.

144. Esmer Islamov, "Uzbek Officials: Preliminary Results of Investigation into Violence May Be Ready in Four Days," *EurasiaNet: Eurasia Insight,* April 1, 2004, 2, at www.eurasianet.org/departments/insight/articles/eav040104_pr.shtm.

145. Islamov, "Uzbek Officials," 3.

146. Jacquelyn K. Davis and Michael J. Sweeney, "Central Asia in U.S. Strategy and Operational Planning: Where Do We Go from Here?" (Washington, DC: Institute of Foreign Policy Analysis, February 2004), ii.

147. Davis and Sweeney, Central Asia, iii.

148. Bruce Pannier, "Central Asia: Is Uzbekistan the Source of Regional Extremism?" *EurasiaNet: Eurasia Insight,* April 30, 2004, 2–3, at www.eurasianet.org/departments/insight/articles/eav043004b_pr.shtml.

149. Ariel Cohen, "Bush Administration Backs Uzbek Response to March Militant Attacks," *EurasiaNet: Eurasia Insight,* April 14, 2004, 1, at www.eurasianet.org/departments/insight/eav04140a_pr.shtm.

150. Cohen, "Bush Administration," 2.

151. Bruce Pannier, "Uzbekistan," 1–2.

152. Arkadiy Dubnov, "Karimov znayet, gde 'zombiruyut' uzbekov" (Karimov knows where Uzbeks are being turned into "zombies"), *Vremya novostey* (Moscow), August 27, 2004.

153. Maksim Yusin, "Tri vzryva v Tashkente. Al-Qa'ida ili mestniye shahidy?" (The three explosions in Tashkent. Al-Qa'ida or local shahids?), *Izvestiya,* July 31, 2004.

154. Yusin, "Tri vzryva."

3

⪻

The Hizb at-Tahrir al-Islami:
A Peaceful Expansion?

It is hard to determine when the Hizb at-Tahrir al-Islami (HTI), or the Hizb at-Tahrir, active in Middle Eastern countries since the 1960s, extended its influence into Central Asia. Nor is it possible to affirm whether the first HTI cells that emerged in the region were local affiliates of a multinational network, and accordingly run from abroad, or constituted a purely local organization set up by foreign emissaries or by residents of Central Asia who had been indoctrinated abroad but returned to the region. Much evidence exists (for example, the fact that the HTI's foreign organizations are well informed about what happens in Central Asia; see, for example, the website of HTI Britain) that allows us to suppose the existence of links between the Central Asian HTI and the foreign Tahriris; however, the extent and character of these links can hardly be fully elucidated. This is explained, first and foremost, by the HTI's well-developed conspiratorial skills, its leaders in Central Asia having for many years remained underground, making no public statements and avoiding making political contacts that may expose them, behavior that is distinct from that of the Islamic Movement of Uzbekistan (IMU). At the same time, the HTI orients itself toward peaceful, political methods of opposition against the regime.

THE EMERGENCE OF THE HTI

An examination of the history of the HTI's emergence in the Middle East is beyond the scope of this work. We can only briefly mention that the HTI was founded in 1953 in Jordan by a Palestinian judge, Taqi al-Din Nab-hani (1909–1977), a member of the Palestinian branch of another Islamic movement, one that had existed since 1928—the Muslim Brotherhood (*al-Ikhwan al-Muslimun*).

Examination of Nabhani's life work allows us to trace the intricate link between Islamism and Arab nationalism. Nabhani's students note that he sympathized with the ideas of Arab nationalism, like many Arab intellectuals who were his contemporaries.[1] However, he belonged to those intellectuals of Mashriq to whom secular nationalism, which underlay major nationalist movements of the Arab world such as Nasserism, Ba'thism, and the Movement of Arab Nationalists (MAN), was unacceptable. According to Suha Taji-Farouki, the HTI, as far as its political structure is concerned, has much more in common with Arab secular nationalist movements than with the major Islamic political movement, the Muslim Brotherhood.[2] Nonetheless, there is enough evidence to suggest that Nabhani initially belonged to the Muslim Brotherhood, and some Arab researchers even viewed the HTI as an offshoot of the Muslim Brotherhood.

After Nabhani's death, his position as leader of the HTI was occupied by 'Abd al-Qadim Zallum (pseudonym, Abu Yusuf), a Jordanian national of Palestinian descent. Zallum died on April 26, 2003, and was succeeded by another Palestinian, 'Ata Abu al-Rushta (pseudonym, Abu Yasin), who had spent time in prison in Jordan and had been linked to the party since 1955.[3] The idea of jihad, as set out in the works of the HTI founders, was inspired by the Prophet Muhammad's struggle for the propagation of Islam. The Prophet's teachings and behavior were interpreted by the HTI founders in a modern context, so from the beginning they were far from being real Salafis, though many other features bring them close to the Wahhabis, for example, their goal of creating a world Muslim Caliphate and their deep hostility toward the Shi'a.

The Hizb at-Tahrir declares that "its aim is to resume the Islamic way of life and convey the Islamic call to the world." This means "bringing the Muslims back to living an Islamic way of life in Dar al-Islam (the domain of Islam) and in an Islamic society—such that all of life's affairs in society are administrated according to Shari'a rules, and the viewpoint in it is the *halal* (lawful) and the *haram* (prohibited) under the shade of the Islamic state, which is the Khilafa (Caliphate) State."[4]

The most puzzling aspect of the HTI ideology is its adherence to the idea of the Caliphate. Even in the context of the early 1950s, the Caliphate seemed anachronistic. The time of the Caliphate and the Caliphatists seemed to have long passed, for the last upsurge of the Caliphatists' activity in the 1920s was followed by an obvious loss of interest in the outdated ideas of the Caliphatists. A trend toward the creation of nation–states was clearly manifested by the growth of the national liberation movements in the Middle East after World War II. However, the utopian Caliphatism of the HTI cannot be adequately understood in isolation from the no less utopian conception of a single Arab nation, underlying Nasserism, Ba'thism, and the MAN (in spite of its apparent unfeasibility, this conception gave birth to short-lived unifying projects such as the United Arab Republic). The project of an Islamic Caliphate as an ideal based on the notion of Islamic *umma* was undoubtedly juxtaposed against the project of a single Arab state as an ideal based on the notion of a single Arab nation. Nabhani expanded the borders of an ephemeral hyperstate from the Arab (envisaged by nationalists) to the Islamic world, expecting to win over to his project more adepts than Arab nationalists could to theirs. His belief in the centrality of Islam in politics also had the potential to attract that segment of the nationally oriented population of the Arab world to which secularism was alien. Therefore, one can hardly reproach the founders of Tahrirism because their "understanding of the Caliphate is decidedly ahistorical."[5] On the contrary, the Caliphatism of the HTI was quite historical in the sense that its emergence was historically linked to the conflict between Islamism and secular nationalism. The fact that after half a century, the Caliphatism of the HTI managed to become an instrument of political mobilization far beyond the confines of the Arab world—for example, in Central Asia, at a time when secular Arab nationalism seems to have exhausted its resources—speaks for itself. In one of his statements in April 2004, the leader of Shi'a radicals in Iraq, Muqtada al-Sadr, declared: "Our aim consists in liberating *the capital of the Islamic Caliphate* [italics mine]— we want to free sacred an-Najaf from the clutches of the occupiers."[6] Thus the Caliphatist idea can rather unexpectedly emerge in slogans that are assigned to inspire and mobilize people in the Middle East.

The documents that are being currently distributed through the HTI website explain that the HTI is "a political party whose ideology is Islam." They read: "The oppressive rulers in Iraq, Syria, Lybia, Uzbekistan, and others have killed dozens of its members. The prisons of Jordan, Syria, Iraq, Turkey, Egypt, Lybia, and Tunisia are full of its members." The HTI believes none of the existing Muslim states can "truly" represent Islam and the Islamic system of government.

The argument in favor of precisely such an arrangement is simple: such a state did exist at the time of the Prophet Muhammad, and this circumstance in itself is a guarantee against the appearance of the ills of modern society—corruption, inequality, and injustice. The Islamists from the HTI admit that the construction of the worldwide Caliphate may be started in any individual country and then spread to other states.[7]

This is how the HTI visualizes the organization of the worldwide Caliphate, as stated in a leaflet made public in Dushanbe in December 2003.[8]

In the name of God the Merciful and the Compassionate

Structure of the Islamic Caliphate State

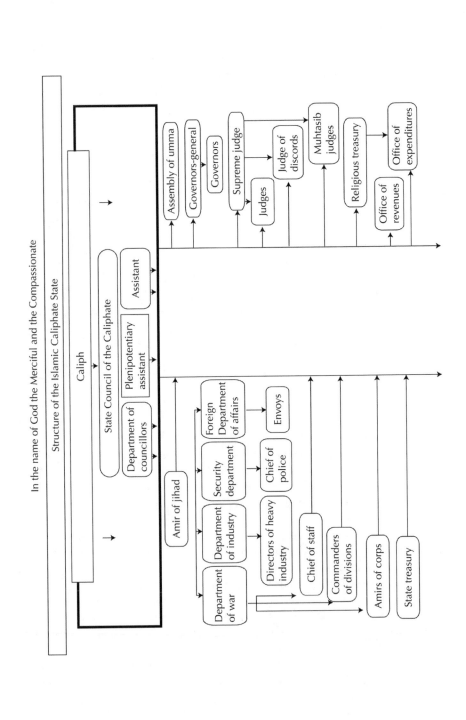

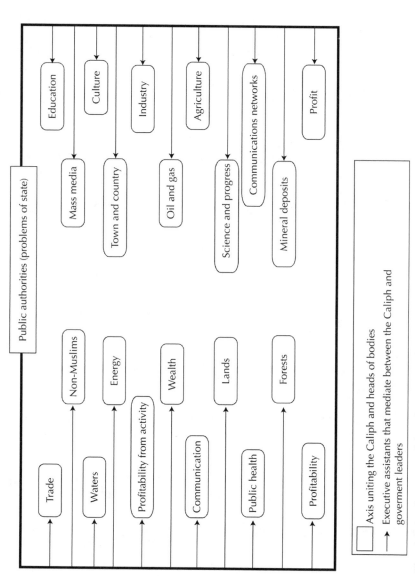

Public authorities (problems of state)

Education
Culture
Industry
Agriculture
Communications networks
Profit

Mass media
Town and country
Oil and gas
Science and progress
Mineral deposits

Non-Muslims
Energy
Wealth
Lands
Forests

Trade
Waters
Profitability from activity
Communication
Public health
Profitability

☐ Axis uniting the Caliph and heads of bodies

→ Executive assistants that mediate between the Caliph and
government leaders

Figure 3.1. Structure of the Islamic Caliphate State

The HTI is often believed to be intolerant toward other schools of thought in Islam. However, such claims leave its leaders indignant. The HTI leaders disagree with Rashid's statement that "HT leaders ignore the fact that the Ottoman Caliphate allowed many Islamic schools of thought to flourish, and even tolerated non-Muslim communities in places like the Balkans, all of which is contrary to HT beliefs."[9] HTI leaders regard this statement as an attempt to distort the HTI's image. They assert that "the Party accepts the existence of schools of thought today and under the Islamic state, such as Hanafi, Maliki, Hanbali, Shafi'i, Zaydi and Ja'fari schools." *The Islamic State,* one of the publications that the HTI disseminates, declares:

> The Muslims are united under the Islamic *'aqidah* and by the fact that the Qur'an and the Sunnah are the source of the Shari'ah evidences, principles, and verdicts. None of them has differed on this issue at all. However, due to *ijtihad,* they have differed in their understanding of the Qur'an and the Sunnah, and as a result of this divergence, *madhahib* has emerged, as have different sects. This was due to the fact that Islam encouraged Muslims to make *ijtihad,* inevitably leading to the disparate interpretations of their meaning. Differences emerged in the understanding of the concepts related to creeds and in the methods of extracting verdicts, as well as in the verdicts and opinions themselves. This resulted in the emergence of alternative Islamic sects and *madhahib.*[10]

This means that the HTI theoreticians acknowledge *ijtihad* and do not consider some trends in Islam infidel, as the "real" Wahhabis do. This explains their disagreement with Rashid concerning his assertion that "also like the Wahhabis, the HTI is violently anti-Shia; the group would expel all Shia Muslims from Central Asia if it came to power."[11]

In response to Rashid's book, the British HTI cites the aforementioned publication *The Islamic State,* which states: "All the sects and *madhahib* which embrace the Islamic *'aqidah,* and believe in the Qur'an and Sunna . . . these sects and *madhahib* are all Islamic, their advocates are all Muslims, and they are subject to Islamic laws."[12]

RELIGION AND POLITICS IN THE HTI'S IDEOLOGY

Two opposite views have been expressed concerning the type of training that HTI members receive. According to one, HTI members are so uneducated and guided by blind faith alone that any dialogue with them is impossible. According to the other, the theoretical training of HTI members is so formidable that entering into arguments with them is hopeless: this is feared, for instance, by members of the official Islamic institution of Tajikistan.[13] The former mufti of Kyrgystan asserts that "there are many well-educated and proficient propaganda specialists" in the HTI,[14] and that the official Muslim clerics are not able to debate with them effectively. Along the same lines, it should be noted that, first, as mentioned above, the HTI includes people with different levels of education and social standing. And here the Islamists' cadre structure highly resembles that of the leftist and nationalist groups. First, similar to all organizations of this type, many rank-and-file members, in addition to others, come from the lower strata of the population and have little interest in theory. At the same time, there is also a small intellectual elite.

In one of Nabhani's books published in Britain, the founder of the HTI explains that the first party cell was formed by persons "with an outstanding intellectual capability," and this cell began to multiply, though slowly. New people were bound "completely by the ideology." "The thinking of this first circle (the leadership) will be deep, and its method of revival fundamental."[15]

Second, the theoretical background of HTI members often bears a strictly religious character. It is a futile and hopeless affair for a secular researcher, often a Christian, to engage in theological arguments with a Tahriri who is well versed in the matters of his religion. Although a pious and religiously educated Muslim treats Christians with respect, as "people of the Holy Scripture," he nevertheless believes them to be "deviationists," if only because, in his view, "the belief in Christ as God Incarnate is a deviation from monotheism—no man can be God." Nevertheless, it is acknowledged that, for Christians, this belief is a matter of faith. In the same way, the idea of the Caliphate can be an object of faith for a Muslim, and only a fellow Muslim who interprets sacred texts in a different way can dissuade him from it. Disputes among Muslims themselves, champions of various doctrines and conceptions, largely concern exegesis, the interpretation of sacred texts. Third, some people are indeed guided exclusively by faith, following their teachers and preceptors. In such cases, the interviewer may also feel disappointed with fruitless attempts to find any common sense in the pronouncements of a member of the movement he has had the good fortune to meet. Those who tried to reeducate the Tahriris in prisons were unable to do so. I asked members of the official clergy allowed to take part in the reeducation process about the results of their discussions with the arrested Tahriris, and in most cases the arrested proved to be steadfast in their convictions. One of these clerics told me that the arrested Tahriris would be happy to die for their beliefs.

Moreover, recent research into the HTI's theoretical conceptions has not been able to clarify whether or not the party is guided solely by obsolete dogmas from books by Nabhani. The texts circulated on the Internet are intended mostly for educating HTI members and bringing them within the orbit of ideas whose acceptance is a definite marker for the Tahriris. In these texts, one can identify a number of uncomplicated dogmatic tenets designed to mobilize the Tahriris to concerted behavior. Just as in the early twentieth century it was enough for a rank-and-file Russian Bolshevik to arm himself with the slogans of the socialist revolution without necessarily grasping the rudiments of Marxist theory, and just as for a member of the Movement of Arab Nationalists in the 1960s it was enough to understand the need for unifying the entire Arab nation (*umma*), so for present-day Tahriris it is enough to come to believe in the idea of the Caliphate in order to be able to identify his affiliation with the IMU to another Caliphatist.

Aspiring to redeem the Islamic ideal exclusively through the installation of a Caliphate regime, a vision that presumes a paramount role for the caliph, the Caliphatists are drawing closer to the Iranian Shi'a conception of *vilayat-e faqih*, according to which the power of Islam, personified in the rule of *faqihs*, is the guarantor of the realization of the Islamic ideal. This gives occasion to certain researchers to regard the Caliphatists as greater authoritarians than many Salafis. In using the term *Caliphatist* in this connection, I consciously combine HTI supporters with other modern adepts of the idea of the Caliphate, in particular Jama'at al-Muhajirun. An in-depth comparison of the views of the HTI and al-Muhajirun is beyond the scope of the present study, but it is useful to get some general idea about the former.

Shaykh Omar Bakri Muhammad, currently the supreme judge of the Shari'a Court in the United Kingdom and the leader of al-Muhajirun, first associated himself with the Muslim Brotherhood, then joined the HTI in Lebanon, and afterward became the founder of this organization in the United Kingdom. In one of his recent interviews, he said that al-Muhajirun first had come on the scene on March 3, 1983.[16] The movement was established in Mecca, but Shaykh Muhammad launched it as a separate organization from the Muslim Brotherhood in Jedda on March 3—the fifty-ninth anniversary of the destruction of the Ottoman Caliphate—"with the help of a team of thirty-eight brothers who had been previously recruited by the shaykh to the HTI. As the shaykh said: "Some of these people were previously affiliated to Juhaiman al-'Utaiba[17] and some were Salafis." The shaykh called his new group al-Muhajirun (those who perform *hijra*, or migration), thus likening them to the followers of the Prophet Muhammed, who migrated from Mecca to Medina and by that migration laid the foundation of the Islamic state. This story shows how interrelated and transnationally wide all modern radical Islamic groups are and how often and easily the same people transfer from one group to another.

It is also hard to answer the question concerning the extent to which the Central Asian Tahriris are "internationalists" and the extent to which they are devoted to the idea of building an Islamic state in one or more states in Central Asia. This applies to the entire HTI. For the sake of comparison, one can refer to an assessment of Usama bin Ladin given by Olivier Roy. The French expert believes that the notorious terrorist "is not interested in the Islamic revolution: he wants the West to collapse first."[18] The HTI is another matter. Its objective is an Islamic revolution on a global scale, and the first step toward that end is the establishment of Islamic rule in a separate country or group of countries—a process that is directly analogous to the theory of revolution of Marxists and Arab nationalists. But it remains unclear in what way the Tahriris are going to achieve the overthrow of the existing regimes.

At the same time, within the party itself, as far as I can judge from some fragmentary evidence, there exists a certain religious theoretical and political discourse. Educated members of the movement engage in debate, and differences emerge, leading to ideological differentiation, a joining and regrouping of forces, a process that is to be fully expected in the case of a clandestine, antiestablishment movement. Islamic revolutionaries, like all others, need to have and do have their own ideological and political doctrine.

Shaykh Omar Bakri Muhammad argues that after Shaykh Nabhani's death in 1977, the HTI "experienced severe persecution by all regimes, and this led to retreat and stagnation."[19] On the split that occurred in the HTI in 1997, Shaykh Muhammad has said that "a man called Abu Rami and his followers" dismissed 'Abdul Qadim Zallum, who at that time led the organization from one secret location and established another. The Zallumis became HT Camp 1, which is stronger than HT Camp 2, which includes the followers of Abu Rami, the so-called *nakithun* (renegades).

For the people of Central Asian states, it is important what positions on religious questions a particular Islamic movement adheres to. As mentioned above, Hanbalism, especially in its Wahhabi interpretation, meets resistance from the bulk of believers and from the religious class, for whom traditions, especially those associated with the cult of saints (*ziyarat*, etc.) are an enduring value. There is an impression that HTI ideologists are trying to evade the theological and legal questions of Islam, including those referring to ritual, which allows them to avoid controversy with the believers. On these questions Nabhani is considered to have taken a position independent of the four *madhhabs* of Sunnism. The vagueness and eclecticism of the HTI's theological and legal platform enables it to retain its transnational status and gain supporters among Muslims belonging to different varieties of Islam. Nevertheless, a number of researchers believe that Nabhani was an adherent of Hanbalism on questions of law, rejecting in particular the tribal laws (*'urf*) and customs (*'adat*) that are conventional in Central Asia. Even if this is the case, this is hardly known to the masses of HTI followers in the region, since the instructors, as far as I know, do not touch upon this subject during lectures. The appreciation of other Salafis, including the jihadists, can be considered evidence of the theoretical strength of the HTI's tenets in the eyes of many Muslims. A great part of the appeal of the HTI to Central Asians, as mentioned earlier, lies in its transnational character. "Rejection of the nation–state as a concept (it was of course accepted as elemental political fact) . . . informs aspects of al-Nabhani's state-model," writes Suha Taji-Farouki. "The promotion of a single, universal Caliphate itself constitutes an implicit denial of the legitimacy of the modern nation–state."[20] I find it quite appropriate in this regard to mention the paradoxical observation by Graham Fuller: "Ironically, the Islamists are actually pursuing a modernizing course here—the effort to *move away* from the parochial nation–state toward regionalization."[21]

THE HTI AGAINST "CAPITALISM" AND DEMOCRACY

Within the framework of this study, it makes sense to touch upon only certain doctrines of the Tahriris, those that allow us to understand their ideological and political program. In particular, I refer to the renewed idea of Islam as a "third way," similar to the conception of the Green Book of Mu'ammar al-Qaddafi. The pamphlet *The American Campaign to Suppress Islam*, circulated via the website khilafa.com, speaks of the existence of three ideologies in the modern world: Marxism–Socialism, which "ended internationally," as well as the remaining two—"Islam and Capitalism." The pamphlet emphasizes the significance of Islam as an all-embracing doctrine that exists in the world as long as the Islamic *umma* will exist, even after the demise of the Khilafa State in 1924. Capitalism is viewed as an ideology of *kuffar*—infidels, including traitors from the Islamic world, who force their own people "to succumb to the yoke of *kufr*."[22] An anti-capitalist pathos today would seem to have little chance of being attractive. However, it has something in common, not only with the leftist ideas of the past, but also with the slogans of modern antiglobalists. The authors of the pamphlet, first published in 1996, seemingly ignore a multitude of works written on the subject of Islam and capitalism, as well as the fact that the greater part of present-day Islamists are well adapted to the capitalist economic system, which is hegemonic in the world today. The views set out in the pamphlet are archaic—they repeat the ideas expressed by the Islamic reformers in the late nineteenth and the early twentieth centuries. However, they are also somewhat innovative. Let us examine the main points in the critique of capitalism by proponents of this view. What is of interest is not only the sources of displeasure among the authors, but also what they see (or what he sees) as an Islamic alternative to these "Western concepts." The West imposes its conceptions on the Muslims out of "fears that the Islamic *umma* would make a return again and destroy its influence and interests not over its land, but over the whole globe."

The campaign to suppress Islam "through forcing the Muslims to embrace Capitalism" is based, as the authors assert, on "four slogans which essentially constitute the core of Capitalism: democracy, pluralism, human rights, and free market politics."[23] So the notion of Islam as opposed to capitalism is clear in HTI thinking. Do its authors reject democracy, and if so, why? According to the text, democracy is unacceptable for Muslims because "it makes the human being and not the Creator as the legislator."[24] Democracy in this view is a way toward a refusal "to follow the law of Allah," and people who accept democracy fall into the category of *kafir* (infidel, nonbeliever), *zalim* (oppressor, tyrant), or *fasiq* (transgressor). In fact, the list of democracy's sins does not go beyond putting "man in the place of the Creator," while "the remaining claims of democracy have no actual reality." Thus in democratic societies "people do not rule themselves," but in reality "are ruled by a certain group of influential people, such as the prominent capitalists in the United States and the aristocrats in England" (the British capitalists are for some reason not considered to be influential). In passing, it is said that "neither do claims to equality, justice, and accountability of the rulers" have anything in common with reality.[25]

Abdel Salam Sidahmed and Anoushiravan Ehteshami have spoken about "an inherent contradiction between the *absolutist* nature of Islamist ideology and the *relativist* character of democracy." In this view, it is a contradiction "between a force that sees itself as a custodian of the divine message, hence as having a monopoly on the truth, and a system built on relative truths and opinions." As Sidahmed and Ehteshami have observed, most of the Islamic radical movements "are happy with democracy as long as it provides them with freedom of organization and power."[26]

Equally unconvincing is the critique of pluralism, the main defect of which, in the opinion of the Tahriris, is that it "emanates from the Capitalist doctrine of detachment of religion from the worldly life." Furthermore, pluralism is guilty of the fact that it permits "the establishment of parties and movements that can call for a *kufr* doctrine or idea . . . on a basis prohibited by Islam, such as patriotic and nationalist parties."[27] This underscores the HTI's open hostility toward secular nationalist movements (this has been inherited from the era of confrontation between secular Arab nationalist movements on the one hand and the Muslim Brotherhood and other Islamist groups on the other). This hostility is caused, first, by the fact that such parties do not bear a religious character and do not endorse the conception of an Islamic state and, second, by the fact that they call for the creation of nation–states (even if this is a pan-Arab state), thereby fragmenting the Islamic *umma*. Finally, pluralism allows movements to exist "that call for things which Allah prohibits, such as sexual perversion, adultery," groups "defending gambling, drinking alcohol, abortion, and the use of women as sexual objects."[28]

A section on human rights says that only "Islam has prescribed the correct relationship between the individual and the community as a symbolic and fulfilling relation, and not a relation of incoherence."[29] In this section, the authors do not simply repudiate Western conceptions of human rights, but they also offer "a true," Islamic interpretation of the rights of individuals and society. The reasoning contained in this section even includes a sociological discourse: "The correct definition of a society is a group of individuals who share a permanent relationship." The champions of pure Islam call erroneous the view "of the Capitalist ideology on the nature of society, as well as its conception of human nature and the relationship between the individual and the community." Even more clear, the radical Islamists assert, is capitalism's "erroneous understanding of the function of the state."[30] In the final account, all freedoms (of belief, expression, ownership, and personal freedom) allegedly lead to bringing man down to the level of the animal, while society is governed by "hardship, disorder and unending anxiety." Freedom of belief does not exist in Islam because Muslims "are obliged to embrace the Islamic 'Aqeedah."[31] As for freedom of opinion, its realization encourages "immorality among women, vice, profanity, and corruption."[32]

Those reading the aforementioned pamphlet are not left with the slightest doubt that a Muslim is not allowed "to express any opinion that contradicts Islam." This point seems to be the key in this section. It also criticizes the Western conception of freedom of ownership, which "contradicts Islam and is therefore forbidden for the Muslims to accept." As a result of freedom, claims the HTI, "wealth is concentrated in the hands of a few." The resemblance to Marxism here is particularly striking. The populist nature of this critique is clearly calculated to attract the underprivileged strata of the population. Finally, on personal freedom, the Tahriris can say nothing positive either. They condemn the "capitalist" concept of personal freedom, arguing that the tenet that "every human being has the right to live his private life as he wishes unless he transgresses the private lives of other people" gives moral sanction to extramarital relationships, as well as the "practice [of] sexual perversion"; in short, "for these Capitalists, the concept[s] of *halal* and *haram* [do] not exist when it comes to personal conduct."[33]

The HTI is against pornography, telephone sex services, strip clubs, and generally all those elements of culture they identify as products of Western civilization and as perversions incompatible with the moral values of Islam. Also, the passages on these subjects are designed to win support among a population that broadly condemns these phenomena. The invocation of the traditional values of Islamic civilization and the Islamic way of life performs a great mobilizing function. The mention of *halal* and *haram* means that the authors' angry diatribes may primarily be addressed to Muslim states. Muslims cannot accept the principles of personal freedom, the authors claim, precisely because it "allows what Allah has forbidden."[34]

Free market policies likewise come under attack. They are designed "to open the markets of all the world states to their superior quality products and investments coming from the West. Such a policy will perpetuate the developing countries' economic and commercial subordination to the wealthy nations and will prevent them from building their economies on strong foundations."[35] This section suggests all the more that the HTI clearly calculates to fill the ideological niche vacated by the Communists. Although Islam, HTI theorists argue, "prohibits imposing customs on traders who are citizens of the Islamic state," it is unlike "the Capitalist concept" of "Free Market Policies," just as it is unlike socialism, though there are similarities between their slogans, and just as Shura in Islam cannot be associated with "democracy."[36]

"Only the *Khalifah* can re-unify you," runs the HTI message to Muslims, "to fight back mischief and evil. The *Khalifah* will return you to the true identity that Allah has designated for the Muslims—the best nation ever brought to mankind."[37]

For all the primitiveness, vagueness, and to a certain extent, archaism in the argument employed by contemporary HTI ideologists,[38] they successfully make use of both the invocation of sacred texts and social demagogy to garner support.

THE APPEARANCE OF THE HTI IN CENTRAL ASIA

Many experts from the region hold that the HTI did not appear in Central Asia until the late 1990s. Others claim that the HTI appeared there earlier and only came to public attention at the end of the 1990s. Saniya Sagnaeva writes that in South Kyrgyzstan the HTI "has become known" since late 1999, "when first arrests started after the Tashkent explosions, which affected not only the citizens of Uzbekistan hiding in the south of Kyrgyzstan, but also local citizens accused of belonging to the HTI."[39] Muhiddin Kabiri, deputy chairman of the Islamic Revival Party of Tajikistan (IRPT), claims that the HTI arose in Central Asia following the breakup of the Soviet Union. An expert from Uzbekistan, Bakhtiyar Babajanov, writes that the "peak of activity" of the HTI fell during the period 1998–2000.[40]

A former official of one of Uzbekistan's law enforcement agencies, Mirsaid, told me that as early as the mid-1980s, evidence on the appearance of Tahriri literature in the territory of the then Soviet republic had been documented. These included HTI ideological pamphlets translated into Uzbek (for instance, *Nizomi Islom*) and issues of the journal *al-Wa'y*, also in Uzbek. And the first clandestine Tahriri cells, he claimed, had been registered in the regions of the Ferghana Valley and in Tashkent in the early 1990s.[41] Be this as it may, the first HTI cells sprang up in Uzbekistan, then the party spread its influence to two other Central Asian republics, Kyrgyzstan and Tajikistan. The Ferghana Valley has become the focus of its activity. Uzbeks predominated and possibly continue to predominate in its membership. Based on evidence from the same Uzbek source, the bulk of the party is made up of unemployed young men, students, petty traders, and a section of the intelligentsia, while the HTI's intellectual framework consisted of young people with higher education who could not satisfy their "opposition ambitions" through legal political activity.[42]

An interesting piece of information on the HTI's formation in Uzbekistan is contained in a paper by one of the former IRPT leaders, Davlat Usmon, that formed part of a symposium published with the assistance of the Institute of Peace and Security Politics of the University of Hamburg. According to Usmon, that part of the Islamic Movement of Uzbekistan that in January 1992 did not join the then established Islamic Revival Party of Uzbekistan (see chapter 2) became part of the Hizb at-Tahrir al-Islami after the creation of the HTI's first cells there "and, as indicated by reliable sources, has no links with the IMU group in Afghanistan."[43] Usmon's version of events is based on a completely accurate conception of the existence in Uzbekistan until the 1990s of some kind of a common, amorphous "Islamic movement" from which activists began to join specific Islamic organizations as these were formed. This is consistent with the general organizational scheme, the merging and sprouting mentioned in chapter 1, and the flow of people between organizations. Some observers take this last phenomenon as evidence of links among these organizations (closely related as they are in terms of human capital), but such links can be completely absent. Moreover, erstwhile comrades and friends, having for whatever reason landed in opposing camps, sometimes become not only rivals, but enemies.

In general, Usmon believes that the HTI emerged in Central Asia, not due to the intrigues of outside forces, but as a result of misguided policies of Central Asian governments. He says: "Riding a wave of mass discontent, the Islamic radical organization Hizb at-Tahrir al-Islami came into being, calling for the creation of an Ottoman-like Caliphate. This makes the Tahriris the descendants of pan-Turkism."[44] He adds, "This is a product of the actions on the part of the authorities of Central Asian countries vis-à-vis their political opponents."[45]

What follows from this passage is not only Usmon's negative attitude toward the Central Asian regimes, especially the Karimov regime in Uzbekistan, but also his opposition to such a core element of HTI doctrine as Caliphatism, which Usmon vaguely associates with pan-Turkism and is traditionally given a hostile reception by both secular nationalists and Islamists.

In Uzbekistan, the HTI gained universal notoriety after the events of February 16, 1999. The Uzbek leadership was completely unprepared for such a turn of events and initially had no public explanation of who might have organized these terrorist acts. In a telephone conversation with the Israeli minister for industry and commerce, Natan Sharansky, President Karimov even blamed the terrorist acts on Islamic extremists from the Hizbullah party, probably meaning the HTI.[46] Other high-ranking officials named "Wahhabis" and the Hizb at-Tahrir as among those responsible. However, during the interrogation of those who were arrested for allegedly perpetrating the acts, it was discovered that it was the IMU, not the HTI, that had orchestrated them. During the trial, as was mentioned in chapter 2, Tahir Yuldashev and Juma Hojiev (Namangani), as well as the disgraced leader of the Erk party, poet Muhammad Salih, were named as the main instigators of the crime.

The testimony given by HTI members arrested by the Uzbek government provided an important, if far from flawless, source of data on how the HTI had been formed. According to information flowing from the court proceedings, the first party cells had been organized by 'Isam Abu Mahmud Qiyadati and Abd al-Qadim Zallum, who are referred to as "subjects of Jordan wanted by the Jordanian authorities."

Babajanov asserts that the Uzbek affiliate of the HTI emerged after the swift liquidation of Islamic extremist organizations of Namangan—Adolat, Islam Lashkarlari, and Tawba—by the security agencies of Uzbekistan in the early 1990s.[47]

Russian human rights activist Vitaly Ponomaryov writes that HTI activity in Uzbekistan can be traced from 1995, which is corroborated by the data of the Uzbekistani law enforcement agencies: the indictment in the case of the Tahriris in 1999 stated that HTI ideology was imported into Uzbekistan by the Jordanian Salah al-Din in 1995, and it was during the same period that H. Nasyrov and N. Saidamirov founded the Uzbek HTI affiliate and then its regional branches.[48]

It is notable that experts from the region mostly have to rely on materials obtained from the law enforcement bodies. This narrows the scope of their research, making it somewhat dependent on information supplied by the special services. Nevertheless, the statements of the arrested Tahriris suggest the information on HTI activity is not the fabrication of the Interior Ministries of Uzbekistan or Kyrgyzstan.

It cannot be asserted that HTI literature was only being brought into the region from the outside, although much of it was imported from the countries of the Middle East. There is evidence of this literature being published locally, at least from the late 1990s. Thus in April 1999, security forces uncovered in Osh, Kyrgyzstan, an underground print shop and confiscated one thousand copies of the book *The System of Islam* in the Kyrgyz language and a layout of a new issue of the journal *al-Wa'y* (Conscience). In the opinion of one Kyrgyz researcher, this attested to the presence of highly educated Kyrgyz citizens in HTI ranks.[49]

The minutes of the aforementioned court proceedings were compiled in a fragmentary and haphazard manner, but still it is possible to derive information from them and adumbrate a general pattern. In the summer of 1991, 'Isam Abu Mahmud visited Namangan, attending Gumbaz mosque and communing with the believers. Buses were booked and Mahmud, together with the believers, set off for Andizhan. In the Andizhan Jum'a mosque, Mahmud declared that a local section of the Hizb at-Tahrir party was being created. Abdurashid Kasymov was appointed leader of the section, and he took an oath there and then. The party's sections in other towns of the Ferghana Valley were set up in about the same fashion. They arose, as the minutes say, in Tashkent and in other Central Asian republics, Russia, and Ukraine.

During the first stage of activity, the organizers strictly forbade the believers to intervene in the work of government bodies and politics. But from 1992 to 1994, Abd al-Qadim Zallum and 'Isam Abu Mahmud were supposedly bringing HTI political literature—*The Statute of Islam, Taqqatul,* and *The State of Islam*—into Uzbekistan. A periodical—*al-Wa'y*—began to be published in the republic, and according to the party functionary Abdulla (the name is an assumed one), the publication now appears in the English, Urdu, Arabic, Russian, and Uzbek.[50]

ORGANIZATIONAL STRUCTURE OF THE HTI WORLDWIDE

Based on evidence given by the Tahriris who were arrested, one may reconstruct a general outline of the history of the Surkhan Darya branch of the HTI to illustrate the structure of HTI.

During his studies in the *madrasa* of the cathedral mosque of Andizhan, Abdulhamid Bekmuradov became acquainted with Hafizulla Nasyrov, like Abdulhamid, a native of the town of Denau, Uzbekistan. Both of them were taught religion by Abduwali *qari* (Mirzaev). After they finished their studies in 1995, Bekmuradov received from Nasyrov a book, *The Statute of*

Islam, by the party's founder, Nabhani. The book made a strong impression on Bekmuradov, and he decided to join the party. A year after, in the autumn of 1996, Bekmuradov swore allegiance to the party in the presence of Nasyrov.

Subsequently, Bekmuradov became the first Hizb member in the Surkhan Darya region and soon, with Nasyrov's help, set up a *halaqa* (circle) of three persons. In three years' time, in the Surkhan Darya region there existed a ramified network under Bekmuradov's leadership, including a *mas'ul* by the name of Bakhtiyar, under whose supervision there were six *naqibs*. Each *naqib* had three or four assistants, with a total of 135 *mushrifs*, 183 HTI members, and 337 *darises*.

Thus, according to Uzbek private sources, the party is built on the principle of a pyramidal hierarchy. It comprises several levels, and the party's primary cell is the *halaqa* (circle, local unit), comprising up to five persons.

Ahmed Rashid, referring to his conversation with one of the HTI activists in Central Asia, "Ali," writes that the HTI operates through secret, decentralized, five- to seven-man cells, which he calls *da'ira* (circle), rather than *halaqa.*[51] Whatever the real name and the real number of members of one "circle," it makes no difference as far as the principle of its action is concerned.

The cells are marked by strict discipline. The novices who come to a *halaqa* do not administer an oath immediately. Only after a lay brother who has passed a course of study firmly decides to associate his life with the party does he take an oath. Rank-and-file members are obliged to carry on propaganda work, familiarizing their acquaintances, neighbors, and colleagues with the party's aims and tasks. In the case of arrest, they are obliged to confess that they are party members. This requirement, however, does not apply to the leaders. Should an HTI member deny membership upon being arrested, the cell will expel him from its ranks. Iron discipline reigns in the organization: the office of an arrested *mushrif* or *mas'ul* is occupied by an organization member trained beforehand, who is forthwith notified of his new position. The remaining members of a *halaqa* accept the replacement of a leader without demur. In cases where a member refuses to follow an order, apostates are menaced with various punishments, for example, the suspension of party membership for a certain period of time, which entails a ban on attending meetings.

Based on evidence obtained from Uzbekistan government channels, the following persons were apparently HTI leaders for the Central Asian region:

1992–1996—Abdurashid Hozhimatovich Qasymov, b. 1960 in the Andizhan region, sentenced to twelve years in prison
1996–1999—Hafizulla Muzhahedovich Nasyrov, b. 1971 in the Surkhan Darya region, sentenced to twelve years in prison

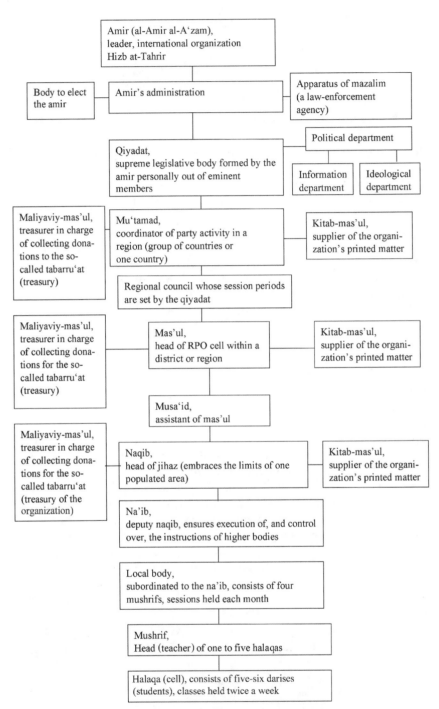

Figure 3.2. Organizational Structure of Hizb at-Tahrir al-Islami

1999–2000—Nugman Omonovich Saidaminov, b. 1972 in Tashkent, died of a heart attack in 2000

2000–2001—Istam Igamberdievich Khudoiberdiev, b. 1957 in the Surkhan Darya region, sentenced to twelve years in prison

2001 to the present—Abdurahim Abdurafukovich Tukhtasinov, b. 1970 in the Andizhan region, wanted by police

It is hard to ascertain if the Uzbekistani law enforcement agencies succeeded in arresting all the highest leaders of the Central Asian HTI and if the above-named persons were in fact such leaders. Doubts exist because if the police had in fact consistently managed to destroy the brain centers of the HTI, for all the conspiratorial skills of its leadership, the party would probably have been deprived of the capacity to act at all.

As I was told by IRPT insiders in Tajikistan, even they are in the dark about HTI leaders. This is consistent with information on some other countries. Thus the identity of the amir of the Pakistani HTI, as written by the authors of the International Crisis Group (ICG) report on the HTI, is unknown, and only one leading member of the HTI is known to the public—the official spokesperson, Naveed Butt.[52]

In addition to Central Asian governments, certain students of the HTI also accuse it of collaborating with the IMU. Ahmed Rashid wrote: "The HT members live in IMU camps and receive military training from the guerrillas. Kyrgyz officials report that during the IMU offensive in the summer of 2000, they discovered HT literature on the dead bodies of several IMU militants. Clearly there are strong links and cooperation between the rank and file of both groups, especially when members come from the same village or town."[53] But the HTI leaders always denounce all speculation about their relationship with the IMU. The HTI of Britain asserts that the HTI is "an independent Islamic political party and does not make any alliances with other groups. . . . The Hizb at-Tahrir is a political party that engages in intellectual and political work and does not involve itself in militant actions."[54]

It is hard to give an unambiguous reply to the question of whether all Caliphatists, and in particular the Hizb at-Tahrir al-Islami, are Salafis of a jihadist type. An analysis of their doctrinal precepts shows that they can only to some extent be deemed Salafis, insofar as they, like all sects, were inspired by the models of Islam from the times of Muhammad and the righteous caliphs. However, they do not preach the idea of *takfir* (as the Wahhabis do) and do not have a Wahhabi fixation on *bid'a*, which seems to be of no interest to them. The Caliphatists seemingly cannot be considered champions of violent jihad, as they have so far proceeded from an adherence to the principle of installing Islamic rule through peaceful means. But if the use of peaceful tactics is only an early stage of opposition, with violent struggle to follow, as some researchers suggest, this gives every reason to deem them jihadists. Such a suggestion is supported by the fact that the founder of the HTI, guided by an analysis of the experience of the Islamic state of the era of the Prophet Muhammad, speaks of three stages of political struggle:

1. The stage of culturing: "finding and cultivating individuals who are convinced by the thought and method of the party." They will then carry on the party's ideas.
2. The stage of interaction with the *umma*, in order "to establish Islam in life, state, and society."
3. The stage of taking over the government "and implementing Islam completely and totally, and carrying its message to the world."[55]

The Caliphatists, especially against the backdrop of "quiet Wahhabis," are exceedingly politicized. For them, the Saudi regime is historically unacceptable, irrespective of the degree of its adherence to pure Islamic norms and values. The Caliphate is the only possible alternative to the existing states, and in order to build it, one must ultimately ensure the departure of their ruling regimes. It is hard to believe that the Caliphatists expect to avoid violence in doing this.

The Tahriris also differ from the jihadist Salafists by calling for a dialogue with the Central Asian regimes that the Salafis label as infidel, pursuing their removal and elimination. These major differences may complicate any cooperation between the HTI and the IMU. Their relationship might be similar to the relations between two main groups of Islamists in Egypt. There the Muslim Brotherhood is opposed to the Al-Jama'a al-Islamiyya (militant, jihadist Islamic groups), mainly due to the former's rejection of the use of violence as a means of opposition. Furthermore, many attempts were made by the Muslim Brotherhood to accommodate itself within the existing political system without trying to overthrow the regime. In contrast, the Al-Jama'a al-Islamiyya turned this objective into its main political goal.

My conclusion is akin to the observation by Dekmejian, who noted the polycentric character of the contemporary Islamist movement. Despite their cohesiveness and pervasiveness, Islamist movements, in his view, emerge in response to local conditions,[56] so it is unlikely that they would join a common cause or, we might say, unite under the banner of the World Islamic Caliphate.

THE ROLE OF HTI NETWORKS

An analysis of the HTI's organizational structure indicates that that party was able to set up an effective patronage-type network. This distinguishes it from other Islamic organizations and may influence its political trajectory in the long run. Patronage and clan networks play a distinctive role in the social and political lives of Central Asian societies.

The patronage and other networks mentioned here cannot be fully understood without a separate discussion of the category of "network" in which analysts have taken a keen interest in recent years, especially after the events of September 11, 2001, widely acknowledged to be the result of transnational terrorist networks' activity. Perhaps this circumstance, or the mere in-depth study of the subject, has led to analytical generalization with respect to the network category. Michael Hudson writes: "A crucial structural feature of the new global and regional environment is the emergence of informal, transnational networks as an agent for change—and a challenge to American unipolarity."[57] In his approach, Hudson is inspired by Coleman,[58] who refers to examples of "culturally bound—networked—communities, such as the wholesale diamond market or the Cairo bazaar, in which a sense of community engenders trust and thus promotes collectively productive action."[59] In Hudson's view, the informal *hawala* money-transfer networks, which are believed to be a part of the "money trail" to fund al-Qa'ida, belong to the same category. Detailed analysis conducted by several authors attests to the importance of the network infrastructure in this part of the Islamic world, and this conclusion can equally be applied to the Central Asian reality. Among others, Islamist networks are regarded as particularly successful. As Hudson argues, "Islamist networks appear to originate in the 'old school ties' of schools and universities," and the same is true of the Arab nationalist movements that utilized alumni and student networks for their transnational political projects.[60]

However, the leaders of such an important pan-Arab movement as the Movement of Arab Nationalists, for example, did not at all limit themselves to the use of "school ties." This movement also made active use of pan-Arab labor unions and the oil fields of Kuwait, where workers from many Arab countries were employed and indoctrinated by MAN ideologists.

But if we are to speak exclusively about Islamist networks, the mosques and seminaries have been their main instruments for recruitment, and for their creation and expansion. As shown by the experience of all the Middle Eastern and Central Asian countries, the Islamist networkers have made the mosques and *madrasas* the strongholds of their organizational activity. For example, the vital role of the Deobandi *madrasa* in India in the formation and development of the Islamist network is widely known. The Islamic radical authorities, who did not necessarily use the mosque or the *madrasa* for networking and did not network themselves, served as the next major instrument of networking by providing ideological resources for organizers to deploy. In the pre-Internet era, their lessons and sermons were disseminated among Muslims on audiocassettes (see chapter 2), which have not lost their popularity in a number of countries to this day. To audiocassettes should be added videocassettes and TV broadcasts, which appeared later, while the Internet, which has slowly entered the world of Islam, has brought a new instrument of network recruitment that is even more effective, though not yet widespread. The global information revolution has become an agent of transformation for networking activities, having opened up truly global vistas for them.

Afghanistan, to which natives of various Middle Eastern states flocked to join the bands of mujahedeen struggling against the Soviet invasion, became the major location of recruitment. Not only were many of them initially not enrolled into Islamist networks, but likewise they had a rather pragmatic motivation, expecting simply to earn good money.

ARRESTS AND PROTESTS

In Uzbekistan, the Tahriris managed to create in the mass consciousness the image of a party operating deeply underground, merciless to renegades, and even impervious to repression. However, the minutes from the trial proceedings reveal that this understanding of the HTI's exceptional clandestine nature is exaggerated.

The rank-and-file Tahriris do not seem to be such skillful conspirators, if one recalls that lists of members of the regional branch were discovered during a search in the house of the *musa'id* Taniev (deputy leader of the Surkhan Darya regional organization). From reading the transcripts of court sessions, it becomes clear how ordinary believers, in principle loyal to the authorities, ended up among the ranks of this clandestine party.

People attend a mosque and listen to the imam's sermon, and sometimes they stay on in the mosque after the *namaz*, conversing about religion and the times of the Prophet and the first four faithful caliphs. In and of itself, this cannot be regarded as criticism of the regime, as nothing is said directly about the situation in the country and government policy. Then the imam, whom the believers trust, says that one has to go to Kyrgyzstan and Kazakhstan, where people are perishing in spiritual darkness, not knowing Islam, and one has to preach. This would be *sawab*, a deed pleasing to God. In the process, the preceptor strictly orders the believers not to speak about politics in their sermons. When some believers or even HTI members become aware that the authorities condemn the party about which they have been told in the mosque or which they have been persuaded to join, they themselves come to the district police, confess their mistake, and ask for pardon—the court materials tell of several cases of this kind. After the penitents promise to abandon the HTI, their names are recorded and they are released with no restrictions placed on their movements. However, after the explosions in Tashkent in February 1999, the authorities began massive arrests of these same individuals. The Uzbek police did not bother to search for party members in hiding and apprehended first of all those who had already repented and whose names had already been known. As a matter of secondary importance, they detained those who were pointed to as "Wahhabis" in the *mahallas*. To get on the "Wahhabi" lists, it was enough to behave in a way not accepted in the *mahalla* or to carry on propaganda espousing an Islamic way of life among neighbors. Therefore there were few HTI leaders among those arrested and convicted, as the former remained more carefully hidden than the rank-and-file members. The police and the National Security Service are not prepared to uncover the party networks operating underground. Instead of subtle intelligence work to reveal the clandestine operators, police prefer to cast a wide net and then extort the needed evidence from the accused, using methods that draw criticism from human rights activists. Most of the court sentences have been passed on the basis of the defendants' confessions.

The inefficacy of combating Islamists in general is also influenced by the fact that the republic's law enforcement bodies have a poor understanding of religious matters and religious parties and movements. The Uzbek secret services have managed to "clean up" the party's networks in some regions; however, many analysts believe the greater part of the leadership has managed to evade arrest. Having preserved its "head," the party may again rebuild its branches. Some researchers believe that the HTI has succeeded in sheltering a very substantial portion of its cadre from arrest.[61]

One may presume that a great share of HTI membership consists of women. Women have participated in numerous demonstrations; however, these participants are mostly relatives of those arrested for allegedly belonging to these Islamist organizations.

Nonetheless, when mass arrests of those suspected of organizing the July 1999 explosions in the Uzbek capital led to simultaneous demonstrations by women in two cities—Tashkent and Andizhan—the action was well prepared and coordinated from a single center. The women approached the city hall buildings in small groups, and as soon as the police detained them, others came to replace them.

Exactly the same kinds of demonstrations were held simultaneously in several towns and cities of Uzbekistan on September 4, 2001. The demonstrators were few—in Tashkent about ten women with children appeared near the building of the city hall and made an attempt to stage a demonstration. It was cut short by secret service officers, who blocked all the entrances to the city hall and, having forcibly put the women on buses, drove them away. A women's action in the town of Karshi, in which about sixty women took part, ended in the same way.

There is evidence that, after the mass arrests of Tahriris in Uzbekistan, their wives at first went to demonstrations demanding that their husbands be freed and then were gradually drawn into clandestine activity. "Seeing how her husband is treated by the police, a woman becomes convinced that she is following the right path. She becomes the continuer of his ideas," said a woman living in Tashkent, Munawwar, in a conversation with Sanobar Shermatova.[62]

Vitaly Ponomaryov uses the example of Uzbekistan to conclude that the number of women members of the Hizb at-Tahrir in Central Asian countries is on the increase: "Women in Uzbekistan have organized protest actions against the abuse and torture of their husbands. In the coming one or two years, women's role in that organization will grow." According to Ponomaryov, owing to the increased number of women in the ranks of the Hizb at-Tahrir, the actions of that movement will become more effective: "If men carry on any kind of actions, the authorities apply repressive measures against them without further thought. But when dealing with women, government bodies begin to waver before using force."[63] My contacts in Uzbekistan also reported cases when children under the age of fourteen disseminated HTI leaflets, not fearing criminal persecution.

The most famous Hizb at-Tahrir woman member in Uzbekistan is Musharraf Usmanova, who, in July 2002, was sentenced in Tashkent to two years in jail. She was released in the courtroom in consideration of her being pregnant and because she had six children. In this case, the Uzbek court, infamous for its harsh sentences aimed at Islamic oppositionists, displayed humanity, apparently anticipating the negative response a more severe verdict might evoke in the West, where the human rights lobby and the press had written about Usmanova's case. Be that as it may, the human rights activists' predictions that the Uzbek authorities will be forced to treat women with greater indulgence than men are coming true.

"SIMULATED MOURNING"

Islamic groups are winning the sympathy of the population by creating a cult of martyrs out of those who fell victim to persecution by the regime for their religious convictions (this mainly concerns Uzbekistan). Although the population is cowed by the tough policies of the authorities, and most individuals are not inclined to risk their lives and freedom for the sake of values preached by the Islamists, over the long term, the regime's hard-line approach is likely to produce outcomes favorable to the Islamists. The "simulated mourning" of these victims is limited in its effect, as the bulk of the population of the republics where Islamists are actively operating does not have access to modern electronic communications media.

Nonetheless, materials from the Internet are circulated in these republics via illegal channels. For several years already, HTI websites have featured the story *Who Killed Farkhad Usmanov?* highlighting the photograph of the body of a well-known imam's son who had been arrested on June 14, 1999, for possession of an HTI leaflet and subsequently died in custody. Bruises and other marks on the body suggested that he had been tortured. On the one hand, Usmanov's death was a show of intimidation vis-à-vis potential HTI supporters. On the other hand, it fostered mobilization, albeit delayed, that was further enhanced by the activity of women participating in the mourning ritual. Information from international human rights organizations expressing their concern over such cases is also being used by the Islamists to create among the population a negative image of the authorities as enemies of Islam and persecutors of the believers.

It would be wrong to contend that in combating the Islamists the Uzbekistani authorities resort to harsh repression *alone*. The state is also waging a public relations campaign, strenuous efforts are being made to develop a moderate, tolerant Islam that conforms to the traditions of Central Asian society, and Islamic education is being developed. A positive role is played by the Islamic University established in Tashkent (a symbiosis of secular and religious education), headed by a vice premier of the government of Uzbekistan. The publication of religious literature is permitted, although a system of stringent censorship causes resentment on the part of the religious class. However, the hope that it will be possible to hold political Islam in check by opposing it with moderate Islam loyal to the establishment is ultimately illusory. Present-day Syria is an example. In 1982, government forces brutally disposed of Islamic rebels in the city of Hama, killing about ten thousand people, and since then the government has been successful in checking the Islamic movement. So that the Islamists would not have the opportunity to portray the government as "an enemy of Islam," the Syrian authorities promoted the development of Islam, built mosques, supported religious education, and so forth, while keeping religion under state control. But of late, there is indication that this strategy may backfire against the secular regime. After the American-led invasion of Iraq, one can attest to a resurgence in mosque attendance, especially among the youth, and the "Islamic appeal" has grown in influence. A substantial section of citizenry is becoming convinced that, at present, Islam is under threat from the outside and that Islam is the only force they can resort to to defend themselves. The sense of threat intensifies the motivation, while the availability of mobilization infrastructure—the mosques and religious seminaries—can facilitate the recruitment of Islamist supporters.

Reverting to the question of victims of persecution by the authorities in Uzbekistan, one should also address the evidence brought forth by the Bureau of Democracy, Human Rights, and Labor of the U.S. Department of State in its *Reports on Human Rights Practices*. One such report, dated February 23, 2000, for instance, in addition to the case of the above-mentioned Usmanov and one other case, wrote of "unconfirmed but credible reports of at least 13 other deaths by torture or beating," most of them on charges related to alleged support of radical Islamic groups.[64]

In the Middle East, observers have long noted the special significance of the mourning ritual as a vehicle of mass protest for Islamic movements. Central Asian societies are similar in this respect to the Middle Eastern ones. Munson recalls that in Iran "during the winter and spring of 1978, the revolution evolved out of a cycle of mourning marches for demonstrators killed by troops and police." Had the shah not shown such cruelty in dealing with the demonstrators and chosen alternative means of crowd dispersion that were less violent, his forces "would not have kept creating martyrs to be mourned."[65] In fact, it is now believed that more humane tactics would help prevent the mourning marches from being transformed into a full-fledged revolution. Zbigniew Brzezinski reported that the State Department and the U.S. ambassador in Tehran in October 1978 opposed sending crowd-control devices to the shah's government (apparently for fear of hindering negotiations with the National Front moderates). Cruelty in suppressing demonstrations, during which troops and police killed thousands of unarmed people, did not help in containing the rebellion that was flaring up. There were many politicians who later reproached the shah for failing to show greater resolve in repressing the opposition. According to Munson, this argument (in particular, Brzezinski, the U.S. national security advisor at the time, was a proponent of a harder line toward the opposition) "overlooks the outrage provoked by the massacre of 'Black Friday' on September 8, 1978."[66]

Thus the appearance of an Islamic political opposition in Iran created a dilemma: how to combat mass insurgency that the authorities perceive as menacing. Certainly, it is difficult to draw parallels between the shah's Iran of the Cold War era and the present-day Central Asian regimes. However, a similarity nevertheless exists. What was at stake in both cases was the survival of a secular regime friendly to the West, and the United States in particular (although the latter was critical of the internal policies of the Central Asian regimes). In both cases, a bloc of Islamic radical activists was the main opposition force. The Central Asian governments, such as the shah's government, are confident that although the West is critical of their internal policies, and in particular their authoritarian, undemocratic methods of dealing with the opposition, it is even less interested in seeing the militant Islamists' coming to power. The experience in Algeria, where the government deployed the military to suppress the Islamists at the moment they appeared close to winning office through democratic elections, further bolsters the Central Asian governments' assessment concerning Western policy priorities. Nevertheless, doubts concerning the effectiveness of reliance on forceful methods in restraining the Islamists are considerable.

THE HTI TURNS TO VIOLENCE?

Khalifatlik (The Caliphate) and other books disseminated by the HTI in Uzbekistan set out the final objective of the HTI's struggle—the construction of an Islamic state on a global scale. The party's ideologists proceed from the assumption that this struggle, which must culminate in the creation of the Caliphate, comprises several stages. The first is propagation of the party's ideas, the creation of cells, and the broad enlistment of the masses into HTI ranks. It is expected that the second stage, which occurs once the idea of the construction of the Caliphate begins to win over the masses, will see a bloodless revolution during which the people will demand that the country's leaders leave their posts. Then, during the third stage, general elections for the caliph will be held in which adult Muslim men and women will take part.

Let's refer in this regard to the aforementioned Nabhani book, a passage of which reads:

> The ideological Hizb will proceed in these stages so as to start implementing its ideology in society:
>
> First: The stage of study and culturing in order to develop the Hizbi culture.
>
> Second: The stage of interaction with the society, so that the society becomes aware of the ideology, the (acceptance of the) ideology becomes the public traditions of the society, and the whole community perceives it as its ideology and defends it collectively. In this stage, the *umma* starts her struggle against those who stand as obstacles in the path of the implementation of the ideology, such as the colonialists and their tools such as the ruling classes, those who prefer living in the dark, and those fascinated by the foreign culture. The *umma* starts this struggle because the *umma* adopts the ideology as her own and views the Hizb as her leader.
>
> Third: The ruling stage, by acquiring the authority throughout the *umma* in order to implement the ideology upon the *umma*. From this stage, the practical aspects of the Hizb will manifest themselves in life's affairs. Calling to the ideology will remain the main task of the state and the Hizb. The ideology will be the message that the *umma* and the state will carry.[67]

Administration of the Caliphate is marked by patriarchal simplicity—full power belongs to the caliph, but a council, the *shura*, is elected that has a consultative function: the caliph may consult with it, but is not obliged to fulfill its recommendations. The remaining officials are appointed by the caliph: two assistants, one of whom is engaged in the administration of public services, while the other heads the caliph's administration, governors, and judges. The caliph is also the commander-in-chief and decides on questions of war and peace with neighboring countries.

While remaining within this framework, the Central Asian HTI leaders seemingly renounce the use of violent methods of struggle, let alone terrorism, to achieve their objectives.

However, Bakhtiyar Babajanov asserts that in 2001–2002, the sharply negative attitude toward the HTI and groups of a similar orientation (who remain loyal to the current Central Asian regimes), the hostility of the state itself, and the antiterrorist operation in Afghanistan strongly altered the HTI's position. Its printed materials, hitherto moderate, now increasingly began to call for "war and self-sacrifice" along with the "overthrow of the present-day infidel governments serving America and the Jews" and so forth.[68] Such calls are, in particular, contained in the journal *al-Wa'y*, no. 149, as well as leaflets from October 26, November 12, and December 10, 2001.

An earlier article published in *al-Wa'y* (June 2001), justifies violent jihad, a position that is not typical of the HTI, particularly during that period. True, some of my Uzbekistani contacts expressed doubts about the authenticity of this article, which in their opinion could have been fabricated by those who wanted to portray the HTI as an organization oriented toward violent and even terrorist methods of struggle. Here is an abridged translation of this article from Uzbek:

SHAHID BULISH AMALIYOTLARI
(General Principles of Self-Destruction in the Name of Allah)

Information agencies have circulated information on the "fatwas" issued concerning acts of self-destruction in the name of Allah, committed by certain Muslims against Jews in the occupied territories of Palestine. Some of these "fatwas" permit the performance of such actions against the military and prohibit their performance against civilians. Some other "fatwas" assert that the theologians issuing the fatwa could not find juridical grounding according to Shari'a allowing such deeds, and therefore they fear that acts of self-destruction in the name of Allah may become an embodiment of suicide.

Given the importance of these problems, we shall expound their juridical foundations according to Shari'a, so that both the dying and the surviving person can know the exact proofs.

According to Shari'a, the methods of waging the struggle against the infidels—*kafirs*—are unlimited. . . . A Muslim is allowed the use of any methods and means in the struggle against the infidels, if they are employed for the killing of the infidel—*kafir*.

A Muslim should use all methods for the struggle against the infidels. In such cases it does not matter if he fights the enemy at a distance arms in hand or face to face, struggles empty-handed or opens the gates for Muslims after having penetrated into the enemy camp, or if he guides his shot-down plane into a point where the infidels are concentrated without parachuting from it or blows himself up to inflict damage on soldiers in enemy camps, or else blows up himself and the infidels after having tied a belt round himself with explosives built into it—all this is permitted, for these means are aimed at struggling against the infidels. . . .

A Muslim who has blown himself up to destroy the enemies is also deemed to have performed jihad, and this is not only akin to the prosecution of hostilities with arms, but also is the most important and the greatest manifestation of manly conduct of war. . . . And therefore when a Muslim blows himself up for the sake of killing the enemy, he by command of Allah unquestionably becomes a *shahid* (one who has sacrificed himself in the name of Allah), if the act in question was committed in the name of Allah.

. . . If the enemy is using weapons of mass destruction, as is the case nowadays in Palestine, we shall also undoubtedly put these weapons into operation. . . . In such cases there is no difference whether the enemy or civilians will be destroyed as a result of the use of explosive substances. . . .

If a woman is a warrior, her killing is also permitted according to Shari'a. . . .

If an elderly man has the opportunity to help the enemy, for example, he expresses his opinion and recommendations on warfare or shows the ways to kill Muslims, such people have to be killed. . . .

If the enemy is destroying our warriors, children, women, and old men by using missile systems, planes, cannon, and other weapons, we should use similar means and, in particular, use explosive substances. In such cases there is no difference whether we shall be killing enemy soldiers or together with them destroying their children, women, and old men.[69]

In light of this passage, the thesis on the HTI's exceptional peacefulness and complete renunciation of violent methods of struggle apparently does not hold. It is called into serious question by both the analysis of various researchers from the region and the statements revealed by the publications and documents themselves (although one of the Tahriris tried to persuade the author that the most militant leaflets of recent times might be fabricated by the "enemies of the HTI" with insidious objects).

The Tahriris feature pieces in issue nos. 138–143 of *al-Wa'y* say that jihad must be the last resort of the HTI's struggle for the sake of Islam. Certainly, there are enough reasons to classify the Tahriris as jihadists.

However, available materials offer no convincing evidence that, as Baba-janov claims, the HTI has started to use violent methods solely. An Uzbek expert gives only one piece of evidence, citing an HTI leaflet dated October 11, 2001—"the vague definitions of jihad that sounded earlier have now acquired the meaning of violent struggle against the 'infidels.'"[70]

Worthy of note is that intensification of HTI activity is associated with the carrying out of IMU actions. In particular, increased Tahriri activity in the Jalal-Abad region was noted at the time of the Batken events of 1999. Six citizens of Uzbekistan who distributed leaflets with appeals to jihad were then detained in the regional mosque and subsequently handed over to the police of the Namangan region of Uzbekistan. Although it is hard to determine whether these jihadists belonged to the HTI, the spokesmen for the Uzbek law enforcement agencies asserted that this was the case. This and other incidents suggest that the authorities of Central Asian republics have begun to impose successful control over the mosques, which are routinely used by all Islamic extremists to win supporters.

When in August 2000 IMU gunmen again invaded the southern regions of Kyrgyzstan, increased HTI activity was again noted in the Jalal-Abad region, where twelve HTI activists were detained. However, does the party members' detention mean that the party itself has begun to act more vigorously? Two alternative explanations are that the law enforcement bodies are more adept at uncovering the Tahriris and that the latter have become less cautious and are acting more openly.

The local press remarked that, at the end of the 1990s, the Tahriris were able to spread their influence to the northern regions of Kyrgyzstan. In particular, in 1999 it reported that three jihadists from the HTI stood trial in the village of Novopokrovka, near Bishkek.

It is interesting to note the attitude toward the HTI of Shaykh Muhammad Sadiq Muhammad Yusuf. At the beginning of the 1990s, he administered the Directorate for the Muslims of Uzbekistan (see chapter 2), but in 1993, after conflict with the authorities, he was forced to emigrate to the Middle East and to live in Lybia. In 1999, he received an invitation to return home. Muhammad Sadiq says:

> President Islam Karimov has said that the Uzbek state would struggle against ideas with the help of ideas, against obscurantism with the help of enlightenment. Had these words been translated into practice in Uzbekistan, there would be no Hizb at-Tahrir in the country now. One can imprison a human being, but one cannot imprison an idea. . . . The youth argues: if we are Muslims, what should a Muslim be like and what is the religion of Islam? But it finds no answers at school, in institutions of higher learning, or elsewhere.

The shaykh claims that the Hizb at-Tahrir and organizations similar to it profit from this failure by urging the youth to join their ranks; and after they are already there, no one will be able to convince people that the radical, Tahriri treatment of Islam is erroneous.

According to Shaykh Muhammad Sadiq, "despite persecution, members of the Hizb at-Tahrir have nonetheless published and disseminated fifty books in Uzbekistan, are publishing a journal, circulating leaflets, and carrying on daily grassroots work, even while they are in custody." Further, "those people who are in charge of religious matters in Uzbekistan, while on the government payroll, have not yet published a single book challenging the ideas of the Hizb at-Tahrir. If they could not write a book themselves, they might have translated from Arabic the already extant works that prove the falsity of these ideas." Shaykh Muhammad Sadiq believes that the lack of freedom of religion and access to information is pushing Muslims to embrace the very banned Islamic groups that the authorities take such pains to combat. "At the same time, those who want to diffuse true Islam have no right to do so, as it is forbidden by law. Such is the absurdity of the current situation."[71]

The Kyrgyz press reported in 2000 that the HTI proposed to independent journalists of the republic's southern regions that they cooperate with the HTI in publishing "objective information" in the mass media on the party's activity in the Ferghana Valley, promising that the HTI representative in Kyrgyzstan would supply them with the party's literature already in print.[72]

At the international conference "Islam and Modern Times: Prospects for the Future," held on September 7, 2000, one of the main Islamic luminaries of Kyrgyzstan, Sadykjan Haji Kamaluddin, addressed the conference in the presence of Kyrgyzstan's President Askar Akaev, among others. When he called on Uzbekistan's President Islam Karimov to start negotiations with the Islamic Movement of Uzbekistan in order to settle the conflict peacefully, the assembled religious figures from Central Asia, Transcaucasia, the Arab countries, and Russia greeted his statement with applause.

Nonetheless, the Uzbek authorities continue to believe that even HTI members are taking a direct part in terrorist activity. Thus, not long before the February events in Tashkent, the Tashkent prosecutor's office and police attempted to seize an armed terrorist who then blew himself up with a grenade. According to police evidence, Bakhtiyar Mahmudov was an HTI member who had undergone training in one of the fighting camps of Chechnya and, together with a group of terrorists, had been preparing an explosion at the Charvak reservoir dam.[73]

On May 1, 1998, the Uzbek parliament toughened laws related to religious activity. In accordance with this legislation, all the mosques of Uzbekistan have to be registered with government bodies; however, in order to be registered, a religious community must total no less than a hundred members (only ten members were needed to get registered in accordance with the previous law). Membership in unregistered religious organizations entails criminal punishment. The law enforcement agencies oblige the *mahalla* committees to identify not only residents belonging to the HTI, but also those sharing its ideas, and to inform the authorities of the employment and means of livelihood of members of these residents' families.[74]

Despite such massive persecution, the number of Tahriris in Uzbekistan remains significant. The exact number is difficult to pin down; however, independent observers estimate it at ten thousand, the judge presiding during the trial mentioned fifteen thousand, while other sources give exaggerated figures of up to sixty thousand.[75] However, the HTI's activity after September 11, 2001, began to decline. According to Kasym, a native of Khavast, Syr Darya region, at present, fewer HTI leaflets are disseminated than before.[76] The leaflets are brought from Tajikistan in small consignments of several dozen copies. Children and youths from border *kishlaks*, familiar with local surroundings, are hired to transport the leaflets by foot or on bicycles and illegally cross the Uzbek–Tajik border, which not only is guarded by the Uzbek border guards, but is also mined in some places on the Uzbek side. Couriers run the risk of being caught by the police or border guards, being shot while trying to escape, or hitting a mine. A courier receives the paltry payment of fifty to seventy soms per errand ($1 = 1000 soms), but can run four to five errands a day. The fact that the leaflets come from Tajikistan fosters residual tensions in relations between the two Central Asian republics. Uzbek government officials have a deeply ingrained, sharply negative attitude toward Tajik Islamists, including those who have been integrated into the power structure, and reject the Tajik experience of institutionalized interaction between secular and religious political forces. Commenting on Said Abdullo Nuri, the spiritual leader of Tajik Islamists, one of the officials of the Directorate for the Muslims of Uzbekistan (DMU) ominously told me in a conversation, "Wait, this Nuri will yet show himself."[77]

Worthy of note is that each of the Central Asian republics (even at the level of average citizen) accuses its neighbor of providing bases for Islamic radicals and charges that it is from the neighbor's territory that subversive literature is being spread; Tajikistan has accused Uzbekistan of this and vice versa.

ATTEMPTS TO CREATE AN UZBEK
VERSION OF AN HTI-TYPE MOVEMENT

The doctrine of the HTI had been brought to Central Asia from abroad, and since then the local branches of this party had been under the strong influence of the broad international agenda of the foreign headquarters, betraying the HTI's Middle Eastern roots. At the same time, the HTI did not address many grievances and needs of the local population. That is why some Uzbek adherents of the HTI attempted to formulate their own doctrine and organizational structure, which resembled those of the HTI but conformed to the social imperatives and traditions of Central Asians. Such an attempt was undertaken by HTI member Akram Yuldashev, who in about 1996 founded Akramiyya in Andizhan, a movement named after Yuldashev himself. Babajanov mentions that the movement's members referred to themselves as Iymonchilar ("believers"), while others call them Akramiyya, as well as Khalifatchilar ("Caliphatists").[78] The idea of the Caliphate found in Yuldashev's book *Iymonga yul* (The path to true faith), which consists of twelve lessons, makes this group similar to the HTI. A. Yuldashev's views as expressed in his book demonstrate his adherence to Salafi Islam; his ideal is the norms of life as they were in the days of the Prophet and the first four caliphs. According to Babajanov, A. Yuldashev suggested the following stages of operation to his followers:

1. The *Sirli* (hidden, clandestine) stage—the selection and education of the movement's activists in *halaqas* (circles).
2. The *Maddi* (material) stage—the formation of the financial base (every member contributes one-fifth of his income to the common treasury—*bayt al-mal*).
3. The *Ma'nawi* (spiritual) stage—the constant "spiritual association" with a circle of fighting brethren.
4. The *Uzwi maydan* (organic influence)—entrenchment of the organization inside the power structures through the infiltration by the organization's activists or recruitment of officials.
5. The *Akhirat* (final) stage—the transfer of all the power in society to the leader of the group.[79]

The emergence of such ideas clearly represents an attempt to create an "Uzbekified," grassroots version of HTI doctrine and organizational structure that would match the specific socioeconomic and cultural environment in this republic. While most of Yuldashev's concepts draw upon the HTI's ideas, there are also some innovations, for example, the notion of *jama'a*, "a special production—and distribution—community."[80] The groups' leaders seem to want to introduce some elements of a socioeconomic program into their doctrine, which might seem more attractive than the purely philosophical teachings of the HTI, which lack any practical solutions to the acute problems that the country is facing. Cells inside *jama'a* have to be organized in accordance with professional specialization (the *halaqas* of shoemakers, tailors, etc.), and every Akramite is supposed

to bring his wives and children into his group. Group members are expected to practice endogamy within Akramite communities.[81] Hence, it is
obvious that Yuldashev develops ideas borrowed from the HTI and, in
recognition of the inherited collectivist instincts of the rural Uzbeks,
brings them into accord with the culture of the *mahalla*. We do not know
to what extent Yuldashev was successful in recruiting followers into his
movements, since adequate field information is not available. The
Akramiyya cells supposedly exist in the Andizhan region, Osh (Kyrgyzstan), Namangan, Kokand, and some other regions of Uzbekistan.[82] The
Akramiyya followers are persecuted, and the movement's founder has
been arrested.

Whatever the fate of Akramiyya, its experience lends support to the
suggestion that the set of originally foreign ideas professed by the HTI has
found fertile ground in Uzbekistan. Hence, this attempt to create a domestic version of the Caliphatic movement might not be the last should
the Akramiyya fail to mobilize the population.

Within Uzbekistan's law enforcement agencies, information is circulating concerning a wing of the HTI that split from the party, forming a
new structure—the Hizb an-Nusra (Party of Support). It is not yet
known whether this new party has the same ramified network as the
HTI. When I asked one of the Tashkent human rights activists whether
such an organization really existed, he replied that he knew next to
nothing about it but was sure that the Hizb an-Nusra was formed by the
local special services in order to uncover those who sympathized with
the Salafis. However, an officer of the Uzbek police service, K., claimed
that the Hizb an-Nusra was a wealthy organization that clearly had a
good financial backing that was suspected of originating in the United
States.[83] According to this official, the Hizb an-Nusra is also involved in
drug trafficking.

THE HTI COMES TO TAJIKISTAN

Although, as we have already noted, it is customary to assume that even
in Tajikistan and Kyrgyzstan the HTI rallies mostly Uzbeks, there is evidence to suggest that in the northern, southern, and western regions of
Tajikistan it includes a great many Tajiks. HTI followers even exist in the
Kulyab zone, where the Islamic Revival Party of Tajikistan, for instance, is
unable to conduct operations.

In Tajikistan, the influence of political Islam is strong mostly in the
south and east of the republic, first and foremost in the Gharm regions.
But the fact that the HTI has managed to gain a foothold specifically in the
north and the west of Tajikistan largely refutes conventional belief on the

exclusively secular mood of the inhabitants of this part of the country. Most probably, the HTI filled "the Islamist" niche vacated because the IRPT was not allowed to pursue its work in the northern and western regions. The same conditions that impel the population to embrace the Islamic alternative to the existing order have here, as in other Central Asian republics, influenced the relative success of the Tahriris. These factors include the unresolved socioeconomic problems (unemployment, poverty), the corrupt nature of the state, the dominance of criminal mafia clans, and the poor performance of the official Islamic bodies. The IRPT, which for some time now has been soliciting the government (its partner in national reconciliation) for posts and privileges, was also clearly losing to the Tahriris. The absence of normal religious education in the country, state interference into the affairs of religious communities, and not least the active work of preachers trained in the countries of the Near and Middle East, as well as in other Central Asian republics, fostered the inflow of adherents of the HTI. Naturally, the HTI's success was also due to the attractive nature of slogans calling for equality, justice, and most importantly in war-weary Tajikistan, the use of only peaceful methods of struggle.

The idea of social justice traditionally occupies a prominent place in the rhetoric of Islamic movements. The Central Asian reality, with its inequality, corruption, and rigid authoritarianism, presents fertile ground for political mobilization based on slogans of justice. Broadly speaking, those whom the Islamists manage to persuade fail to notice that they never offer concrete solutions to problems, especially in the socioeconomic domain. What makes their propaganda attractive is the very invocation of "absolute" values, which, given the dire circumstances, are extremely seductive. What is suggested is not a concrete solution to a problem (for example, eliminating unemployment, financial normalization of the economy) but the reconstruction of an "ideal" society in which such problems simply cannot exist. The simplicity of any utopian project makes it understandable; it becomes a matter of faith, and one does not have to ponder its internal logic as one does with more practical alternatives. Nor does the absence of a program discourage the Islamists themselves, as coming to power is so obviously an end in itself for them. "Absolute" arguments are quite enough, for what happens after they come to power is of secondary importance. In principle, no ingenious, specifically Islamic solutions to complex socioeconomic problems exist. Hopes are pinned on expropriating public funds that have been egregiously embezzled, as well as on redistributing a part of the national income to the poor, a traditional Islamic practice. Thus the Islamic project is invariably connected with the recreation of a traditional society. However, this idea does not repel the relatively modern segments of society, who have their own political agenda and expect to raise their social status as a result of this project's realization.

Central Asian governments juxtapose to the Islamists' social demagogy their own social programs and understanding of Islam, without overlooking traditional social institutions in the process. Relying heavily on such institutions, and even encouraging their development, allows the state to attenuate social discontent somewhat and prevent it from turning into political action. Moreover, the state is thus able to "cut" the ground from under the feet of the Islamists, who might otherwise overwhelm these institutions.

In relation to this, it is important to discuss the extent to which the national HTI organizations in various Central Asian republics differ from each other. In general, the relative independence of the national HTI organizations allows them to diverge strongly concerning the tactical issue of political struggle, as well as the party's programmatic principles. Substantial distinctions in political culture, general civilizational peculiarities, and the fact that different schools of Islam prevail in various countries are all important factors in this divergence. Therefore, Yemen, Uzbekistan, and Tajikistan, for example, hardly fall onto the same analytical plane. In terms of attitude toward democracy, an activist from Osh states: "Democracy means freedom of opinion and freedom of business activity—all this is in contradiction to Islam."[84] However, the antibusiness orientation of one Osh Islamist can scarcely be projected onto society as a whole; aside from the well-known restrictions on loan interest, which are easily circumvented by the Islamic banking system, and the interdictions associated with the ethical norms of Islam concerning, for example, the sex industry and gambling—interdictions that exist in Western societies as well—there is no modern Islamic current that would fully deny free enterprise.

Contrary to IRPT leaders, the main HTI ideologists, as has already been mentioned, deem democracy to be anathema to Islam. Among the books circulated by the Tahriris in Tajikistan, Zallum's *Demokratiya— nizomi kufr* (Democracy—a godless order) states that democracy is an instrument that allows humanity to fulfill its wish of ridding itself of the absolute power of the Almighty and going beyond the framework of enactment ordained by Him, whereas "Allah is the only enactor."[85] Speaking of the "four freedoms"—of conscience, opinion, property, and personality—the author writes that "none of them is recognized in Islam. . . . All these species of freedoms are entirely at variance with the principles of Islam."[86]

The Tahriris criticize the IRPT leadership for its positive attitude toward democracy, which the former see as a deviation from Islam. In particular, they censure Nuri's book *Human Rights and Islam.*

The HTI's condemnation of the IRPT, which "has sold out to the government, betraying the interests of Islam," has borne its fruit: 1999–2000 saw an outflow of members from the IRPT into the HTI. The exodus later ceased, possibly out of fear of reprisals, since all IRPT members are in the limelight, and it is therefore difficult for them to conceal their defection to the HTI.

Developing a position toward the HTI was a painful process for the IRPT. "The revivalists" saw in the HTI a rival that successfully targeted their constituency. At the same time, the IRPT initially did not wish to engage in criticism of the HTI for fear of fomenting discontent among their own followers as well. Still, the IRPT had to make a choice after the authorities detained several IRPT activists on charges (unfounded, from the IRPT's perspective) of belonging to the HTI. Only in 2002 did IRPT chairman Said Abdullo Nuri neatly state in an interview with the newspaper *Najot*: "I believe that this group has no right to operate in Tajikistan from the standpoint of both Shari'a and [secular] law. . . . We regard it as an illegal party."[87] Noteworthy is an additional argument put forth by the IRPT leader: "In Tajikistan, a party with a religious character is already active, and therefore it is not necessary for another such party to be created and to become active." To put it differently, the IRPT had no qualms about expressing its desire to monopolize political Islam. It is nevertheless obvious that the fundamental political principles of the two organizations are radically different: the HTI stands for changing the existing regime, while the IRPT has consented to become its integral constituent member; the HTI advocated the creation of an Islamic Caliphate, while the IRPT has expressed no such aspiration and generally considers that conditions are not yet ripe for the formation of an Islamic state in Tajikistan.

The IRPT also undertook practical steps aimed at preventing the growth of HTI influence. For example, in the Sogdian region, special propaganda groups were formed to begin a dialogue with the populace concerning the negative consequences of HTI activity.[88] IRPT activists also participated in this endeavor. However, all signs suggest that this activity has not been successful and will soon be discontinued.

EFFORTS TO OPPOSE THE PARTY IN TAJIKISTAN

The IRPT leadership, which began to fear that cooperation with the authorities would yield no benefits after reconciliation, was encouraged by the government's opposition to the HTI. At the same time, the party that had embarked on a course to form "a humane, democratic, and law-governed society" in Tajikistan felt the need to dissociate itself from government actions that could manifestly be interpreted as human rights violations or even as infringements of religious freedom. The IRPT could not but support the standpoint of independent observers and international organizations who noted that the punishments meted out to HTI members and supporters were incommensurably harsh relative to the offenses. In particular, the court sentenced one resident of the Tursunzade district, in whose home HTI leaflets had been discovered, to three years' imprisonment. IRPT leaders fully understood the futility of attempts to eliminate the HTI solely by means of severe repression.

The Islamic Revival Party of Tajikistan deems that one of the main differences between the IRPT and the HTI is that the former is "national and liberal," while the latter is "transnational and clandestine," thus precluding the possibility of interaction between them. Nevertheless, in the Central Asian republics, at the initiative of government bodies, rumors are being constantly spread concerning the alleged close cooperation between the IRPT and the HTI.

After the attacks in Tashkent, the HTI stepped up its work in the region. More leaflets began to appear in which the party criticized the authorities, while at the same time addressing the daily needs of the population. This is in marked contrast to previous publications, in which the HTI paid much attention to Middle Eastern problems, such as support for the Palestinians and criticism of Zionism.

But even among the leaflets and other print materials that the HTI circulates, there occur materials that are clearly "custom-made." Moreover, it is not clear who the target audience for these materials is. For instance, a leaflet circulated on March 27, 2002, and that was probably translated into Tajik from Uzbek, was devoted to the examination of the activity of OPEC and called for exerting pressure on the authorities to change the world price of oil. This material clearly can be traced back to the Middle East.

But the Central Asian Tahriris are always stressing their local roots. "Many people believe that foreign money is behind our activities," says an HTI member in Khujand.[89] "This view is mistaken. Our struggle is funded primarily from local sources. You cannot imagine how many people donate money to fund us." I am sure that this is an enormous overstatement; however, a certain familiarity with the Islamic organizations of Central Asia enables one to feel that the dues paid by active HTI members and the donations of private persons do indeed account for a sizable portion of the HTI's budget.

Tajik analysts, like their colleagues throughout Central Asia, note the clandestine character of the HTI's activity, which is partly explained by the sophistication of its organizational structure, borrowed from the experience of the illegal organizations of the Middle East. Here, as in Uzbekistan, the primary HTI cell is the *halaqa*, whose members, except for the leader, know only each other and nobody from other circles or higher

Two suspected members of the Hizb at-Tahrir al-Islami—Husayn Khojakulov and Kamol Ibrahimov—are arrested in Tajikistan (April 2000).

ranks. Circle leaders form an organizational unit at the next level up, and so forth. As a result of the HTI's conspiratorial nature, the identities of its higher leaders remain unknown to the Tajik authorities. Repression strikes mostly rank-and-file circle members, who possess insignificant information about the party's activity.

Nonetheless, the Tajik authorities, just like their Uzbekistani counterparts, rely largely on repressive methods in combating the HTI. According to the former public prosecutor of the Sogdian region, K. Mukhabbatov, the first case against the Tahriris in the region was in 1999. In the
ensuing three years, a total of 108 criminal cases were brought before the
courts in relation to 130 "leaders" and "active participants" in the HTI on
charges of "appealing for the violent takeover of state power and the
overthrow of the political system" and also "fomenting ethnic and religious strife." "Leaders" received prison terms ranging from eight to
twelve years, while "active participants" received sentences of three to
five years.[90] The authorities of the Sogdian region possess information
that its territory was repeatedly visited by "emissaries from Uzbekistan,"
but admit that they could not detain them. That said, an incident was
noted where members of Uzbekistan's law enforcement agencies, in
breach of the law, seized residents of the Soviet district of the Sogdian region of Tajikistan, brought them to the Ferghana region of Uzbekistan,
and then convicted them.[91] Similar incidents took place in Kyrgyzstan.

In the process, the Tajik authorities have proceeded from the assumption that the HTI has infiltrated the republic from neighboring Uzbekistan. For example, a law professor from Dushanbe has called for a dialogue with HTI rank-and-file members, as they are not aware of "all the
consequences of their participation in the realization of insidious designs
of foreign emissaries." In his assessment, the HTI has been "entrenched in
the Turkic-language districts of the Ferghana Valley and found a social
base there among people disaffected with the Karimov regime's confrontation with the believers."[92]

Tajikistan fears Uzbekistan's regional ambitions and views the hegemonic aspirations of certain unspecified "forces" in the Uzbekistani
leadership as a threat comparable to that of Islamic radicalism. An analyst from Tajikistan believes that the threat comes from a political clash
in Uzbekistan, "where underground Islamic parties and organizations
pursuing the goals of the construction of an Islamic state in the form of a
Caliphate struggle with forces aspiring to regional hegemony."[93] This
discourse demonstrates how intertwined religion and ethnicity are when
they are equally used for political purposes, especially for mass mobilization.

In the law enforcement agencies of Tajikistan, it is believed that the tactics of Hizb at-Tahrir members are similar to those of the IRPT during its
formative period. Thus for the Tahriri, as was the case with the IRPT, the
initial stage is characterized by a plan to seize power by attracting people
with its ideas and enrolling them into the ranks of the party through
promises to resolve the current socioeconomic difficulties. Thus, like the
IRPT in its own time, their main gambit is for the youth, the intelligentsia,

and women, who, after certain psychological training, can all become active propagators of HTI ideas. It is important to note here that the main contingent within the ranks of the party is made up of persons who in the past studied at religious schools or graduated from similar institutions.

From October 1988 until the end of 2002, through concerted efforts of Tajikistan's law enforcement bodies, 334 Hizb at-Tahrir leaders and activists were identified and detained, nine of whom were citizens of Uzbekistan.

During house searches, a great quantity of subversive literature was confiscated, including *Nizomi Islam, Khirad, Gurukhbandi dar Hizb at-Tahrir, Minhoji Hizb at-Tahrir,* and *al-Wa'y.* In accordance with articles 187, section 2; 189, section 2; and 307, section 2, of Tajikistan's Criminal Code, 121 criminal cases have been brought against the detainees before the courts. The investigation of 110 criminal cases concerning 149 persons has been completed and submitted to the judicial bodies. The judicial bodies have considered 106 criminal cases concerning 140 persons, as a result of which the accused have been sentenced to various length terms of imprisonment in a strict-regimen penal colony.

HTI leaders are among those detained. Thus the regional Tahriri leader (*mas'ul*), Abdujalil Yusupov, was detained in the Sogdian region, while Arobiddin Urinov, who was also a *mas'ul,* was apprehended in the Lenin district. Also detained were thirteen *naqibs,* leaders of the party's regional cells; fifty-three *mushrifs,* leaders of *halaqas* consisting of five persons; and forty-five distributors of literature.

During the searches, the supply channels for extremist religious literature and HTI leaflets were uncovered. Analysis of police materials allows us to conclude that the Tahriri literature comes to Tajikistan from Uzbekistan through the Sogdian region, and partly through the Tursunzade and Shaartuz areas, with the bulk of the publications translated into the Tajik language and prepared by skilled, politically competent professionals—the ideologists of Islamic radicalism.

Security agencies have carried out "preventive" work with eighty-one party supporters and have given forty-two persons official warnings and put public prosecutors on notice about them. The Ministries of Security and the Interior, which are responsible for the condemned Tahriris, keep them in separate cells to prevent them from influencing other prisoners.

Police officers hold meetings with the personnel of enterprises and institutions, organize lectures and conversations, orchestrate TV and radio broadcasts, and publish articles in the press in order to warn the population about Hizb at-Tahrir ideology and prevent its spread.

The Tajik authorities are focusing on the HTI as a major threat. In the words of Saidamir Zuhurov, deputy prime minister of Tajikistan, "the probability of the Tajik–Afghan border being overwhelmed by IMU militants or the Taliban disturbs me today to a lesser extent than the increasing danger coming from the Hizb ut-Tahrir party."[94]

Certain representatives of Tajikistan's official circles were in favor of starting a dialogue with the Tahriris, but they remain a clear minority. The fact that in Tajikistan dialogue with HTI members is not only accepted, but already being pursued, signals that the authorities there are trying to backtrack from the traditional strategy of combating Islamic radicalism exclusively with forceful methods.

Is government dialogue with the party as such possible? In the short run, probably not. The HTI's position concerning the prospects of cooperation with the regime is not clear, either. It would seem illogical for this party to cooperate with a regime that it is striving to overthrow; however, there is much evidence that attests to the HTI's readiness not only to carry on dialogue with the authorities of Central Asian republics but also to cooperate with them in one form or another.

THE HTI'S KYRGYZ SAGA

In Kyrgyzstan, the HTI operates predominantly in the south, and the overwhelming majority of its members are Uzbeks. Twenty-five hundred HTI members have been listed by the republic's Interior Ministry, but these figures cannot reflect the genuine number of followers that the party maintains. Local experts note that HTI members are mostly unemployed young men twenty to thirty-five years of age. In contrast to Uzbekistan, in Kyrgyzstan highly educated people can hardly be found among the HTI's ranks.[95]

Scholars and practitioners have always been concerned with the question of the social base of Islamist movements. The main conclusion that can be drawn from the materials available to researchers is that it is impossible to generalize the insights gained with investigation of a single country during a single period. In some cases this social base is made up of individuals from the lower social classes, while in others it is composed of highly educated youth. Egyptian political scientist Saad Eddin Ibrahim, who with his colleagues studied a group of thirty-four Islamic militants in Egypt, observed of the subjects' fathers that twenty-one (62 percent) were civil servants, four (12 percent) were high-level professionals, another four (12 percent) were small merchants, three (9 percent) were small farmers owning between six and eleven acres, and two (6 percent) belonged to the working class.[96] Researchers into the Egyptian Muslim Brotherhood noted that their main social base in the 1960s–1970s consisted of university graduates coming from the middle and lower strata, from the provinces, who had exceedingly high expectations regarding their career but were unable to find adequate jobs or become fully integrated in society. In Egypt under Nasser, members of these strata had limited access to education. In other countries and at other times children from poor families had no chance to attend university. On this basis, Munson argues that most militant Islamic students were from either traditional or modern middle-class families, and according to a 1979 survey of students at Cairo University's Faculty of Arts, "belonging to political parties was more for the sons of the rich and middle classes and less for the sons of the poor and the very poor classes."[97] Unfortunately, we have no accurate data on the social makeup of the Central Asian HTI. Further, it is generally hard to judge precisely which strata of the population of the Central Asian republics is most predisposed to the ideas of radical Islam.

At the end of the 1990s, as reported by the Kyrgyz press, some more radical extremist organizations became noticeable in Kyrgyzstan, in particular, Tabligh, Uzun Sokol (The long-bearded), Islam Lashkarlari (Warriors of Islam), Nur (Light), and Akramiyya. These organizations were active in Osh and the Jalal-Abad region.[98] According to information from the republic's Interior Ministry, during a period of only two years, about twenty HTI envoys were detained in the southern regions, and literature with appeals for the violent overthrow of the authorities was confiscated.[99]

Officers of the Kyrgyz law enforcement agencies believe that the party's popularity is explained by its solid financial base. They say that the HTI enlists new followers solely by offering material incentives. However, Chief of the Investigation Department of the Jalal-Abad Regional Procurator's Office Rasul Umarov notes that detained HTI members firmly champion their convictions and do not wish to renounce them. "To date, three criminal cases have been opened with respect to six members of the Hizb at-Tahrir party. They do not conceal their membership in that party. Last year, thirteen criminal cases for fanning religious strife were opened with respect to seventeen persons. None of them repented, and all of them are still convinced that they are following the path ordained by Allah."[100]

Many people, even those who are not religious, sympathize with the party's ideas and believe they are right. Entrepreneur Zhipar K. does not attend mosque, nor does he perform the *namaz,* but he is not against the implementation of Shari'a legislation. He says that he was summoned to the police and asked "to give them five thousand soms." They threatened Zhipar with a tax audit and fire code inspection, which would surely uncover violations. "If we lived according to Shari'a, such extortionists would not exist."[101]

A number of experts hold that mistrust of state, and particularly the police, generates among the people sympathy toward the Tahriris as fighters for "the faith and the truth." This reasoning also holds that it is only for fear of being victimized for their convictions that they do not join the ranks of that party. Sabir, who lives in Jalal-Abad, is thirty-two. He became an HTI member four years ago, when he swore an oath upon the Qur'an. He told me that a person joining the ranks of the party must take an examination during which he has to convince HTI members that he is a true Muslim who observes all the *ayats* of the Qur'an and follows the path ordained by the Prophet. According to Sabir, his parents were initially against his joining the party, but then he managed to convince them that nothing bad would be taught there. Sabir mentioned to his parents the example of his school friends: two of them had become addicted to drugs and did not work; one had been left by his wife, who took her child with her. But upon entering the party, they began "leading decent lives."

Sabir once asked the imam of the local mosque to allow him to hold a conversation with the believers at the mosque during a Friday prayer, when the greatest number of people assembles. The imam refused to do so. After that, Sabir was detained by police, who demanded an explanation from him.[102]

In Kyrgyzstan, women constitute more than 10 percent of the total HTI membership, which as estimated by Kyrgyzstan's Security Council numbers a few thousand followers. One of the party activists claims that he knows about 150 women residing in the Jalal-Abad region who are members of the party.

A vigorous inflow of women into the ranks of the Hizb at-Tahrir corresponds with an intensified crackdown on that organization. The following women's stories allow us to understand why women, traditionally remote from politics, found themselves in the ranks of underground militants.

A thirty-three-year-old housewife, Zamira, Uzbek by nationality, lives in Jalal-Abad. At present, she is a *daris*, which means that she is taking classes and preparing herself to join the Hizb at-Tahrir. The woman was brought into the ranks of the movement by her husband, Rahimjan. Zamira believes that the HTI aims for justice in the world, an idea that she upholds. In her opinion, all the present ills in the country stem from rule by the wrong form of government, and the only way out is the creation of an Islamic state with a caliph at its head. In an interview, she said: "Now, there is no equality in the country. We see how comfortably high-ranking government officials live. Things should not be like this, and we want to change it."[103] Another underground militant, Zamira's neighbor, Rano, is the wife of HTI member Tahir. Rano had earlier become a *mushrif*, a preceptor of pupils, or *darises*. Rano claims that it is easier to propagate the ideas of the Hizb at-Tahrir among women: "First, women are much more religious than men; second, most women are out of work, and therefore they are less exposed to 'negative worldly influence.'"[104] According to Rano, it is easier to enlist young women into the party. Older ones do not wish to follow the laws of Shari'a, such as the interdiction of communing with men or the imperative to wear a headscarf fully covering the hair. These women, having received an atheist upbringing and free higher education in Soviet times, are impervious to the party's ideology.

The party's women activists say that they are not concerned with numbers or trying to enroll as many people as possible. For them, the main goal is to clarify religious questions to people and to tell them about the situation in society. Rano believes: "It is not obligatory that all with whom we converse should join the HTI; it is more important that they understand the need to live by the laws of Shari'a."

The authorities of Central Asian republics and the advocates of the secular model of state are particularly concerned by the fact that the Tahriris are succeeding in drawing schoolchildren and university students into their ranks. This, among other things, was stated by the head of the Jalal-Abad department of the Kyrgyz National Security Service, Marat Imankulov, in Jalal-Abad at the end of October 2003. He noted the dangerous growth of religious extremism in that region, mentioning in particular that before the start of the month of Ramadan, which fell on October 26, the Tahriris circulated leaflets calling on the population to come out against the authorities in the Suzak and Bazar-Qurghan districts of that region.[105]

The active role of women in the Islamic movement is possibly explained by their greater social vulnerability as a result of the destruction of the system of customary family values and ties by modernization. As has been observed by Hardacre, "Women are thus powerfully attracted by fundamentalism's interpersonal networks that invoke the language of kinship and in which the religion itself is portrayed as a family."[106]

As an example of the HTI's particular attention to the role of women, I cite the content of one of the party's leaflets:[107]

In the name of God the Merciful and the Compassionate
WOMEN'S DISCIPLINE IN THE PARTY

Just as in the Hizb at-Tahrir men obey discipline, so do women as well. Just as the Party's documents, rules, and procedures are applicable to men, so are they to women. In the same way do women, equally with men, observe the necessary requirements of Islam. Everything that is present in the Party's books, documents, and other sources, men and women fulfill equally. However, in view of the fact that the Party and political life requires the observance of things that are not necessary, one is obliged to constantly observe complete purity and an unblemished record; for that reason in the Hizb at-Tahrir the discipline of women,

(continued)

being also related, along with certain generally accepted principles, with special principles, by virtue of the latter includes certain restrictive conditions, which should be observed without question and accurately. In view of the above, women's discipline in the Hizb at-Tahrir is confined to the following principles:

1. Women's circle may be organized by women alone. In the same way, women alone may head circles. If a man is to be found who is closely related to all the women of the circle [*mahram*], it is permitted for him to head them.
2. All local committees, which supervise women's circles and govern women and their party activity, must consist of women. Under no circumstances is the presence of men permissible there.
3. Admission of women into the Party is effected only by women. A woman is admitted into the Party by the female leader of the local organization [*jihaz*] intended strictly for women and composed of women, or members of that organization. Admission of women [into the Party] by men is absolutely unacceptable with a single exception: admission of a woman may be effected by the amir or deputy [*wakil*] sent by him.
4. In the case of complications in creating a local organization [*jihaz*] out of women, the regional council [*majlis-i wilayat*] in place of a [nonexistent] local organization may appoint a woman who, while supervising women's circles, will admit them into the Party.
5. Monthly circles and meetings arranged for women must consist strictly of women. It is completely impossible for men to take part in them. On this question, there is no difference between a person taking the floor in a circle and a circle participant. In the same way, a woman must not take part as a speaker or even as a participant in monthly circles and meetings arranged for men.
6. It is inadmissible for a woman to carry on a discussion or maintain communication with men, pay a visit to them, or do this jointly with men. It is equally inadmissible for her to form part of the same membership of deputies [*wakils*] in which men take part. She may carry on a discussion with, maintain communication with, or pay a visit to only women and together with women. The membership of deputies must consist only of women.
7. A woman is not to be entrusted with governance of a district [*mintaqa*]. This can be done under no circumstances. A district is not entrusted to her, and she cannot be responsible for it. It would likewise be wrong to appoint her only to be in charge of certain houses or certain neighborhoods, even if she [is to carry out her functions] for women and together with women. On the contrary, she ought to avoid any kind of permanency, a stable timetable, and any constantly recurring situation.
8. A woman should not become a leader of the Party's regional secretariat or an employee of a department or library, or perform Party functions similar to these. The regional Party department, library, and functions

related to them refer to the Party's general [*umumi*] management, its library, and similar functions.

9. It is inadmissible for a woman to become financially responsible for a city, region, or the entire Party. It is equally inadmissible for her to become a calculator and collector [of funds]. However, it is admissible for her as a female leader to collect the requisite funds from women alone, that is, in her own circle.

10. It is inadmissible for a woman to become an agent [*mu'tamad*] of a region or amir of the Party. However, it is admissible for her to become generally [*umumi*] responsible for women of the region and contact with an agent. If there is no such [woman who is] generally responsible, the neighborhood female leader [directly] gets in touch with the agent.[108]

These are the special principles that regulate women's discipline in the party. Other principles bear a general character, embracing both men and women. In keeping with them, women equally with men distribute documents, books, and so forth. Like men, women champion the truth and combat falsehood, oppose unjust power, and resist oppressors. Women as well as men suffer arrest and torture, are persecuted by the authorities, and live in secret. A woman, like a man, carries on a battle of ideas and a political struggle. Besides the ideas set forth above, all the party principles and functions pertain to both men and women. Therefore, women have to keep a zealous watch over the observance of absolute caution, constant purity, and an unblemished record.

THE MOBILIZATION PROCESS

The successful mobilization of the population of Kyrgyzstan, which endures enormous hardships and injustices in everyday life, is promoted by the HTI's main precepts. In Saniya Sagnaeva's opinion, these are "a just order and equality of all members of society" and "the idea of solidarity of all Muslims."[109] An additional factor greatly contributing to the successful mobilization of the population is the orientation to nonviolent methods of struggle, among which propaganda occupies the most prominent place. The Kyrgyz author, Orozbek Moldaliev, considers the HTI to be more dangerous to the national security of Kyrgyzstan than the IMU for a number of reasons. The HTI works mainly with the Kyrgyz youth, it understands the real problems plaguing society, and it uses effective means of mobilization—pamphlets and leaflets.[110] But the HTI, as most Islamist political parties, can hardly provide solutions to the hardships the local populations are suffering from, especially hardships that are socioeconomic in character. Those Central Asian writers who either represent the official point of view or have strong links with the establishment tend to exaggerate the dangers of the HTI. In Kyrgyzstan, despite the HTI's sharp criticism of the entire existing order in which it seeks to ensure a change, the party shows a willingness to pursue dialogue with the government, addressing appeals to the authorities and acting as if it were not an underground party that rejects the existing state order. For its part, the ruling regime does not limit itself to repression against the HTI, either. According to a message on the Internet, Chairman of the Committee for Religious Affairs under the Government of Kyrgyzstan Mamedyusupov allegedly expressed the government's willingness to consider the HTI's application for registration. However, this was soon refuted by the committee chairman himself. Despite all rumors, the government has not ceased legal prosecution of the Tahriris.

In Kyrgyzstan, there are influential public figures who have come out for a more tolerant attitude on the part of the authorities toward the HTI. The ombudsman of the republic, Tursunbai Bakir Uulu, says that the ban on the party is not at all justified from a legal point of view, as there is no law indicating a restriction of its activity. Sharing the Kyrgyz government's concern over HTI activity, the ombudsman disapproves of the government's punitive actions: "The fight against [the HTI] must be based on legal methods. The organization's members are mostly citizens of Kyrgyzstan, who, in accordance with the Constitution, have the right to [express] their views."[111] Does the position of the ombudsman reflect the existence of sympathies for the Islamists among the Kyrgyz elite, or is it only resentment, natural for a man of his station, against such actions on the part of government bodies that go beyond the framework of law? In fact, the Kyrgyz parliament discussed the question of passing tougher laws against the activity of radical Islamic organizations, but deputies failed to agree on the enactment of such legislation. Some deputies believe that mass arrests of the Tahriris may only cause Islamic extremism to intensify. According to Deputy Alisher Sabirov, "if we toughen punishments, in a couple of years we shall be dealing with experienced criminals, fanatically battling for the ideas of Islamic Caliphate."[112] For Sabirov, to date, the authorities are oriented solely toward arresting all those suspected of belonging to the HTI.

However, there are many fewer criminal cases in Kyrgyzstan than in Uzbekistan or Tajikistan. In the Osh region, where HTI activity is most noticeable, only a small number of Tahriris—twenty-four persons—have been tried, and only seven have been sentenced to jail. At the same time, the terms of punishment have been mild—two to four years imprisonment, with the majority of those convicted being simply fined less than U.S. $200. In all, only a little over five hundred HTI members have been identified in the Osh region.

According to media reports based on information from the Kyrgyz authorities, about two thousand HTI activists are allegedly operating in the republic, with the numbers of party members constantly growing. As of June 2003, the Kyrgyz law enforcement agencies opened 193 cases against persons suspected of belonging to the HTI.[113]

A Kyrgyz author Botobekov believes that the IMU is borrowing HTI methods.[114] He cites reports that appeared in the Russian mass media about some operational rules for Namangani's group. For example, members are required not to use their own names, but to address each other by assumed names or numbers.[115] But such rules exist in almost all underground movements, and there is no reason to believe that they have been borrowed by the IMU from the HTI.

Still, many Kyrgyz government officials claim (as do all other Central Asian governments) that there is a direct link between the HTI and the IMU. Arrests do not dampen the HTI's popularity but impel its members to hide themselves more effectively. Also, there have been mass protests against the arrests of the Tahriris in which both women and men have taken part. Thus, more than two thousand people gathered at the funeral of an HTI activist who had died in an Uzbekistani prison and was proclaimed a *shahid*. The funeral took place in the small town of Karasu, located on the other side of the Kyrgyz–Uzbek border, and the crowd gathered in spite of the fact that the people had not known beforehand that he would be brought home for burial.

On September 12, 2002, Kyrgyzstan's Interior Minister Kutuev announced that a clash between militants of the Islamic Movement of Uzbekistan and government troops in the Chatkal district of the Jalal-Abad region resulted in the killing of seven militants who had on them, among other types of literature, HTI leaflets.[116] Regular reports on contacts between the HTI and the IMU in early September 2000, with Taliban representatives taking part as a third party in such meetings, have been issued by the Kyrgyz special services.[117] A number of analysts supported that thesis. Botobekov believes that "the Islamic Movement of Uzbekistan, nurturing far-reaching plans for the seizure of power, has now focused its efforts on the creation of the 'inner underground,' relying on the religious and political Hizb at-Tahrir organization."[118] And HTI leaders possess far greater religious learning than IMU leaders, which helps them to persuade people. According to the former head of the State Commission for Religious Affairs of Kyrgyzstan, Zh. Zhorobekov, "many HTI activists know theology well; they are past masters of psychological methods of persuasion and agitation."[119]

Sagnaeva also speaks of the weakness of the authorities' counterpropaganda against the HTI. The imams' reluctance to engage in open activity is probably due to the fact that they feel insufficiently prepared to engage in polemics. The statement by the Mufti of Kyrgyzstan, Kisambai-Aji, who tried to convince the Tahriris that their activities contradicted Islam, had no impact on them. The "people's squads" organized by the government to prevent the Tahriris from posting their leaflets were not effective, either. Besides the helplessness of the authorities, another factor behind state fecklessness is the abuses perpetrated by officials in the process of enforcing measures taken against the Islamists; these abuses include extortion, blackmail, bribe taking, and the settling of personal accounts.

The Central Asian governments hold the HTI's links with IMU functionaries today to be fully "documented." Among the evidence that they cite are the results of the raid of the home of Anarbaev, a Tahriri functionary from Tajikistan's Sogdian region. Among the items discovered were an arms cache, forbidden literature, and a letter from Juma Hojiev (Namangani) calling on the Tahriris to join forces for common struggle. Authorities also point to a meeting, held in 1997 in Islamabad, Pakistan, at which representatives of Tabligh, Tahir Yuldashev, and three delegates of the HTI of Uzbekistan discussed how to build an Islamic state. At that time, Yuldashev argued the need for an armed takeover in Uzbekistan to the Tabligh and HTI representatives. The Tahriris failed to support the IMU leader. In 1999, after the February attacks, HTI leaders allegedly agreed to pool efforts with the IMU to bring about jihad. The spokesmen for the Uzbek authorities claim that, as part of the Namangani band that invaded the territory of Kyrgyzstan jointly with other IMU members, there were Afghan, Tajik, and Uighur militants, in addition to radically minded "leaders of regional structures" of the HTI who had come there from Uzbekistan. Ilham Izzatullaev, a native of Kokand and an active HTI functionary, was among the persons detained by Kyrgyz police on suspicion of complicity in the explosion in one of the rooms of Inexim Bank in Osh. He joined the IMU in 2001 and served in the band of the field commander "Abdurahman." However, the flow of Islamists from one organization to another is quite common. Rather than attesting to the proximate positions of these organizations, it suggests quite the opposite: that the Islamic radical was dissatisfied with the HTI's moderation and opted for an organization directly aiming at armed struggle.

Beyond any doubt, the Tahriris entertained contacts with all the radical Islamist movements, including those who engaged in terrorist activity. The Uzbekistan police possess information that in February–March 2002, one of the HTI coordinators for the CIS countries sent several emissaries to Tajikistan to meet representatives of Usama bin Ladin and the Taliban movement, ostensibly in order to apprise them of the HTI's support for their actions. In Tajikistan, such information has not been confirmed. In fact, one of the operatives of the local law enforcement agencies expressed doubt as to the necessity of such a meeting for the HTI, even if it really supported bin Ladin and the Taliban.

There would be more grounds to rank the HTI among aggressive jihadists, if a corresponding position had been expounded in its documents. However, HTI statements are either contradictory or, as the Tahriris themselves assert, fabricated revelations of their "jihadist choice." The aforementioned article on the "general principles of self-sacrifice," published in the HTI periodical *al-Wa'y*, is an example of the contradictory type.

THE HTI AFTER SEPTEMBER 11

As was discussed in chapter 2, after September 11, the Central Asian governments, having allied themselves with the United States and other Western countries in the struggle against terrorism, sharply stepped up repression of Islamic radicals, who also lost a significant part of the assistance that they had been receiving from abroad.

Despite the repressive measures taken by the state, in 2001–2002 Hizb at-Tahrir leaders and supporters continued and even intensified their agitation and propaganda activity among the population. In particular, after the start of the antiterrorist operations in Afghanistan in October–November 2001, and in connection with events in the Middle East, in April and early May 2002 they distributed religious extremist leaflets with an anti-American, anti-Israeli, and anti-Karimov slant. Distribution occurred in Uzbekistan, especially in densely populated regions, in crowded places such as markets, in the buildings of ministries and departments, and also in the diplomatic missions of foreign countries and organizations accredited in Central Asia. The literature appealed for support for the Arabs of Palestine and jihad against the United States, Israel, and the Karimov regime. The leaflets had mostly been produced in Uzbekistan, and during the last months of 2002 there was evidence of their being distributed through the Internet and by subsequent photocopying.

In Tajikistan, four activists of the HTI were detained and condemned in October 2002 in the cities of Dushanbe and Khujand for complicity in the distribution of such leaflets. Earlier, in April and the beginning of May 2002, six leaflet distributors were detained for similar activity in the same cities.

Based on evidence from the law enforcement bodies of the Central Asian republics, a meeting was held between representatives of the *qiyadat* and functionaries from the republics of Central Asia in the town of Urumqi of the Xinjiang-Uighur Autonomous Region of the People's Republic of China (PRC) in March 1992 (the preceding meeting of representatives of the *qiyadat* of the Hizb at-Tahrir and their functionaries in Central Asia took place on September 25, 2001, in Bishkek, in which Al-Salai

Muhammad, a Jordanian national who is one of the HTI coordinators for the CIS countries, took part). One of the topics of discussion in Urumqi was how to intensify the religious propaganda activity of the local Tahriris, given the increased determination and coordination on the part of world powers to curb the activity of religious extremists. One outcome of the meeting was that a Kyrgyz citizen, Muhammadyusuf Mamasadykov (b. 1973) a native and resident of Osh, was appointed leader of the Hizb at-Tahrir in the Central Asian region.

In government circles of the republics of Central Asia, there was a consensus that the religious and political situation in these republics had become aggravated after the meeting of Tahriri leaders in the PRC. In particular, the Tahriri functionaries in Uzbekistan mobilized to identify National Security Service and the Interior Ministry operatives who are directly in charge of combating religious extremism, in order to be able to take repressive measures against them after the installation of a theocratic state in the territory of Uzbekistan. On August 16, 2002, Kyrgyz police exposed the illegal activity of clandestine Tahriri cells in the Bazar-Qurghan district of the Jalal-Abad region. In particular, in the houses of Tukhtakhanov and Tukhtasinov, Tahriri leaders and native residents of the village of Arslanbob in Jalal-Abad, authorities discovered and "legally documented" three live grenades, an unregistered small-caliber rifle, and 395 live cartridges, as well as a great number of extremist literature, leaflets, and audio- and videocassettes issued by the Hizb at-Tahrir.

In the process, on the eve of the Kyrgyz Independence Day, Kyrgyz law enforcement agencies discovered a mined cache, allegedly containing a large consignment of weapons and ammunition that were to be utilized for carrying out sabotage and terrorist actions in Bishkek with the aim of destabilizing the sociopolitical situation in the republic. The governments of Central Asian republics made use of these facts to prove that the HTI had begun to actively prepare for terrorist activity.

In Uzbekistan, at the same time that the HTI had begun to pay more attention to the immediate concerns of the populations of Central Asian republics, materials prepared in the HTI's international centers and devoted to international problems continued to be circulated. This allows us to come to the following conclusions. First, the HTI in Uzbekistan continued to be an affiliate (though possibly with a high degree of autonomy) of the international HTI organization. Second, the HTI views the events in Palestine, Afghanistan, and Iraq as instruments of political mobilization.

Events involving Iraq in the spring of 2003 occasioned the publication of several HTI materials. On March 20, 2003, the leaflet *Answers to Questions*[120] was sent to Uzbekistan to help local HTI functionaries carry on work with rank-and-file members. As an example, I shall cite several questions and answers contained in the leaflet (translated from Uzbek).

On the same day, a leaflet with an appeal "Stop the crusade!" was circulated in Uzbekistan.[121]

Question: What happened in Baghdad? What is the cause of the U.S. entry into Baghdad and the surrender of the Iraqi guards without a fight?

Answer: In the mass media there are different versions of the disappearance of Saddam Hussein. Almost all of them are improbable. It should be noted that Saddam's power was held up by fear and diktat. The army and the people were backing Saddam as they were afraid of him. The guards were not sure if their President was alive or dead, and therefore they abandoned the war.

Saddam's warriors had no faith; therefore they could not battle as *shahids*. If they had had genuine faith, then, despite the death of their leaders, they, armed with their faith, would have fought to the end, to victory or death.

Question: Why does the USA threaten Syria? Is not the Syrian government a U.S. underling?

Answer: Earlier America had given its underlings room to maneuver and had not demanded open expression of submission. Presently, the USA is demanding from its underlings an open form of submission.

If Syria does not hold talks with Israel, as the USA demands, does not cease its attempts at putting pressure on the east coast of the Lake of Tiberias, and does not persecute the so-called undesirable patriotic organizations, the probability of U.S. forces entering Syria to subdue the region is great.

Should Syria not make an open display of submission, the USA will look for other stooges in the region, ones that will accept its demands without demur.

Syria demands room for maneuver; while secretly being a U.S. underling, the Syrian authorities are making a sham display of resistance to the USA for domestic consumption. However, the USA is demanding open submission from Syria, and therefore threatening it.

Assessing the events taking place in Iraq, its authors call the United States and Britain "invaders of Islamic states" and their actions "the fourth crusade against the Muslims." They call on Muslims to overthrow the governments of states backing the United States and Britain, as well as certain Islamic states that, instead of rebuffing the Americans in the name of jihad, lend them assistance by giving them access to their territories and military bases.

Furthermore, the leaflet points out that U.S. President George W. Bush allegedly started "a war against Muslims" on September 16, 2001, with the words: "the American people begin to understand this crusade."

An additional leaflet was called *A Call by the Hizb at-Tahrir—Only with the Caliphate Will You Achieve Victory!*[122] Addressing themselves to Muslims, the authors call on them to strive toward the creation of a worldwide Caliphate. In particular, they point out that every aggression against Muslims ends in favor of the invaders.

You are being humiliated by America, Britain, Russia and even India. The Jews together with other states, great and small, occupy the territories of

Afghanistan, as before they did Palestine, Kashmir, Chechnya, and now you are being humiliated in Iraq. You have tried various forms of government: kingdom, republic, hoping to achieve well-being. However, you are being deprived of all benefits, including your material and human potential.

And is it not time to create a Caliphate as the only way out of this darkness?" The writers appeal to all Muslims to help the Hizb at-Tahrir and urge them to visit the HTI's website.[123]

International problems continued to be the object of HTI attention after the end of the military campaign in Iraq as well. Thus a leaflet dated May 24, 2003, reads:

In view of the fact that America is the leader in the international arena, it was able to justify its aggression against Iraq as a just cause. With this act, the USA brought the world back to an era of "might makes right" and the laws of the jungle. The USA forced the UN Security Council to pass Resolution 1483 of May 22, 2003, which conferred a stamp of legitimacy on the U.S. and British takeover of Iraq.

A person analyzing developments in the world and, in particular, in the countries of the Islamic belt can see that the USA, having become the sole leader on the international arena, steers policy in any direction it deems necessary. If one is to take note of the events taking place in the world and particularly in the countries of the Islamic world, one may point out the following:

1. Being the founder of the UN after World War II, America is using this organization to adopt laws and decisions justifying its geopolitical encroachments and international conspiracies.

2. The USA has become complacent as a result of its power and might. For this reason, it has ceased to take account of the interests of other countries should they run counter to U.S. interests. It does not recognize international treaties where interests of the USA are not placed above those of others: for fear of inquiry into the crimes of its soldiers, the USA has refused to sign a treaty on the creation of an organization to investigate war crimes. Moreover, the USA opposes international laws; so that goods imported from Europe cannot compete on its internal market with American goods, it has imposed customs duties on European commodities.

3. America has begun to seek the condemnation of the countries of the Islamic belt on the basis of standards that it has invented by itself. The unexpectedly easy conquest of Afghanistan and Iraq has served as an impetus for this. Having damaged Muslim unity, the USA has started to make plans to fragment their countries. The events in Afghanistan and Iraq are a confirmation of this. The way for this is being paved by politicians expatiating upon the extension of the line of security on the Arabian Peninsula, the war on terrorism, women's rights, and the modernization of curricula that give rise to "extremist ideas."

4. The rulers of Muslim countries have thrown the problems of the *umma* into the American basket and entrusted America with the solution of 99 percent of their problems. The USA is resolving problems in favor of the *umma*'s enemies, first of all distracting their attention with the seizure of Muslim lands in 1967, as well as on the basis of the Road Map of Tenet and Mitchell on the Palestinian problem, the Cyprus and Greece plan, the Machakos treaty for South Sudan, and also UN resolutions on Kashmir. And they intend to settle the Chechen issue jointly with Russia. The USA has overrun Central Asia and the Caucasus, and now Afghanistan and Iraq. This is not to speak of the Arabian Peninsula and the Gulf.

5. Other countries are unable to save the world from American expansionism. There are several reasons for this, and we shall cite but a few:

a) Such countries as France, Germany, and Russia, who do have influence on the world arena, themselves stand for a capitalist system advocated by America.

b) China, which is developing along a noncapitalist path, is influenced by its mentality. Therefore, for China, the development of its own system is more important than the outrages unleashed upon the world by America.

c) America fears the unification of the European Union but has achieved its collapse in three ways:

1. EU enlargement through the incorporation of the countries of Eastern Europe. These countries, being dependent on America, have become a spearhead that has ushered in America's influence within the European Union. This was noticeable when they supported America's invasion of Iraq.

2. The continued existence of NATO despite the demise of the Warsaw Treaty.

3. Britain's position. It does not wish to merge into a single union with the European states and become "dissolved" in that union like Luxembourg. Britain still lives in the euphoria of a "great power." Thus it contributes to the weakening of Europe, and as a result, no country can face up to America.

Hey, Muslims!

This deed is within your powers. The key is the creation of a state under the name of the Caliphate.

Only the Caliphate can throw America and Britain from the international arena, face up to America's dominance on the world arena, and free the world from America's atrocities.[124]

Propaganda in favor of the Caliphate remains a high-priority task for the HTI. Another leaflet, entitled *Victory Will Come with the Caliphate*, dated April 13, 2003, says (translation from Uzbek):

[H]elp Allah and observe Shari'a. It is then that you will establish the Caliphate and be victorious. Should not the words of the Prophet be borne out: "He who will die without having come to believe will die an ignoramus"?

Swear an oath to the Caliphate, for with it alone will you save yourselves from ignorant death; with it will you be able to fight and defend yourselves. "The imam championing it is able to fight and with it to save himself."

You, the army and the mighty people?! Your blood is on the wrong track; instead of the pointless and godless existence, do you not want to be pure along the path of Allah?

Should you too not keep to the path along which the Prophet found refuge for himself, helped people, and converted his peoples to Islam? Help Allah and his Prophet to establish the Caliphate, for in this righteous way our people will again become the people of Islam. It is then that your service to Allah will turn into shining pages.

Only the Caliphate will save you from dishonor and humiliation. It has all the means to restore respect for you. It is the regime that Allah, master of the worlds, prescribed, having linked all the victories to it.

Only with the Caliphate will you be able to pay them back for the aggression in Iraq, for the fact that children have joined the war, and for the flesh-creeping terror that has filled their ingenuous faces and pure hearts.[125]

The HTI's new upsurge of interest in international problems and criticism of the foreign policies of Central Asian regimes drew fresh accusations that the HTI is a mouthpiece for international radical Islamist forces. The Uzbek authorities made new statements characterizing the HTI as an organization hostile to Uzbekistani national interests, set up and supported from abroad. Iran, understanding the notion of "abroad" as a reference to itself, denied complicity in rendering any kind of assistance to the HTI. As early as May 1998, the state-run Iran Radio criticized the president of Uzbekistan for suppressing Muslims, saying that he did not differentiate between "Islamic extremists" and "Islamic reformists."[126] In this way, Tehran was responding to Karimov's cool and critical policy toward Iran, which Tashkent accused of supporting the Islamist forces.

Though there is no doubt that the HTI maintains broad foreign links, the degree to which HTI activity in Central Asia is financed from abroad has thus far remained an open question. As mentioned earlier, an HTI member in Khujand asserted that it was not foreign money but local donations that constituted the main source of funding of the party's activity. This HTI member also added in an interview that some of these donations were coming from very wealthy Central Asian individuals.[127] We are not able either to confirm or to deny such statements.

The primary source of financing for Tahriri activity is widely believed to be membership dues. Every member of the party is obligated to make a monthly payment to the party treasury (*tabarru'at*). The size of the payment depends on the member's property and income (5 to 20 percent). In addition to the membership dues, the Tahriris receive financial backing from the so-called *mu'ayyids* (sympathizers) and *ansar* (helpers). These are not members of the Hizb at-Tahrir, and they do not take a direct part in "active measures" such as recruitment of new members, the circulation of leaflets, and participation in what are referred to as *ochik da'wats*. However, they render material and other aid to the Tahriris (for instance, they make available their apartments and homes for classes, meetings, and refuge for wanted Tahriris). Each Tahriri has to recruit *ansar* and *mu'ayyids* whose identities he alone knows.

Despite the constant growth of alarmist reports on HTI activity, many questions remain unanswered. Has the HTI at present identified new objectives, and has it changed its views concerning the means to achieve them? How do the activities of various HTI religious organizations differ? Is there evidence of the party's alliance with other Islamic organizations or at least of coordinated action? Who makes up the party's social base in various countries, and what place does the "national" agenda (say, the Kashmiri problem) occupy in the HTI's program? Some members of the mass media have claimed that during a meeting that took place in Tehran in June 2003 between the presidents of Uzbekistan, Tajikistan, and Iran, the question of Tehran's terminating support for the HTI and the radical Islamic movements in Central Asia was raised. However, official sources have not confirmed that there was ever any mention of this topic. Moreover, there is no evidence that Tehran supports the HTI; in fact, it is unlikely that a Shi'ite Islamic state would support a Caliphatist Sunni movement based on the idea of *vilayat-e faqih*.

Since September 11, the HTI has been increasingly and more persistently accused of allying itself with Islamic militant organizations. According to a British consultant, "there are already indications that some Hizb at-Tahrir cells, for example, have begun to engage in the drug trade and have sought to establish links to the IMU."[128] In contrast to these accusations, there is no evidence that supports the HTI's alleged drift toward militancy, and the party has for a long time remained legal in most Western countries, despite calls from Uzbekistan to ban it. In early 2003, Germany was the first European state to ban the HTI for distributing anti-Semitic tracts.[129]

Many Western human rights organizations appealed to President Karimov to show tolerance and not to persecute a party that has renounced the use of force in realizing its political goals. Still, many of those arrested in Uzbekistan, according to International Crisis Group (ICG) interviews, belong to the HTI. At the same time, there have also been arrests of certain individuals who have a general interest in certain Islamic teachings, even when they have no relation to any radical political program, as in the case of the Turkish mystic philosopher Bediuzzin Said Nursi (1873–1960).[130]

There have been even more cases in which the accusation of membership in the HTI has been used to oppress individuals who have criticized the government. On February 18, a court in Tashkent sentenced the journalist Ghaizat Mekhliboev to seven years in prison on charges of anticonstitutional activities (article 159), involvement in religious extremist organizations (articles 216 and 244-2), and inciting religious hatred (article 156).[131] His publications in the local press allegedly contained HTI ideas. Mekhliboev admitted his knowledge of HTI ideology, but denied any possession of HTI material, which is considered illegal in Uzbekistan. This sentence was interpreted by human rights organizations as a sign of the authorities' intolerance of criticism.

An amnesty in Uzbekistan was announced in December 2002, and a number of religious prisoners were released, but we can hardly suggest that this represented a shift toward a more tolerant position with respect to the Islamists. All Central Asian governments continue to be afraid of the HTI, and they believe it poses the utmost danger to their secular regimes, thus exaggerating its potential effects.

A CHANGE IN THE POSITION OF INTERNATIONAL ACTORS

The shift in the policy of many of the world's states toward the HTI, represented by its being listed as a terrorist organization in 2003, has made it easier for Central Asian governments to combat radical Islam and the Islamic opposition in general.

A ban imposed on the party in Russia in February 2003 was largely dictated by the wish to accommodate Islam Karimov. The implication was that the ban would be followed by repressive measures against the HTI. On June 10, the Russian authorities announced that they had launched a crackdown against the HTI in Moscow. The Federal Security Service (FSB) had arrested fifty-five leaders and members of the Moscow HTI group and found plastic explosives, hand grenades, dynamite, and detonator cords at their headquarters. FSB spokesman Sergei Ignatchenko said in an interview: "We have no doubts or illusions about their actions. We had intelligence information about their preparations. They were training fighters to send to Chechnya." Ignatchenko also accused members of the HTI group of providing support for possible terrorist acts in Moscow—calling them the "Muslim brothers" of al-Qa'ida.[132] The arrested leader and members of the HTI had come to Moscow from Uzbekistan and Tajikistan to escape local government repression. The authorities did not disclose any details about them, but announced that among those arrested were Alisher Musaev, head of the Moscow HTI branch, and Akram Dialov, a leading HTI activist. This significant shift in Moscow's position toward the HTI coincided with a similar turn in Washington's position. This suggests that Moscow's and Washington's policies were probably coordinated.

According to mass media sources in Pakistan, Pakistani authorities had been receiving "some advice" from Washington to place restrictions on the HTI. It was understood that "the advice came in response to reports that the Hizb has been inciting public opinion against the US and the Musharraf administration" at gatherings and through the distribution of handbills, pamphlets, and other literature.[133] A number of arrests had been made in Pakistan on numerous occasions, and Pakistani agencies had begun infiltrating HTI meetings and making an effort "to learn about its structure and aims."

The HTI is believed to have appeared in Pakistan in late 2000. In early 2001, Hizb at-Tahrir members opened a branch and a print shop in Peshawar whose tasks included designing Islamic ideological strategy that is destined to be carried over to Central Asian states from Pakistani territory. For their political purposes in Pakistan, the Tahriris employ such religious groups as Jami'at-i-Ulema-i-Islami.

In fact, the Pakistani authorities have let it be understood that the campaign against the HTI is connected exclusively with its anti-U.S. agenda, and not with convincing evidence concerning its participation in terrorist activity, a question that still remains murky. Earlier, President Musharraf had banned such jihadist groups as Lashkar-e Tayyiba, Jaysh-e Muhammad, and Harakat ul-Mujahidin. Information agencies have reported on their resurgent activity in Indian-held Kashmir, and these banned organizations remain on the U.S. watch list.[134]

The HTI's activity in Turkey has begun to be severely restricted by the Turkish authorities. The HTI is carrying on agitation work there in the country's poorest regions. Turkish HTI leaflets state that in the near future a Caliphate modeled on the state of "righteous Caliphs" will be created, and that Turkish citizens are not recommended to celebrate Republic Day on October 29. In 2002, a number of operations against religious extremist and terrorist organizations were carried out in Turkey. Among those detained was the Turkish Tahriri leader, Ahmet Kilickay.

DECLINING ACTIVITY BUT CONTINUING POTENTIAL

For all the reasons discussed above, in the opinion of a number of observers, the HTI is encountering difficulties and as a result experienced a decline in its overall activity in 2003–2004.

Based on information from an Uzbek professor who maintains ties with the Islamic opposition, Alexander Shevyakov reports that the popular influence of that organization is on the wane.[135] As a consequence, squabbles and splits are allegedly rampant within the HTI leadership. However, the possibility that this struggle is a façade designed to help the Islamic radicals weather these difficult times cannot be discounted.

Informants in the Ferghana Valley whom I met on my trips there in 2003 are saying that people are intimidated by measures taken against individuals who harbor the slightest sympathies for the HTI and other radicals. It goes without saying that individuals are reluctant to provide direct assistance or join their ranks. Furthermore, as a result of mass repression, members of radical Islamic organizations have gone deeper underground and decreased their activity. People frustrated with their day-to-day difficulties are no longer as responsive as they once were to the radicals' appeals. To begin with, the risks have become greater, people do not see much benefit from supporting the Islamists, and they no longer believe (as many of them did before) that Islamists will manage to build a just and prosperous Islamic state as they have been telling people they would for fifteen years. Nonetheless, sympathies for Islamic radicals do exist in the region; they remain the only force challenging the regime; and sentiments of protest are voiced in the form of support for the Islamists, even by those who cannot be called devout and obedient Muslims. Alexander Shevyakov cites a study by the Ijtimoiy Fikr foundation that shows that among native, Muslim Uzbeks, who comprise 97 percent of the population, very few actually observe all the prescribed rites.[136] Mosques are attended mostly by old people and by very devout young people. Only one out of four youths under the age of thirty performs ceremonies and rituals prescribed by Islam. But one can hardly interpret this as representing a decrease in religiosity.

It would be more accurate to speak of dormant, hidden religiosity— open religiosity has been discredited by the entire course of events in the country, the region, and the world, and might also be seen as dangerous due to the policies of the authorities, who regard Islamic radicalism as an existential threat and are therefore interested in seeing religiosity decrease in general. Dormant, suppressed religiosity had already poured forth in a mighty wave of Islamism after the breakup of the Soviet Union, and a similar upsurge could take place in Uzbekistan in the future.

There exist several reasons why the HTI (and religious opposition more generally) remains virtually the sole channel of expressing sentiments in opposition to the regime. First, the religious part of the population distrusts the official clergy, which finds itself under the tight surveillance of the authorities. At the same time, confidence in those who invoke "true Islamic values" and suffer for the faith due to state persecution is traditionally high among this segment of the population.

Second, secular opposition parties—Birlik and Erk—have almost completely lost the capacity to act. Officially, they were banned, and until recently they conducted no illegal work among the populace; also, their websites are inaccessible to all but a few isolated members of the intelligentsia. In addition, the leaders of these parties, residing in exile, have effectively lost touch with Uzbekistan and have scant knowledge of the problems that worry ordinary citizens.

Third, the HTI leadership recently, and for the first time, started actively to address the everyday needs of the Uzbeks, using economic and environmental problems to fan opposition sentiments and gain popularity. To a disgruntled population, the Tahriris looked like the only group championing their rights. An example was the picketing, organized on three occasions in Samarqand in early 2003, of a tobacco factory owned by an Uzbek–British–American tobacco company. During the protest, the picketers, the greater part of whom were women and children, threw stones at the building and tried to set fire to it. The formal grounds for picketing were concerns about ecological problems: the factory's influence on the environment and health of local residents. The factory had been in existence there for about sixty years; previously it used outdated equipment to produce Belomor cigarettes, and ironically, the most up-to-date American equipment had been installed there shortly before the controversy began. According to the leader of the local ecological foundation, the riots at the factory in Samarqand had been organized by the HTI, whose cell incited the people with leaflets and also agitation.

Fourth, in the first half of 2003, the HTI successfully utilized for political mobilization the anti-American and anti-British feelings that had appeared in the region in connection with the events in Iraq. In the context of the new political situation, the HTI's traditional anti-American and anti-Israeli rhetoric, in essence alien to Uzbekistanis, who were already rather bored with it, began to resonate. Slogans of solidarity with unjustly aggrieved Muslims became even more popular due to the fact that the operation in Iraq was endorsed by the Uzbek authorities (the secular opposition did not protest the operations, either). The use of the situation in Iraq as an instrument of mobilization continued even further after the downfall of Saddam Hussein's regime. It was no accident that the picketing of the British–American tobacco factory coincided directly with preparations for the military operation in Iraq.

Despite the fact that the Middle East is very peripheral in importance to Central Asians, issues related to the Middle East, as many scholars agree, can be easily used for the purposes of political mobilization against the West and Western influence in Central Asia.[137]

Fifth, it is possible that the HTI has begun to succeed in using interclan rivalry to its advantage. In the case of the disturbances at the Samarqand tobacco factory, members of certain local clans obviously had an interest in their execution. As my Samarqand interlocutors told me, these clans were dissatisfied because all the profits from the lucrative tobacco business were going to the capital. Understandably, clans believing themselves to be excluded in the division of power and opportunities in the business sphere may come to side with the Islamists. And, in the words of a Cabinet of Ministers of Uzbekistan official who requested that his identity remain undisclosed, even in government institutions, including the presidential administration, there are "secret supporters of the Wahhabis."

That explains the intensified "Wahhabi" hunt in Uzbekistan, in the *kishlaks* of the Ferghana Valley, and elsewhere. Periodically, Salafi literature is discovered here and people suspected of its propagation are arrested—even the most central institutions are not immune. Thus in the spring of 2003, a search in the Academy of Sciences of Uzbekistan led to the discovery of leaflets and the detention of a group of people suspected of maintaining links with the Salafis.

In other words, despite a certain reduction of HTI activity and the HTI's partial loss of popularity, the party still has considerable political potential. This, among other things, is attested to by leaflets devoted to the internal problems of Uzbekistan, in which a more skillful manipulation of information is discernible. Persistent reference in the leaflets to President Karimov as "the Jew" reveals HTI leaders' intention of portraying him as someone who is "alien" to Uzbekistan and hostile to Islam. In the assessments of many Uzbeks and Tajiks with whom I had the chance to discuss this, these tactics are not fully effective, as the Muslim peoples of Central Asia have always enjoyed normal relations with Jews; in particular, the Bukharan Jews were well integrated into local society, and no significant manifestations of anti-Semitism were observable there.

An example of the HTI's characterization of Karimov as "the Jew" comes in one of the HTI leaflets, dated May 30, 2003 (abridged translation from Uzbek).

On May 16, 2003, officers of the Kashka Darya National Security Service brought the corpse of Arif Alimkhanovich Eshanov, b. March 14, 1965, father of four children, to his house on Said Sultanov Street in Yanghiyul. On the corpse were traces of awful tortures to which Arif Eshanov had been subjected. As a result of repeated beatings, the whole body had turned into one continuous bruise. Some parts of the body were scorched; the left shoulder and an armpit had traces of the application of red-hot metal and a flat iron. Wedges were driven between the fingers. Inserted under the nails and in many parts of the body were needles or an awl. His ribs were broken. Let Allah enter our brother in the ranks of *shahids*, and let him accompany the prophets and saints. They are such good interlocutors.

This awful murder took place after Sayfiddin Numanovich Muminov, a native of the Surkhan Darya region living in Denau on Abdulla Avloni Street, house no. 33, b. May 25, 1967, and Salimzhan Atabaev, a native of the Surkhan Darya region, Denau, living on the Kizil Fargona public farm, and also Sherzoda Abdumajidovich Malikov, b. April 27, 1973, went missing after being led away by the Kashka Darya officers of the Interior Ministry.

Over the course of four years, the Jewish underlings of the Jew tortured to death more than sixty members of the Hizb. Tortures and murders during interrogations became business as usual for the Jew (let him be damned by Allah) underlings. Each year, prisoners are in growing number beaten, placed into punishment cells for the observance of the *namaz*, and infected with various diseases through forced injections; Hizb activists are vilified in the eyes of their comrades, and also subjected to torture so that they should ask for pardon or leave the Hizb.

In Uzbekistan, the Jew and his servitors have devised a new plan for the mass murder of the staunchest young Hizb activists. Having announced that, in detention facilities, the lads that are firm in their faith begin to teach other lads, they incarcerate those who are firm in their faith with prisoners serving punishment for numerous murders and other heinous crimes in the Zhaslik jail UYa 64/71 of Karakalpakia. The aim of this tactic is to foment conflict between these groups, then to bring the troops in and destroy everybody, particularly Hizb members. The Jew (let him be damned by Allah) and his government, in expectation of a good opportunity to implement these plans, is preparing "appropriate conditions" for them. For this purpose, in the middle of May a whole group of high-ranking officials, among whom were the former adviser on the question of Judaism Abdulaziz Mansur,[138] Assistant Chief of the Main Department of Detention Centers Zuhriddin Husniddinov, as well as Chairman of the Directorate for the Muslims Mufti Abdurashid *qari* Bahromov and Anvar *qari* Tursunov, came to Zhaslik. Having gathered the lads from the Hizb, they tried to persuade them to renounce the idea of Islamic life under the Caliphate; they tried to persuade them to ask for the Jew's pardon. After the lads flatly refused to do so, the prison chief, Kulimbetov, told them, "The case is closed. Whether you renounce your idea or not, you will not leave this place alive. We shall leave nobody alive. I have killed two people among you, and no one has done anything to me. The state protects me. And it will protect me this time as well."

Chairman of the Directorate for the Muslims of Uzbekistan, the Mufti of evil Abdurashid *qari* Bahromov, has issued a fatwa on the arrest of members of the Hizb and for members of their families to sever all ties with them. In his statements on the radio and TV, he staged a real attack on the Hizb at-Tahrir and its ideas. In the process, he distorted the *ayats* and the Hadiths. All that Allah called a duty of the Muslim he called sin, and all that was called a sin he called a duty of the Muslim. Anvar *qari* Tursun issued several fatwas so that the officers of the National Security Service and the Interior Ministry could torment Hizb members during interrogations.

Now they are preparing a fatwa for the mass murder of Hizb members; moreover, to commit this murder, the Zhaslik leadership and its officers have received from the Jew (let him be damned by Allah) a "white prayer." Each of them, knowing that the Hizb at-Tahrir relies only on the principles of Islam, has exchanged them for the filthy Jewish life. They know very well that all the thoughts of the Hizb are Islamic, that neither in the thoughts nor in the acts of the Hizb is there even a drop of what is alien to Islam, and that everything it

(continued)

does is in accordance with the precepts of the Prophet. All we can do is to repeat the words of Allah: "The faithful, do not make friends of Jews and Christians! They are friends of somebody else. That of you who is their friend is himself one of them" (5:51). The regimen is toughened in all prisons in Uzbekistan, especially for Hizb members. One such institution is a maximum-security jail, Korovul Bazar UYa 64/25, located in the Bukharan region. A special code of behavior has been established for lads from the Hizb there. As soon as they are imprisoned, they are prescribed to do four things. To pray to the Jew's (let him be damned by Allah) portrait, to thank it, to sing a hymn, and abuse themselves with the dirtiest words. He who obeys these prescriptions is not beaten and not forced to work. In view of the fact that all these requirements contradict Islam, the youths avoid fulfilling them. As a result, their torments become ever more intolerable. At present, thirty-five Hizb members transferred from various prisons of the Navoi region are kept in the closed jail of Korovul Bazar.

One more prison institution where the regimen has been toughened is jail UYa 64/36, for inmates sick with tuberculosis, located in the Navoi region. Here, injections are made with syringes used for AIDS patients, the healthy are placed with the sick, mass starvation is organized, people sick with tuberculosis are left without any treatment, and all kinds of other horrors are practiced. And the conditions for Hizb members are even harder than those for other inmates.

We have already said that a special regimen has been established for Hizb members in prisons of Uzbekistan. The requirements the ordinary detainees must comply with do not extend to members of the Hizb. A handful of infidels has installed the Jew's (let him be damned by Allah) regimen or one with elements close to it for them. For the enforcement of this regimen, the prison chiefs are given broad powers. Thus in order to torture Hizb members until their very death, they constantly receive fresh conditions and orders from the Jew (let Allah damn him). The fact that the Jew (let Allah damn him) masterminded all these deeds is admitted by everyone—by their bloody police, by the cruel prison leadership, the politicians of America, Britain, and Russia who support them with material and other resources, and by human-rights organizations and the foreign media.

Indeed, since America made the Jew its strategic partner, it has supported all his crimes against the Muslims. The mass media have reported that the USA has again allocated to the government of the Jew (let Allah damn him) more than one million dollars in aid. To date, the amount of aid to strengthen the Jew (let Allah damn him) and his criminal government has reached tens and hundreds of millions of dollars. Although these resources have been earmarked for different purposes, it is no secret to anyone that all of them have been assigned to strengthen the Jew (let Allah damn him) and his bloody police in order to keep Muslim lands in devastation. Governments akin to America and Britain are encouraging the Jew by erecting one difficulty after another in Muslim countries and dropping tons of bombs on the civilian population, destroying infants, women, and old people. Now he is carrying out their plans in a rage, killing children and endlessly crippling our generation. To his masters, he represents all the horrors that he is perpetrating against Muslims as insignificant and unworthy of attention.

The Muslims of Uzbekistan! . . .

Allah has informed us, those who have come to believe, that Jews and *mushriks* are the most hostile to our faith. Today this *ayat* has a profound meaning. In all directions, the Jew is attacking us, those who have come to believe. The purpose of his attacks is to restrict the Islamic religion to a few rites performed for show, to deal a blow against the family so as to lessen the number of Muslims, to openly indulge in debauchery, to break down the economy so as to sell at bargain prices the main wealth of the people—cotton and gold—to the infidels, to attack the private property of the Muslims, to subdue all the educational institutions—elementary, high school, and college—to Western views, thereby colonizing our generation from within, and raising henchmen friendly to the West. The unremitting statement of the Jew "We shall not stray from this path" clearly shows that attacks on their part will not cease. In order to guarantee the continuation of this loathsome policy of oppression already pursued for more then ten years, a session of the Olii Majlis (parliament) has adopted a law on people's representatives, in reality people's traitor deputies, that accords guarantees of lifelong immunity to the Jew and his depraved family. This treason on the part of the deputies makes it possible for the Jew (let Allah damn him) and his family to attack the Muslims until death. According to that law, the Jew and his depraved family will until death be leeches on the body of the Muslims.

The Muslims of Uzbekistan!

Hizb at-Tahrir
Uzbekistan, 30 May, 2003[139]

The Arif Eshanov story is used by the Tahriris for political mobilization, just as the martyring in prison of another Tahriri, Farkhad Usmanov, was previously used for this purpose. In June 2002, leaflets of HTI Britain began to be circulated in London under the title *Who Killed Farkhad Usmanov?* Since then, this material has also been disseminated on the HTI websites.[140] "The *shahids'* blood cries for vengeance: jihad is necessary," says the leaflet entitled *Just Another Game of the Servants of Satan—The US and Britain.*[141] It continues:

We ask Allah to reward Arif Eshanov and other brethren of ours with the best rewards—to turn his blood into *shahid*'s blood for their service to Islam and the Muslims, for exhorting the treasonous, hypocritical, and depraved leaders to enter the rightful path, for their open appeal to rally under the banner of the Caliphate. We ask Him to give them a high rank and place them together with the prophets, the righteous, and the *shahids*. We also ask Allah to turn their blood into joyful news for the Muslims, to make them heralds [announcing] that the Caliphate unifying all Muslims is in the offing, that the rays of Islam, extending along the globe, are strengthening the law of the faith. . . .

The Muslims of Uzbekistan!

Uzbekistan is the land of Islam and an inseparable part of Islamic lands. The people living in this region took an oath to Allah, His Prophet Muhammad, His sacred book the Qur'an, and the afterlife as a Muslim people. Did the followers of the Prophet, in performing the *namaz* TOGETHER, not come TOGETHER to perform jihad?

Our time has come to defend the *umma*. . . .[142]

Muslims!

Violence against the Islamic *umma*, done quietly, is spreading more and more. The mentally degrading West, using the help of its minions and material resources for the strike, cannot conceal its hostility toward Islam and the Caliphate. As examples of this, one may cite the closure of the Hizb office in Germany and the entry of Russia's President Putin onto the path of enmity in November and December.[143]

After the March 2004 violence began in Uzbekistan and the Uzbekistani authorities accused the HTI of being involved in it, the HTI headquarters in London reacted immediately. The HTI's statement released on March 29 read: "Hizb at-Tahrir does not engage in terrorism, violence or armed struggle. . . . Dr. Imran Waheed . . . said: 'The finger of blame for these explosions must point at the tyrannical Uzbek regime which has orchestrated such events.'"[144]

Many Central Asian public figures assert that, despite strong repression in Uzbekistan, the HTI is more powerful and influential there than in any other Central Asian republic. Sadykzhan Kamalov, former mufti of Kyrgyzstan and currently president of that republic's Islamic Center (he is an ethnic Uzbek from Qarasu in the south of Kyrgyzstan) has a different opinion. He said in an interview that the influence of the Kyrgyzstan HTI, which includes two thousand to three thousand members, is growing, and in addition to ethnic Uzbeks who constituted the absolute majority of the Tahriris several years ago, an increasing number of Kyrgyz and even Russians are being recruited.[145] Kamalov believes that though the overwhelming majority of the Tahriris are "marginal social elements" who failed to adjust to the new economic situation, the top tier of the HTI consists of an "entirely different pedigree": all of them received a good education at prestigious universities and are fluent not only in Russian, but in English and Arabic as well. This observation corresponds with what we know about different HTI national organizations in the Middle East, as well as about some other similar Islamic organizations, even those practicing a much more militant brand of terrorism such as al-Qa'ida.[146] In the view of the former mufti, Kyrgyzstan surpasses all other Central Asian republics in terms of the HTI's influence. It is followed by Uzbekistan, Tajikistan, then Kazakhstan.[147]

Though the level of Islamization in Kazakhstan remains low, all my interlocutors in this republic told me that its southern regions have been witnessing the growth of the influence of Islam during recent years. They linked this phenomenon to the worsening living conditions of the population (though Kazakhstan is one of the most successful, if not the most successful, post-Soviet republic in terms of economic growth) and the influx of migrants from the bordering republic of Uzbekistan, who are much more religious than the Kazakhs. The exodus of Uzbeks was especially massive after the Uzbek government's crackdown following the February 1999 Tashkent bombings, and the observers linked the spread of the HTI cells in southern Kazakhstan to this wave of migration.

In April 2004, the court of Chimkent sentenced Rahmatulla Ibodullaev to four years' imprisonment for the production and distribution of HTI literature.[148] But HTI leaflets continued to be found in the Chimkent region in great quantity. This afforded new ground to speak about the growth of Islamist influence in Kazakhstan, as the leaflets now also began to be found in the cities where Islamists had not earlier been heard of, for example, in mostly Russian-populated Pavlodar. Still, it is difficult to say whether the arrests that were made in southern Kazakhstan in the beginning of 2004 indicate the real growth of influence of the HTI or signal the growing activity of the Kazakh security services, which as their counterparts in all other republics of Central Asia are searching for Islamic activists, sometimes ordinary believers suspected of links with or sympathies toward the HTI.

Reports of the human rights organizations suggest that this may be the case. Kazakhstan and Kyrgyzstan became the primary destinations for the Uzbek believers who started to flee Uzbekistan as a result of a new Uzbek government security sweep carried out in response to the late March 2004 attacks on Islamic insurgents. Surat Ikramov, chairman of the Tashkent-based Independent Group of Human Rights Defenders, observed that among those who fled from this republic were followers of the Islamic radical groups, "along with those who are not connected to these groups." The Kazakh authorities tried to restrict the immigration: at least five hundred Uzbek citizens were prevented from entering Kazakhstan because they didn't have proper travel documents, as the Kazakh state news agency Khabar reported on April 11.[149] Again, as in 1999, fear of repression pushed many citizens of Uzbekistan out of this republic, and again, the Central Asian politicians expressed their concern about possible negative consequences of repression in Uzbekistan for the whole region of Central Asia.

All Central Asian governments now strengthened their security measures to keep Islamist activities in check. In Kyrgyzstan, new Muslim communities, in order to perform their religious duties, require special approval from the Muslims Spiritual Directorate.[150]

In summary, in three Central Asian republics, despite repression of the Hizb at-Tahrir and, after September 11, 2001, diminished assistance from abroad and the decreased appeal of radical Islamism, the party was able not only to maintain, but also in part to build up, its power. This is explained, first of all, by extremely serious socioeconomic problems, including poverty and unemployment, the lack of real prospects of the situation improving, government incompetence, corruption, and—against this background—the lack of other political alternatives, except the Islamic one. The final collapse of the Soviet welfare system exacerbated the hardships. Central Asian peoples' desire to open borders between their states made the Caliphatist appeal of the Tahriris more attractive. The historic memory of Central Asians also provides a source of inspiration for the Tahriris, as has happened with Middle Easterners (Sheikh Omar Bakri Muhammad, as mentioned earlier, launched the al-Muhajirun project in Saudi Arabia on the anniversary of the collapse of the Ottoman Caliphate).[151]

At the same time, in order to be an acceptable partner in dialogue with the governments and become a legitimate political force, the HTI will at a minimum have to renounce three postulates: the creation of a worldwide Caliphate as its main objective, its aggressive anti-Semitism, and any manifestations of a reorientation toward the use of illegitimate methods of struggle.

NOTES

1. Suah Taji-Farouki, *A Fundamental Quest: Hizb al-Tahrir and the Search for the Islamic Caliphate* (London: Grey Seal, 1996).

2. Taji-Farouki, *Hizb al-Tahrir*, 7.

3. International Crisis Group (ICG) interview, Imran Wahid, spokesperson, Hizb at-Tahrir, United Kingdom, June 5, 2003, London, in "Radical Islam in Central Asia: Responding to Hizb at-Tahrir," *ICG Asia Report*, no. 58 (June 30, 2003): 3.

4. Hizb at-Tahrir al-Islami website, at www.war-against-terrorism.info (accessed December 7, 2003).

5. "Radical Islam in Central Asia," 3. It is also wrong to say that the Caliphate "as a single entity under the command of a Caliph who receives obedience from all and has religious authority has not existed at least since 850 AD" (3). In the Abbasid Caliphate, the caliph wielded supreme secular and religious power until the middle of the eleventh century, when the Seljuk sultans deprived him of the powers of supreme secular ruler; but the Umayyad Caliphate later revived in Andalusia.

6. See Anatoly Goldovsky, "Voina tol'ko nachinaetsya" (The war is just beginning), at www.gazeta.ru/print/2004/04/14/09_117853.shtml.

7. Hizb at-Tahrir website, at www.war-against-terrorism.info (accessed December 7, 2003).

8. The leaflet was stealthily placed in my mailbox.

9. Ahmed Rashid, *Jihad: The Rise of Militant Islam in Central Asia* (New Haven, CT: Yale University Press, 2002), 122.

10. "The Inaccuracies of the Book *Jihad: the Rise of Militant Islam in Central Asia*, written by Ahmed Rashid, Yale University Press, 2002," 1, at www.war-against-terrorism.info/waragainst/articles/article14.htm (accessed December 7, 2003).

11. Rashid, *Jihad*, 123.

12. "Inaccuracies," 2.

13. These two extreme views constitute opposite poles in assessing the HTI's theoretical background, but middle-ground assessments exist as well.

14. Igor Rotar, "Hizb at-Tahrir Today, An Interview with Sadykzhan Kamaluddin (Kamalov) by Igor Rotar," *Terrorism Monitor*, March 11, 2004.

15. Taqiuddin an-Nabhani, *Hizb at-Tahrir* (London: Dar al-Khilafah, 2001), 26–27.

16. "Al-Muhajirun in the UK: An Interview with Sheikh Omar bakri Muhaamad," *Spotlight on Terror*, special supplement to *Terrorism Monitor*, March 23, 2004.

17. The leader of an extremist uprising in Saudi Arabia in December 1979.

18. Olivier Roy, interview in *Terrorism Monitor*, November 20, 2003, at www.Jamestown.org (accessed December 7, 2003).

19. "Al-Muhajirun in the UK," 8.

20. Suha Taji-Farouki, "Islamic State Theories and Contemporary Realities," in *Islamic Fundamentalism*," edited by Abdel Salam Sidahmed and Anoushiravan Ehteshami (Boulder, CO: Westview, 1996), 42.

21. Fuller, *Political Islam*, 19.

22. Hizb at-Tahrir al-Islami, *The American Campaign to Suppress Islam* (London: al-Khilafa Publications, 1996), 9. The pamphlet is also available on the website, at www.khilafa.com (accessed December 7, 2003).

23. Hizb at-Tahrir al-Islami, *American Campaign*, 9.

24. Hizb at-Tahrir al-Islami, *American Campaign*, 15.

25. Hizb at-Tahrir al-Islami, *American Campaign*, 17.

26. Abdel Salam Sidahmed and Anoushiravan Ehteshami, "Introduction," in *Islamic Fundamentalism*, ed. A. S. Sidahmed and A. Ehteshami (Boulder, CO: Westview, 1996), 13.

27. Hizb at-Tahrir al-Islami, *American Campaign*, 18.

28. Hizb at-Tahrir al-Islami, *American Campaign*, 18–19.

29. Hizb at-Tahrir al-Islami, *American Campaign*, 21.

30. Hizb at-Tahrir al-Islami, *American Campaign*, 23.

31. Hizb at-Tahrir al-Islami, *American Campaign*, 25.

32. Hizb at-Tahrir al-Islami, *American Campaign*, 27.

33. Hizb at-Tahrir al-Islami, *American Campaign*, 31.

34. Hizb at-Tahrir al-Islami, *American Campaign*, 32.

35. Hizb at-Tahrir al-Islami, *American Campaign*, 36.

36. Hizb at-Tahrir al-Islami, *American Campaign*, 37.

37. Hizb at-Tahrir al-Islami, *American Campaign*, 41.

38. It can be assumed that the brochure under study, displaying certain signs of having been written not in Nabhani's time but relatively recently, dates not from 1996 but from an earlier period. In any case, its last section refers not to the World Trade Organization but to the General Agreement on Tariffs and Trade.

39. Saniya Sagnaeva, "Religiozno-oppozitsionnie gruppy v Kyrgyzstane" (Religious opposition groups in Kyrgyzstan), in *Religioznyi ekstremism v Tsentral'noi Azii: Problemy i perspektivy* (Religious extremism in Central Asia: problems and prospects) (Dushanbe: Organization for Security and Cooperation in Europe, 2002), 64.

40. Bakhtiyar Babajanov, "Religiozno-oppozitsionnie gruppy v Uzbekistane" (Religious opposition groups in Uzbekistan), in *Religioznyi ekstremism*, 55.

41. Mirsaid, conversation with the author in Tashkent, September 18, 1996.

42. Babajanov, "Religiozno-oppozitsionnie gruppy," 55.

43. Davlat Usmon, "Mirnyi protsess i yego vliyaniye na razvitie Islama i islamskikh tsennostei v stranakh Tsentral'noi Azii" (The peace process in Afghanistan and its influence on the development of Islamic movements in the Central Asian states), in *O sovmestimosti politicheskogo Islama i bezopasnosti v prostaranstve OBSE* (On the compatibility of political Islam and security in the OSCE space), ed. Arne Seifert and Anna Kreikemeyer (Dushanbe: Sharqi Ozod, 2003), 86.

44. Davlat Usmon, "Samoponimanie, zadachi i tseli islamskoi politiki v Tadzhikistane i Srednei Azii" (Self-awareness, tasks, and objectives of Islamic policies in Tajikistan and Central Asia), in *O sovmestimosti*, ed. Arne Seifert and Anna Kreikmeyer, 51.

45. Usmon, "Samoponimanie," 54.

46. ITAR-TASS, 0201-18, 12:02—Israel-Uzbekistan-president-terrorism, version 1.

47. Babajanov, "Religiozno-oppozitsionnie gruppy," 85.

48. Vitaly Ponomaryov, *Ugroza islamskogo ekstremizma v Uzbekistane: mify i real'nost'* (The threat of Islamic extremism in Uzbekistan: myth and reality) (Moscow: Memorial, Pravozashchitnyi informatsionnyi tasentr po pravam cheloveka v Tsentral'noi Azii, October 1999), 9–10.

49. Uran Botobekov, "Vnedrenie idey partii "Hizb at-Tahrir al-Islami" na yuge Kirgizii (The implantation of the ideas of the Hizb at-Tahrir al-Islami in South Kyrgyzstan), in *Islam na postsovetskom prostranstve: vzglyad iznutri* (Islam at the post-Soviet space: a view from the inside), ed. Alexei Malashenko and Martha Brill Olcott (Moscow: Moscow Carnegie Center, 2001), 141.

50. Abdullah, interview with the author, November 21, 2002.

51. Rashid, *Jihad*, 119.

52. "Radical Islam in Central Asia," 13. Butt is an electrical engineer educated at the University of Chicago, probably indoctrinated in the West.

53. Rashid, *Jihad*, 133.

54. "Inaccuracies," 3.

55. Taqiuddin an-Nabhani, *Structuring of a Party* (London: Al-Khilafah Publications, 1999), 33.

56. Hrair R. Dekmejian, *Islam in Revolution: Fundamentalism in the Arab World* (Syracuse, NY: Syracuse University Press, 1995), 3–4.

57. Michael Hudson, "Managing Unruly Regions in an Age of Globalization," *Middle East Policy* 9, no. 4 (December 2002): 68.

58. See James Coleman, "Social Capital in the Creation of Human Capital," in *Social Capital: A Mulifaceted Perspective*, ed. Partha and Ismail Sirageldin (Washington, DC: World Bank, 2000).

59. Hudson, "Managing Unruly Regions," 69.

60. Hudson, "Managing Unruly Regions," 70.

61. See, for example, Babajanov, "Religiozno-oppozitsionnie gruppy," 58.

62. Munawwar, interview conducted by Sanobar Shermatova on behalf of the author, Tashkent, November 3, 2002.

63. Vitaly Ponomaryov, interview, November 2002.

64. US Department of State (Uzbekistan), Country Reports on Human Rights Practices—1999, 2, at www.state.gov/g/drl/rls/hrrpt/1999/369.htm (accessed December 12, 2003).

65. Henry Munson, *Islam and Revolution in the Middle East* (New Haven: Yale University Press, 1988).

66. Munson, *Islam and Revolution.*

67. Nabhani, *Hizb at-Tahrir,* 33.

68. Babajanov, "Religiozno-oppozitsionnie gruppy," 55–56.

69. *al-Wa'y,* no. 170 (June 2001).

70. Babajanov, "Religiozno-oppozitsionnie gruppy," 58–59.

71. Shaykh Muhammad Sadiq Muhammad Yusuf, interview conducted by Sanobar Shermatova, October 7, 2002.

72. *Vecher,* April 17, 2000.

73. Oleg Yakubov, *Volchya staya* (A pack of wolves) (Moscow: Veche, 1999), 236–39.

74. Dilip Hiro, "Politics—Uzbekistan: Karimov Keeps His Gun Ready for Islamists," *World News, Interpress Service,* IPC/DH/RJ/98: 1; Botobekov, "Vnedrenie idey," 136.

75. *Karavan,* July 12, 2002.

76. Kasym, interview with the author, April 7, 2003.

77. Conversation with the author, September 3, 2003.

78. Babajanov, "The Ferghana Valley: Source or Victim of Islamic Fundamentalism?" *Political Islam and Conflicts in Russia and Central Asia,* Conference Paper no. 24 (Stockholm: Swedish Institute of International Affairs, 1999), 119.

79. Babajanov, *Ferghana Valley,* 12.

80. Babajanov, *Ferghana Valley,* 12.

81. Babajanov, *Ferghana Valley,* 121.

82. Babajanov, *Ferghana Valley,* 121.

83. K., conversation with the author in Tashkent, August 31, 2003.

84. "Radical Islam in Central Asia," 6.

85. Abd al-Qadim Zallum, *Demokratiya—nizomi kufr* (Democracy—a godless order), 57, at www.hizb-ut-tahrir.org (accessed December 14, 2003).

86. Zallum, *Demokratiya,* 69. These ideas, originally worked out by Nabhani and Zallum, migrate from one publication to another, including different translations of a book by the founder of the HTI. In a British edition entitled *Democracy Is a System of Kufr,* it reads:

> The democracy which the *Kafir* West promotes in the Muslim countries is a system of *Kufr.*
>
> It has no connection whatsoever with Islam. It completely contradicts the rules of Islam whether in the comprehensive or partial issues, in source from which it came, in the 'Aqida from which it emanated, in the basis on which it is established and in the thoughts and systems it has brought. Abdul Qadim Zallum, *Democracy Is a System of Kufr* (London: Al-Khilafah Publications, 1995), 5.

87. *Najot*, no. 33 (2002).

88. Muhiddin Kabiri, conversation with the author, December 13, 2002.

89. Interview with the author in Khujand, December 14, 2002.

90. Qurbonali Mukhabbatov, "Religiozno-oppozitsionnie gruppy v Tadzhikistane: Hizb at-Tahrir" (Religious opposition groups in Tajikistan: the Hizb at-Tahrir), in *Religioznyi ekstremism*, 86.

91. Mukhabbatov, "Religiozno-oppozitsionnie gruppy," 87.

92. Ashurboy Imomov, "Nepreryvnyi dialog—vazhneishii sposob resheniya problemy ekstremizma" (Sustained dialogue—the best way to resolve the problem of extremism), in *Religioznyi ekstremism*, 175.

93. Komeb Jalilov, "Faktory rosta ekstremizma: regional'nyi kontekst" (Factors in the growth of extremism: regional context), in *Religioznyi ekstremism*, 159.

94. Davron Vali, "Banned Islamic Movement Increasingly Active in Tajikistan," *EurasiaNet*, May 9, 2002, at www.eurasianet.org/departments/insight/articles/eav090502.shtml.

95. Sagnaeva, "Religiozno-oppozitsionnie gruppy," 64.

96. Munson, *Islam and Revolution*, 96.

97. Munson, *Islam and Revolution*, 96.

98. *Vecher*, May 28, 1999.

99. Botobekov, "Vnedrenie idey," 133.

100. Rasul Umarov, interview with the author, October 20, 2002.

101. Zhipar K., interview with the author, Jalal-Abad, December 15, 2002.

102. Sabir, interview with the author, Jalal-Abad, December 17, 2002.

103. Zamira, interview conducted by Sanobar Shermatova on behalf of the author, Jalal-Abad, October 14, 2002.

104. Rano, interview conducted by Sanobar Shermatova on behalf of the author, October 19, 2002.

105. *Chuiskie izvestia*, October 31, 2003.

106. H. Hardacre, "The Impact of Fundamentalists on Women, the Family and Interpersonal Relations," in *Fundamentalists and Society: Reclaiming the Sciences, the Family and Education*, ed. M. E. Marty and R. S. Appleby, Vol. 2 (Chicago: University of Chicago Press, 1993), 141.

107. The leaflet was stealthily placed in my mailbox in Dushanbe in December 2003.

108. In this document, there are words borrowed from Arabic that are not conventionally used in Tajiki, for instance *lajna*—committee (Tajiki *kumita*). Also newly coined is the word *waraqa* (literally "paper"), which seems to denote a leaflet.

109. Sagnaeva, "Religiozno-oppozitsionnie gruppy v Kyrgyzstane," 65–70.

110. Orozbek Moldaliev, "Islamic Extremism in Central Asia," *Central Asia and Caucasus*, no. 5 (2000): 36.

111. Alexei Sukhov, "Po mneniyu kirgizskogo pravozashchitnika, zapret na deyatel'nost radikal'nykh islamskikh organizatsyi ne imeet zakonnykh osnovaniy" (In the opinion of the Kyrgyz ombudsman, the ban on the activity of radical Islamic organizations is legally unfounded), *EurasiaNet*, October 19, 2002, 1–2, at www.eurasianet.org/russian/departments/insight/articles/eav100903ru.shtml (accessed December 14, 2003).

112. Sukhov, "Po mneniyu," 2.

113. Sukhov, "Po mneniyu," 2.

114. Botobekov, "Vnedrenie idey," 143.

115. Oleg Komarov, "Kto on, Juma Namangani?" What Is He, Juma Namangani?" *Nezavisimaya gazeta,* August 24, 2000.

116. *Delo N,* September 13, 2000.

117. Zh. Zhorobekov, "Chto pitaet ekstremizm?" (What feeds extremism?), *Vecherni Bishkek* (Bishkek), July 19, 2001.

118. Botobekov, "Vnedrenie idey," 139.

119. Zhorobekov, "Chto pitaet ekstremizm?"

120. Hizb at-Tahrir al-Islami, *Answers to Questions,* March 20, 2003.

121. Hizb at-Tahrir al-Islami, *Ostanovit' krestovyi pokhod!* (Stop the crusade!), March 20, 2003.

122. Hizb at-Tahrir al-Islami, *A Call by the Hizb at-Tahrir—Only with the Caliphate Will You Achieve Victory!*

123. Hizb at-Tahrir al-Islami leaflet, *Hizb at-Tahrir al-Islami,* at www.hizb-ut-tahrir.org.

124. Hizb at-Tahrir al-Islami leaflet, May 24, 2003.

125. Hizb at-Tahrir al-Islami, *Victory Will Come with the Caliphate,* April 13, 2003.

126. Hiro, "Karimov Keeps His Gun," 3.

127. Author interview, December 14, 2002.

128. Tamara Makarenko, "The Changing Dynamics of Central Asian Terrorism," *Jane's Intelligence Review,* February 2002, 4.

129. *ICG Asia Report,* no. 46, February 18, 2003, 6.

130. *ICG Asia Report,* no. 46, February 18, 2003, 6.

131. Khilafah Digest, February 28, 2003 (London: Al-Khilafah, 2003).

132. Peter Baker, "Russia Cracks Down on Banned Islamic Party," *Washington Post Foreign Service,* June 11, 2003, A20.

133. *Gulf News,* June 12, 2003, at www. khilafah.com (accessed February 28, 2004).

134. "US Asks the Pakistani Government to Ban Hizb at-Tahrir," *Daily Pakistan,* June 15, 2003.

135. Alexander Shevyakov, "Religioznaya situatsiya v Uzbekistane" (The religious situation in Uzbekistan), unpublished manuscript.

136. Shevyakov, "Religioznaya situatsiya."

137. As Burke says, "What makes the ground so fertile in the Middle East is that the U.S. is seen as humiliating the Islamic world." Jason Burke, "Al Qaeda Today and the Real Roots of Terrorism," *Terrorism Monitor,* February 12, 2004, 2.

138. He was an adviser on questions of religion, a well-known translator of the Qur'an into the Uzbek language.

139. Hizb at-Tahrir al-Islami leaflet, May 30, 2003.

140. The HTI in Britain in that period organized rallies and pickets near the premises of the embassy of Uzbekistan in London, delivering petitions in favor of those sentenced for "religious extremism."

141. Hizb at-Tahrir al-Islami, *Just Another Game of the Servants of Satan—The US and Britain* (May 31, 2003).

142. Here and in other passages in leaflets, the *ayats* of the Qur'an and the Hadiths are often adduced as proof of the rightness of HTI appeals.

143. Hizb at-Tahrir al-Islami, *Just Another Game*.
144. "Hizb at-Tahrir Denies Involvement in Uzbekistan Blasts," *Nineteen Twenty-Four*, April 29, 2004, at www.1924.org/campaign/index.php?id=1169_0_28_0_C.
145. Rotar, "Interview with Kamalov," 1–2.
146. Let's remember that the top leaders of al-Qa'ida represent the most wealthy and well-educated groups of Middle Eastern society. Usama bin Ladin, as is widely known, is a successful Saudi millionaire, and his deputy Ayman al-Zawahiri belongs to a family of famous Egyptian intellectuals, rectors of universities.
147. Rotar, "Interview with Kamalov," 3.
148. Alexei Matveev, "Ekstremisty ugrozhayut Kazakhstanu" (Extremists threaten Kazakhstan), *Gazeta SNG*, April 22, 2004.
149. "Human Rights: Uzbek Crack Down on Muslims Prompts Some Believers to Flee," *EurasiaNet*, April 16, 2004, 1, at www.eurasianet.org/departments/rights/articles/eav0416004b_pr.shtml.
150. "Human Rights: Uzbek Crack Down," 2.
151. This historic memory, for instance, includes active participation of the Central Asian Muslim intellectuals in the 1920s international Caliphatist conferences. The Bolshevik government at the early stages tried to use Caliphatists for the promotion of its own political goals. For instance, when in the first half of the 1920s the Soviet Union established ties with the Sharif of Hijaz, the Bolshevik leaders decided to demonstrate their support to the Hijazi Caliphatists. In June 1925 Georgiy Chicherin, people's commissar for foreign affairs, instructed Hakimov, Russian representative in Hijaz, to continue contacts with the local Caliphate committee not because of Moscow's sympathies with the idea of the Caliphate but because the Caliphate movement was playing an important part "in the struggle of the Muslim peoples for complete liberation." Chicherin to Hakimov, June 18, 1925, Archiv vneshei politiki Rossiiskoi Federatsii (Archives of the Foreign Policy of the Russian Federation), fund 0127, inventory 1, folder 2, file 14, sheet 49.

4

⌒⌒

Islamists in Government: The Case of the Islamic Revival Party of Tajikistan

In the history of Tajikistan, the Islamic movement cannot be separated from the story of the violent conflict that took place in this country in the 1990s, because Tajik Islamists constituted the core group of one of the opposing sides. Throughout the different periods of its history, the Islamic movement in Tajikistan has undergone serious evolution, in which seven discrete stages can be distinguished.

The first period of this movement covers the 1970s and 1980s, when several small underground Islamic organizations, focused on religious education and the dissemination of the Muslim Brotherhood's ideas, came into being in the republic.

The second period began in summer of 1990 with the birth in the USSR of the Islamic Revival Party (IRP), in which representatives of Tajikistan actively participated, and ended in November 1991, when the national Islamic Revival Party of Tajikistan (IRPT) was established. During this period, the Tajik Islamic activists built their main power base in the Gharm–Karategin group of regions, and since then they have been strongly committed to the interest of the regional elites of this group of regions. This period was also the beginning of direct confrontation with the ruling regime. Initially this confrontation was provoked by the February 1990 events in Dushanbe. The next stage of confrontation began upon the failure of the August 1991 coup in Moscow and ended with the election of Rahmon Nabiev as president of Tajikistan in November 1991.

The third period followed this election. In May 1992 President Rahmon Nabiev and the Supreme Council (parliament) reached an accord with an alliance of the Islamic and democratic opposition groups.

Nabiev's forced resignation in September 1992 marked the beginning of the fourth period, which witnessed the most intensive and brutal armed clashes between the contending camps, ending with the victory of the Kulyabi–Leninabadi–Hissari clan over the alliance of Islamic–democratic forces in December 1992. These events are usually labeled "civil war," due to the scale of violent conflict between different regional and political segments of Tajik society and the devastation it caused to this republic.

The fifth period—from the end of 1992, when the Islamists fled to Afghanistan, until summer 1997—was marked by violent clashes between Islamic guerrillas and government forces on the border and inside the country and, at the last stage, by the beginning of talks between the opposing sides. By launching the negotiation process, the IRPT expressed readiness to give up its strategy of armed struggle against the regime and its willingness to become a legal parliamentary party. The government, for its part, was gradually realizing the necessity of coming to a power-sharing agreement with the Islamists.

The sixth period lasted from the signing of the agreement between the conflicting parties on June 27, 1997, until the beginning of real integration of the Islamists into the power structures in 1999, after which a new, seventh period of intensive cooperation started.

ETHNIC AND SOCIAL FRAGMENTATION

The story of Islam and politics in Tajikistan cannot be properly understood without reference to the deep fragmentation with which Tajik society has been marked throughout its history. Most of the Western scholars who have written on Tajikistan have stressed the importance of various elements of diversity that made the dynamics of the independent history of this state different from those of all other Central Asian nations. The clear lines of geographical, economic, social, ethnic, subethnic, cultural, and linguistic heterogeneity along which the people are divided do not coincide; they overlap and intercross, forming the mosaic of the Tajik society.

Although the Tajiks constitute the majority of the population (about 70 percent), they are hierarchically divided into many groups and subgroups whose fragile coexistence relies upon a complicated balance of interests, distribution of wealth, and power sharing. Regionalism, or localism, is one of the prevailing features of the Tajik mentality and political culture. Any upsetting of the shaky balance caused by dramatic turns in the history of the people who inhabit this territory has always exacerbated dormant tensions, thus leading to acutely conflictual relationships.

As far as the ethnic composition is concerned, the Uzbeks, the second largest group after Tajiks, make up as much as 25 percent of the population of Tajikistan. They speak a Turkic language different from Tajiki, which is of the Western branch of the family of Iranian languages. The Uzbeks are dispersed over many regions of Tajikistan, but quite naturally many of them populate some regions adjacent to Uzbekistan (the Sogdian, formerly Leninabad province) and are linked to their kin across the border with many ties. The Uzbeks here are far from being homogeneous: they are divided into subethnic groups and tribes that maintain their own identities—for instance, the Lokai tribe, which always maintains a distinct identity. Also living here is a small number of Kyrgyz, a group of Central Asian Arabs who have already lost their language, and a group of Iranians (Iranis). There were many other ethnic groups among the population of Tajikistan, including Russians.

The southwestern part of the Gorno–Badakshan Autonomous Region, which lies in the Pamirs, is inhabited by several local ethnic groups distinct from the Tajiks who have multiple identities based on their ethnic affiliation, the language they speak (all these languages belong to the eastern branch of the family of Iranian languages), and confessional affiliation (the Yazgulemis, Rushanis, Khubis, Bartangis, Oroshoris, Shugnanis, Ishkashimis, and Wakhanis). The majority of the Pamiris are Ismailis, whereas all Tajiks are Sunni Muslims, mostly of the Hanafi school.

The Tajiks are settled on the plains and in the mountains; the natural barriers that prevented interaction between these two supracommunities by accentuating economic, social, and cultural differences between them fostered the emergence of their specific identities. Massive population transfers have altered this reality but created a deep identity crisis within certain groups and communities. These transfers were the result of collectivization and industrialization and of repression against the *basmachis*, who continued their resistance through the 1930s. When the highlanders from the Karategin cluster of regions were resettled in the plains as a result of the Vakhsh River Valley irrigation project, which deprived them of their traditional habitat, the transfer marginalized this population group. And it is not surprising that these new settlers with their grievances and concerns became the pivot of the Islamist movement starting from the late 1980s.

The Tajiks are historically divided into two main groups: the Northerners and the Southerners. This division was entrenched in the nineteenth and twentieth centuries. The North, the present-day Sogdian region, was part of the Russian Empire from 1886 to the revolution of 1917, while the southern regions—the present-day Khatlon region and the Gharm and Hissar zones—were part of the Bukharan Amirate, which was Russia's protectorate and did not undergo even the limited modernization that the North did. The isolation in which the amirate found itself, due both to historical circumstances and geographical conditions (the Zerafshan mountain range separates the South from the North), fostered the conservation of archaic forms of social structure there, hindering economic development and exchanges with neighboring regions. The southern part incorporated the even more isolated high-mountain Badakhshan, whose annexation to the Russian Empire at the end of the nineteenth century changed but little the traditional way of life prevalent there.

Today these two large groups have split into smaller ones that basically coincide with the existing administrative regions: in the North, the communities of Khujand, Urateppa, the former inhabitants of Samarqand, Bukhara (these two cities were not handed over to Uzbekistan until the mid-1920s), Isfara, Panjikent, and others; in the South, the communities of Darvaz, Karategin, Kulyab, Kurghanteppa, and so on.

These communities are subdivided into district-size groups, which are further divided into city- or village-size entities. Within these municipalities are neighborhood-size units (*mahalla*), each identified by the name of the legendary founder of the settlement, the common vocation (merchant, mulla, etc.), or a local object of note (a fortress, orchard, mountain, etc.). A neighborhood community, in its turn, consists of several family-related groups called *avlod, top, urug, qawm*, and so forth, their members claiming common ancestors.

A common denomination for blood-kinship communities among the Tajiks is the extended, or greater, family, in which a few generations of relatives from the male line having their own families live together or close to each other. As described by the Russian ethnographers who studied Tajikistan, extended families in Northern Tajikistan living in one household are called *top*, while several *tops* kindred to each other make up an *avlod* (the Arabic for "sons"). The Tajiks also include their deceased relatives from the male line in such a patronymy as *avlod*. Among the Yazgulemis, such a patronymy is called *qaum*; among the Wakhanis, *tukhm*; among the Matchis, *heish*; and among the other mountain Tajiks, *toyfa* or *qynda*. The *mahalla*, which can also be characterized as the territory of community residence, is in some regions also called *guzar*.[1]

The *avlod* worship the deceased familial ancestors, the *arvoh* (Arabic for "spirits"). Among the mausoleums, or *mazars*, to which the Tajiks make pilgrimages, there are many where the family founders are buried. These *mazars* cement familial solidarity, which remains in force despite the modernization to which Tajik society has been subjected.

Olivier Roy aptly remarked that under the Soviet regime collectivization brought about a systematic territorialization of traditional solidarity groups within the framework of the *kolkhoz* (collective farm). "The *avlod*, the *mahalla*, and (in the tribal zones) lineage segments were reincarnated in the subdivisions of the *kolkhoz* (the *uchastok* or *kolkhoz* section, which was itself divided into brigades, with each division having its own territory and its own habitat, called a *khutur*)."² Thus, on the one hand the *kolkhoz*, "as a new tribe," was an attempt at modernization of traditional social networks and structures, replacing them with new, territory-based ones; but on the other it fostered their preservation and social perpetuation, rather then their destruction; and there are also lines of differences within Tajiki between groups of northern, central, southeastern, and southern dialects.

Divisions along the borders between Sufi brotherhoods can be added to this diversity. The main two Sufi brotherhoods in Tajikistan are Naqshbandiyya and Qadiriyya, which comprise the majority of the population. Sufi brotherhoods as organizations do not play a very significant role in Tajik society, and one can hardly separate the Sufi networks from other traditional patronage networks that exist there, for example, the different status groups that form a quasihierarchical structure similar to those found in some Middle Eastern societies.

Many of the aforementioned groups and communities are vertically stratified: some families and clans have inherited the high status of pirs, ishans, sayyids, ashraf, and *khwaja* (the same as khoja, or people of aristocratic descent), as opposed to *fuqaro* (the poor, ordinary people). The *khwaja* and *fuqaro*, in Roy's view, constitute the fundamental division in the Ferghana Valley.³

The Bukharan Amirate, for instance, was subdivided into *vilayets* or *bek*-governed entities, their borders coinciding with the regions of modern Tajikistan. Essentially, over the course of many centuries, areas that later became part of Tajikistan had enjoyed a large measure of autonomy. Moreover, politics within *bek*- (or *beg*-) ruled localities were defined by a patron-client system that provided protection from the central government. These traditional relationships were to prove viable. The existence of this hierarchical system of segmentation strongly resembles *nesting* in tribal societies, based on the segmentary-lineage organization,⁴ although strictly speaking, Tajik society cannot be classified as such.

Due to such fragmentation, the Tajiks are guided by a system of multiple, or segmented, identities. Being included simultaneously in several multilevel solidarity groups, the Isfarans, for instance, identify themselves as Tajiks as contrasted with the Uzbeks, as Northerners versus their compatriots from the South, and as Isfarans in their relations with Khujandis, and they defend the interests of their regional clans, *mahallas*, *avlods*, *tops*, and so on, descending by the pyramid of identities. This identity system is obviously a serious obstacle to national consolidation.

DISTRIBUTION OF POWER

Although the Tajiks represent the most ancient nation of all modern ethnic groups in Central Asia, they never had a state in present-day boundaries before the Soviet era. The establishment of a new statehood system
in the 1920s was dominated by the ethnic principle. The difficulty of this
task was due not only to the lack of clear-cut borders between the ethnic
settlements, but also to the rudimentary level of the peoples' national
awareness and the unfinished nation-forming process. Both Turkic- and
Iranian-speaking ethnic groups identified themselves as Muslims. The
use of a particular language or dialect was therefore not a certain determining factor of ethnic identity.

"No one would take it upon himself to refer to the population of Samarqand as Tajik. For several centuries Samarqand and Bukhara were the economic and cultural centers of Uzbek Khanates. Because of the cultural
and economic relations with Persia maintained by these cities and thanks
to the refinement of the Farsi language, everyone believed that speaking
Farsi was a sign of good breeding." This was how one of the advocates of
Uzbek identity described the situation in the course of a debate held in
Uzbekistan in 1929.[5]

In the view of a Kazakh ethnographer, the Iranian-speaking peoples of
Central Asia, the Tajiks, and the nationalities inhabiting the areas adjoining
the Pamirs (Yazgulemis, Rushanis, Khufis, Bartangis, Oroshoris, Shugnanis, Ishkashimis, Wakhanis, and Sarryagnobis), widely differing in the linguistic, confessional, economic, and cultural respects, were ordered in the
mid-1920s to unite into a nation that had never previously existed as such.[6]

Under the Soviet regime, which preserved the old territorial divisions
practically intact, these relationships determined, to a certain extent, the
composition and structure of the new ruling class (*nomenklatura*). Apart
from clan, family, and community ties crucial for personnel appoint-
ments, great importance was attached to the contacts developed by the
protégés in the course of their work. The emergence of the Soviet state
and Communist Party's local *nomenklatura* led to the formation of a new
patronage network that existed alongside the traditional ones.

The core of the ruling class consisted, more often than not, of people
coming from a single region. This determined the allocation of posts in the
system of state government. For example, senior Communist officials all
came from the Leninabad (now Sogdian, with its capital at Khujand) region in the North. The Northerners controlled the Ministries of Agriculture, Economic Affairs, and Trade. The Southerners held posts in the Ministries of Culture, Education, and the Interior.

The preeminence of the Khujandis was not accidental. They had encouraged the growth of educated urban strata and of industry, while the

southern part of the country remained mostly an agricultural province. Historically, a Tajik autonomous unit was established within Uzbekistan, which was an entirely agricultural area in the 1920s. Khujand and the adjacent part of the Ferghana Valley were transferred to Tajikistan only in 1929, when it received the status of a Soviet republic. It was only natural that this more developed region, faster growing and with a better-educated populace, came to play a greater role in administration. Its representatives assumed political power and control over resources.

Community–cultural ties were built into Tajikistan's political system, determining the composition of the ruling class and its internal dynamics. Many conflicts resulted, but they were deferred by compromise at the top level or by Moscow's interventions. This "traditional" balance of power began to crumble under the impact of the *perestroika* reforms accompanied by the sweeping politicization of the public. Not wishing to wait until their Communist bosses left the stage of their own accord, novices and second-tier Communist officials set out to capture the positions of power. Backroom deals were no longer able to stifle the imminent conflict. Moscow, suffering from similar pressures, was unable to play its traditional role. Relying on community and cultural ties, various groups began, often successfully, to seek public support. Regional elites, ready to seek the redistribution of wealth and power, started the process of mobilizing their communities.

Islam has always been one of the components of Tajik identity. It did not cease to be so even during the Soviet period of Tajikistan's history, though the level of religiosity was different in various parts of the republic. During World War II, the Soviet leadership needed to foster the country's patriotic mobilization, and Stalin reshaped his policy toward religious institutions, hoping that the clergy could play a role in rallying the people for resistance against the Nazi occupation. In the course of this "partial liberalization," as was mentioned earlier, a governing body of the Muslims of Central Asia, called the Spiritual Board, was established in Tashkent in 1943, and later branches subordinate to the Spiritual Board, called the qaziates, were established in all Central Asian republics. The Spiritual Board was headed by the mufti and therefore called a muftiate; meanwhile the qaziates were headed by *qazis*, or Shari'a judges (this word is pronounced in Tajiki as *qozi*). During the war, clerics were given more freedom to talk to believers, and that paved the way for a limited re-Islamization, which continued after the war.

During the Soviet period, underground prayers were offered at home and in public places, such as village clubs and *chaykhanas* (tea houses), and several private underground circles appeared where youngsters were taught Islam and Arabic. Shirin Akiner suggests that as early as the 1970s, groups that had previously been concerned with rituals and religious texts began to favor "a more political agenda."[7] In the author's view, this manifested two trends: one, "apparently drawing inspiration from the works of Muslim leaders abroad, took root among marginalized urban youth"; the other, village-based, was centered on "traditional mentors and bound together by local family-community networks." It still remains unexplained why and how these two trends materialized. What is known for sure is that from the 1960s some Tajiks who had graduated from the universities, where they had studied Arabic, and subsequently had received training abroad or worked as interpreters, contributed to the dissemination of knowledge about Islam and Islamic thought through private meetings and explanations of Arabic books that were brought from abroad and circulated by them. In the Gharm cluster of regions, religiosity was much higher than it was in other parts of Tajikistan.

THE BIRTH OF THE ISLAMIC REVIVAL PARTY OF TAJIKISTAN

In the course of the rise of regional elites, Islam became one of the main instruments for political mobilization. Beginning in the 1970s, several clandestine Islamic organizations were already working in Tajikistan, especially in the South, most of them running private schools of Islam like the one run by Hindustani (see chapter 2). In 1978, an underground youth organization was created to study and disseminate the ideas of the founders of political Islam, such as the father of the Muslim Brotherhood, Hasan al-Banna. The founder and leader of this organization was Said Abdullo Nuri (b. 1947), a disciple of Hindustani who later, in March 1987, participated in a demonstration in support of the Afghan mujahedeen and was arrested and sent to prison, where he spent two years.

On the eve of the collapse of the Soviet Union, many opportunities were opened to Soviet Muslims. Although the party leadership of Tajikistan was not ready to abandon its atheistic policy, the rapid liberalization in Russia provided a good opening to the proponents of political Islam in Tajikistan.

Two of them—Davlat Usmon and Saidibrahim Hadoev—took part in the constituent conference of the all-USSR Islamic Revival Party in Astrakhan, held on June 9, 1990. On their return to Dushanbe, they appealed to the Supreme Soviet—the main legislative body of Tajikistan—asking for permission to hold a constitutive regional conference of the IRP in Tajikistan, since the IRP leaders were planning to set up regional branches in all Central Asian republics. Their appeal was studied at one of the Supreme Soviet's sessions and rejected, because religious organizations were prohibited by law from participating in political activities. The organizers, who had been put under surveillance, were unable to hold a conference in Dushanbe. No mosque, no club could host it, because security agents had established tight control over all mosques, theaters, clubs, and other places in the capital that determined Islamists might use as a venue for their conference. Instead, they managed, using conspiratorial tactics and passing information only to a limited circle who they knew shared their ideas, to hold the conference in a mosque in one of the rural areas near Dushanbe.

On October 6, 1990, the conference established the Tajik branch of the IRP. Later Davlat Usmon told me that that conference was a real breakthrough in the process of Islamic revival in Tajikistan.[8] Meanwhile, the authorities confirmed the ban on the newborn party, and its organizers were fined. But this only helped the banned Islamic opposition to acquire more popularity.

By that time, significant changes in the position of Islam had already started to take place in many Central Asian republics. As two Russian scholars put it: "The two processes merged—enlightenment from below and reorientation of the communist leadership from fighting Islam to restoring Moslem culture, supporting religious and national traditions, and developing religious education."[9] New mosques and *madrasas* began to function; links were established between Soviet Muslims and their coreligionists abroad. The first secretary of the central committee of the Communist Party of Tajikistan, Kahhar Mahkamov, was the only Central Asian leader who still maintained his atheistic position. A young and well-educated head of Tajik Muslims, qazi kalon Akbar Turajonzoda (b. 1947), even declared that the first secretary "would be denied Moslem burial after his death."[10]

According to the IRPT Statute, the IRPT set for itself the following objectives:

* The spiritual revival of the citizens of Tajikistan.
* The economic and political sovereignty of the republic.
* Political and legal rights with a view to realizing Islamic norms in the life of the Muslims of the republic.[11]

Among the tasks set by the party statute, in particular, were:

* The expansion of Islam and its propaganda by all available means and the mass media among the population of the republic.
* The involvement of Muslims in the economic, political, and spiritual life of the republic.[12]

The Islamic opposition entered into an intensive dialogue with the newborn organizations of the democratic opposition: the Rastokhez society, the

Democratic Party of Tajikistan, and La'li Badakhshon. The Rastokhez society was organized in September 1989 by a group of young and middle-
aged Tajik academics, writers, poets, and journalists headed by Tahir
Abdujabbor, a native of Asht in Northern Tajikistan. The main goal of
Rastokhez—the revival of genuine Tajik culture—found some response
among the Tajik intelligentsia and students, but the organization did not
grow into a political party. It had a loose organizational structure and a
limited number of followers, because by reviving memories of the glorious
Tajik past, those enlightened intellectuals were not able to address the real
grievances and concerns of most Tajiks.

The Democratic Party of Tajikistan (DPT), created on August 10, 1990,
declared itself a political party; from the very beginning it united a certain
number of educated people, mostly middle-aged members of the intelligentsia and state employees, who proclaimed as their main goal the
achievement of the independence of Tajikistan. The chairman of the party
was Shodmon Yusuf, a researcher at the Academy of Sciences, a native of
Vakhio (Darvaz). But given the conservatism of the overwhelming majority of the population, such slogans as "democracy" and "anticommunism" could hardly become a platform on which the broad masses of
Tajiks could unite, especially outside the capital and several major cities.
Students might form a potential power base for the DPT, but the party did
not succeed in winning mass support, even among this group of the urban population. Both Rastokhez and the DPT were ethnically inclusive.

La'li Badakhshon (the Pearl of Badakhshan), which appeared in September 1990, was an exclusively regional political movement aimed at
serving the interests of the Badakhshani elites and seeking wide autonomy for their region. It had no plans to become a nationwide party. Its
chairman was Amirbek Atobekov. All the newborn democratic movements were secular and in the beginning seemed critical toward the idea
of an Islamic state in Tajikistan. Their leaders represented groups of well-
educated people who had not been integrated into political life and were
determined to use their opportunities to enter politics, because they felt
that the time for the old Soviet-type *apparatchiks* was over.

All these new political parties appealed to different layers of Tajik identities. This again relates to one of the most intriguing issues—the relationship between three levels of identities among the Tajiks: pan-Persian,
pan-Tajik, and local (regional). Was this relationship conflictual, or could
these identities coexist, with each of them prevailing in a particular context? We can find both situations where these identities either contradict
each other or are simultaneously shared and expressed by their bearers.
Olivier Roy mentions two possible approaches to Tajik nationalism. One
is to take "the Soviet ethnic view," according to which the Tajiks are the
descendants of the Sogdians conquered by the Arabs, Persianized, and

subsequently Turkified: "Occasionally it is noted that Uzbeks are often Turkified Tajiks."[13] Roy's assertion is not quite accurate, however. First, such an "ethnic view" was not a common one among the Soviet ethnographers. Second, even if we accept this view, it is not clear why Roy suggests that "this leaves open the question of relations with Iran and the Persian-speaking population" and why the Sogdians have been resuscitated. The pan-Persian identity was advocated by some intellectuals and politicians for limited periods; for example, the revival of the "Persian heritage" and the replacement of Cyrillic script with Arabic/Persian were the demands of some famous Tajik poets and writers in the early 1990s. But at the same time, a different nationalistic view was formulated by other Tajik intellectuals, who regarded the Tajik culture as superior to the Iranian one and opposed "the new cultural Iranization." Actually, they were frightened by the assertiveness and arrogance of some Iranian representatives who in the early 1990s too enthusiastically tried to teach the Tajiks "the true Persian language" and missed no opportunity to demonstrate the superiority of Iranian culture. This case is similar to that of Azerbaijan: the first wave of Azeri nationalists in the late 1980s and the early 1990s called for a single Turkic loyalty and proposed to consider Azeri and Turkish as the same language (Azeri and Turkish are even closer than Tajiki and Persian), but later "narrow Azeri nationalism" took over. Stressing an identity different from the Turkish one was especially important because the twin country was stronger and more ambitious, thus threatening the interests of Azeri nationalists. For Tajik nationalists, the Iranian twin brother looks no less threatening. Sectarian difference—the Tajiks are Sunnis and the Iranians are Shi'ites—made the Tajiks' fears even stronger. But the Sogdian dimension of the Tajik identification process cannot be totally dismissed. Rastokhez and the Democratic Party of Tajikistan, at the initial stage of their activity, considered Sogdian heritage one of the pillars of their nationalist concept. The government of Tajikistan in 2001 renamed the Leninabad region the Sogdian, and the Tajik intelligentsia has made references to the Sogdian heritage.

The second approach mentioned by Roy involves viewing the Tajiks as the heirs of the great Persian and Sunni civilization of Central Asia.[14] The main argument for this theory was made in an article by Hoji Akbar Turajonzoda in 1995 where the former qazi kalon stressed the importance of Persian culture and history for the Tajiks, rather than Shari'a and the Islamic state. But it should be taken into account that the qazi kalon at that time was enjoying Iran's hospitality and that, as a Sunni cleric, he could not equate the Islamic component of the Tajiks' Sunna-based national identity with the Iranian Shi'a-based one. So far, the Persianness of Tajik nationalism has not always properly served the interests of new elites seeking a universal and powerful religious instrument for political mobilization.

In the early 1990s, the competition between the old and the new elites was both generational and political, but some analysts viewed the platforms of the democratic movements as a mere instrument for challenging those in power. Shirin Akiner called their leaders "self-styled democrats" because, "in the context of Tajikistan at that period, the term was little more than a label by which the new contenders for power sought to distinguish themselves from those already in office." Akiner goes as far as suggesting that "the manifesto of the Communist Party of Tajikistan, as set out at the 22nd Party Congress (January 1992), was arguably more in keeping with Western concepts of democracy than were those of *Rastokhez* and DPT."[15]

Although some newcomers to local political life were opportunists who sought office, there were some who had clearly idealistic motivations and sincerely sought to bring democracy and prosperity to Tajikistan. All the newborn democratic opposition movements began to cooperate on the basis of anticommunism, trying to capitalize on the discontent of the population.

The ranks of the opposition in Tajikistan, then, at the beginning of the 1990s included both Islamists, proponents of an Islamic state, and secular nationalists who favored rapid radical changes and advocated democracy. However, despite growing politicization, the public at large had so far proved unprepared to accept the ideas of both groups. At the same time, for most villagers, Muslim identification was their only comprehensible communal connection apart from tribal identity, and this meant many of them were automatically potential voters for the Islamic forces. This situation was promoted by the natural process of revival of national culture and religion. For a long time, like other religions in the former USSR, Islam had been persecuted under the propaganda and the repressive machinery of the atheistic Soviet regime. The people were deprived of the opportunity for normal spiritual growth. Controlled by the central and local authorities, the official clergy did not enjoy public trust. The gap between the Tajik Muslims and the old ruling elite was growing, despite attempts by some high-ranking officials (even with the *perestroika* reforms under way) to arrest the spiritual rebirth and the community's return to the traditional values of Islam.

If religious mobilization in the region is coupled with economic (no less than social) mobilization, then it is competition that causes religious mobilization, just as in cases of ethnopolitical mobilization.[16] Competition here should be understood more broadly than rivalry between ethnic groups: this is a rivalry of a wider range of groups, stretching from ethnic and regional ones to traditional patronage networks. Here it is pertinent to draw a parallel with the discourse of the proponents of ethnic competition theory (Susan Olzak, Joane Nagel, and others). In accordance with this theory, the weakening and collapse of territorial and social barriers among groups cause ethnic mobilization. Among the processes that attest to such a collapse, for instance, urbanization, industrialization, immigration, economic depression, and changes in the dominance of certain ethnic groups in particular occupations are mentioned.[17] These conditions were exactly the causes of ethnoreligious (or, more precisely, quasiethnoreligious) mobilization of the Gharmis throughout the period starting from their forced migrations to the valleys.

What took place in this case is delayed mobilization, which emerged as a consequence of accumulation effect and was triggered by the processes that unfolded in Tajikistan at the turn of the 1990s: deep depression, the changing roles of regional groups (including particular group dominance in occupations), and so forth. The religious mobilization of the Gharmis was inseparable from mobilization of quasiethnic forces (if we use this term with reference to the distinct, self-identifying regional subdivisions of the Tajiks), but it was the regional elites who directed this twofold mobilization, and it was their interests that were served first and foremost by the wave of protest and rebellion raised by the Gharm-Karategin clans under the slogans of Islamic revival.

THE OUTBREAK OF THE CONFLICT

The dramatic events that occurred in Tajikistan in 1990 triggered conflictual relationships between regional elites and their political rivals. On February 11, 1990, a crowd of people assembled near the headquarters of the Communist Party to demand the expulsion of all Armenians and to protest rumored government intentions to give permanent refuge to thousands of them. It is still unknown what forces were behind this: Azeris involved in the clans' struggle; the emerging nationalist opposition groups; or any external powers, such as Iran, who might have tried to exploit the situation in Dushanbe for the purpose of expanding their influence under nationalist and religious slogans. Rastokhez played an important role in the February demonstrations.

As a result, that same day, the authorities deported about two hundred Armenians from Dushanbe. The IRP used the outburst of nationalist feelings to rally more supporters. But, its efforts notwithstanding, the party was not able to overcome the narrow localism of its power base, which was confined to the Gharm-Karategin cluster of regions. The rising nationalist sentiments made the party think about departing from the all-Soviet IRP and creating an independent Tajik party. Some Tajik analysts report that the IRP from the early days of its existence was an "anti-systemic" party aiming at bringing about the downfall of the Communist regime and that from those days on, it started accumulating weapons and training fighters for a future guerrilla war.[18]

A highlight of the second stage of confrontation between the opposition and the authorities was the resignation of Kahhar Mahkamov, who had been elected by the Supreme Soviet (Council) as president in November 1990 while still retaining his post as Communist Party first secretary. He was on the verge of openly supporting the antidemocratic August 1991 coup in Moscow, thus giving the opposition a credible and popular reason to attack him. Also, the coalition he had held together failed to provide effective support. Among the reasons for Mahkamov's resignation was that his ostentatious atheism was increasingly viewed as an anachronism even by the ruling elite.

On September 7, 1991, Mahkamov, under strong pressure from the popular movement he was unable to resist, had to step down. The Supreme Council appointed Qadruddin Aslanov, a nominal figure, as acting president pending elections. During his short rule, Aslanov dissolved the Communist Party and declared Tajik independence, following some other Soviet republics. The Communists, still powerful, reacted sharply, and Aslanov on September 23 was replaced by CP first secretary Rahmon Nabiev, who declared a state of emergency and abolished Aslanov's decree dissolving the Communist Party.

This led to the election of Rahmon Nabiev as president in November 1991. Initially, Nabiev maneuvered quickly and skillfully. Remembering his predecessor's errors, he immediately restored the more viable coalition of Leninabad and Kulyab, rivals in the past. Relying on this regionalist North–South axis, the coalition guaranteed the stability of the ruling class as a whole. In response, the opposition also assumed an organizational form.

With the approaching collapse of Soviet rule, all competing regional elites intensified their struggle for the redistribution of wealth and power. The IRP was a unique instrument for the Karategin economic, political, and religious elites to challenge the traditional holders of the main shares of wealth and power. Under the pressure of mass public meetings, the Supreme Council annulled the old law that banned the establishment of religious political parties.

Now the official head of the Muslims of Tajikistan, qazi kalon Hoji Akbar Turajonzoda, decided to take the side of the Islamists openly and reallied himself with the IRP, though he did not join the party. For the first time in Central Asia, "the parallel" political Islam and the official clergy, who in all other republics remained rivals, joined hands against the ruling regime.

Turajonzoda was one of the most brilliant exponents of the Central Asian religious class. His family came from Samarqand. Due to his origins, he was especially popular in Zerafshan, Aini, and Matcha and also among a part of the population of Dushanbe; but contrary to the opinion of certain researchers, he did not command a support base in the Gharm group of regions—Karategin, Tavildara, Kofarnihon—and in the Leninabad region, nor did he fully control any sizable part of Dushanbe's population. At the time, among all the leaders of the emerging Islamic opposition in the central part of Tajikistan, Rezvan Sodirov enjoyed the greatest popularity.

Hoji Akbar Turajonzoda had not himself been a disciple of Hindustani. It was his brother Nuriddin who had been a student of Hindustani for fourteen years. Their father had been a close friend of Hindustani's and on Saturdays usually invited the Maulawi to his home, and during the meetings, conversations about religion lasting many hours were conducted.[19]

On October 26, 1991, after the Supreme Council, frightened by the mass meetings, adopted a new law that abolished the old law that had banned religious parties, a new, officially recognized conference was held, resulting in the creation of the Islamic Revival Party of Tajikistan (IRPT), which was registered on December 4, 1991. The conference elected Muhammadsharif Himmatzoda as its chairman and Davlat Usmon and Saidibrohim Hadoev as his deputies. In its documents, the party did not put forward the idea of the creation of an Islamic state and stressed as its goal the establishment of a democratic state based on the rule of law, with a multiparty "government of national trust." Judging by these documents, the IRPT was oriented toward peaceful means of struggle and power sharing, though it did not exclude making preparations for a guerrilla war.

During the presidential elections of November 24, 1991, the IRPT formed an alliance with Rastokhez, the DPT, and La'li Badakhshon called the Union of Democratic Forces, which supported a united candidate— the democratically oriented film director from Badakhshan Davlat Khudonazarov, who lost the election to Nabiev.

For the first time in Central Asia an Islamic organization: (a) became an officially registered political party; (b) formed a coalition with secular democratic forces; and (c) participated in presidential elections. The character of the opposition's regional support was partly to blame for its electoral setback. It was believed that the alliance of such different forces would garner widespread support. Owing to its links with movements led by intellectuals, the Islamic Revival Party of Tajikistan consolidated its position in Dushanbe, while the nationalists and democrats gained an outlet to the countryside, the Islamists' stronghold. However, its success in uniting the discontented elements in southern Tajikistan resulted in the opposition's failure to acquire an all-Tajikistani image. Unlike the governing North–South coalition, the opposition retained, in the public opinion, a southern bias.

The IRPT was not a homogeneous group of people united by a set of ideas, a unifying and binding program, or a clear vision of its relationships with other segments of Tajik society. As my personal interviews with some IRPT activists during those days showed, some of its leaders understood that the idea of an Islamic state would not be supported by the majority of the population, and they saw a coalition as a long-term strategy rather than a tactical step to prepare future attacks on the mainstream leaders. This was not typical of the more aggressive thinking of some other leaders, who considered a violent clash with the mainstream inevitable. These leaders were determined to start a rapid Islamization of Tajik society, and some measures taken by them, such as broadcasting the *azan* (a call to prayer) five times a day, showed the secular segments of the society that, once in power, the IRPT would not waste time in implementing Islamic reforms.

The presidential elections failed to diminish the intensity of the political struggle in Tajikistan. The leaders of the Islamic–democratic bloc proclaimed themselves a political opposition to the ruling regime. They launched an intensive political campaign against the government in their newspapers, such as *Charoghi Ruz, Minbor-i Islam,* and *Adolat.* Hunger strikes and mass rallies of supporters became instruments of political pressure used by the opposition against the government. In March 1992, Safarali Kenjaev, chairman of the Tajikistan Supreme Council, accused Interior Minister Navjuvanov of abusing his office. In response, the opposition accused Kenjaev of the same offense. As an ethnic Pamiri, Navjuvanov was supported by other Pamiris. The opposition organized an unsanctioned rally at Shahidon Square in Dushanbe, which lasted from March 26 until April 23 and from April 25 until May 5, 1992. The government reciprocated by calling a similar rally in Ozodi Square, transporting its supporters by bus from Kulyab.

The Shahidon rallies, which went on for two months, brought together all those dissatisfied with the government who favored radical changes in the political system in Tajikistan. Representing different organizations and factions, the majority of those involved in the rallies belonged to "the weak regional groups," mainly Pamiris, Gharmis, Karateginis, and some representatives of Kurghanteppa, who were seeking higher social status. More antisocial elements from these regions who were ready for any sort of violent action joined the gathering.

In turn, the Ozodi rally, where the majority consisted of Kulyabis and Northerners, also included some antisocial elements who at this stage supported the government out of regional solidarity. Some of these later played a decisive role in the emerging civil war on the side of the mainstream forces. Among them was the future commander of the Kulyabi

A rally of the Islamic opposition at Shahidon Square in Dushanbe in May 1992.

militia, Sangak Safarov, who had spent twenty-three years in jail, as well as several former racketeers and black-market dealers.[20]

In the end, President Nabiev sacrificed Kenjaev, even though he had run his victorious presidential campaign. The parliament accepted Kenjaev's resignation but soon restored him to office under pressure from the Kulyabis. However, the maneuvering by Nabiev and the parliament only worsened the situation. The Shahidon and Ozodi rallies ended in a violent confrontation. Afraid of disloyalty among the law enforcement agencies, Nabiev on May 1 called for the formation of a National Guard. On May 5, the opposition took over the television station and the presidential palace. The president responded by forming National Guard units of his Kulyabi supporters, who received more than 1,800 automatic rifles.

Mounting and uncontrollable tensions forced President Nabiev to begin talks with the opposition. As a result, a government of national reconciliation, to include eight representatives of the opposition, was formed. Davlat Usmon, as a representative of the IRPT, became deputy prime minister. The opposition received the important post of chair of the republican State Committee for Radio and Television. The agreement provided for the establishment of a national Majlis that would set aside half of its seats for the opposition.

In a new first for Central Asia, an Islamic party entered the government. The Islamists found a favorable climate in the countryside, where self-identification on grounds of religion was well established and could be used as a mobilizing factor, especially in the regions with an identity crisis. Moreover, the discontent and feeling of deprivation that the Islamists played up was strongly flavored with interregional rivalries and distrust. In the southern areas of Tajikistan, people blamed the proliferating troubles not on the administration in general, as is usually done, but more specifically on its higher functionaries of Leninabadi origin. Representatives of Kurghanteppa, the Gorno-Badakhshan Autonomous Region, and Gharm found themselves upstaged in the politics. Kurghanteppa was partly inhabited by the so-called *muhajereen*, or migrants, the natives of other parts of the republic (Gharm, Kulyab, and Leninabad) who were re-settled in the course of the region's planned development in the 1920s; they were still clinging to their ancestral self-identification. It was Kurghanteppa that became the scene of the most ferocious fighting during the emerging civil war.

THE OUTBURST OF VIOLENCE
AND CONSERVATIVE STABILIZATION

The May 1992 agreement did not defuse the situation. In an effort to prevent bloodshed, Davlat Khudonazarov asked the Kulyabis to leave Dushanbe. However, this move was insufficient, allowing armed groups of Kulyabis to enter the opposition-backed Kurghanteppa area, where bloodshed ensued. Several regions, one by one, declared disobedience to Dushanbe—first Kulyab, then Leninabad, and then the Hissar Valley. In effect, the country found itself divided into separate entities confronting each other. The Kulyabis organized themselves into armed militias called the Popular Front under the command of Sangak Safarov, one of their most militant leaders.[21]

The large-scale military confrontation between the supporters of the Islamic–democratic bloc, mainly from Gharm and other regions in the South, on the one hand and the bloc of Kulyabis and Khujandis representing the old regime on the other continued through the summer and fall of 1992. The civil war enlarged the already deep divide in Tajik society, and the triumph of regionalism threw the country back to the feuds of a previous era. The drama of a fragmented society could not be overcome by the nation itself, and for the foreign actors the burden of mediation later proved to be burdensome and costly.

Armed clashes between the units of the Islamic opposition and the Kulyabi militia became especially bloody from the end of June. In the South,

Sangak Safarov with a group of fighters from the People's Guard in 1992.

an increasing number of Islamic militants penetrated into Afghanistan to bring arms from there. Sometimes Afghan instructors would come with them. According to Russian experts, five hundred to six hundred mujahedeen were active in the territory of Tajikistan in summer–fall of 1992.[22]

President Nabiev's subsequent conduct during the war aroused general indignation. The regime's inability to control developments was becoming increasingly manifest. The president's numerous demands for the surrender of arms were absolutely ignored. The opposition was hastily arming itself, using, like the Kulyabi group, various channels of arms supplies. The situation was increasingly slipping out of control. The opposition laid all responsibility for failure to reconcile the warring factions of the society on the president. Under strong pressure from the opposition, President Nabiev unwillingly tendered his resignation on September 7, 1992. The "Agreement between the President of the Republic of Tajikistan Rahmon Nabiev and the Youth of Tajikistan," published the same day, left no doubt that Nabiev was threatened by force.[23] Actually, Nabiev was taken hostage by this group of aggressive youngsters at the Dushanbe airport. The president's powers were transferred to Akbarsho Iskandarov, a forty-one-year-old Pamiri who had previously taken over from Safarali Kenjaev as chairman of the Supreme Council.

Armed strife generated many acute new problems. Among them was the mass exodus of ethnic Russians, although this had begun before the developments took a dramatic turn. Among the main provocations of this emigration, apart from growing political instability, was the compulsory introduction of the Tajik language in daily practice and official use. As elsewhere in Central Asia, in Tajikistan ethnic Russians were integrated into the community only to a small extent. Forcible Russification under the Soviets allowed ethnic Russians to fare well without knowing local languages or customs. The new, compulsory status of the Tajik language meant the loss of the opportunity for ethnic Russians to receive a higher education. From an economic point of view, the massive outflow of Russian specialists was a telling blow to Tajikistan, which did not have enough indigenous people in skilled trades and professions. The increasing internecine strife also provoked other ethnic groups to flee. Uzbeks started to leave, and many Tajiks moved from Dushanbe and Southern Tajikistan to Khujand.

As almost always happens in internal ethnopolitical conflicts (or quasi-ethnopolitical ones, as in Tajikistan), the threat of annihilation of a group was a powerful driving force of violent conflict at a certain stage of the conflict's escalation. In June 1992 Kulyab found itself blockaded by forces supporting the Islamic–democratic bloc, but this helped rouse the population to fight the government. The Kulyabis seized Kurghanteppa, and on September 21, at the closed session of the Presidium of the Supreme Council and the Cabinet of Ministers, they spelled out their demands. Among these were, in particular, the ouster from their posts in the national reconciliation government of persons nominated by the opposition (Vice Premier Davlat Usmon, Chairman of the Television and Radio Committee M. Mirrahimov, Deputy Chairman of the National Security Committee D. Aminov, and qazi kalon Turajonzoda) and the cessation of radio broadcasts of the *azan*.[24]

The tragic course of events greatly undercut the potential of the executive branch. The situation in Dushanbe revealed the gradual deterioration of all municipal services and the absence of general order. Transportation services were interrupted and bread and meat supplies became very irregular. Crime mounted; residents did not venture out after dark and preferred not to use their cars. A shortage of petrol and fears that their cars might be attacked by armed criminals further discouraged movement. Official departments and offices switched to shorter hours, and the government assumed a passive stance. Dispirited officials came to work for a few hours only to shuffle paper. There was a genuine bureaucratic paralysis.

In this situation, Kenjaev's October 24, 1992, attempt to reinstall the pre–May 7, 1992, government, which did not include the opposition, now had a chance to succeed. The day before, rumors were circulating about a likely attack by an armed group led by Sangak Safarov. This group included many criminals who were notorious for their atrocities in Kurghanteppa. Ethnic Russians were particularly afflicted by the international alarm that had been raised and were effectively exploited by Safarov to counter the opposition's invocation of Tajik nationalism.

At the end of 1992, together with my colleagues, I started working on the selection of participants for the inter-Tajik dialogue we were planning to hold within the framework of the American–Russian Dartmouth conference. One of those who welcomed this idea was Saidhoja Azizov from Kulyab, who gave me a document for protection stating: "The People's Front of Tajikistan. Pass. V. V. Naumkin, a member of the press–Center of the People's Front of the Republic of Tajikistan is allowed to freely move in the territory of the Republic and in the zone of combat operations. All commanders are obliged to provide him with all assistance and to protect him. October 25, 1992."

But this time, support for the leadership change came from military units in the Hissar and Regar Districts. The leaders of the Islamic–democratic bloc alleged Uzbeks (from Uzbekistan) had a hand in the events. The Uzbek involvement was a time bomb that could explode without warning. Attempts to channel the conflict into the field of Tajik–Uzbek relations would have the most tragic consequences for the whole of Central Asia. The attempted coup was stopped by the joint forces of armed city residents, riot control police, and the troops of the National Security Committee. Following the abortive coup, Russia's 201st Motorized Infantry Division, stationed in Tajikistan, took control of the approaches to Dushanbe.

Meanwhile, the economic crisis in Tajikistan entered a new stage. In the South, where armed conflicts did not cease, agricultural and industrial production came to a halt. Crops remained in the field. Bread, other essentials, and electricity were in short supply, and people were starving. This encouraged armed groups to expand into neighboring, wealthier areas, thereby enlarging the conflict zone. Tajikistan thus became increasingly fragmented, with a number of regions forming their own armed forces and ignoring central government authority. The situation was worsened, particularly in the capital, by a large influx of refugees as a result of the clashes. Tens of thousands of desperate, angry, homeless, and dispossessed people were a source of further tensions.

The crisis directly affected other former Soviet republics and Tajikistan's neighbors, including Russia. Early in November, the presidents of Kazakhstan, Uzbekistan, and Kyrgyzstan and the Russian foreign minister met in the Kazakh capital of Alma Ata with Tajikistan's acting president, A. Iskandarov, to prevent a further escalation of tensions. They backed Iskandarov's idea to form a Council of State composed of representatives from all parties, movements, and regions of Tajikistan. It was also decided to help Tajikistan with food and other essentials. The 201st Division would remain in Tajikistan as a peacekeeping force, to be joined later by troops from other CIS members. The meeting supported the proposal to convene the Tajik Supreme Council session, to be recognized as the legitimate authority by all parties to the conflict.

Iran played a positive role in pacifying the conflict, though Tehran sympathized with the IRPT and obviously would not have objected if an Islamic state had been created in Tajikistan. But in general Tehran did not want to risk its good relations with the northern neighbors, Russia first of all, and demonstrated a pragmatic and cautious attitude toward the situation. At the same time, various groups in Afghanistan were supplying weapons to the warring parties in Tajikistan. Some Tajik groups were trying to cross the border from Tajikistan into Afghanistan in search of weapons. All this made pressure on the Tajik–Afghan border, which was also a CIS border, unbearable.

Not all the suggestions of the Alma Ata conference met with Tajikistan's approval. For instance, the Kulyabi grouping emphatically rejected the idea of the Council of State, which was not created, despite several attempts. The Supreme Council's Presidium and the republican government resigned, to facilitate a compromise in parliament.

A session of the Tajik Supreme Council began near Khujand on November 16, 1992. The high-running passions in the republic affected the session from the very outset, resulting in the surfacing of new complications. The session accepted the resignation of Iskandarov, chairman of the Presidium. Emomali Rahmonov, former head of the Executive Committee of the Kulyab Regional Council, was elected as successor to Iskandarov, and Abdumalik Abdullajanov from the North was nominated premier. The session asked that a CIS peacekeeping force be sent to Tajikistan. Forces loyal to the new government (which did not include any representatives of the Islamic–democratic bloc, but mainly consisted of the militia from Kulyab) had by the end of the year managed to seize control over the southern areas.

In early 1993, government forces carried out mop-up operations. Strong resistance on the part of the opposition was still present in the areas along the Tajik–Afghan border. Inhabitants of regions loyal to the Islamists and the democratic parties fled the country to avoid acts of revenge on the part of the Kulyabis. The first reports received by the government of Tajikistan in the aftermath of the civil war showed that more than 400,000 people were displaced and not less than 10,000 people had been killed.[25]

THE IRPT IN EXILE

More than 100,000 Tajiks escaped to Afghanistan along the Pyanj River. The Tajiks in refugee camps urgently needed aid, which was provided by the UN (through the UN High Commissioner for Refugees) and by some Islamic states. Thousands were recruited by the IRPT, which was developing its links with Islamic states. Some militias were established or funded by Islamic foundations from Saudi Arabia and supported by Pakistani intelligence and some Afghan political leaders. Groups of Islamic fighters—mujahedeen—began to shell frontier posts in Tajik territory. A number of Russian and local border guards were killed as a result of these attacks.

To unite all Islamic opponents of the Dushanbe regime, who included modernists and extremists, IRPT members and nonmembers, and traditionalists and reformists, and to develop their international connections and broaden the scope of foreign support for their struggle, the Islamic opposition leaders in 1993 established a new political framework, the Movement of Islamic Revival of Tajikistan (MIRT). This step also made it possible for such prominent figures as former qazi kalon Hoji Akbar Turajonzoda to occupy leading posts in the Islamic opposition movement, their high reputation and wide international connections thus serving the movement's cause. After the events, in 1993 Turajonzoda lost his post: the new authorities abolished the qaziate and replaced it with the muftiate, having appointed a loyal imam, Hoji Fathullo Sharifzoda, as mufti who had not been organizationally associated with the IRPT. The creation of the MIRT also made it possible to combine efforts of the IRPT and the other Islamic forces that opposed the government in Dushanbe. Said Abdullo Nuri was elected MIRT chairman, Turajonzoda became first deputy chairman, and Muhammadsharif Himmatzoda (official IRPT chairman) deputy chairman. The national–democratic opposition parties found themselves junior partners of the Islamists, though nominally, all of them now became equal participants of the newly formed United Tajik Opposition (UTO). They were helpful in rallying support in Russia and the Western world. In the end of 1993, a Coordinating Council of the

Democratic Forces of Tajikistan in the CIS was inaugurated in Moscow; it was led by Otahon Latifi, a famous journalist and former *Pravda* correspondent who was later assassinated in a chain of terrorist acts against representatives of both camps. This committee was considered an offspring of the UTO.

As for the political situation in Tajikistan, the victory of the alliance led by the Kulyabi forces did not bring peace and stability to the republic. The new regime purged its opponents and their supporters from government service, along with people who originated from the regions that provided the basis for the opposition. Members of the militias arrested and killed people in revenge. The government could not control the situation in a number of regions. The regime was widely criticized abroad for violations of human rights and its unwillingness to start negotiations with the opposition, which in response resorted to military pressure on the regime. New tensions emerged among "the winners" themselves. For instance, during the civil war, the Uzbeks had taken the side of the Kulyabis. Then, after many Gharmis had emigrated, the relations between the Uzbeks and the Kulyabis worsened sharply. At the same time, the rivalry between the inhabitants of the Kulyab and Leninabad regions also became aggravated.

After their victory over the Islamic and national–democratic opposition, the Kulyabis began to seize key government posts. Their influence prevailed among the army, police, and security forces. The Kulyabis forcibly acquired houses and flats in Dushanbe as well as other towns, evicting inhabitants who had moved from other areas. Militia members who had been instrumental in achieving victory began to claim the fruits of that victory and wanted to secure guarantees for their own regions, as the 1992 events demonstrated the vulnerability of all. Nevertheless, only representatives of the local elite and people with connections to organized crime acquired their desired privileged positions in the state. The bulk of the population of Kulyab, including military volunteers, had to bear the burden of the economic crisis, the more so since the region has always been underdeveloped.

The inhabitants of Hissar and Regar claimed their share in the new interregional balance of power. The populations of these western areas were more than half Uzbek. It is believed that the Regar volunteers were the main force behind an attempted coup at the end of October 1992.[26] As a result of the settling of scores among different clans, the aforementioned leader of the Popular Front, who had played a decisive role in the battle against the Islamists, Sangak Safarov, was killed, along with a group of other field commanders. The Islamists who fled to Afghanistan, Pakistan, and Iran started to train their forces in camps in Afghanistan, receiving aid from Islamic governmental and nongovernmental sources, but mostly from the Afghan government of President Burhanuddin Rabbani and Defense Minister Ahmad Shah Masoud, both ethnic Tajiks. Training camps were created in Kunduz and Taloqan in the northeastern part of Afghanistan, and some Islamists were being trained in Iran, at the bases of the Islamic Revolutionary Guards. Their detachments, led by well-trained and experienced field commanders, infiltrated the territory of Tajikistan, created bases in Karategin and Tavildara, where the local inhabitants were supporters and kinsmen of the Islamists, and opened a guerilla war there against the new government. Government forces were unable to take control of these mountainous territories with populations alien to "the winners." The IRPT during those days was oriented toward armed struggle but did not exclude the possibility of negotiations.

It would be wrong to suggest that the cleavage between the warring camps in Tajikistan completely coincided with the cleavage between the rival regions. On the side of the opposition stood some prominent representatives of the Kulyab region, including Saidibrohim Gadoev from Kulyab itself, Saidumar Husaini from Muminabad, Sabzali Sharifov from Dangara (President Rahmonov is also a native of Dangara), and Mullo Abdurrahim from Kulyab, who after the reconciliation became director of the Agency to Combat Illicit Drug Turnover.

There were instances where religious figures from the Kulyab region fought on the side of the Islamists. A small group of Kulyabi ishans took part in the rallies at Shahidon Square, then left for Afghanistan and, after the reconciliation, returned home. Among them were Domullo Muhammadi from Kumsanghir and Ishan Abdo. In the same fashion, certain natives of Gharm fought on the Kulyabi side. A number of religious figures on both sides were killed, including the main Naqshbandi authority from Kurghanteppa, Saidatraf, who had been imprisoned until 1994. He was a candidate for election as qazi kalon.

"THE SECOND CIVIL WAR"

The Islamic guerrillas who retreated into the regions adjacent to the Pamir Mountains proclaimed the "Islamic Republic of Gharm" there. Government forces agreed to stop their offensive in this region in exchange for guarantees of loyalty provided by the Gorno-Badakhshan authorities, in spite of the remaining links between the local opposition and the IRPT.

By the summer of 1993, the opposition had regrouped and reorganized its armed detachments, which used the northern regions of Afghanistan as their main base. They started attacks on the Russian border guards who were protecting the border between Tajikistan and Afghanistan. One of these attacks, on July 13, 1993, resulted in the killing of twenty-seven Russian troops and the wounding of several others. It impelled Russia to strengthen its efforts to prevent escalation of the nascent war. Apart from diplomatic activities, Russia bolstered the CIS peacekeeping force. This decision had been made earlier, during the meeting of defense ministers of Russia, Kazakhstan, Kyrgyzstan, and Uzbekistan, but it was not implemented until this tragic event. The peacekeeping force consisted of the Russian 201st Motorized Infantry Division, already stationed in the republic, one battalion from Kazakhstan, one battalion from Uzbekistan, and one company from Kyrgyzstan. This force was deployed in Tajikistan in October 1993.

The neighboring states were also motivated by a possible spillover of the conflict. In July 1993, at a summit of the Organization of Economic Cooperation (ECO) in Istanbul, President Burhanuddin Rabbani of Afghanistan initiated an agreement on the formation of a committee to include representatives of Afghanistan, Tajikistan, Uzbekistan, and Russia to find solutions to all existing disputes, including that of the situation on the Afghan–Tajik border. On July 28, 1993, Russia's President Boris Yeltsin issued a decree that confirmed previous Russo–Tajik agreements on the protection of the border between Tajikistan and Afghanistan by the Russian border guards. The United Nations was also exerting growing pressure on Tajikistan, fearing an escalation of violence in the absence of political will among the conflicting parties to negotiate a solution, and fearing further worsening of the acute humanitarian crisis, which required massive international aid.

But in spite of consolidated efforts of the foreign actors concerned over the rapid aggravation of hostilities, everything suggested the conflicting sides did not actually want peaceful settlement of the intra-Tajik conflict and spoke about peace only to appease outside forces. Both the Islamic opposition and the government included "doves" and "hawks," the latter opposed to any move toward compromise and unwilling to make any concessions to their adversaries in the name of peace. The hawks were well aware of their inability to withstand strong pressure from the outside world and tried to secure better bargaining positions for future talks by achieving some military success. The armed confrontation escalated. By 1994, the main opposition military contingents had been deployed along the border with Tajikistan in the Afghan cities—Kunduz, Taloqan, Hojagar, and Faizabad—on several "fronts": the Kabadiyan front (1,000 troops), the Pyanj front (over 3,000), the Kulyab front (3,000) and the Badakhshan front (2,000).[27] Apart from these contingents, the opposition had 4,500 underground guerrillas in Dushanbe, 2,000 in the Kulyab region, 3,500 in Kurghanteppa, and 7,000 in Gorno-Badakhshan.[28]

On the one hand, the military build-up in the opposition camp made hawks in the government more responsive to the international efforts to put an end to the conflict, and on the other, the leaders of the MIRT—the dominant force in the UTO—understood that they could not achieve their goals by resorting to military force and would probably lose popular support.

THE BEGINNING OF TALKS AND PROSPECTS FOR PEACE

By that time, the situation had already reached a critical point. There were about 145,000 Tajik refugees in Russia and 634,000 in other CIS republics and Afghanistan.[29] A statement by the permanent representative of Tajikistan in the United Nations read that the armed clashes in 1992–1993 resulted in more than 50,000 people killed in Tajikistan.[30] The conflicting parties in Tajikistan held the first round of official talks in Moscow on April 5–19, 1994, under the auspices of the UN and in the presence of observers from the Commission on Security and Cooperation in Europe (CSCE), Russia, and some other countries. The delegations of the Dushanbe government and the UTO were not led by first-rank officials; agreements were limited to the agenda for the next rounds of talks. The talks demonstrated a deep difference between the positions of the conflicting parties. The second round of talks, held in Tehran, did not result in any significant achievement, either. The opposition continued to launch raids from the territory of Afghanistan and inside Tajikistan in an attempt to destabilize the domestic situation and force the government toward concessions. During the first six months of 1994, the armed formations of the opposition made 129 attempts to break through the border from Afghanistan and shelled the positions of the Russian border guards 149 times.[31] On August 19, 1994, a group consisting of two hundred fighters attempted to destroy the twelfth post of the Moscow border guard detachment, which was simultaneously attacked by three hundred fighters from inside Tajikistan. Brutal clashes took place in Gharm, Tavildara, and some other places. The government demonstrated its readiness to make concessions to the UTO by granting amnesty and freeing some people from the list of twenty-nine arrested fighters presented to it by the delegation of the UTO, which reciprocated with its own reconciliatory steps.

Just before that, Dushanbe had decided to hold presidential elections and adopt a new constitution. The international organizations, the Western powers, and Russia all were critical of these plans, predicting that under the existing circumstances the elections would not be democratic, free, and fair. The skepticism was due primarily to the fact that there were still hundreds of thousands of Tajik refugees and displaced persons living abroad who would not have an opportunity to take part in the elections. The CSCE and the UN missions urged the authorities to change the rules for the nomination of candidates and ensure political freedoms. Under pressure, the government decided to postpone elections from September until November 6. It also agreed to raise the level of representation at the talks.

In September a consultative meeting between high-level delegations of the government and the opposition was held in Tehran, organized by Russia and Iran. The meeting in fact became a new, additional round of talks, which led to an agreement on a cease-fire to be monitored by UN observers, on the release of prisoners, and on other confidence-building measures. The U.S. government was actively encouraging a negotiated settlement, democratization, and the provision of humanitarian aid to the Tajiks. It expressed its growing interest in the search for peace and stabilization. In its concurrent resolution 302 in September 1994, the U.S. House of Representatives expressed its anxiety about this situation.

On October 20, 1994, the third round of official talks began in Islamabad, Pakistan. The delegations were headed, respectively, by First Vice-Chairman of the Supreme Council Abdulmajid Dostiev and MIRT First Deputy Chairman Hoji Akbar Turajonzoda. This round confirmed that the process of reconciliation still faced many obstacles. The parties agreed to prolong the cease-fire for another three months, and the government agreed to release a group of prisoners.

The disagreements between the government of Tajikistan and the leaders of the UTO were sharp, and the possibility of reconciling them seemed problematic. On the most fundamental issue—that of power in the republic—the UTO invariably stuck to the demand of creating a National Accord Council, which was to be formed by the two sides on the parity principle and given legislative powers for a term of two years. The council was to form a provisional government consisting of competent and neutral persons.[32] For its part, the existing government did not intend to leave the political arena, believing that there were no grounds for doing so. It thought it best to rely on the legitimation of the regime, and after conducting a referendum on the new constitution and election of a president, where the required support was naturally received, it held a presidential election on November 6, 1994.

Although in Afghanistan the IRPT leaders were predominantly oriented to ethnic Tajik groups, aware that without a solid rear in that neighboring country they would not become an influential political force, they reached out to other groups as well. "In the fall of 1996," writes Alexander Knyazev (Russian TV and Broadcasting Company correspondent),

when the Taliban launched its northward blitzkrieg, the Tajik opposition had to choose between the ethnically kindred Rabbani-Masoud group (within whose zone of influence they were living with their camps in the provinces of Tahar, Kunduz, and Balkh, which they controlled) or to side with the Taliban whose radical opinions struck a chord in the hearts of many opposition leaders. Finally, they established contacts with both camps: Davlat Usmon, head of staff of the armed detachments, met the Taliban leaders, while Hajji Akbar Turajonzoda announced that he supported President Rabbani.[33]

In effect, Emomali Rahmonov became president, elected by popular vote. But the opposition did not recognize either the legitimacy of the election itself or the legality of Rahmonov's election to the presidency, and it continued to press its claims. Hoji Akbar Turajonzoda made a statement broadcast by the opposition radio station, the Voice of Free Tajikistan, in which he said that the opposition had to intensify its armed struggle against "the regime in Dushanbe." Despite the signed Agreement on a Temporary Cease-fire, the termination of military actions, and a moratorium on the movement of troops, clashes on the border and inside the republic sporadically continued. The officers of the Russian border guards accused the opposition of violating the Tehran cease-fire agreement, while the leaders of the opposition laid the blame for it on the Russian frontier troops.

In January 1995, on the eve of new parliamentary elections fixed for February, Rahmonov made a statement on the need for an armistice with the opposition as the decisive factor of stabilization. But the situation was not conducive to the achievement of this aim. Early in 1995, the tacit neutrality between the border guards and the Badakhshan self-defense forces on the Tajik–Afghan border was broken, with the resulting loss of some thirty frontier troops. The UN special representative for Tajikistan, Ramiro Piris-Ballon, discussed the possibility of holding consultations in Moscow with the official government and the commander-in-chief of the armed forces of the UTO in the North of Afghanistan, Said Abdullo Nuri. Meanwhile, the Russian air force bombed the opposition bases in the North of Afghanistan, as the Tajik conflict began to rise to a regional level.

The election of the Majlis-i Oli (parliament) held in the country was proclaimed by the opposition to be illegitimate, since a considerable part of the population had no opportunity to take part in it. The atmosphere of confrontation led to another military incident, this time in Badakhshan. As a result of firefights, twenty-four Tajik and Kazakh servicemen were killed. Soon after that, President Islam Karimov of Uzbekistan held a meeting in Tashkent with representatives of the opposition and made proposals toward the solution of the conflict. The proposals, however, were not supported at the meeting of the three Central Asian states. Besides the president of Uzbekistan, the meeting was attended by the presidents of Kazakhstan and Kyrgyzstan. On April 19, political consultations between the official Dushanbe and the opposition were officially opened in Moscow. During the opening of the consultations, however, the head of the Russian Foreign Ministry, Andrei Kozyrev, threatened a large-scale use of force if incidents similar to the one that had taken place in Badakhshan were repeated. The talks were frustrated, and the opposition appealed to Piris-Ballon to arrange talks in another state.

In May 1995, President Emomali Rahmonov of Tajikistan met in Kabul with the leader of the UTO, Said Abdullo Nuri, the meeting brought about on the initiative of Russia. At last, an agreement was reached to prolong the armistice and hold the next, fourth, round of talks in Almaty. The temporary lull was facilitated by the visit of the Ismailite leader Aga Khan IV on a peace-making mission to Tajikistan in June (the majority of the Tajik Ismailites living in Badakhshan were backing the opposition). Simultaneously, the fourth round of intra-Tajik talks took place in Almaty, bringing no results: the government delegation rejected all proposals of the opposition, as well as the peace-making initiatives of President Nursultan Nazarbaev of Kazakhstan, without offering an alternative compromise solution.

A way out of the deadlock seemed to have been found when Emomali Rahmonov met Said Abdullo Nuri in Tehran on July 19, 1995.[34] The leaders instructed their representatives to consider in the fifth round of talks the question of forming a Consultative Forum of the Peoples of Tajikistan, with the opposition as a full participant.[35] It turned out, however, that the government did not intend to invest this forum with any administrative powers, while the opposition, although it did agree to preserve the existing institutions of the republic, the presidency first of all, over a transition period, could not imagine the Forum without its real participation in the national government.

Clashes between government and opposition forces continued. The battle in Tavildara (at the foot of the Pamirs) resulted in forty-eight (according to other estimates, fifty-seven) of the government troops being taken prisoner. Yet the fifth round of talks was agreed upon during consultations in the Iranian city of Meshhed in November. It was scheduled to be held in Ashgabad and Tehran on November 30, but clashes between the government troops and the opposition, including the use of the air force by the official Dushanbe government, continued in the mountainous areas of Tajikistan throughout November, again causing the date of the talks to be put off. They finally took place in Ashgabad at the end of December 1995, but yielded no results.

A growing dissatisfaction began to be voiced by "the third force" represented by the Leninabad (including Khujand) and Hissar elite residing in the country and seemingly integrated in the regime, although they were gradually ousted by the Kulyabis. An uprising occurred in several areas of the republic simultaneously in January and February 1996 (led in the Hissar region by the ex-mayor Ibod Baimatov, in Kurghanteppa by

Government troops suffer losses during the fighting over Tavildara in June 1996.

Colonel Mahmud Khudoiberdiev). The president was able to cope with the crisis by removing a number of odious figures of Kulyabi origin from the government.

The state of "neither war nor peace" continued in the republic throughout the first six months of 1996. The sporadic skirmishes between government troops and the opposition developed into real military operations, although of a very limited nature, in the Tavildara area.

The bloc of Islamists that was formed in Afghanistan incorporated different people, including those who were involved in drug trafficking and were closely linked with international militant Islamic organizations. Islamic extremists from Uzbekistan also joined the ranks of the Tajik fighters. Juma Khojiev-Namangani and his supporters were participating in the military actions of the IRPT, but Khojiev-Namangani kept his own agenda in mind—to overthrow the Karimov regime in Uzbekistan. The government of Uzbekistan therefore had its own score to settle with the IRPT, which it blamed for "harboring terrorists."

Let us once more look at the document of an Uzbek law-enforcement agency cited in chapter 2:

The United Tajik Opposition and its leader, Said Abdullo Nuri, have longstanding and well-established ties with the Islamic extremists presently

coming under the flag of the Islamic Movement of Uzbekistan (IMU). Moreover, this movement is the brainchild of the Islamic Tajik opposition, having
been nurtured in the blood of the peaceful citizens of Tajikistan in the years
of the civil war. It is also known that the bandit groups headed by Tahir Yuldashev through 1998 fought as part of the armed formations of Mirzo Ziyoev in Tajikistan against government forces and in 1998 took part in punitive operations in the Sogdian region of the Republic of Tajikistan. In the
process, one of the IMU ringleaders, Juma Hojiev, performed the role of a
messenger between UTO leader Nuri and IMU leader Yuldashev in the territory of Tajikistan.
    Wide-ranging and multilevel contacts between the UTO and the IMU have
now been established and are being reinforced. In particular, bands of Uzbek
Islamists in Tajikistan under the direct patronage of UTO leaders, particularly Said Abdullo Nuri, are freely moving in the zones controlled by the opposition and continue to be supplied with arms, munitions, food, and financial resources, both through their own channels and from UTO sources. The
followers of extremists who have been coming from Uzbekistan from early
1999 on, were, as in former years, undergoing special commando and terrorist training in the camps of the Tajik opposition.[36]

Exacerbated by deep economic crises, the ongoing political rivalry between regional elites prevented the stabilization of the situation in Tajikistan. The Rahmonov group's relationship with Uzbekistan, which had
greatly contributed to the victory of the regime, soured.

THE DYNAMICS OF CONTINUING TENSIONS

Roy believes that the basis of political mobilization in Tajikistan has always been regionalist, not ideological or religious. He provides many examples that, in his view, prove this idea, including equal reverence for
Sufi pirs by the opposing parties to the conflict. One of the examples concerns qazi kalon Akbar Turajonzoda, who Roy calls "the spiritual leader
of the Tajik opposition" (which is not an accurate label).[37] Turajonzoda's
father, Ishan Turajon, as mentioned above, was a *murid* of Hazrat Ishan
Khaliljon, a famous pir from Kurghanteppa.
    After Turajonzoda left it, the government of the winners, dominated
by the Kulyabi clan, likewise appointed as a mufti an offspring of a Sufi
family, but a Naqshbandi one, Fatullah Khan Sharifzoda, who was assassinated in January 1996. "Sharifzoda's father, Damullah Muhammadsharif," Roy writes, "was highly respected (by the qazi as well). Sufi
solidarity is here expressed not in a political affiliation but in the mutual
respect which the families have for each other." Data are cited indicating that Turajonzoda appointed Muhammadsharif to serve as *sar khatib*
(incumbent of the mosque) of the Hissar region in 1988, and when

Muhammadsharif's son was assassinated, Turajonzoda denounced the crime.

However, this and similar examples in no way exclude the possibility of Sufi solidarity being used for political mobilization. The conflict in Tajikistan had been waged not between different Sufi brotherhoods but between regional political elites and not at all due to the general nature of Sufi relationships. The very fact that religious figures belonging to the most revered Sufi families (including Sharifzoda) were murdered makes this statement not very convincing. The fact that Turajonzoda (long before the outbreak of the conflict) appointed a respected Naqshbandi pir an incumbent of the mosque is of no importance at all, because, as the head of the Muslims of Tajikistan, the qazi kalon was engaged precisely in appointing ministers of religion of various origins, while the fact that he condemned the murder of the mufti in 1996 is within the limits of normal human ethics (the qazi kalon himself had never taken part in military operations, nor had he commanded them). Besides, from the beginning of negotiations between the UTO and the government, Turajonzoda proved himself a champion of reconciliation. He became easily integrated into the government, showing himself, in the estimation of both the Islamists and "the party of power," a strong politician. He virtually ceased religious activity and can hardly be named "the spiritual leader of the Tajik opposition" (it would be more correct to say "the Islamist opposition"), which, incidentally, he had not been a part of since the first days of its emergence. This leader willingly left the ranks of this opposition when a chance was given to him to start a career as a high-ranking government official.

Sufism in Tajikistan, indeed, "duplicates and simultaneously transcends tribal segmentation."[38] However, this is characteristic of Sufism in general, in all countries where it exists. The brotherhoods mentioned here (Naqshbandiyya and Qadiriyya) themselves bear a supranational character and are present in a large number of states. Nevertheless, there is nothing unusual in the fact that the people of one settlement, neighborhood, or village would affiliate themselves with only one Sufi brotherhood—more precisely, a branch of it—and consider themselves followers of a certain regional pir. It was thus not surprising that the Naqshbandi pir of Hissar, Domullo Muhammadsharif Hissari (d. 1990), "had been able to establish a very broadly-based network of disciples in Uzbek Ferghana (Kokand and Namangan)," because Uzbeks constitute a high percentage of the population of Hissar and Regar, the western region of Tajikistan, adjacent to Uzbekistan.[39]

Examples of political mobilization on the basis of Sufi solidarity can be found in the Tajik conflict, as well as beyond Tajikistan. These cases do not imply a particular political ideology: during the Caucasian war in the nineteenth century, the core group of the Chechen leaders who fought

against Russia were Naqshbandis, but most of the leaders of Chechen separatists today are Qadiris. After all, all Tajiks are Muslims, and the Islamic
factor played a major role in the conflict. While admitting the paramount
role of the antagonism of regional elites, one could deny the importance
of cleavage along the line of supporters versus opponents of the Islamic
state. The Islamists' joining hands with the democrats was "an alliance of
convenience" and can hardly last long.

Roy mentions that Sufi brotherhoods "recruit in both Turcophone and
Persian-speaking populations without distinction."[40] But there is nothing
unusual about this in Sufism, which has never been an ethnicity-based
movement. Knowing the long history of Naqshbandiyya, which started in
the fourteenth century, one can hardly imagine that the Naqshbandi
brotherhood could have been other than a group that embraces Muslims
of varied ethnic descent. It is not surprising, therefore, that Pir Muhammadsharif Hissari was "able to establish a very broad-based network of
disciples in Uzbek Ferghana (Kokand and Namangan)," especially given
the fact that the population of Hissar is mixed, and many of the Hissaris
are ethnic Uzbeks (or, to put it better, Turcophones).

The broadly shared affiliation does not exclude "local Sufi solidarity" in
case of competition and rivalry among regional elites. The fact that each
local group has its own object of worship at the tomb of a local saint only
facilitates the possibility of appealing to this kind of "segmental Sufi solidarity." If a pir of a particular order is outside the given local community,
this means only that he plays the role of symbol of its solidarity, but does
not dilute it in any way. The fact that Sufism in Tajikistan has not become
a basis for the mobilization of Islamists, who in the years of conflict
mostly represented the Gharm-Karategin group of regions, is explained
not by the impossibility of its marriage to regional identities, but by the
specific agenda of this movement, which appealed to all Muslims. Having two faces—"narrow" and "broad"—and having incorporated traditional norms, beliefs, and rituals, Sufism could not totally meet either the
demands of regional elites who were seeking a specific ideological cover
or of fundamentalists who wanted a more puritan religion and were more
uncomfortable with "the impurity" of Sufi Islam, which has incorporated
many local traditions, beliefs, and rituals.

On the one hand, the intragroup solidarity of Tajik communities fostered the transformation of the civil war in Tajikistan into a clash among
regions; on the other, the political and ideological differences among those
who took part in it and the absence of hard-and-fast boundaries between
kindred territorial groups did not allow these differences to be characterized as clashes solely among regional communities.[41]

Spokesmen for the IRPT leadership disagree that the inter-Tajik conflict
was interregional. In D. Usmon's opinion, this was a clash of opposing

views and ideas preached by "the new people" and "the old people." "The new people coalesced around the IRPT and the old ones around the CPT."[42] It is clear that it is to the advantage of Islamist leaders to show themselves as the champions of an idea and not as the mouthpieces of regional elite interests. No matter how strong "the localist drive" in the Tajik conflict was, it was not the general populace of the region (who were manipulated and mobilized by the elites) who skillfully addressed their own grievances, concerns, and fears. Instead, it was mainly the regional elites, who were so persistent in striving for self-expression and a share of power and wealth. But the importance of the ideological dimension of conflict cannot be underestimated either.

PEACEFUL SETTLEMENT

Under strong domestic and international pressure, the two sides drafted a document on the creation of a Commission of National Reconciliation (CNR), which was signed by President Rahmonov and UTO leader Nuri in Moscow on December 23, 1996; the functions and powers of the commission, as well as its composition, were to be defined in the course of future negotiations.[43]

While the politicians were signing these hard-won agreements, the situation on the ground underwent a drastic change. The field commanders, who had made effective progress in dividing the spheres of influence, began to lose interest in the interminable and hopeless internecine strife. Of late, their primary concern had been to "legalize" and consolidate the gains of the civil war. Politicians had actually been outrun by the pace of developments. The meeting held on September 15–16, 1996, between the Tajikistan State Commission and the field commanders of the Karategin area can be seen as an attempt to catch up to some extent with the brisk process of the semifeudal partition of some of the country's areas. The composition of the UTO delegation at the meeting testified to a clear-cut division of functions and control among the field commanders, who were not interested in the appearance of new forces, which might call for a redivision. The UTO was represented by Mirzohoja Nizomov, commander of the Karategin area (delegation chairman); Mahmadruzi, commander in charge of Tajikabad; Eshoni Aziz, deputy commander in charge of Komsomolabad; Mirzohoja Akhmadov, commander in charge of Gharm; and Kosimjon, commander in charge of Komsomolabad. The talks were held with UN mediation. "Agreement was reached to effect the following measures prior to the settlement of political questions at the coming inter-Tajik negotiations: to remove the checkpoints in the Jirgatal and Tajikabad areas; to reconstitute agencies in charge of the interior and security matters in these two areas; to permit members of the UTO armed forces to stay in these areas without their weapons; the two sides guarantee the free movement of transport on the Dushanbe-Jisgal route; the two sides undertake to jointly discuss and resolve all outstanding questions."[44]

The large-scale offensive mounted by the Taliban forces in Afghanistan, who seized Kabul, radically changed the course of events, and this was bound to affect the situation along the border. Moreover, shortly before the next round of inter-Tajik negotiations, the UTO resorted to its well-tried tactic of hard pressure on the Dushanbe leaders so as to obtain more concessions at the negotiating table. In contravention of the September agreement, the opposition's armed forces seized the territory of the Gharm group of regions. The confrontation in the republic did not stop even after the breakthrough in the negotiations. On June 27, 1997, a General Agreement on Peace and National Accord was signed in Moscow by Tajik president Emomali Rahmonov, United Opposition leader Said Abdullo Nuri, and the UN envoy for Tajikistan, Gerd-Dietrich Merrem.

An attendant Protocol of Mutual Understanding was also signed at the Russian Foreign Ministry by Rahmonov and Nuri in the presence of the Russian and Iranian foreign ministers. The Tajik sides agreed to convene in Moscow before July 7 the first meeting of the Commission on National Reconciliation in order to work out a draft law on general amnesty to be submitted to the existing Tajik parliament.[45] The CNR chaired by Nuri was to consist of twenty-six persons, split equally between opposition and government representatives. Fresh parliamentary elections would be held after a transition period of twelve to eighteen months, but until the transition period ended, at least 30 percent of the portfolios in the Tajik government would be occupied by opposition representatives. Opposition forces would be integrated into government force agencies, and 460 armed opposition fighters would go to Dushanbe to protect opposition leaders. Given the nature of the inter-Tajik conflict and Tajik society itself as a clan-based society, the settlement reached between the government and the opposition was, on the one hand, an agreement between the secular and the Islamic tendency and, on the other, a clan pact.

THE IRPT IN GOVERNMENT

The parties to the negotiations on March 8, 1997, signed the Protocol on Military Questions, which specified the process of disarmament and reintegration. The implementation of the Protocol faced many difficulties that were finally overcome due to the constructive spirit of government and opposition leaders, the IRPT above all. Representatives of that party were incorporated in the central and local government bodies according to the

30 percent quota stipulated by the agreement. The IRPT's armed formations underwent a process of stage-by-stage reintegration into the country's military, police, and civil government bodies. The agreement was at the brink of collapse because "the party of power" was firmly opposed to the appointment of one of the most prominent Islamic field commanders, Mirzo Ziyoev, known as "Jaga," as defense minister. The opposition insisted on this appointment. The level of trust had not yet reached a point that would allow "the party of power" to lose control over the armed forces. Only after the government realized that the tensions exacerbated by the sharp debate over this appointment would inevitably lead to a new confrontation was Ziyoev appointed minister for the emergencies.

In conformity with the Protocol on Military Questions, about 5,400 former fighters of armed UTO groups were given amnesty and reintegrated as a result of certification in 1999. Most of these people became servicemen of Tajikistan's army. A small number of oppositionists were enrolled for service in the Ministry of the Interior, the Ministry for the Emergencies, and the Committee on the Protection of the State Border. Particularly significant was the appointment of former field commander Ni'matullo Bilolov (before the events with the militia in the Gorno-Badakhshan Autonomous Region) as head of one of the regional police departments. After returning from Kunduz, Bilolov had served in several groups of UTO representatives on the Commission on National Reconciliation. Also, several militants charged with protecting Nuri were enrolled in the presidential guard. The total number of civilian refugees who came back from camps in Kunduz and Mazar-i Sharif as a result of the understandings has exceeded eighty thousand.

Work in the Commission on National Reconciliation in search of a legal formula of coexistence between the secular and religious elements in Tajikistan's political system proceeded with difficulty, the two sides reluctant to retreat from their positions. For instance, the opposition proposed that in Article 1 of the constitution Tajikistan be defined as a "democratic" and "law-governed" state, whereas the government insisted that the term "secular" necessarily be present in the formula. When the talks reached deadlock, the president of the republic and the UTO leader agreed on the formation of a joint commission, in which the government would be represented by Mahmadsaid Ubaidulloev and Talbak Nazarov, and the opposition by Hoji Akbar Turajonzoda and Muhammadsharif Himmatzoda. After protracted private talks between Ubaidulloev and Turajonzoda, the two sides agreed on a compromise formula: to guarantee simultaneously the secular character of the state and the religion's political activity. As a result of a nationwide referendum of September 26, 1999, a provision allowing the creation of religious political parties was incorporated into the new version of the constitution.

Hoji Akbar Turajonzoda, United Tajik Opposition deputy leader, returns to Dushanbe on February 28, 1998, after five years of exile in Iran.

Nonetheless, the opponents of concessions to the Islamists attempted to stage a comeback when dealing with the question of amendments to the law on political parties. The Majlis-i Oli passed a new law whose Article 4 prohibited the establishment and activity of political parties of a religious character precisely at the time when the CNR was still discussing amendments to the constitution. To defuse the crisis, the president had to institute an interagency commission, upon whose decision the parliament revised the law, granting religious parties the right to function. However, as noted by the advocates of an Islamic tendency, "new restrictions were imposed on them in such an important question as relations with nonpolitical religious organizations."[46]

On August 12, 1999, according to the provision of the Protocol on Political Questions, the Supreme Council lifted the ban on the IRPT and other opposition parties, and the IRPT legally resumed its activity in Tajikistan. On September 18, 1999, the IRPT held its second congress, which reelected Said Abdullo Nuri as its chairman. Muhammadsharif Himmatzoda and Mirzoyusufi Fozil became his deputies, while Sayid Umari Husayni became the party's general secretary (*dabiri kull*). The publication of the IRPT's organ, the newspaper *Najot*, was resumed.

As pointed out by Davlat Usmon, after the party's second legalization in 1999 and the adoption of the new program and statute, it has become clear that the realization and revival of Islamic morality and norms was relegated to the background by the party.[47] The IRPT defined its objectives as:

- Ensuring the development of economic, social, and cultural life in the republic.
- Ensuring the development of democracy, rights, and social regulation.
- The development of Islamic values, as well as national and human values, among the people of Tajikistan.
- Raising the political and cultural level of the population, especially women and youth, through their participation in political activity and state government.
- Safeguarding the unity and integrity of the territory of Tajikistan.
- Ensuring unity and fraternal relations among the peoples of Tajikistan.
- Ensuring the political, economic, and cultural independence of Tajikistan.
- Realizing its aims through the public authorities and legislative bodies with the participation of members of parties in their activity.

This list is so comprehensive and general that it is not possible to judge from it that the IRPT is an Islamic party.

The IRPT also took part in the presidential and parliamentary elections. At a party congress in September 1999, Hoji Akbar Turajonzoda called on his colleagues to rally their support around Emomali Rahmonov, threatening to quit the MIRT if they did not do so. Having failed to convince the IRPT not to nominate its own candidate, Turajonzoda left the movement. At the end of the electoral campaign, IRPT nominee Davlat Usmon, then minister for the economy, asked the party leadership to boycott the election, accusing "the party of power" of having violated the electoral law, but the party leaders refused to do this. As some IRPT members have told me, the real reason Usmon did this was his fear that he would not gain much support as a presidential candidate. IRPT leaders thought that even if such violations had taken place, it was not a sufficient reason to endanger the party's peaceful and constructive cooperation with the mainstream and risk a new round of violence. Davlat Usmon won 2.1 percent of the vote. Two IRPT candidates (6.8 percent), including Muhammadsharif Himmatzoda, were returned to the country's parliament. After his defeat, Usmon left the party. Tajik researcher Saodat Alimova noted in 2002 that Davlat Usmon, who had graduated from the Diplomatic Academy in Moscow, might try to create a new political party, but at least as of the beginning of 2004 this had not happened.[48] According to the data of the IRPT itself, the party membership was now roughly twenty-five thousand.[49] However, this may well be an overestimate. The IRPT enjoys the greatest support in the Gharm, Kofarnihon, Matcha, and Isfara districts and in places of concentrated residence of immigrants from the Gharm zone (the Vakhsh and Kumsanghir districts).

"The party of power" and the opposition, which had been at war, now started to govern the country together. They constructively solved many problems that appeared in the course of the national reconciliation process, especially in the relationship between armed formations. They stopped all feuds that had been tearing the country apart for years, and the refugees were able to come back to their homes.

The experience of peaceful reconciliation between a secular government and an Islamic political opposition, which resulted in the integration of such a party in the government, was a unique example for Central Asia. The ruling alliance remains stable. The fate of this historic experiment will be of immense importance for the Islamic world. The IRPT demonstrates its loyalty to "the party of power" and to President Rahmonov. When its members are expressing their concerns about some undemocratic practices of the ruling Kulyabi elite, the tension is usually mitigated by the cautious reaction of the IRPT leaders. The party has officially supported the concept of a secular state, but fears that the IRPT can in the future embrace the idea of an Islamic state are still shared by many members of "the party of power."

THE ROLE OF TAJIKISTAN'S ISLAMIC CLERGY

The IRPT's return to government and the rehabilitation of political Islam in Tajikistan again posed the question of the role the Islamic clergy played or could play in government and what clergy generally represented in the postconflict period. Let us examine the main groups forming part of the clergy.

Conventionally assigned to the official clergy are those clerics who have official religious status or professionally perform the functions of imams, qazis, *'ulama*, and so forth. These people are intimately linked with the authorities and are loyal to them, manage the affairs of mosques, including their own incomes and the donations of believers, and represent Tajik Islam at the official level. Earlier, the principal figure in that group was the qazi kalon (until 1988, Abdullo Kalonzoda, then Hoji Akbar Turajonzoda), but in 1993 the qaziate was transformed into the muftiate, and Hoji Fathullo Sharifzoda becoming the mufti of Tajikistan. However, he was killed as a result of a terrorist act in 1996. After that, the Muftiate was abolished, and Muslim affairs began to be administered by the Council of the 'Ulama (its chairman to date being Amonullo Ni'matzoda). In the time of qazi kalon Turajonzoda, when the official clergy held great leverage, its best-known representatives included the Ni'matzoda, Mullo Faizullo, and Hoji Habibullo in Dushanbe; Huseinjon Musozoda, Ibadullo Kalonzoda, and Muslihiddin Mukarramzoda in Khujand; Ismail Pirmuhammadzoda in Hissar; Haydar Sharifzoda in Kulyab; and Ishoni Saidjon in Kurghanteppa. Today certain former representatives of the official clergy appointed to senior government posts do not pursue ecclesiastical activity but continue to carry the authority of clerics; these include Hoji Akbar Turajonzoda and Odilkhan Aliev, the latter from Khujand.

The reform wing in Tajikistan's clergy comprises all imams, *'ulama*, and other figures who have in one form or another departed from traditionalism and are oriented toward the politicization of Islam. This wing manifested itself with the start of Gorbachev's *perestroika*, being at variance with Turajonzoda. According to Turajonzoda's assistant, Abdullo Hakim, the following people can be assigned to this wing of the clergy: the leader of the former UTO and IRPT chairman Said Abdullo Nuri, IRPT deputy chairman and delegate to the Majlis-i Oli Davlat Usmon, Muhammadjon *qari* Ghufronov (who lost his life during the civil war), Eshon-i Kiyomiddin (Ghoziev), Mullo Kalandar (chairman of the IRPT organization of the Khatlon region), Maulawi Mahmadali (chairman of the IRPT Auditing Commission), Maulawi Abdulhai, Mullo Qosim, Mullo Abdurrasul, and others. Among the younger generation of exponents of this wing are Muhiddin Kabiri (IRPT first deputy chairman), Sayyid Umar Huseini (IRPT secretary-general), Maulawi Ghaibnazarov (former deputy labor

minister), Mullo Sa'uddin (Rustamov), and Mullo Navid (Mirzohodi Mirzomuhammadiev, former deputy culture minister).[50] The profusion of
"has beens" in this list does not inspire optimism about a successful integration of IRPT activists into government bodies. According to IRPT data,
of fifty-three functionaries of the highest rank (deputy minister and
above) who received their posts in accordance with the General Agreement, by early 2003 only twelve remained; the rest had been dismissed for
one reason or other.

The next group of Tajikistan's Islamic clergy is the so-called traditional
clergy. These are authoritative ishans, 'ulama, shaykhs, mudarrises, and
others. According to Abdullo Hakim, among the main features of this
stratum of the clergy is that its members:

- stick to traditional, conservative positions on matters of religion;
- observe all the traditional rites;
- mostly belong to kinsmen of ishans or sayyids (descendants of the
  Prophet or other noble families);
- are not enthusiastic about politics and do not actively cooperate with
  the authorities;
- do not support the policy of centralized state management of religion
  and stand mostly for maintaining "polycentricity" in Tajik Islam;
- distance themselves from the official and reforming clergy;
- do not have an organizational framework for their activity.[51]

In the recent past, the now deceased Ishoni Abdurrahmanjon, Ishoni
Tajj, and the family of Ishoni Eloki carried incontestable authority in the
Obi-Gharm and Faizabad districts and part of the Kofarnihon district; else-
where, the persons of influence were: in the western part of Kofarnihon,
the now deceased Domullo Sharifi Hozori and, in the Kulyab region, the
now deceased Ishoni Sangi Kulula and other ishans and 'ulama. Tremen-
dous authority is carried in the eastern portion of the Hissar Valley (in the
Kofarnihon and Lenin districts and part of the city of Dushanbe) and in the
Zerafshan Valley (in the Sogdian region) by Ishoni Turajon (the father of
Hoji Akbar Turajonzoda) and Ishoni Nuriddin (Hoji Akbar's elder
brother), in the Karategin Valley by Domullo Hikmatullo and Ishoni
Saidashraf, in the southern portion of the Khatlon region by Domullo
Muhammadi, in various parts of the Hissar Valley by Ishoni Abdukhalijon
and Ishoni Kalon, and in the Zafarabad, Gancha, and Matcha regions by
Ishoni Mirzo and Ishoni Yusuf and others.

It is also conventional to consider separately the so-called rural clergy.
These are clerics catering for the spiritual needs of the dwellers of kishlaks,
the overwhelming majority of whom are semiliterate people with a rather
primitive knowledge of religion. In religious questions, they are close to

the traditional clergy and, as pointed out by Tajik researchers, are marked by political passivity. In the localities, in their *kishlaks* and neighborhoods they exert a considerable influence upon the population.

Naturally, the different strata of the Tajik clergy carry different social weight and markedly differ as to the influence they exert on political and public life. Their relationship with the IRPT is very contradictory: among the clergy, there are both uncompromising opponents of any involvement of religion in politics and supporters of the IRPT, along with individuals secretly sympathizing with more radical groups.

NEW HOPES AND OLD FEARS

The IRPT's legalization and the inclusion of its representatives in government bodies, as President Rahmonov's supporters believe, has resulted in a decrease in their political ambitions and neutralized the risk of open resistance. "The party of power," which consists mainly of representatives of the Kulyabi clan, even now is convinced that it can modify the actions of IRPT leaders. This is obviously manifest in the position taken by the party leadership concerning the liquidation of the Sanginov–Muakkalov bandit groups, in the expulsion of Juma Namangani's units of extremists beyond the Tajik borders, during the prosecution of an antiterrorist operation in the Islamic State of Afghanistan, and a number of other political measures taken by the government.

Several groups from the Islamic opposition opposed the General Agreement and refused to obey the rules of the Protocol on Military Questions, which required them to disarm and be incorporated into official structures. They continued acts of violence in Tajikistan, and all attempts by the IRPT leaders to make them obey their orders failed. Some of these holdouts joined up with Juma Namangani. Two groups, one led by Rahmon Sanginov, nicknamed "Hitler," and another by Mansur Muakkalov, first were absorbed into the government army, but then, having been exposed as bandits involved in kidnapping and bank robberies, escaped and continued acts of violence in different regions of Tajikistan. After a month of fighting with the Tajik army, in August 2001 Sanginov's group of about a hundred men was defeated, and the commander was killed along with forty-five of his men.[52] Muakkalov was also killed during a special operation against his group, some of the group's members were killed, and others were arrested. The IRPT leader clearly took the side of the government during these events.

In May 2002, after an investigation, eighty-two members of these gangs were put on trial on charges of hostage taking, terrorism, murder, and belonging to illegal armed groups. The Supreme Court's military tribunal in

The start of the military operation to neutralize the Sanginov–Muakkalov band in Tajikistan on June 22, 2001.

February 2003 sentenced nine of them to death by firing squad, handed down sentences to seventy-two of them ranging from eighteen months to twenty-five years in prison, and released one for health reasons.[53]

Cases of rebellion against the government by Islamic field commanders who had already been incorporated into the force agencies of the republic, once again, were not numerous. In addition to Sanginov and Muakkalov, Mullo Abdullo Rahimov was a commander who demonstrated disobedience and left his service. In an interview, a senior officer in the Ministry of Defense told me that there had been several other minor cases in which former mujahedeen were leaving military service due to low salaries.

The dynamics of the death penalties in Tajikistan left an impression that the remnants of the civil war were still strong. The OSCE mission in Dushanbe said that some 240 people were sentenced to death in 2002, while the number of people receiving the death penalty had increased over the previous three years.[54] Is this just because there are still many war criminals who have been killing people for a long time and simply cannot stop, or because the Tajik authorities use the situation to settle scores with these opponents? The Tajik authorities point out that there are many cases where former guerrillas have been involved in serious crimes.

Said Abdullo Nuri

The head of the Tajik Military Court told RFE/RL about two former rebels of the UTO who were executed in February 2003. A. Rasulov and A. Khalov had massacred a family of thirteen people, including a baby and a pregnant woman.[55]

Societies that have survived civil wars usually have large numbers of people who cannot integrate into normal, peaceful life. At the same time, human rights groups complain of a lack of fair trials in the republic. As stated in a summary of the Institute for Peace Research and Security Policy at Hamburg University, compiled on the basis of written reports made in Tajikistan on the instructions of the OSCE, "the texts submitted by the IRPT and other moderate Islamists clearly show that the change in their profile, that is, a transition from hitherto radical positions to a moderate, reforming tendency (national Islam) continues."[56] The IRPT, for example, has condemned the terrorist acts of September 11 and dissociated itself from terrorism as a method of political struggle. The parties representing IRPT in the dialogue on Tajikistan's various political forces organized in Dushanbe by the OSCE in 2002 also condemned the antidemocratic, repressive actions of the Central Asian regimes (except for Tajikistan), believing that they create a more favorable ground for agitation by radical Islamists. They called the exclusion of religious parties,

Muslim authoritative persons, and Islamic politicians from political life "a major mistake" of these regimes.[57]

"The party of power" in 2002–2003 took into account the fact that the IRPT even now remains the most active and efficient opposition party and that its main efforts are aimed at the strengthening and expansion of its structural subdivisions at regional and district levels, which cannot but cause anxiety among members of the progovernment National Democratic Party (led by Emomali Rahmonov). The NDP was especially troubled that the IRPT relies for support mainly on the youth, women, and intellectuals.

The IRPT leadership, for its part, was now concerned about the conflict that had arisen in the party leadership on account of past election returns—which were unfavorable to the IRPT—their decreased authority among the ordinary believers due to the party's accession to power, and the IRPT's loss of supporters to the IMU, the Hizb at-Tahrir, and other radical religious-cum-political groups. Thus the IRPT leaders have introduced amendments to the tactics of political struggle, directed toward restoring the party's influence among the religious part of the population, recruitment of new members, preparation for the upcoming elections, and a search for potential allies in the political struggle. In the second elections to the Majlis-i Namoyandagon (Lower Chamber—Council of Representatives) of the Majlis-i Oli, IRPT leaders nominated their candidates for the Asht and Kolkhozabad voting districts. However, they failed to achieve the desired results.

The IRPT has not lost its links with the international Islamic movement. Tajikistan's law enforcement agencies controlled by the Kulyabi grouping seem to believe that the IRPT continues to maintain links with the radical section of the international Islamic movement as well.[58] Foreign Muslim government and nongovernmental institutions, spokesmen for these agencies have assured, continue to remain the sponsors of the legalized Tajik Islamists. The material and financial support for the IRPT, they claim, as a rule is camouflaged by donations of religious literature and consumer goods (proceeds from whose sales become the party property), the allocation of grants for the construction of mosques and prayer houses, and the conduct of religious and humanitarian work (support for orphan children, the families of the slain mujahedeen, etc.). With direct assistance of foreign sponsors, the IRPT is sending the most highly trained young party members for study in the theological institutions of Iran, Pakistan, Saudi Arabia, and other Muslim states.

According to one of the senior officials of the presidential apparatus, representatives of the IRPT's radical wing, dissatisfied with the "passivity" of the political leadership, are harboring the intention to oust Nuri from his post or set up a new Islamic party.[59] These radicals sympathize with the IMU, al-Qa'ida, and other Islamic extremist organizations. Considerable differences exist even among moderate leaders of the Islamic movement in Tajikistan. This is demonstrated by the following example. According to Olimova, several groups of Islamic leaders are currently participating in the legal political process.[60] They are (1) Islamic leaders who have occupied posts in the government and distanced themselves from the IRPT, "expressing their disagreement with the idea of an Islamic party" (Turajonzoda); (2) leaders who have occupied posts in the government in accordance with the quota allocated by the General Agreement and two members of parliament elected from the IRPT; (3) leaders who have occupied their posts in accordance with the quota but left the IRPT and, under pressure, joined the National Democratic Party of Tajikistan, led by President Rahmonov (Minister of Industry Zayd Saidov); (4) Islamic leaders who have not occupied any official posts (S. A. Nuri); and (5) influential Islamic leaders (outside the IRPT) who have remained loyal to the regime throughout the civil war (Chairman of Shuro-i Ulamo, or the "Council of the 'Ulama," Muhammadsharif Ni'matzoda).

On the one hand, government circles consider the experience of reconciliation with the opposition and, even more, the incorporation of the leaders of moderate Islamists into government as important achievements worthy of imitation in other Central Asian states. On the other hand, they continue to distrust many of these leaders, keeping a zealous watch on their activity. Conversations with individual members of the Kulyab clan show that they speak with alarm and irritation on the development of propaganda tactics by the IRPT and the practical application of such forms as seminars, debates, and round tables to influence the particular social strata and the international community's image of the IRPT. These members distrust the party's portrayal of itself internationally as oriented toward constitutional methods of political struggle, having a highly professional cadre potential with the requisite scientific-cum-practical training, and thus having the ability to perform the functions of public management in a self-sufficient manner.

Cited as an example were some of the following measures carried out by the IRPT, which to all appearances became the subject of close attention from their new partners and simultaneous political rivals.

- At the end of 2000, on the initiative of the leadership of the Isfara town IRPT cell, a scholarly conference of the women's branch of that party on the subject of "The Role of the Woman in the Transformation of Society" was organized in the town of Isfara, in which about one hundred women took part.
- On May 18, 2002, an academic seminar on the subject of *Sharob wa zararhoi* (the problem of alcohol and its damages) was held at the

premises of the Sitora cinema in the city of Dushanbe, organized by the Frunze district IRPT branch, in which about fifty party members took part.

• On June 15 of the same year, on the initiative of the IRPT leadership, a roundtable was held in the headquarters of that party, devoted to the fifth anniversary of the signing of the General Agreement on peace, on the subject of *Sulhi tochikon va samarahoi* (Tajik reconciliation and its results), in which representatives of other parties, as well as the UN and the OSCE, took part.

Asked whether such conference violated existing legislation, the interlocutor replied that the organization of all such conferences, as a rule, conforms to the law, but their conduct above all "pursues the aim of Islamization of society, laying the ground work for the creation of an Islamic state in the Republic of Tajikistan."

Probably, the stepped-up IRPT activity in the Sogdian region, and above all in the Isfara district, instills in their electoral rivals the fear that at the following elections the IRPT could crowd out the NDP. According to the same interlocutor, the IRPT in the town of Isfara "creates a semblance of loyalty to the existing system and the policies of the state." "For the realization of their plans and intentions to Islamize society and broaden the sphere of their influence among the various strata of the population," party activists "make use of every possible public event (weddings, religious ceremonies, funerals, etc.), attracting a great number of people, which contravenes the existing regulations." For example, so-called Islamic weddings have started to become the norm in recent years, attended by what on the face of it seem to be edifying sermons, but ostensibly exhibiting far-reaching objectives. It is IRPT members and activists who in most cases address the audience at these "weddings."

What causes serious discontent in government circles is the intensified IRPT activity among women of the Isfara district, who are called upon to raise the coming generation. Women's assemblies (*ma'vizes*) held by *otuns* (senior women), at which their Islamic indoctrination is being conducted, have become more frequent. The law enforcement agencies have repeatedly warned the inhabitants of the *kishlak* of Chorkukh—two Islamic woman activists—of such a violation of the law, and the court has fined one of them for teaching children Islamic dogma outside the framework established by law.

The Isfara district has probably become an object of discord because the high religiosity of the inhabitants of this part of the North makes it easier for the Islamists to win support. It has been noted that several

IRPT activists from among the inhabitants of the Isfara district were nominated to leading posts in that party. Thus one native of Chorkukh, Vokhindkhon Kosiddinov, the former chairman of an IRPT town cell, was nominated IRPT vice president, while another, Nabiullo Dovudov, is a member of the control and auditing commission of that party. Naimjon Samiev ("Bobosome") is now head of the IRPT department of culture for the Sogdian region, while the IRPT activist Khodi Fattoev serves as *imam-khatib* of the mosque Khoja Ustodi Wali in Chokrukh. Some of the most hard-line representatives of the Kulyabi grouping in the leadership even believe that it is precisely the Isfara district that can become a "trial base" for the project of an Islamic state for the IRPT. Such an explanation obviously pursues the aim of enhancing distrust of the IRPT in government circles so as to bury the reconciliation and bring about the outlawing of the Islamists once again. Another aim is to strengthen control over the northern part of the country, with which the political elite of southern clans has an old rivalry.

Trying to limit the spread of political Islam, the government does not admit persons who received religious education abroad for service in mosques, believing them to be infected with a virus of Islamic radicalism. However, it cannot prevent them from conducting private study and conversations with the believers within their homes. To a certain extent, though to a much smaller degree than in Soviet times, a phenomenon of a parallel or informal Islam is observed here, which in the right situation may become more attractive for the people than the official one.

The IRPT functionaries are also dissatisfied by the existing system of controlling religious life. However, many clergymen who do not fall into the orbit of the IRPT influence and who during the civil war had sided with "the party of power" are likewise dissatisfied. They believe that an authoritative Spiritual Board must be established to unite and supervise religious life in the country, and that the board should have the appropriate broad powers to perform its task. The government has until now avoided taking such a step, fearing a recurrence of the past, when the Qaziate led by Turajonzoda went out of the state's control and launched a struggle in support of political Islam. The current Council of the 'Ulama, in the opinion of many imams, is insufficiently representative, authoritative, and most important, does not possess any powers. The greater part of the clergy believe that a Spiritual Board as a supreme body for the management of religious affairs might, on the one hand, stand for the interests of the believers and the clergy, sustaining the requisite level of competence in ministers of Islam, and on the other help the state to solve constructively all the questions of relations with religious institutions (not only Islamic ones).

THE IRPT: A FURTHER GROWTH OF INFLUENCE?

The tendency toward the growth of IRPT influence in 2002–2003 was also marked in the territory of the Gorno-Badakhshan Autonomous Region, where the grassroots cells of that party did not function earlier. Since the overwhelming majority of residents of that region are Ismailis, the influence of the IRPT here has always been insignificant. Nevertheless, the party has been working at shaping its image as a spokesman of the interests of all Muslims of Tajikistan. The IRPT functionaries carry on organizational and propaganda work among the youth, particularly among students of the Khorog State University and other educational institutions, the unemployed, and members of the Muslim clergy, pursuing the aim of both replenishing its ranks and raising the authority of the party in the region. According to government officials, they have found evidence of Iran's support for the IRPT activity in Gorno-Badakhshan.[61] Using Iranian assistance, the regional IRPT committee sends members abroad for study, mostly into Iranian Islamic colleges. In particular, the IRPT vice president in the region, M. Broimshoeva, is studying at one of Iran's Islamic colleges.

As in all other regions, in Central Asia the Islamists are devoting a significant part of their efforts to working with youth. This is shown, in particular, by the attention given to youth in the IRPT newspaper. In one article, the author writes that the clergy should display more zeal in spreading the truth about Islam among young people and, together with the public, bring up the youth in the spirit of Islam.[62] Many articles are devoted to the struggle against youth drug addiction and the need to use Islamic culture and education in order to restore in young people "an interest in real life and its moral laws and values." Besides publishing propaganda against drug addiction among the youth, the IRPT authors criticize the HTI, intending to divert the pious youth from the Tahriris and win them over to their side.[63] This is logical: the IRPT can scarcely bank on recruiting into its ranks those youngsters who show no interest in religion and are firmly inclined toward secularism.

The IRPT's attention to Gorno-Badakhshan, "the party of power" believes, is attested to by the fact that A. Aliev has been relieved of the post of chairman of the region's IRPT for "shortcomings and omissions," and for weak organization in his work. As chairman of the party's Regional Committee, A. Aliev issued contradictory data on IRPT activity in the region by overestimating the number of party members from among the residents of the region for the purpose of raising his authority among the IRPT leadership. The leadership decided to replace him with N. Amonbekov, a native of the Shugnan region who had been working in the IRPT's central apparatus and received a theological education in Iran.

In July 2002, during preparation for the IRPT's second congress, Nuri went for a trip to Gorno-Badakhshan for the first time since the end of the Tajikistan war. Speaking at a press conference in Khorog, Nuri exhorted the local population to help the law enforcement agencies "to uncover and suppress attempts to smuggle drugs and arms from Afghanistan, and to liquidate the possible routes of drug trafficking."[64] Thereby Nuri once more showed the authorities that his activity might be very helpful to the government.

Between 2002 and the beginning of 2003, the IRPT carried on vigorous political activity in the Kurghanteppa zone of the Khatlon region. At the end of 2002, "the legal Islamists" held conferences in the region to review their work for the period, elect new leadership, and discuss the results of the party's political activity for 2000–2002. Also, by decision of the IRPT Central Committee and on Nuri's instruction, the party functionaries carried out a qualification exam of the executives of district cells and the Regional Committee. These measures were directed toward the enhancement of agitation and propaganda work among the population, reinforcing party ranks with more highly trained staff, and cleansing the IRPT of incompetent persons. During the conferences, the party functionaries also discussed questions of the party's preparation for the country's forthcoming parliamentary elections and for gaining power in a peaceful way.

In a private conversation with me on December 21, 2002, an informed representative of the Kulyabi grouping claimed that the need to make amendments to Article 5 of the Republic of Tajikistan's law "On Religion and Religious Organizations" was being discussed in the IRPT ranks and that the IRPT members of parliament intended to place this question on the parliament's agenda at the forthcoming sessions or after the next elections. As the interlocutor asserted, if at the elections the IRPT managed to receive a significant number of seats in the country's parliament, it would ostensibly secure the submission of modifications and amendments to Articles 8 and 26 of the constitution, which would result in the strengthening of the party's political platform in Tajikistan and balance its positions with those of "the party of power."

"The party of power" is especially dissatisfied that the IRPT, seeking to attract educated people to its cause, would turn first and foremost to those who had undergone training and received education abroad. Thus it was noted that the IRPT leaders regularly held press conferences for local and foreign organizations on various subjects, met with diplomatic representatives accredited in Tajikistan, and regularly went abroad, mostly to the Islamic Republic of Iran. It could not be ruled out that the radically anti-Islamist elements from "the party of power" would take advantage of these accusations to discredit the IRPT during its future election campaign in order to disrupt it. It is these radicals who in their time called on the leadership not to allow the granting of a 30 percent quota of seats in government bodies to the opposition and, after this decision was taken, did not hide their intention of achieving the speediest rupture of the General Agreement, finding an occasion to call attention to the IRPT's foreign ties. To a certain extent, these radicals made common cause with the Islamic stalwarts who also stood against the General Agreement, which in their view deprived the IRPT of its "Islamic identity."

Incidentally, over the several years that have passed since power sharing began, the number of members of the Islamic opposition who occupied high government posts in the republic has notably decreased for one reason or other.

The authors of the summary at the Institute for Peace Research and Security Policy at Hamburg University expressed the opinion that "if the secular party does not stimulate the Islamists' readiness for reforming themselves by means of a balanced, strategically planned course of compromise, but tries to assume the rights of 'winners,' . . . the moderate Islamist wing could lose influence and disintegrate."[65]

THE IRPT: A NATIONWIDE PARLIAMENTARY PARTY?

The summer and fall of 2003 showed that the IRPT concentrated ever greater effort on transforming itself into a nationwide parliamentary party, while its leaders were prepared to obscure the party's Islamic character even more to achieve this goal. The party's growing activity met with intensified resistance of its old opponents in "the party of power." Sometimes the unfolding events took on a very dramatic quality.

The arrest on May 30, 2003, of IRPT deputy chairman Shamsuddin Shamsuddinov caused sharp discontent in the party. Its leadership appealed to the OSCE, the UN, and foreign missions in Dushanbe to help ascertain the grounds for, and conditions of, this arrest, sanctioned by Tajikistan's Chief Military Prosecutor Sharif Qurbanov.[66] Later, the Prosecutor's Office brought a number of criminal charges against Shamsuddinov, including murder (a murder revealed to have been committed back in 1995). On July 13, senior party member Qasim Rahimov was arrested on a rape charge. The party leadership asserted that these charges were unproved and that the real goal of the arrests was "to discredit the party and to frighten its members."[67]

At the second congress of the IRPT, on September 13, Said Abdullo Nuri was reelected for another four-year term. He told journalists that the current conditions for the functioning of political parties, including religion-based ones, could be considered satisfactory. Nuri clearly did not wish to subordinate the party's strategic interests to the fate of its arrested members and was unwilling to create a conflict because of that, although he did say that Shamsuddinov had been misidentified by government witnesses. For the party, it was more important that it not be openly obstructed in pursuing its work in various regions of the republic, including those in which its influence was minimal. At the same time, the Dushanbe prosecutor Vohidov linked Rahimov's arrest to the arrests of thirteen other prominent persons, chiefly law enforcement officers but also entrepreneurs and foreigners, whose victims were eleven enslaved girls, mostly under fourteen years of age.[68] Chief Military Prosecutor Sharif Qurbanov insisted that Shamsuddinov's political affiliation had nothing to do with the investigation. At the end of 2003, journalists wrote that Shamsuddinov and three of his assistants stood accused of seventy crimes, including treason, organizing a criminal band, illegal border crossing, and polygamy, committed since 1993.[69] The IRPT leaders' supposition that "the party of power" wanted to harass the IRPT was supported when, in the course of 2003, several other members of the party were arrested.

Considering that 2003 was the year of intensified repression against the HTI (see chapter 3), Tajikistani authorities may have launched a massive campaign against Islamists of various affiliations, a move with many motivations, including both electoral interests and international commitments (or, more simply, the wish to please both the CIS partners and the United States). IRPT activists also expressed resentment over the fact that, in late August, unregistered mosques in Dushanbe were not allowed to relay the *azan* through loudspeakers, as these mosques were now considered "illegal places" rather than houses of worship. Shamsuddin Nuriddinov, a religious affairs official in the Dushanbe government, told reporters that "his superiors had communicated a 'request' along these lines to select imams."[70] In the context of the arrests of IRPT members, this was regarded as a component of the campaign to curb the influence of Islam.

In the wake of these developments, Nuri, speaking at a meeting on the occasion of Unity Day on June 27, 2003, stated: "On charges of membership in former opposition bandit units, the law enforcement agencies of Tajikistan detained many IRPT members, and if the process is not interrupted, it may again provoke an armed conflict in the country." Nuri also announced that he had asked the president to stop the persecution and detention of members of the IRPT and other former oppositionists by the law-enforcement agencies, which directly contravened the peace agreement. As for Shamsuddinov's arrest, Nuri called it a prearranged action whose object was the destabilization of the situation in Tajikistan.[71] On receiving the IRPT's appeal, the offices of the international organizations in Tajikistan expressed concern over the arrests. In particular, the permanent representative of the UN secretary-general in Tajikistan and head of the UN Bureau on Peace Construction in that republic, Vladimir Sotirov, at a meeting with the leader of the Sogdian region, also expressed "concern over the tendency of the growth of authoritarianism in Tajikistan" in regard to the arrests.[72] IRPT functionaries privately told me that during negotiations of the Military Protocol, the more experienced governmental party had simply managed to exclude some high-ranking members of the IRPT (including Shamsuddinov) from the list of those who would be spared criminal persecution.

The advocates of resolute suppression of the Islamists also tried to compromise Nuri himself. During a round table on "Political Parties in Contemporary Tajikistan" held on September 16, Nuri answered the journalists' questions concerning the publications on the TIA-Hovar website of a feature on his complicity in the murder of the head of the Bobojonoghafur district of the Sogdian region, Sobirjon Begijanov. The feature, by Sukhrob Orom, said that Begijanov, appointed to that post on Nuri's recommendation, was allegedly killed for disobedience in May 2001 on Nuri's orders. For his part, Nuri said that "this case was the work of the special services, whose aim was to discredit Tajik society," and he stressed that he had made a request to the appropriate bodies to examine the situation.

A particularly strong resistance by "the party of power" with respect to IRPT activity was observable in Kulyab—the heartland of the ruling clan. The IRPT conference that took place there on October 11 was to be reconvened on May 15. But it turned out that a condition for its holding was the provision to the authorities of a dossier on all IRPT members in Kulyab, which was not required of other parties. An article by Turko Dikaev spoke about the similarity between that measure and the authorities' instruction to submit to the *hukumat* lists of names of all parishioners when registering a mosque or a house of prayer.[73] Nuri behaved with dignity. When on May 15 conference delegates were already seated in the hall, on hearing the demand of the hakim of Kulyab, he announced the postponement of the conference. The authorities backed down. According to Dikaev, a viewpoint prevailed that the legal activity by the IRPT was in any case preferable to the organization going underground. Nuri's one-and-a-half-hour speech was a surprise not only to the official representatives (who grudgingly had to welcome the delegates) but also to IRPT members themselves. The party leader called on his followers to observe all commandments of Islam but leave religious sermons and propaganda of religion to the mullas. "We are not mullas," said the chairman of the Islamic party, Mullo Nuri. "We are a party concerned with only one thing: how to make the people's life better, how to assist our beloved country to stand firmly on its feet within the shortest time possible."[74]

On October 13, 2003, during a meeting with an official of the UN Department on Political Questions, the IRPT chairman stated that, at the forthcoming parliamentary elections, the IRPT would advance its own economic program. Nuri called the HTI's activity "illegal and harmful."[75] Clearly, ensuring the IRPT's participation in the forthcoming elections was a priority task for the IRPT. Nuri noted that the laws on elections to the Majlis-i Oli and the local majlises required "serious alterations." In particular, it was necessary to ensure "real representation of all political parties in all the election committees from the central one down to those in the polling stations," so as to guarantee one "genuine transparency and democratic spirit of the elections." Thus the IRPT leader once more confirmed that it had become a normal parliamentary party. In so doing, Nuri proceeded from the fact that the IRPT was the second most important party in Tajikistan after the ruling Popular Democratic Party. At the IRPT's second congress on September 13, Nuri reported that the party's membership totaled forty thousand and that it had sixty-four grassroots organizations in all regions of the country.[76]

PROSPECTS FOR DIALOGUE

Upholding political Islam, one of the IRPT's highest leaders, Himmatzoda, writes that the existence of a religious political party does not do harm to the state, even if the latter is secular. "The presence of deputies from a religious political party," Himmatzoda believes, "can foster the development of cooperation between religion and state in various fields, among other things, allowing the religion's position to be expressed in drafting and adopting laws on questions where its position is important."[77] Himmatzoda, criticizing the views of those highest representatives of "the party of power" who hold that permission for the creation and activity of political parties having a religious basis runs counter to secular polity, bluntly names such a figure—Abdumajed Dostiev. For his part, Dostiev openly declares that the constitutional norm on religious parties "does not accord with the constitutional definition of the state."

Thus, it is possible to speak of serious differences among the highest leaders of "the party of power" on the question of attitude toward cooperation with political Islam. Whereas Dostiev is an open adversary of allowing Islamists to participate in elections, another influential exponent

of the ruling Kulyabi group, Ibrahim Usmonov, supports their participation. He deems that "displacement, indeed, a policy of repression in relation to religion, encourages the polarization of society and discredits its
political institutions."[78] Characteristic of the secular politicians of this
type is a sincere constructive attitude toward cooperation with moderate
political Islam. But Usmonov, too, sees the danger on the part of "the Islamic factor," consisting in rivalry between the legal and the illegal (the
HTI) parties, and that in terms of propaganda, "the illegal religious party
often acts more effectively than the legal one." He points out that now that
a distrust of the IRPT has appeared, "many people consider it to be a regional, not a nationwide party, linking the activity of some of its representatives with corrupt groups," while the Uzbek-language Muslims of
Tajikistan gravitate more to the HTI than to the IRPT.[79]

Nevertheless, by the beginning of 2004 the IRPT had a great chance of
becoming a genuinely representative nationwide party of a parliamentary
type. In the course of preparation for new parliamentary elections in the
spring of 2004, the IRPT declared its readiness to revive its alliance with
democrats. This time the IRPT's partners would be not only its old ally,
the Democratic Party of Tajikistan, but also the Social Democratic Party
and the Socialist Party. These parties achieved an agreement on joint participation in the forthcoming election in April 2004.[80] One more organization, the Development Party, still not officially registered, would be an observer in this bloc. Later the DPT rescinded its decision.

The future of the Tajik experiment for the incorporation of political Islam into the secular state now depends in many ways on whether the constructive dialogue of secular and Islamic politicians will be successfully
continued—a dialogue able to put an end to the mutual lack of trust inherited from the recent tragic past.

NOTES

1. Valentin Bushkov and Dmitri Mikulsky, *Anatomiya grazhdanskoi voiny v
Tadzhikistane* (The anatomy of the civil war in Tajikistan) (Moscow: Nauka, 1996),
11–13.
2. Olivier Roy, *The New Central Asia: The Creation of Nations* (London: Tauris,
2000), 87.
3. Roy, *New Central Asia*, 19.
4. According to Ernest Gellner: "A vital aspect of segmentary society is *nesting*.
Groups contain subgroups, which in turn contain other subgroups whose relationship to each other is once again similar. . . . The balance of power operates *inside* groups as much as it does between them." Ernest Gellner, "Tribalism and the
State in the Middle East," in *Tribes and State Formation in the Middle East*, ed. Philip

S. Khoury and Joseph Kostiner (Berkeley: University of California Press, 1991), 109–110.

5. Sh. Jabbarov, "Protiv nepravil'nogo ponimaniya natsional'noi politiki," *Za partiyu*, no. 4 (1929).

6. Nurbolat Masanov, "Natsional'no-gosudarstvennoe stroitel'stvo v Kazakhstane: analiz i prognoz" (National and state construction in Kazakhstan: analysis and forecast), in *Natsionalizm i bezopasnost' v postsovetskov prostranstve* (Nationalism and security in the post-Soviet space) (Moscow: Nauka, 1994), 47.

7. Shirin Akiner, *Tajikistan: Disintegration or Reconciliation?* (London: Royal Institute of International Affairs, 2001), 30.

8. David Usmon, conversation with the author, March 9, 1993.

9. Lyudmila Polonskaya and Alexei Malashenko, *Islam in Central Asia* (Reading, England: Ithaca, 1994), 114.

10. Polonskaya and Malashenko, *Islam and Central Asia*, 117.

11. IRPT Statute of 1991, pt 1.3.

12. IRPT Statute of 1991, pt 1.4.

13. Roy, *New Central Asia*, 122.

14. Roy, *New Central Asia*, 123.

15. Akiner, *Tajikistan*, 40–41.

16. See, for example, Rima Wilkes and Dina G. Okamoto, "Ethnic Competition and Mobilization by Minorities at Risk," *Nationalism and Ethnic Politics* 8, no. 3 (Autumn 2002): 1–23.

17. Susan Olzak, *The Dynamics of Ethnic Competition and Conflict* (Stanford, CA: Stanford University Press, 1992), 32–47.

18. Muzaffar Olimov and Saodat Olimova, "Politicheskii islam v sovremennom Tadjikistane" (Political Islam in modern Tajikistan), *Islam na postsovetskom prostranstve* (Islam in the post-Soviet space) (Moscow: Moscow Carnegie Center, 2001), 195–96.

19. Abdullo Rahmamo Hakim, Turajonzoda's secretary, conversation with the author, March 23, 2003.

20. Born in 1928, Safarov was first sentenced back in 1951 for carjacking. In 1957 he ran over a pedestrian, and in 1964, in a drunken brawl, he killed a customer at a lunchroom where he was working as a cook; one year was added to the sentence passed for this crime for organizing a prisoners' mutiny.

21. Saidhoja Azizov, professor of mathematics at the University of Kulyab, during our meeting in the end of 1992 claimed that he had played a leading role at the first stage of creating the People's Front.

22. Bushkov and Mikulsky, *Anatomiya*, 65.

23. This strongly resembles the aforementioned organization of Islamic youth in Uzbekistan (see chapter 2).

24. Bushkov and Mikulsky, *Anatomiya*, 69–70.

25. Erkin Rahmatullaev, *Mirotvorchestvo OON v Tadzhikistane* (UN peacekeeping in Tajikistan) (Moscow: Center for Strategic and Political Studies, 2001), 75.

26. Author interviews with members of militias, October 1992.

27. *Krasnaya zvezda*, March 23, 1994.

28. Bushkov and Mikulsky, *Anatomiya*, 80.

29. *Nezavisimaya gazeta*, December 4, 1993.

30. Rahmatullaev, *Mirotvorchestvo*, 75.

31. Rahmatullaev, *Mirotvorchestvo*, 77.

32. Documents of the first round of the inter-Tajik negotiations.

33. Alexander Knyazev, "Afghanistan: Religious Extremism and Terrorism. The Year 2000," *Central Asia and the Caucasus*, no. 5 (2000): 82.

34. *Sadoi mardum*, July 19, 1995.

35. ITAR-TASS, July 20, 1995.

36. Untitled internal document, in the author's possession, of an Uzbek law enforcement agency.

37. Roy, *New Central Asia*, 149.

38. Roy, *New Central Asia*, 149.

39. Roy, *New Central Asia*, 148.

40. Roy, *New Central Asia*, 148.

41. Speaking of the segmentary-lineage organization, E. Gellner writes: "This means in effect the existence of cohesive social groups that ensure order by joint effort. They have a high military participation ratio, to use S. Andreski's phrase, in practice all adult males take part in organized violence and share the risks involved. Gellner, "Tribalism," 109.

42. Davlat Usmon, "Samoponimanie, zadachi i tseli islamskoi politiki v Tadzhikistane i Srednei Azii" (Self-awareness, tasks, and objectives of Islamic policies in Tajikistan and Central Asia), in *O sovmestimosti politicheskogo Islama i bezopasnosti v prostaranstve OBSE* (On the compatibility of political Islam and security in the OSCE space), ed. Arne Seifert and Anna Kreikmeyer (Dushanbe: Sharqi Ozod, 2003), 50.

43. ITAR-TASS, January 5, 1997.

44. *Sadoi mardum*, September 21, 1996.

45. ITAR-TASS, June 27, 1997.

46. Hakim Rahnamo, "O sosushchestvovanii 'svetskogo' i 'religioznogo' v Tadzhikistane" (On the coexistence of the "secular" and the "religious" in Tajikistan), in *O sovmestimosti*, ed. Seifert and Kreikmeyer, 155.

47. Usmon, "Samoponimanie," 52.

48. Saodat Olimova, "Religiozniye korni terrorizma" (The religious roots of terrorism), *Kazakhstan–Spektr* no. 3 (2002): 28.

49. Author interview with IRPT leaders.

50. Abdullo Hakim, O Polozhenii Islama v Tajikskom Obshchestve (On the Position of Islam in the Tajik Society). Manuscript presented to the author in 2003.

51. Hakim, O Polozhenii.

52. Rashid, *Jihad*, 109.

53. *Daily Time*, February 27, 2003.

54. Farangis Najibullah, "Rights Groups Say Executions Increasing," *Radio Free Europe/Radio Liberty*, March 10, 2003, at www.eurasianet.org/departments/rights/articles/eav030803.shtml.

55. Najibullah, "Right Groups."

56. Summary of Reports from Tajikistan. Center for OSCE Research, Institute for Peace Research and Security Policy at the University of Hamburg (2002), 3.

57. Summary of Reports from Tajikistan.

58. Conversations with one of the senior officers of the Interior Ministry, Dushanbe, January 7, 2003.

59. Conversation with a senior official of the presidential administration, Dushanbe, January 9, 2003.

60. Olimova, "Religiozniye," 25.

61. Private meetings between the author and government officials.

62. Salahiddin Ayubi, "Hey, You in the Mosque! Have You Called on the People to Do Good?" *Najot*, April 20, 2000. See Kiemiddin Sattori, "Tajik Press about the Youth and Islam," *Central Asia and the Caucasus* 2, no. 15 (2002): 127.

63. On the unacceptability of the HTI to the IRPT, see chapter 3. A. Rasizade believes that Nuri labeled Hizb at-Tahrir members extremists "in view of Uzbek–Tajik antagonism," given that the group includes mainly ethnic Uzbeks. Alec Rasizade, "The New 'Great Game' in Central Asia after Afghanistan," *Alternatives: Turkish Journal of International Relations* 1, no. 2 (Summer 2002): 50.

64. *Aziya plus*, July 31, 2003.

65. Summary of Reports from Tajikistan.

66. Justin Burke, "Tajik Islamic Party Appeals to OBSE, UN over Arrest of Deputy Leader, June 8, 2003," *EurasiaNet: Tajikistan Daily Digest*, September 22, 2003, 1, at www.eurasianet.org/resource/tajikistan/hypermail/news/0010.stml (accessed December 1, 2003).

67. Edward Weihman, "Tajik Islamic Party Demands Release of Detained Members," *EurasiaNet: Tajikistan Daily Digest*, November 12, 2003, 1, at www.eurasianet.org/resource/tajikistan/hypermail/news/0010.stml (accessed December 1, 2003).

68. Edward Weihman, "More Arrests in Tajikistan Linked to Rape Case, August 11, 2003," *EurasiaNet: Tajikistan Daily Digest*, November 12, 2003, at www.eurasianet.org/resource/tajikistan/hypermail/news/0010.stml (accessed December 1, 2003).

69. Kambiz Arman, "Opposition in Tajikistan Lies Low after High-Profile Arrest, November 12, 2003," *EurasiaNet*, at www.eurasianet.org/departments/rights/articles/eav111203_pr.shtml (accessed December 1, 2003). See also Timur Onica, "Criminal Charges Filed against Tajik Islamic Party Official, October 7, 2003," *EurasiaNet: Tajikistan Daily Digest*, November 12, 2003, 1, at www.eurasianet.org/resource/tajikistan/hypermail/news/0010.shtml (accessed December 1, 2003).

70. RFE/RL Newsline, September 10, 2003; Arman, "Opposition in Tajikistan."

71. *Vechernii Dushanbe*, July 4, 2003.

72. *Aziya plus*, July 10, 2003.

73. *Aziya plus*, October 23, 2003. The journalist reported that before the conference, many Kulyabis advised him not to go "to that assemblage of bearded fanatics."

74. *Aziya plus*, October 23, 2003.

75. *Aziya plus*, October 16, 2003.

76. *Vechernii Dushanbe*, September 19, 2003.

77. Muhammadsharif Himmatzoda, "Politicheskie metody i protivorechiya pri uregulirovanii otnoshenii mezhdu gosudarstvom i religiei" (Political methods and contradictions in the settlement of relations between state and religion), in *O sovmestimosti*, ed. Seifert and Kreikemeyer, 93.

78. Ibrahim Usmonov, "Opasnosti dlya vnutrennei stabil'nosti Tadzhikistana" (Dangers for the internal stability of Tajikistan), in *O sovmestimosti*, ed. Seifert and Kreikemeyer, 198.

79. Usmonov, "Opasnosti," 197.

80. Amniyat Abdulazizov, deputy chairman of SDP, *Radio Free Europe/Radio Liberty Tajik Service*; quoted by Bruce Pannier, "Tajikistan: Former Opposition Planning to Renew Coalition, *Eurasia Insight*," April 9, 2004, 1, at www.eurasianet.org/departments/insight/articles/pp040904_pr.shtm.

Conclusion

Since the end of the 1980s, and especially after the collapse of the Soviet state in 1991, Central Asian societies have witnessed a steady process of Islamic revival. This process was stronger in some parts of the region—particularly in Uzbekistan and Tajikistan—than in others. A retrospective survey of the Islamic culture that flourished in the great centers of Central Asian civilizations shows how intimately Hanafi Islam became interconnected with traditional rites and customs, particularly those of the Sufi brotherhoods. Even after the Russian conquest, and despite Russia's policy of containing Islam, religiosity remained significant. After the nineteenth century, when Islamic political parties were established in the region, Islam's involvement in politics increased with the downfall of tsarism, but it then ceased entirely under Bolshevik rule.

The atheistic Soviet state harshly repressed religious believers, the 'ulama, Sufi brotherhoods, and the system of religious education in the 1930s, and it placed what was left of Islamic institutions under tight control. However, a private, underground system of spiritual education remained and helped Islam survive. As a result, Central Asian Islam has maintained an uninterrupted tradition of religious knowledge. Most of its informal teachers stuck firmly to the Hanafi tradition, but some were attracted to the ideas of radical Islamic thinkers. The same can be said of several individual representatives of the official clergy as well.

As a result, despite the domination of Hanafi Islam, elements of a more puritanical and rigid school of Sunnism were embedded in local religious thought by the end of Soviet rule. To a certain extent, this helped bring about the emergence of Islamic political groups in the early 1990s. Most observers underestimated this phenomenon at the time, and as a result, they were surprised by the emergence of Islamic radicalism in some Central Asian societies at the end of the Gorbachev era.

To adequately understand Islamic radicalism, however, we have to take into account all of its roots and causes. My investigation suggests that poverty, unemployment, relative deprivation, social inequality, the collapse of the welfare system, corruption, and harsh authoritarianism have created fertile ground for recruiting new members to the ranks of Islamic radicals who offer simple solutions to everyday problems. But these factors are not the only causes of Islamic extremism, as the case of Uzbekistan confirms.

The importance of Uzbekistan in the process of re-Islamization can be explained, first, by the higher religiosity of Uzbek society; second, by the fact that most of the historic centers of Central Asian Islamic culture are located in its territory; and third, by the nationalistic policies of its government in the post-Soviet period. Uzbekistan has been building its new identity through the "eradication" of the entire period of Russian and Soviet domination, the return to the historic origins of its indigenous culture, which is inextricably linked to Islam, and the glorification of great spiritual and military leaders of the past.[1] This pattern has paved the way for the retraditionalization of society (a trend that is used effectively by Islamists for recruitment). It has also enhanced the regime's authoritarian tendencies and complicated the process of modernization. But, even in these conditions, active supporters of political Islam still represent only a minority of the population in Uzbekistan, as throughout all of Central Asia.

It was Max Scheler who developed the notion of *ressentiment* to describe the grievances of minority groups obsessed with inequality and inferiority.[2] The Islam-oriented part of Central Asian society is overwhelmed by this *ressentiment* and feels that it is discriminated against and deprived of justice. The call of radical Islamists for equality and justice is thus particularly appealing to these people, and as a result, proponents of violence within the body of political Islam receive popular support.

An essential aspect of the rise of militant Islamism in the region was its relationship with organized crime. Income from drug trafficking, hostage taking, and looting helps fund extremist groups. Extremism in turn creates conditions in which criminal groups can flourish because it destabilizes society and exerts pressure on governments. Local traditional networks—regional groups, extended families, clans, and so on—are exploited by both secular authorities in the government and radical Islamists, both of whom compete to dominate these networks. The traditional networks benefit in turn from Islamism both in the form of ideological inspiration and the organizational framework needed to further their interests.

One of the most important questions about Central Asia's Islamic radicals is how to determine which factors—external or internal—exert the greatest influence on the dynamics of extremist mobilization. Our study of local historical roots and the international context of Islamic radicalism in Central Asia suggests that external and internal causes are in dynamic balance and complement each other. External factors have been, and probably will continue to be, very important. International Islamist groups channel aid from Middle Eastern Salafi centers to militants in the region. This aid is used to indoctrinate Central Asian youth and to train Central Asian guerrillas, who may then be used for missions other than the Islamization of Central Asia (for example, fighting on the side of the Taliban in Afghanistan).

This study of the three main political Islamic movements in Central Asia does not exhaust the topic of religious radicalism in the region. However, it does show how diverse these movements can be from the point of view of their tenets, organizational structure, objectives, power bases, international links, and modes of action. A theoretical discourse using the framework of this triad may be helpful for developing a general approach to the study of the present and future of political Islam in the region, and for developing a typology of radical Islamic movements globally.

The influence of globalization on Central Asia's Islamists is growing. To paraphrase John Esposito, the "globalization of communication, technology and travel" not only fosters the formation of a "transnational identity" among Central Asian Islamists but also is an inexhaustible reserve of potentialities. Resentment of barriers between states and the dominance of local barons explain the attractiveness of transnational ideologies, even utopian ones such as Caliphatism.

At the same time, however, our research indicates that the theories and concepts expressed in printed and disseminated materials of militant Islamists are not of primary importance in the recruitment of members and supporters. Other mechanisms for addressing, influencing, and recruiting individuals are more important—mechanisms that operate through traditional social institutions and networks.

What do all radical Islamists, regardless of the diversity of their organizations, want? Like any organized political group, they want power. What makes them "Islamist" is the fact that they want to use that power to build an Islamic state based on Shari'a, which is the priority objective of their political agenda. It is true that there is no convincing example of a successful Islamic state in the modern world. But this does not make the idea less attractive, because a genuine model of the first Islamic state created by the Prophet Muhammad himself with all its greatness is available. This vision of the authentic Caliphate is contrasted with the deeply imperfect present-day regimes of the region's nation-states and the widespread injustice in today's Islamic societies. It also helps foster a belief that immediate action is absolutely necessary to overcome that injustice.

Building a perfect Islamic state is for radical Islamists what building communism was for the Bolsheviks. It requires sacrifices, and it may cost many lives. The Caliphatists, moreover, are sure that it will be impossible to establish the Caliphate in one place because it would not be allowed to survive by the existing world order, which radical Islamists are convinced is ruled by their enemies—Zionists supported by today's sole super-power, the United States. And the overwhelming preponderance of power in the world international system is in the hands of the non-Islamic, unjust, corrupt, and morally degraded West. The Islamists fear that the West, with its financial–economic power and resources, will at-tack the foundations of Islamic societies, destroy their traditional Islamic values through globalization, and allow hostile norms of behavior to pen-etrate society. Protecting the Muslim world from this civilizational offen-sive is thus a critical objective.

Nevertheless, we have seen that some political Islamic groups are able to make deep transformations, transformations that change their very character. The Islamic Movement of Uzbekistan is a national Uzbek or-ganization set up in 1996 by Islamic militants who in the early 1990s be-gan their political activities in the Ferghana Valley under the influence of Salafi mullas. Initially they tried to take power locally, but they were driven into Tajikistan by the Karimov government. Once in Tajikistan, they took an active part in the civil war there against the alliance of secu-larist forces and earned a reputation as fearless and ruthless warriors. Since then the IMU has been involved in numerous terrorist acts and criminal activities, although it is hardly a mere criminal gang. It has its own theoretical tenets, and although those tenets are ambiguous, they have helped the IMU to attract a considerable following and to inspire militancy. The IMU has also deliberately avoided being associated with any particular school of Sunnism, in an effort to make itself acceptable to adherents of various *madhhabs*. But elements of Salafism are apparent in their "doctrine" as well. The IMU's fixation on overthrowing the Karimov regime is what primarily sets it apart, making it distinctive from most other violent Islamic groups in the Islamic world.

The IMU's focus on seizing power in Tashkent corresponds with the centrality of Uzbekistan for the future of Islam in Central Asia. Although the IMU does not have an extensive international agenda, its scope of ac-tivity has a transborder character. It by far surpasses all other groups of Central Asian Islamists with respect to the range of links with foreign or-ganizations, which include the Taliban and al-Qa'ida. After September 11, the IMU suffered its greatest defeat, and its remnants fled to Pakistan for rehabilitation and regrouping. Its capability was substantially diminished, but the movement has been undertaking steps to reorganize and remobilize.

The Hizb at-Tahrir al-Islami, unlike the IMU, is of a distinctively transnational nature and has a clear-cut global agenda. The main strategic goal of the HTI is to establish a world Islamic Caliphate state, although a first step in achieving this mission may be the creation of a Caliphate within the frontiers of Central Asia. So far the concept of a Caliphate is the sine qua non of the Tahriri doctrine. The HTI's driving force is the idea of justice as embodied in Islamic teachings. Party leaders insist that the HTI has never resorted to violence and is oriented exclusively toward peaceful means of struggle, that is, the propagation of its ideas through the dissemination of printed (and online) materials and education. The HTI has a strictly clandestine organizational structure that makes it similar to leftist and nationalist groups of the past. Some of the leaflets, pamphlets, and other printed materials disseminated by HTI cells in Central Asia are sent there from abroad and translated into local languages. Many of these materials have a strong anti-Semitic flavor. The HTI is believed to have a substantial number of members all over Central Asia, the severe persecution of the movement by the authorities notwithstanding. Outlawed in most states in the West, the Middle East, and Central Asia itself, the party is accused of subversive activities directed at toppling legitimate regimes in the region. The party clearly serves as a tool for expressing protest feelings of the impoverished population. The HTI's adherence to nonviolence remains equivocal to many observers, since some statements in its literature can be interpreted to mean that at some point there will be a transition from the stage of propagation and education to a stage where violent means will be used to overthrow existing governments.

The Islamic Revival Party of Tajikistan began as a national party but was primarily made up of inhabitants from the Gharm-Karategin cluster of regions. It was initially devoted to the pursuit of the interests of elites in those areas who felt discriminated against both politically and economically. The IRPT became the only Islamic organization in Central Asia to be registered as an official political party. It formed an alliance with a number of secular democratic parties and participated in elections. Having consolidated its position, the party entered the government as a result of a redistribution of power in 1992. After the outbreak of the civil war in Tajikistan, the IRPT became one of the warring parties and, in short order, allied itself with many militant Islamist elements from different parts of Central Asia who were known for their bellicosity. The dramatic deterioration of the political situation in Tajikistan, the hopelessness of a continuation of the military confrontation, and pressures from global and regional states led to peace talks and the signing of a power-sharing agreement. Since then the IRPT has been undergoing a process of deradicalization and transformation into a mainstream, legal parliamentary party. In the framework of the peace agreement, it accepted a constitutional provision declaring Tajikistan to be a secular state.

The different Central Asian regimes have thus responded to political Islam in several distinct ways:

- repressing all Islamists, destroying all Islamist networks, and not allowing any political activities under the banner of Islam;
- repressing radical (Salafi, especially jihadist) groups and tolerating others by entering into some kind of cautious dialogue with them;
- repressing radical groups and engaging other Islamist organizations, allowing the latter to be a part of the political establishment (the only case being Tajikistan).

Central Asia governments also do the following to reduce the Islamists' mobilization potential:

- controlling the religious life of the citizenry;
- enhancing traditional, moderate Islam and trying to use it for confronting imported, radical forms of Islam;
- encouraging secularism;
- preventing international Islamic networks and some charity organizations, especially of Salafi orientation, from funding local Muslim communities.

Western criticism of Central Asian rulers notwithstanding, there is a widespread conviction that authoritarian regimes are better able to cope with the threat of terrorism and insurgency, a belief that in turn enhances stronger authoritarianism. The situation can be likened to the former days of the Soviet Union, when Zbigniew Brzezinski and Samuel Huntington wrote that the absence of liberty "does enable the Soviet political system to be strong in ways which are denied to Western liberal democracies."[3] Though one may consider this observation trivial and even irrelevant today, it can be applied to a degree to the realities of Central Asia. Of relevance is a remark by Daniel Chirot: "Why is it that the worst of the Western ideological tradition, its aggressive nationalism and pseudo-scientific totalitarian fantasies, has been adopted so much more easily outside the West than the best of that tradition, faith in genuine democracy? In large part this is because outside the West there never developed strong philosophical traditions that allowed the rights of the individual to stand against those of the community."[4]

It is commonly believed that it is counterproductive to combat radical Islam through repression (not to speak of the complete unacceptability of illegal arrests, torture, and extrajudicial punishment). The idea that repression only generates more protest and leads to a rising tide of Islamic radicalism has already become a ritual incantation for everyone engaged with this problem, not excepting myself. However, I do not want this claim to be merely a moral maxim in my research. To transform it into a political imperative by linking it with the need for democratization, it is necessary to have a clear vision of what circumstances and factors are working in its favor and what factors are working against it. We also need to consider what problems need to be solved and what practical steps are required for its realization.

In particular, it has to be admitted that some of the ways in which the war on terror is being waged in the Muslim world do not always promote a balanced and tolerant attitude toward political Islam. Authoritarian secular regimes benefit from the leading global and regional players by cooperating with them, and they expect that support from these leading players will allow them to ignore the preferences of society and the protests of the opposition in their countries. But the stronger the manifestations of pressure from below, the more reluctant these regimes are to open doors to democratization.

The fact that power is not balanced between different interests and that no consensus exists on how the government should function tends to promote tyranny. None of the Central Asian leaders can stand firm in the face of the temptation to turn to authoritarian means to confront their challenges. Political leaders are well aware that neither the leading Western countries nor other strong actors such as Russia or China are interested in destabilizing the region. But it is precisely the legalization of Islamic opposition, many of these rulers believe, that leads to such destabilization. A ban on the activity of a party such as the HTI by the greater part of the world's states, despite the fact that, until now at least, the HTI has not called for the violent overthrow of governments, encourages those local politicians who favor repressive methods in dealing with Islamists. A rigid position of at least a part of the official clergy, which tends to view political Islam as its direct rival, further fortifies the authorities in their overall preference for violent approaches.

Among the urgent questions demanding a solution, one may mention the definition of the Islamic forces with whom it is possible and necessary to carry on a dialogue. Should the course toward dialogue and tolerance be inclusive, and if not, what restrictions on the scope of this dialogue should be made? One has to delimit the borders of that segment of the Islamists with whom it is inappropriate for Central Asian regimes to negotiate (just as it would be futile to speak of a dialogue between Washington and Usama bin Ladin). What should be done to incorporate non-violent although committed elements of the HTI into the negotiating process? The exclusion of this (so far peaceful) segment will not help do away with radicalism. The same applies to Salafis as a current in Islam, which unites not only jihadists.

But does Western society, which itself has not yet developed an optimal and consensual position with regard to Islam in general and political Islam in particular, and which has frequently pursued inconsistent policies in this respect, have a right to give advice to Islamic governments on what currents and movements in political Islam are acceptable or unacceptable to it? Let us recall that, when Algerian Islamists won the first round of elections in 1991, elections that were conducted in full accordance with democratic procedures, the secular authorities in Algeria staged a military coup to keep the Islamic Salvation Front from power after what was seen as its inevitable victory in the second round. No Western state condemned this undemocratic action, for nobody wanted a radical Islamic regime in power in Algeria. Many experts on the Middle East are convinced that if honest and transparent democratic elections were held in many states in the region, radical Islamists would win and come to power.

My intent is not to deny the need for democratization in the Islamic world. Rather it is to call for a cautious approach toward the transformation of Islamic societies in conditions fostering a rise in anti-Western and antimodernization sentiments (of which the main factor is the failure to resolve the Arab–Israeli conflict).

International organizations and institutions tend to look at the question of the relationship between secular and Islamic forces in Central Asia in the context of regional security. According to a document produced by participants in the informal secular–Islamic dialogue held in Dushanbe in December 2003 under the auspices of the OSCE:

> the creation of a space of stability in Europe presupposes stability in the OSCE's Asian region as well. Such a goal calls for the development of a new model of relationships based on political instead of violent antagonisms. It includes overcoming "the dilemma of mistrust" between secular and Islamic representatives or, at the obligatory minimum, the creation of frameworks that will be able to narrow the space of mistrust and enable the parties to co-exist peacefully.[5]

Accordingly, the dialogue's participants call for measures to enhance trust between these forces: "The task of confidence-building measures is to seek optimum variants of rapprochement between state authority and representatives of religions."[6]

What is unclear in this formulation, however, is whether political Islam, including its radical (but not jihadist) form, can function as a part of "the space of confidence-building measures." For example, having agreed to enter into an alliance with secular authorities, the IRPT found itself in a difficult situation. On the one hand, after several years of cooperation, during which the Islamic party has displayed considerable patience and prudence, mistrust toward it on the part of the secular mainstream in Tajikistan is only very gradually dissipating, and separate groups or individual actors in government bodies are taking measures that may provoke the IRPT to ill-considered actions. On the other hand, the greater the readiness for compromise manifested by the IRPT, the more it is forsaken by its traditional electorate, small as it already is, which is being carried away by the demagogy of the radicals who attack the IRPT for compromising with the authorities. No longer the mouthpiece of protest sentiments, the IRPT has narrowed its power base. It is easy to predict that if this trend continues, the IRPT will fail to overcome the temptation to rejoin the opposition to secular authority or will be forced to do this, as this will be the only way to keep its ideological and political identity and to survive in general. Will the political mainstream of Tajikistan manage in such a situation to display the maturity that will allow a new political system to form in Central Asia, a political system in which the main element would no longer be an Islamic party incorporated into the establishment but a legally functioning oppositional Islamic party?

Given that the basic grievances and needs of the population in the Muslim world are not being addressed effectively by existing governments, and as the traditional societies in the region are experiencing the stresses associated with modernization, Islamic radicalism at least for the foreseeable future will likely remain an inspiration for a large segment of society. However, in the final analysis, the deradicalization of political Islam will be an inevitable result of the Muslim world's integration into the globalizing international commonwealth.

NOTES

1. Uzbekistan, as A. Djumaev believes, has given priority to the development of its state institutions, creating an integral program for building a national government with its own "national ideology of independence," presented by President Karimov himself (Aleksandr Djumaev, "Nation-Building, Culture and Problems of Ethnocultural Identity in Central Asia: The Case of Uzbekistan," in *Can Liberal Pluralism Be Exported? Western Political Theory and Ethnic Relations in Eastern Europe*, ed. Will Kymlicka and Magda Opalski, New York: Oxford University

Press, 2001, 323). Djumaev was program director of the Tashkent branch of the Open Society Institute, which was closed by the authorities in 2004.

2. See Max Scheler, *Ressentiment* (Glencoe: Free Press, 1960).

3. Zbigniew Brzezinski and Samuel P. Huntington, *Political Power: USA // USSR* (New York: Viking, 1964), 413.

4. Daniel Chirot, Modern Tyrants, *The Power and Prevalence of Evil in Our Age* (New York: Free Press, 1994), 413.

5. *Confidence-Building Measures*. Results of studies by participants in an informal secular–Islamic dialogue conducted under the auspices of OSCE (Dushanbe, December 2003), 9.

6. *Confidence-Building Measures*, 10.

Glossary

'adat	customary law
'adolat ('adalat)	justice
'alim (pl. 'ulama)	Islamic scholar
amir	commander; leader; a ruler (monarch) in an amirate
'amma	the common herd
'aqida (pl. 'aqa'id)	Islamic dogmatics
aqsaqal	elder man ("white-bearded")
avlod	(from Arab., "sons") traditional solidarity group in Tajikistan, based on alleged kinship
ayats	verses of the Qur'an
ayil (in Kyrgyzstan)	a nomadic or settled village
'ayyarun	the same as *fityan*
azan	call to prayer
basmachi	literally "robbers"; movement of resistance under the banners of jihad against the Soviet rule in Central Asia in the 1920s and 1930s
bayt al-mal	treasury
beg (bek)	a title; a province governor
bid'a	innovation; in the Wahhabi thought totally inadmissible
chaykhana	teahouse
da'wa, da'wat	the propagation of Islam
da'ira	circle
dabiri kull	secretary-general in the HTI

271

daris	student; disciple
dawra	circle
domulla	honorary title for religious scholars
faqih (pl. fuqaha)	Islamic lawyer
fasiq	transgressor
fatwa	a legal religious judgment issued by a mufti
fiqh	Islamic jurisprudence
firqa	a sect in Islam
fityan	a clandestine association of urban dwellers in the Abbasid Caliphate
fuqaro	"poor "; the traditional lower class in some regions of Central Asia
Hadith	a short story about an act or saying of the Prophet Muhammad
hajj	pilgrimage to Mecca and Medina; one of five main religious duties of a Muslim
hajji (hajj)	a Muslim who has performed hajj; a member of the Sufi brotherhood (Naqshbandiyya)
halal	lawful
halaqa	circle
haram	prohibited
hawala	money-transfer network
Hijra	migration of the Prophet Muhammad and his followers from Mecca to Medina in AD 622, the beginning of the Islamic era
hujra	(Arab.) "room"; a place in the mosque where a student of Islam lives; a private class run by a religious teacher
hukumat (hukuma)	government
'ibadat	religious observances
idtirar (iztirar)	coerced necessity
ijtihad	an opinion of a recognized Islamic scholar on a religious issue
ikhwan	brotherhood, brothers
'ilm	Islamic science
imam	Islamic cleric, literally "he who heads the prayer"
imam-khatib	imam who serves in a big Friday mosque and reads a sermon (*khutba*)
ishan	an honorific title of a Sufi shaykh
Islam Lashkarlari	the religious–political group Warriors of Islam
jadid	(Arab., literally "new") a term used to define the nineteenth- to twentieth-century

	Islamic enlightenment in the Russian Empire (from *usul-i jadid*—new foundations of education)
jama'at	community; a village council
jihad	a holy war for Islam (interpreted also as a human effort)
kafir (plur. kuffar)	godless; infidel
kalam	Islamic dogmatic theology
kalym	the same as *mahr*
Khalifatlik	the Caliphate
khan	a title; a ruler (monarch) in a Khanate
khassa	the selected herd
khatna	a circumcision rite
khoja	Central Asian aristocrat, descendant of the four righteous caliphs (or the first Arab conquerors)
al-Khulafa' al-rashidun	the four righteous caliphs who took over after the Prophet Muhammad (Abu Bakr, 'Umar, 'Uthman, and 'Ali)
khwaja	the same as *khoja*
kishlak	village
kolkhoz	collective farm in the Soviet Union
koracha	"mob"; lower strata of the population in Central Asia
kufr	godlessness
kurultai	congress
ma'vizes	women's assemblies
madhhab	one of the four legal dogmatic schools in Sunni Islam
madrasa	Islamic seminary
maftana	a ritual present to a religious teacher
mahalla	neighborhood
mahr	money paid to the family of a bride
maktab	Islamic primary school
mas'ul	"responsible" member (rank in the HTI)
maulawi	honorary title for a teacher of Islam
mawali	(Arab.) "clients"; non-Arabs converted to Islam in the first centuries of Hijra
mazar	tomb of a saint in Sufism
mu'allaqat	poems of pre-Islamic poets in Arabia
mu'amalat	public and private life of Muslims
mudarris	teacher at madrasa
mufassir	interpreter of the Qur'an; author of tafsir

mufti	religious authority who issues fatwas; in Central Asia head of muftiate (a governing board of Muslims)
muhajir	he who commits hijra
muhtasib	a market inspector, an assistant of an imam
mujaddidiyya	renovationist movement in Central Asia
mujahed	a fighter of jihad
mujtahid	a recognized knowledgeable scholar who has the right to issue ijtihad
mulla	cleric; religious servant
murad	disciple of Sufi shaykh
murid	a pupil of a shaykh or ishan
musa'id	assistant (rank in the HTI)
mushrik	polytheist
mushrif	"supervisor" (rank in the HTI)
mutawalli (mutavalli)	controller of endowments; attendant at a mosque (of lower rank then imam)
nakithun	renegades
naqib	a senior rank within the HTI hierarchy
ok-suyak	"white bone"; aristocratic, higher strata of the population in Central Asia
otun	senior woman
pir	hereditary title of shaykh in a Sufi brotherhood
qadi (or qazi)	Islamic judge
qadim	(Arab., literally "old") a term to define conservatives, opponents of the jadids
qazi	see *qadi*
qari	"reader" who knows the Qur'an by heart
qaum	traditional solidarity group, based on alleged kinship
qazi kalon	great judge; in Tajikistan head of the Qaziate, the board governing the Muslims
qira'a	the recitation of the Qur'an
qiyadat (qiyada)	leadership
quzar	traditional solidarity group, based on alleged kinship
qynda	traditional solidarity group, based on alleged kinship
ra'is	supervisor of public morals; head of a community of adherence of a certain madhhab religious school in Central Asia
ruqu'	a ritual bow during the prayer

Salafism	Islamic fundamentalism; trend based on the idea of returning to the norms and values of the ancestors (*salaf*)
sangha	community of monks in Buddhism
sar khatib	incumbent of the mosque
sayyid (pl. sada), or sharif (pl. ashraf)	descendant of the Prophet Muhammad
sayyil-bayram	a spring festival in Central Asia
shahid	one who sacrifices himself in the name of Allah
shaykh	a savant in Islam; the leader of a Sufi brotherhood (or its branch); a tribal leader
shaykh al-islam	honorary title
shirk	polytheism
shura	council
Sufism	mystical trend in Islam
sura	a part of the Qur'an
tafsir	interpretation of Qur'an
takfir	an accusation in godlessness, anathematization, excommunication
taqlid	"imitation"; following the orders of religious authority
tariqat (tariqa)	Sufi brotherhood
tawba	repentance
tawhid	monotheism
tokivor	donation given during funerals
top	traditional solidarity group, based on alleged kinship
toyfa	traditional solidarity group, based on alleged kinship
tukhm	traditional solidarity group, based on alleged kinship
tuman	ten thousand; district
tura	Central Asian aristocrat; descendant of Genghis Khan
'ulama	see *'alim*
umma	transnational community of Muslims
'urf	tribal law
urug	traditional solidarity group
vilayat	region
vilayat-e faqih	"reign of Islamic lawyer"; the concept of Islamic state in Iran
waliyy al-amr	head of religious establishment (in Hanbalism)

waqf	charity property donated for religious purposes supporting mosques, educational institutions, and so forth
zakat	obligatory donation in Islam
zalim	oppressor, tyrant
zikr	"remembrance"; technical term for a Sufi ritual of repeating the name of Allah
ziyarat	a pilgrimage to the tomb of a saint in Sufism

Index

Abbasid Caliphate, 6, 9
'Abd al-Wahhab, Muhammad, 1, 3, 57
Abdul Ahad, amir of Bukhara, 15, 45
Abdul Ahad, imam of Namangan
  mosque, 58–59, 67, 121n43
Abdullajanov, Abdumalik, 222
Abi Talib, 'Ali b., 14
Abu Bakr, caliph, 1
Abu Hanifa, al-Nu'man b. Thabit b.
  Zuta, imam, xv, 7, 64, 75, 99
Abu Mahmud, 'Isam, 142
Adolat movement, 29, 96–97, 123n43,
  123n45, 124n105, 141, 216
Afghanistan, 46, 202, 219, 222–29, 231,
  236, 243, 251; U.S.-led military
  campaign in, xii
Akramiyya movement, 159–60, 169
'Ali, caliph, 1
Aliev, Odilkhan, 241
Alim Khan, amir of Bukhara, 15, 45
'Allama, Rahmatulla, 122n48
al-Qa'ida. *See* Qa'ida
Andizhan, 52, 58, 60, 78, 80–81, 142–43,
  145, 149, 159–60
Arab Caliphate, xi, 6, 14. *See also*
  Islamic Caliphate
Arab nationalism, xiii, 24, 34n32,
  128–29. *See also* Ba'thists,

Movement of Arab Nationalists,
  Nasserists
Azhar University (Cairo), 41

Ba'thism, 24, 122n56, 128–29
Babakhanov, Shamsuddin, 39, 41, 51,
  68, 119n5
Babakhanov, Ziyauddin Khan Ishan,
  xvii, 39–43, 56, 111, 119n5, 120n13;
  criticism of "popular" Islam by,
  41–43; Uzbek scholars searching for
  "Wahhabi" influence on, 42
Badakhshan, 229–30, 237, 250–51
Bahadur Khan, Sayyid Muhammad
  Rahim II, khan of Khiva, 14
Bakhromov, Abdurashid qari, Mufti,
  113, 189
Banna, Hasan, 27, 208
basmachi movement, 38, 46
Baz, 'Abd al-'Aziz b., shaykh, 2
Bedil, Mirza 'Abd al-Qadir, 45–46, 56
Berkeley Program in Soviet and Post-
  Soviet Studies (BPS), x
Birlik party, 59, 69–70, 186
Bolsheviks, 69, 75, 103; attack "nests of
  ignorance," 41; education and
  language policies of, 20, 38; and
  Muslims, 20, 40–41, 261; promote

the consolidation of ethnic groups,
19
Bukhara, 6, 8, 10–13, 15–16, 18–19,
33n18, 39, 44–45, 49, 114–15, 118,
204, 206
Bukhara, Amirate of, 15, 17; as Russian
protectorate, 13
Bukhara, People's Soviet Republic of,
19
Bukhari, imam, 41
Burhanuddin, mulla, kazi kalon of
Bukharan Amirate, 45
Bush, George W., U.S. President, 117,
126, 179
Butt, Naveed, 145, 196n52

Carnegie Corporation of New York, x
Caucasus, 30
Central Asia, xi–xiii, 46–53, 58–61, 71,
88, 90, 96, 99, 106, 108, 110, 118,
119n12; Bolshevik revolution and,
18; estates prior to 1917 in, 9, 14;
formation of Soviet Republics in,
19; Islamization of, 6–7, 10, 24; late-
twentieth-century Islamic
renaissance in, 46; national-
territorial delimitation (1920s) in,
19; post-Soviet, 22, 29–31; pre-
Islamic customs in, 7–8; Sufi
brotherhoods in, 9–10, 21, 33, 205,
233–34, 261
Chechen separatists, 233–34;
movement of, 31; public executions
and floggings organized by
(1996–1999), 30
Chechnya, 23, 78, 80–81, 97, 103, 108,
157, 180, 184
"clash of civilizations" thesis (S.
Huntington), 27, 35n42
colonialism, 28
Commission of National
Reconciliation (Tajikistan), 235–36,
239
Communist Party, USSR, 21, 66, 86,
120n13, 126n136; atheistic policies
of , 20, 66. See also Bolsheviks
Council of the 'Ulama (Tajikistan), 241

Dartmouth Conference, x
Democratic Party of Tajikistan, 210,
212, 215
Directorate for the Muslims of
Uzbekistan, 113
DMU (Directorate for the Muslims of
Uzbekistan), 113
Domullo Hikmatullo, 242
Domullo Sharifi Hozori, 242
DPT. See Democratic Party of
Tajikistan

Egypt, 23, 27, 34, 66, 129, 146, 168–69
Erk party, Uzbekistan, 69–70, 82,
84–85, 141, 186; leaders convicted,
83–85
Eshon-i Kiyomiddin (Ghoziev), 241

Fatima, the Prophet's daughter, 14
Ferghana Valley, 114, 205, 207, 233–34,
264; Islamic radicals in, xii; Salafis
organize in, 38; underground
teachers of Islam in, 49

Gasprinsky (Gasprali), Ismail Bey,
32n7
General Agreement on Tariffs and
Trade, 195n38
Genghis Khan, 11, 14, 275
Ghazali, Abu Hamid, ix
Ghufronov Muhammadjon qari, 241
Gorbachev, Mikhail, 65
Gur-e Amir Mausoleum, Samarqand,
10–11

Hakim, Abdullo, 241–42
Hakimjan qari of Margelan, mulla,
51–52, 122n48
Hamadani, Yusuf, xv
Hanafism, 38, 42, 74, 261
Hanbalism, 3–4, 42–43, 54, 60, 99
Harakat ul-Mujahidin (Pakistan), 185
Himmatzoda, Muhammadsarif,
122n48
Hizb at-Tahrir al-Islami, xi–xii, 60, 108,
110, 113, 115, 118, 127–200, 265,
267–68; after September 11,

177–184, 264; activity in
Kyrgyzstan, 156–57, 168–71, 173–76;
activity in Uzbekistan, 148–60;
activity in Tajikistan, 163–68;
attitude toward violence, 154–56;
vision of an Islamic Caliphate,
128–34, 153–54, 265; organizational
structure of, 142–48; origins of,
127–28; use of mourning rituals by,
150–51; women recruited by,
149–50, 171–73
Hizbullah, 24, 141
Hojiev, Juma (Namangani), 68, 71,
73–74, 84, 88–89, 92, 94–95, 107–108,
141, 176, 231, 243
Hoji Habibullo, 241
HTI. *See* Hizb at-Tahrir al-Islami
Huseini, Sayyid Umar, 241

IMU. *See* Islamic Movement of
Uzbekistan
Inter-Tajik dialogue, x
Iraq, 7, 26, 179–82, 187
IRP. *See* Islamic Revival Party, USSR
IRPT. *See* Islamic Revival Party of
Tajikistan
Ishoni Abdukhalijon, 242
Ishoni Abdurrahmanjon, 242
Ishoni Eloki, 242
Ishoni Kalon, 242
Ishoni Mirzo, 242
Ishoni Nuriddin, 242
Ishoni Saidashraf, 242
Ishoni Saidjon, 241
Ishoni Sangi Kulula, 242
Ishoni Tajj, 242
Ishoni Turajon, 242
Ishoni Yusuf, 242
Iskandarov, Akbarsho, 219, 222
Islam Lashkarlari, xvii, 58, 66, 96, 141,
169
Islam: fundamentalism in, 1, 3, 32, 113,
275; medieval, debates in, 31;
theology of, 6–7, 9, 15, 132;
traditionalists in, 5–6, 9, 42, 51, 65,
223; underground movements of,
68, 71, 97, 104, 120n24, 121n43, 166,

170, 174–75, 186, 201, 207–8. *See also*
political Islam; "popular Islam"
Islamic Caliphate, 28, 129, 146, 163,
174, 264–65; as an ideal based on
the notion of Islamic *umma*, 129. *See
also* Arab Caliphate
Islamic extremism, 22, 24, 28, 110, 174,
262. *See also* militant Islamism,
radical Islamism
Islamic Movement of Uzbekistan, xii,
37–38, 59, 71–83, 87–110, 114–18,
127, 134, 140–41, 145–46, 156, 167,
173, 175–76, 183, 264–65; after
September 11, 106–9; guerrillas
fighting on the side of the Taliban,
38; ideology of, 96–106; activity in
Tajikistan and Afghanistan, 93–96;
takes hostages in Kyrgyzstan,
89–93; terrorist networks set up by,
80–83
Islamic Revival Party, USSR, xvii, 201,
213
Islamic Revival Party of Tajikistan,
xi–xii, xvii, 30, 71, 73, 88, 92–94, 96,
208–13, 236–43, 245–56, 265–66, 269;
in exile, 223–25; in government,
236–40; and the idea of an Islamic
state, 216
Islamic Revival Party of Uzbekistan,
140
Isma'iliyya, 7
Israel, 2, 177, 179

Jadidists, 5, 17, 38
Jamaat-i-Tabligh (Pakistan), 113
Jamiat-i-Ulema-i-Islami (Pakistan), 71,
185
Jaysh-e Muhammad (Pakistan), 185
jihad, 37, 54–55, 78, 81, 84, 87–89, 93,
98–99, 105–6, 124, 128, 145, 154–56,
176–77, 179, 191–92
jihadism, 2, 4
Jurabekov, Ismail, 85–86

Kabiri, Muhiddin, 139, 241
Kahharov, Abdul Ahad, 51
Kalonzoda, Abdullo, 241

Kalonzoda, Ibadullo, 241
Kamalov, Sadykzhan, former Mufti of Kyrgyzstan, 192
Karakhanids, dynasty of, 10
Karimov, Islam, xii, 66, 68–70, 72, 74, 76–79, 83–88, 93, 97, 110, 117–18, 124n105, 125n128, 229, 231, 264
Kashmir, 180–81, 185
Kazakhstan, xii, 47, 81, 91, 93, 95, 114, 117–18, 148, 192–93
Kenjaev, Safarali, 216–17, 219
Kettering Foundation, x
KGB. *See* Komitet gosudarstvennoi bezopasnosti (Committee on State Security, USSR)
Khachilaev, Nadirshah, 29
Khiva, Khanate of, 11, 14, 16–17; as Russian protectorate, 13
Khorezm, People's Soviet Republic of, 19
Khorezm, region of Uzbekistan, 80
Khrushchev thaw, 49, 51
Khudoiberdiev, Mahmud, 231
Khurasan, province of Iran, 7
Kokand, Khanate of, 13
Komitet gosudarstvennoi bezopasnosti (Committee on State Security, USSR), 38, 51
Kukaltash madrasa (Tashkent), 40, 45
Kulyabi clan (Tajikistan), 224, 230, 232, 243, 247, 259n73
Kulyabi–Leninabadi–Hissari clan (Tajikistan), 202
Kyrgyzstan, xii, xviii, 35n40, 57, 72, 77, 81, 88–92, 94–96, 107–9, 124n116, 125n121, 139–40, 142, 148, 156–57, 160, 166, 168–70, 173–76, 192–93, 196, 222, 226, 229

La'li Badakhshon, xvii, 210, 215
Ladin, Usama bin, 2, 23, 135, 176, 200n146, 268
Lashkar-e Tayyiba (Pakistan), 185

Ma Wara' al-Nahr (Transoxania), Islamization of, 6–7, 10, 39, 53

madrasas, 37, 71, 97–98, 209; in Central Asia before the Russian colonization, 6, 8, 10, 15–16
Makhsum, Abdullajan domulla, 122n48
MAN. *See* Movement of Arab Nationalists
Mangyts, dynasty of, 11
Marxists, 24, 122n56, 135
Masoud, Ahmad Shah, 72, 96, 225, 228
Massari, Muhammad, 2
Maturidi al-Samarqandi, Abu Mansur, xv
Maududi, Abul-Ala, 27, 53–54, 59
Maulawi Abdulhai, 241
Maulawi Ghaibnazarov, 241–42
Maulawi Mahmadali, 241
mazars, 10, 13, 41, 43, 52, 61, 114, 204
Mecca, 41
Medina, 41
Mekhliboev, Ghaizat, 184
Middle East, 22, 34, 37, 40, 49, 161, 164, 177, 187, 192, 199n137, 265, 268; immigrants to Central Asia from, as source of Salafi ideas, 37; radical Islamism in, 24, 262
militant Islamism, 37, 262. *See also* Islamic extremism; radical Islamism
Mir Arab madrasa (Bukhara), 33n18, 39, 49–50
Mirzaev, Abduwali qari, 52, 58–59, 71–72, 80–81, 122n48, 142
Movement of Arab Nationalists, 24, 122n56, 128–29, 147
Muakkalov, Mansur, 243
Muhammad, Prophet, 1, 6–7, 14, 20, 33, 43, 47, 50, 55, 128–29, 134, 146, 148, 159, 170, 181–82, 190, 192, 242, 263
Muhammad Yusuf, Muhammad Sadiq, Mufti, 48, 61, 68, 122n48, 156–57
Mukarramzoda, Muslihiddin, 241
Mullo Abdurrasul, 241
Mullo Faizullo, 241
Mullo Kalandar, 241
Mullo Navid (Mirzohodi Mirzomuhammadiev), 242

Mullo Qosim, 241
Mullo Sa'uddin (Rustamov), 242
Munavvarov, Shaazim, Chairman,
    Uzbekistan Committee on the
    Affairs of Religion, 113, 126n136
Munavvar qari, 126n136
Muslim Brotherhood, 2, 23, 27, 60, 128,
    134, 137, 146, 168, 208
Musozoda, Huseinjon, 241

Nabhani, Taqi ad-Din, xvii, 128–29,
    133, 135, 143, 153, 197n86
Nabiev, Rahmon, xvii, 201–2, 214–15,
    217, 219
Namangan, 33n18, 72, 78, 121n43,
    122n50, 124n105, 124n106, 141–42,
    156, 160, 233–34
Naqshband, Khoja Bahauddin, xv, 12
Naqshbandiyya, 9–10, 12, 33n12, 39,
    53, 62, 114, 205, 225, 232–34
Nasser, Gamal Abdel, 27, 169
Nasserism, 24, 128–29
National Democratic Party of
    Tajikistan, 247
Nazarov, Obidkhan, 71–72
Ni'matzoda Amonullo, 241
Northern Alliance (Afghanistan), 72,
    96, 107
Nuri, Said Abdullo, 89, 92–95, 208, 223,
    229–32, 235–37, 239, 241, 245–47,
    251–55, 259n63

Pakistan, 38, 46, 59, 66, 71, 89, 98, 107,
    109, 114–15, 118, 126n140, 176, 185,
    224, 228, 246
Palestine, 23, 26, 34n32, 100; creation
    of a Jewish state in, 28
Party of Islamic Liberation. *See* Hizb
    at-Tahrir al-Islami
Pirmuhammadzoda Ismail, 241
political Islam, 1, 3, 18, 20–21, 23,
    34n32, 53, 58, 65, 67–68, 73, 88, 93,
    151, 160, 163
"popular Islam," 10, 21, 38, 40–43,
    60
Popular Front of Tajikistan, 30, 218,
    224

Qadimists, 5, 17
Qadiriyya, 9, 31, 62, 234
Qa'ida, 22, 36n46, 67, 109, 116, 118,
    147, 184, 192, 200n146, 264
Qiyadati, Mahmud, 141
Qubra, Najmuddin, xv
Qubraviyya, 9, 33n12
Qur'an, interpretation of, 39
Qurbanov, Sharif, Chief Military
    Prosecutor (Tajikistan), 252–53
Qutb, Sayyid, 27, 53–54

Rabbani, Burhanuddin, 224, 226, 228–29
radical Islamism, 28, 32, 194; in the
    Middle East, 24; Western scholars'
    approaches to and explanations of,
    21–29. *See also* militant Islamism
Rahim, Muhammad, founder of the
    Mangyt dynasty, 11
Rahimov, Mullo Abdullo, 244
Rahimov, Qasim, 252
Rahmonov, Emomali, 73–74, 88, 93,
    222, 225, 229–30, 232, 235–36, 240,
    246–47
Rastokhez society, xvii, 209–13, 215
religious class in Central Asia; before
    1917, 11, 13, 33n12; Soviet policies
    in the 1920s and 1930s toward,
    20–21, 37
Rockefeller Foundation, x
Rushta, 'Ata Abu (Abu Yasin), 128
Rustamov-Hindustani, Muhammadjan
    (Maulawi Hindustani), 27, 43–55,
    208, 215; disciples of, 51–56

Sadr, Muqtada, 129
SADUM. *See* Spiritual Board of
    Muslims of Central Asia and
    Kazakhstan
Safarov, Sangak, 30, 217–220, 224,
    257n20
Salafism, 37–40, 42–43, 51, 68, 98, 114,
    122n48, 264, 275
Salih, Muhammad, 84–85, 141
Salimov, Yaqub, 30
Samarqand, 11, 86, 114, 187, 204, 206,
    214

Sanginov, Rahmon ("Hitler"), 243
Sanginov–Muakkalov bandit groups
(Tajikistan), 243–44
Satimov, Hakimjan, 58
Sa'ud, 'Abd al-'Aziz b., Saudi king, 45
Saudi Arabia, 1, 32n4, 38, 41–42, 46,
66–67, 70–71, 119n7, 223, 246
Saudi Wahhabis, 1–4, 41, 67, 113
Shah-i Zinda ensemble, madrasa in
Samarqand, 10
Shami domulla (al-Shami al-
Tarabulsi), 40–41, 119n6
Shamsuddinov, Shamsuddin, 252–54
Shari'a, 2–3, 38, 42–43, 54, 58–60, 62,
66, 74–76, 97, 101, 106, 109, 112–13,
128–29
Sharifzoda, Fathullo, 241
Sharifzoda, Fatulla Khan, 232–33
Sharifzoda, Haydar, 241
Sharifzoda, Muhammadsharif, 232–33
Shaybanids, dynasty of, 11
Shaybani Khan, 10
Shi'ism, 9; brotherhoods in, 9–10, 21,
33
Spiritual Board of Muslims of Central
Asia and Kazakhstan, 21, 39, 68,
120n13
Stalin, Joseph, 39, 69
Stanford University, x
Sufism, 39–40, 61, 113–14, 122, 233–34;
symbols and rituals in, 62
suicide bombers, attacks in Tashkent
(July 2004), 118
Sunnism, 3, 7, 9, 38–39, 52, 57, 62–65,
261; *madhhabs* of, 7, 9, 62–65
Syria, 40, 129, 151, 179

Tajibai domulla, 122n48
Tajikistan, xii, 38, 47–49, 58, 68–74,
76–78, 80–81, 88–98, 105–8, 113,
122n48, 122n60, 125n120, 200–261,
264–66, 269; armed conflict in,
213–27; ethnic and social
fragmentation in, 202–5;
distribution of power in, 206–8;
General Agreement on Peace and

National Accord in, 236, 242–43,
247–48, 252; Islamic–democratic
bloc in, 202, 216, 218, 220–22;
Islamic movement in, 201–2; talks
to end the conflict in, 227–32,
235–36; prospect for dialogue in,
255–56
Tajiks, 71, 90, 160, 188, 202–6, 208,
210–11, 213, 220, 223, 225, 228, 234
Taliban, 38, 71–73, 85, 94–96, 106–10,
168, 175–77, 263–64
Tatarstan, 17, 23
Tawba (Repentance) group, 66, 70, 96,
105 (sura from the Qur'an), 121,
141
terrorist bombings, in Tashkent
(February 1999), 87–88, 105, 109–10,
115, 149, 193
Timur, xv, 10
Timurids, dynasty of, 10
Turajonzoda, Hoji Akbar, 49, 209, 211,
214–15, 220, 223, 228–29, 232–33,
237–38, 240–42, 247, 249
Turdybai domulla, 122n48
Turkestan, 13, 17–18, 40; annexed to
the Russian empire, 13;
Autonomous Soviet Republic of, 19;
Governorship-General of, 13
Turkey, 46, 66, 71, 84, 117, 129, 185
Turkmenistan, 23, 34n23, 79–80, 84

Ulugh Beg, xv, 10
Ulugh Beg madrasa, Samarqand, 10
'Umar, caliph, 1
United Tajik Opposition, 38, 72–73, 89,
92–96, 223–24, 227–30, 231–33,
235–38, 241, 245
Ush Zhuz party, 18
Usmon, Davlat, 58, 73, 140, 208–9, 215,
217, 229, 239–41
U.S. State Department, xi
'Uthaymin Ibn, shaykh, 2
'Uthman, caliph, 1
UTO. *See* United Tajik Opposition
Uzbekistan, ix, xii, 37–39, 41, 43,
45–49, 51, 53, 55, 57–61, 63, 65–91,

93–99, 101–3, 105–19, 121n43,
121n48, 122n50, 122n60, 124n108,
125n120, 125n121, 125n128, 127,
129, 139–42, 148–60, 162, 164,
166–68, 174–78, 182–84, 186–93, 203,
207, 221–22, 226, 229, 231–33,
257n23, 261–62, 264, 269n1;
government crackdown on Islamic
activists, 38, 71–72, 77–80, 152,
148–53, 188–92; struggle against
Islamic terrorism in, 109–18
Uzbeks, 71, 90, 92, 101, 104, 114,
117–18, 125n127, 202–3, 205, 211,
220–21, 224, 233–34, 259

Vaisov Group (Vaisites), 17
Vohidov, prosecutor (Dushanbe), 253
Volga Bulgaria, 33n12

Wahhabism, 2–4, 32n6, 38, 42–43,
51–52, 57, 80, 119n7
World Muslim League, 2
World Trade Organization, 195n38

Yasavi, Ahmad, xv
Yasaviyya, 9, 33n12, 39, 119n3
Yuldashev, Abduwali, 80, 92
Yuldashev, Akram, 159–60
Yuldashev, Tahir, 52, 57, 59, 66, 68,
70–72, 80–86, 89–90, 92, 94–95, 98,
107–8, 115, 121n45, 232
Yunusov, Abu Turab, 122n48

Zallum, 'Abd al-Qadim, xvii, 128, 135,
141–42, 197n86
Zawahiri, Ayman, 22, 200n146
Ziyoev, Mirzo ("Jaga"), 92–95, 232, 237

About the Author

Professor **Vitaly V. Naumkin** is a Russian author who writes extensively on the Arab world, Islam, Central Asia, and the Caucasus. He is president of the Moscow-based International Center for Strategic and Political Studies, editor-in-chief of *Vostok-ORIENS*, the journal of the Russian Academy of Sciences, head of the Center for Arab Studies, Institute of Oriental Studies. In 2003 he was a visiting professor at the Department of Political Studies, University of California, Berkeley. He is author of about four hundred publications in Russian, English, French, Arabic, Italian, and other languages, including: *Red Wolves of Yemen* (2004), *Island of the Phoenix* (1993), *Central Asia and Transcaucasia: Ethnicity and Conflict* (editor and coauthor, 1994).